Fourth Edition

GEOGRAPHY
AND
GEOGRAPHERS

Anglo-American Human Geography since 1945

R.J. JOHNSTON

Geography and Geographers

Geography and Geographers

**Anglo-American
Human Geography since 1945**

R. J. Johnston
Professor of Geography, University of Sheffield

Fourth Edition

Edward Arnold
A division of Hodder & Stoughton
LONDON NEW YORK MELBOURNE AUCKLAND

© 1991 R. J. Johnston

First published in Great Britain 1979
Second edition 1983
Reprinted 1984, 1985
Third edition 1987
Reprinted 1988, 1990
Fourth edition 1991

Distributed in the USA by Routledge, Chapman and Hall, Inc.
29 West 35th Street, New York, NY 10001

British Library Cataloguing in Publication Data

Johnston, R. J. (Ronald John) *1941–*
    Geography and geographers : Anglo-American human
    geography since 1945. – 4th. ed.
    1. Great Britain. Human geography, history   2. United
    States. Human geography, history
    I. Title
    304.20941

    ISBN 0–340–51755–7

Typeset in 10/12 pt California
by Colset Private Limited, Singapore
Printed and bound in Great Britain for Edward Arnold, a
division of Hodder and Stoughton Limited, Mill Road,
Dunton Green, Sevenoaks, Kent TN13 2YA
by Biddles Ltd, Guildford and King's Lynn

Contents

A Note to the Reader

This comprises a book within a book. The inner volume – Chapters
2–8 – contains a factual record of the history of Anglo-American human
geography. The outer volume, which incorporates Chapters 2–8 with
Chapters 1 and 9, is an attempt to account for that history. Thus the 'outer
volume' is the 'innovative' work, based on the material of the 'inner volume':
Chapter 9 interprets Chapters 2–8 in the light of the material presented in
Chapter 1.

Preface

To the First Edition

Most students reading for a degree or similar qualification are required to pay some attention to their chosen discipline's academic history. The history presented to them commonly ends some time before the present. This has advantages for the historian, because the past is often better interpreted from the detachment of a little distance and there is less chance of hurting scholars still alive. But there is a major disadvantage for the students. In virtually every other component of their courses they will be dealing with the discipline's current literature, and so if the history ends some decades ago, they are presented with the contemporary substance but not with the contemporary framework, except where this is very clearly derivative of the historical context.

This state of affairs is unfortunate. Students need a conspectus of the current practice in their chosen discipline and should encounter a relevant overview which describes, and perhaps explains too, what scholars believe the philosophy and methodology of the discipline presently are and should be. Such an overview will allow the substantive courses comprising the rest of the degree to be placed in context and appreciated as examples of the disciplinary belief system as well as ends in themselves.

As a discipline expands, so the need for a course in its 'contemporary history' will grow too. In the last few decades, for example, most disciplines, and certainly human geography, have expanded greatly, with expansion measured by the number of active participants and their volume of published work. And the more active members there are, almost certainly the greater the variety of work undertaken, making it difficult for individual students to provide their own conspectus of the discipline from their own reading. Hence the need for a 'contemporary history' course at the present time.

The present book is the outcome of teaching such a course for several years, and is offered as a guide for others, both teachers and students. As with all texts, it has many idiosyncrasies. The course on which it is based is taught to final-year students reading for honours degrees in geography, and is probably best used by people at that level since it assumes familiarity with the concepts and language of human geography. Further, my view is that students probably benefit most from a framework after experiencing some of its contents; this book provides the matrix for organizing the individual parts rather than a series of slots into which parts can be placed later, which would be the case if the course were taught early in the degree.

A series of constraints circumscribes the contents and approach of this contemporary history. First, it deals only with human geography, for several reasons. The most important is that I find the links between physical and human geography tenuous, as those disciplines are currently practised. The major link between them is a sharing of techniques and research procedures, but these are shared with other disciplines too, and are insufficient foundation for a unified discipline. (What price a department of factorial ecology?) Further, my own competence, work and interests lie wholly within human geography and although I have been trained with and by and have worked among physical geographers, and have obtained stimuli from this, I am incompetent to write about physical geography. And finally, much of the human geography discussed here is of North American origin, and many geographers there, especially in the United States, encounter no physical geography as it is understood in British universities. To a considerable extent, therefore, human and physical are separate, if not independent, disciplines. Throughout the book, I use the terms 'geography' and 'human geography' interchangeably.

The second constraint is cultural; the subject matter of the book is Anglo-American human geography. Most of the work discussed emanates from either the United States or the United Kingdom: there are some contributions from workers in Australia, Canada, and New Zealand, but the efforts of geographers in the rest of the world are largely ignored. (A partial exception is Sweden, which has major academic links with the Anglo-American tradition; much Swedish geographical work is published in English.) Such academic parochialism in part reflects personal linguistic deficiencies, but it is not entirely an idiosyncratic decision. Contacts between Anglo-American human geography on the one hand and, say, that of France and of Germany on the other have been few in recent decades, so to concentrate on the former is not to commit a major error in separating a part from an integrated whole.

The final constraint is temporal, for the book is concerned with Anglo-American human geography during the decades since the Second World War only. Again, this is in part a reflection of personal competence, for I have been personally involved in academic geography for the last twenty years. But the Second World War was a major watershed in so many aspects of history, not least academic practice, and much of the methodology and philosophy currently taught in human geography has been initiated since then.

This book, then, is a history of Anglo-American human geography since 1945. It does not purport to be an objective history, for such an enterprise is impossible. The material included represents subjective judgements: the stress on certain topics is subjective, too, and so is the organization. But although not objective, nor intended to be, the book is neutral. My own opinions are not stated, and are not intendedly implied in anything that has been written (though some of them may be identifiable). There is no commentary, only a presentation of what I perceive to be the salient features.

Arising out of this intended neutrality is a second characteristic of the book, its dependence on the written statements of others. There are few lengthy quotations, but many short ones. Most arguments have, of necessity, been précised or paraphrased, in which case there may be unintentional distortion of the emphasis in the original. My aim has been to report what others have written, and the contents of Chapters 2–6 depend entirely on the published record, for no use has been made of personal memoirs (however valuable these might be, if a representative set could be collected). A consequence of this orientation is a large bibliography. Some authors are commended by reviewers for the utility of their bibliographies. Mine indicates the material on which the book is based.

Within the terms of reference set, I have not attempted simply to provide a chronology of arguments. As well as describing the changing contents of Anglo-American human geography I have tried to account for them, to suggest why certain things were said and done, by a particular person in a particular place. Such an attempted 'explanation' of events cannot be neutral, and so it has been handled by writing a book within a book. The outer volume is Chapters 1 and 7; the inner is 2–6: the former presents the subjective account, phrased in terms of the models developed by historians of science, and the latter contains the neutral description. The inner book can be read independently of the outer; the contents of Chapter 7, however, are derived from all of those preceding it.

The account provided in the outer book is not idealist (using that term in the same way as in Chapter 5), for in attempting to explain changes in attitudes to philosophical and methodological topics I rely on my own modelling of scientific progress rather than on the views of the change-agents themselves. The modelling is set in the context of other studies of the history of academic disciplines, notably the physical sciences. By the end of Chapter 7, this model turns out to be something of a straw man. I am not the first to use it within human geography, however, and so my presentation, criticism and then replacement of it represent a contribution to the general enterprise of writing the history of geography (and perhaps of other social sciences).

One problem with writing 'contemporary history' is knowing when to stop. There is a constant flow of new material which can be employed in the task, and there is always the probability (sometimes the certainty, using publishers' advertising) of something very useful appearing tomorrow. Eventually, a halt must be called. For this book, it was in mid-1978, although some later material is referenced (because I was privileged to read it before it went to press). By the time it appears, therefore, this book will of necessity be a period piece, although the arguments in Chapter 7 suggest that a few years will elapse before a major revision is needed.

It was Malcolm Lewis who designed the course of which the material in this book became a part; Stan Gregory was responsible for my teaching it. Both are in no way responsible for the outcome. I am grateful to them for the opportunity to undertake what turned out to be, for me, an enjoyable and stimulating task. The comments (direct and indirect) of the various student audiences have helped to redefine the contents in various ways over the years, and I am grateful for these.

Preparation of this book has been helped materially by several people. My wife Rita has, as always, been of great assistance in a variety of ways, not least in reading the whole manuscript twice and giving much advice on the presentation. Secondly, Walter Freeman has read the entire manuscript and given much of his time in discussing both its contents and its context; I am deeply grateful to him for his interest, his kindness, and his continued friendship. Alan Hay, too, read the complete first draft and commented freely and very helpfully on many aspects of the work. Both he and Walter Freeman felt that there is not enough of me and my opinions in the book: I hope that they understand why. The diagrams were produced by Stephen Frampton and Sheila Ottewell, and Joan Dunn has yet again created an excellent typescript out of a messy manuscript. My thanks to all.

I make it clear in Chapter 1 that the progress of any individual's academic career depends considerably on the actions (and sometimes inactions) of others. No academic is an island. Many people have helped me in the last twenty years, but I should like to express special thanks to Percy Crowe, Walter Freeman, Basil Johnson, Murray Wilson, Barry Johnston, Michael Wise, Stan Gregory and Ron Waters.

Autumn 1978

To the Second Edition

The generally favourable reaction to this book, and the continued demand for it, suggests that a successful formula was identified in its writing, and that no basic changes are needed. Nevertheless, it was felt that a second edition was desirable, rather than a reprint. The opportunity has been taken to correct errors, to update (hence expanding the bibliography substantially) the 'inner volume' (to mid 1982; the first edition was written in 1978), and to respond to some of the criticisms, in particular with regard to the contents of the 'outer volume', on which my ideas have changed somewhat.

The preface to a second edition should not be used simply as a response to particular reviews of the first. But the reviews of this book have raised a number of general issues that are worthy of brief discussion here – and which have been taken into account when preparing the revision.

The first point concerns the nature of the entire enterprise. In the original Preface, I stated that although the book was not objective history – 'for such an enterprise is impossible' – it was neutral, in that it contained no personal commentary. In retrospect, this was an over-statement. The book is basically a reconstruction, from published material, of philosophical and methodological debates within human geography; it is more concerned with writing about human geography than with writings that are human geography (as one reviewer so clearly pointed out), and is something of a political history of human geography. In effect, it is an exercise using the philosophy of idealism outlined in Chapter 5 (despite my statement to the contrary in the original Preface). The literature that I review represents the theories (or ideologies) of its authors regarding the nature of human geography. The framework into which I set that literature represents my theory of the history of human geography, which has been constructed – and is continually reconstructed – to ensure that the two cohere (see Chapter 7). It is, then, a personal statement, set in the context of my own socialization as a human geographer.

This orientation has not been changed. I still rely entirely on published evidence for my history – while accepting the value of 'oral history' of various kinds, which is now providing valuable published materials (Browning, 1982; Buttimer, 1983; Buttimer and Hagerstrand, 1980). But the revision has allowed me to remedy some important omissions, and to reorganize certain sections to emphasize more fully the contributions of particular individuals. It is their contributions to philosophical and methodological debates that are the focus of the book. Substantive contributions are widely reviewed in a variety of places – most notably the excellent journal *Progress in Human Geography*. It is not a major purpose of this book to summarize what human geographers have done, but rather to concentrate on how they have done it, and why.

Some criticism has been directed at the book for its separation of human from physical geography; indeed, I have been 'accused' of doing the discipline a political disservice by advancing this separation. I stand by my statement in the original Preface, however – 'I find the links between physical and human geography tenuous, as they are currently practised'. During the 'spatial science' era (Chapters 3 and 4) there was a common interest among physical and human geographers in methodological questions, especially of a statistical and mathematical nature, and the interactions that took place are recognized here. And certain methodological frameworks – notably systems analysis (Chapter 4) – seemed to provide common bonds. These bonds remain, and are presented here. But as each of the two fields has moved away from quantitative description to studies of, first, how (process studies to physical geographers) and, then, why (process studies to human geographers), so the differences between the two have been magnified. There is very little basis for bonds with physical geography in the approaches to human geography discussed in Chapters 5 and 6 of this book. Of course, the subject matter of human geography is closely concerned with that of physical geography, but there is no apparent need (and certainly no published evidence of its realization) for an integration of the two fields as they are currently practised. Some argue that such integration is (or should be) achieved through the study of resources, but a review of the relevant literature (Johnston, 1983a) provides no evidence to support that claim. Human and physical geography overlap. There are benefits to be achieved from that, especially in a pedagogical context, and I would not strongly advocate their institutional separation. But they are separate fields, each overlapping more with other fields than with each other.

Internal to human geography, it has been suggested that my treatment is unbalanced. In particular, cultural, historical and regional geography are ignored, relative to economic, social and political geography. To the extent that this is so, it reflects relative contributions to the literature being reviewed. The focus of this book is philosophical and methodological debate, not substantive contribution.

One of the most fundamental criticisms concerns the underlying rationale for the book, that there is a separate history of human geography worthy of investigation. By presenting such a history, am I not drawing artificial boundaries? To this, I would respond that the boundaries already existed. Human geography is an institutionalized discipline in the countries studied here; at the school level in Britain it is clearly defined by the syllabuses for public examinations. The boundaries around human geography are indeed artificial, because the subject matter of the social sciences should not be compartmentalized. But a desire to break down those boundaries in some way does not detract from the need for a history which, among other things, should demonstrate to students how that desire has developed within the academic community of human geographers in recent decades.

Despite the institutionalization of human geography, there is nevertheless considerable movement through its boundaries, involving contributions by human geographers to other disciplines and vice versa. This may be understated in the book. It takes a variety of forms. The basic flows are of ideas from other fields into human geography. These ideas are assimilated into the recipient discipline, and in return human geographers may seek to demonstrate the results of that assimilation to the source discipline. This is usually done by way of publications in the journals of the latter; there has been more of it in some source disciplines (agricultural history, for example) than others (such as political science; Laponce, 1980). Some individuals have transferred their disciplinary allegiance as a result: there are several British professors of sociology who were trained as geographers, for example. But are they still human geographers, whose work should be reviewed here?

Certainly, inter-disciplinary links are substantial, even if not always apparent, and should not be ignored. Developments in human geography in recent decades have been indelibly influenced by these links — many of them completely informal, because they involved 'World Three' (p. 280) only. But such links do not deny the existence of a discipline called human geography into which many students are socialized each year and whose history is of intrinsic interest.

Finally, why confine the treatment to the 'English-speaking world', basically to Britain and North America? My answer is the same as it was in the Preface to the first edition: competence. The need for a more thorough international survey is clear, however, and small steps have been taken to meet it (Johnston and Claval, 1984). There are other things we are ignorant about. None of the arguments presented here is in any way backed by solid quantitative evidence, where that would be relevant. Gatrell (1982) has pointed to one possible direction, but the routes are wide open. Indeed, the tasks ahead of us are many

> The 1980s promise to be challenging, exciting and fraught years, not least to the academic community. For geographers, the uncertainty is a double one: both in what to study and how to study it (Robson, 1982, p. 1).

In continuing the work on this subject, and in the formulation of the second edition, my debts from the original book remain. I am particularly indebted to my publishers for constant encouragement, and also for stimulating me to provide a companion volume – *Philosophy and Human Geography* – that outlines the philosophies the debates over which are reviewed here. The contributors to *The Dictionary of Human Geography* stimulated me considerably, as did the valuable comments of the kind reviewers of the first edition. To them all, I am extremely grateful. As always, I am deeply indebted to Rita Johnston and Joan Dunn.

Summer 1982

To the Third Edition

When the second edition of this book was prepared in 1982, it seemed unlikely that another would be needed only four years later. Events have proved different, however, for three reasons. First, there has been a continued flowering of geographical scholarship, in all three of the major research paradigms identified here; to retain the contemporary perspective of the book it has been necessary to incorporate these, so that several sections have been substantially rewritten and extended. Secondly, the political response to economic recession in the late 1970s and, so far, the whole of the 1980s has put substantial pressures on researchers to contribute to economic and social change in particular ways, and the reactions of geographers to such pressures have been incorporated in the present narrative. Finally, there has been increased interest in the history of human geography, bringing new insights to the processes of change. These, too, have been incorporated here. The basic thesis of the book has not been altered, however; indeed, re-evaluation of the work of Kuhn (as suggested by Mair's, 1986, critique) has led to greater confidence being expressed in the concepts that he introduced.

The Preface to the Second Edition provides an extended defence and amplification of the approach taken in the book, and no further discussion is intended here. I am grateful to those who continue to comment favourably upon it and consider it a valuable introduction for student use. To them, as again to Rita Johnston and Joan Dunn, my thanks.

December 1986

To the Current Edition

The previous three editions of this book have each been written at approximately four year intervals, so the preparation of this fourth version has increased the turnover time somewhat (by about six months, or 12.5 per cent). The reason for the haste is in large part the continued production of substantial volumes of high quality scholarship by Anglo-American human geographers, and especially the continued vitality of the debate over competing views of the discipline. More than sufficient new material has been produced since the third edition was written 3½ years ago to require the rewriting of several sections of the book and the inclusion of new sections and sub-sections. Within a short period of years, the production of a large number of edited volumes with titles such as *Geography in America, Horizons in Human Geography, Remaking Human Geography, Remodelling Geography*, and *The Power of Geography* all testified to the discipline's vitality and called for a reworking of a book that sets out to provide students of geography with a conspectus of its 'contemporary history'.

The basic organizational framework of the book has not been altered; the contents have simply been updated. But one significant change has been introduced, however. The chapter structure increasingly seemed anachronistic as the debates over the discipline continued, and it was decided to increase the number in order that separately identifiable approaches should be individually treated, and clearly so. Thus the book now has two more chapters than it had in the previous editions, which it is hoped provides a clearer structure within which the debates can be situated.

The Preface to the Second Edition was used to answer some of the criticisms of the book – what it covers and what it excludes; how this material is structured – and the Preface to the Third Edition made brief reference to continuing debates over the material used, and especially its interpretation. Similar criticisms have been made since (notably in Stoddart, 1987) but no detailed response is offered here; the Preface to my book on *Environmental Problems* (Johnston, 1989b) continued that debate, however.

In producing yet another edition of this book I am grateful to those who have reviewed it and made valuable comments (especially Robin Flowerdew), those who continue to cite it and to recommend it to students, and to those who buy it. The four editions have each been commissioned by different editors, and I am grateful to all with whom I have been involved at Edward Arnold for their continued support. As always, my greatest debt is to Rita Johnston, not least for convincing me that I should learn word-processing.

April 1990   R. J. Johnston

1

The Nature of an Academic Discipline

This book is a study of an academic discipline, in particular of its content. But content cannot be discussed fully without an understanding of context, which this chapter provides. In essence, the context is the population involved in the discipline. To study an academic discipline is to study a society, which has a stratification system, a set of rewards and sanctions, and a series of bureaucracies, not to mention a large number of interpersonal conflicts (some academic, some not). To the outsider, academic work may seem to be objective and 'scientific'. But many subjective decisions must be taken: what to study; whether to publish the results; where to publish them and in what form; what to teach; whether to question the work of others publicly; and so on. As with all human decisions, they are made within the constraints set by the society of which the academic worker is a member.

In studying an academic discipline one in effect has to study a society within a society; both are relevant in setting the constraints to individual and group activity. The study of the society within a society involves a focus on two questions; 'how is academic life organized?'; and 'how does academic work, basically its research, proceed?'. The first two sections of this chapter are concerned with those two questions. Use of the term 'society within a society' strongly implies that academic life does not proceed independently. It is not a closed system but rather is open to the influences and commands of the wider society which encompasses it. A third question to be asked, therefore, is 'what is the nature of the society which provides the environment for the academic discipline being studied, and how do the two interact?'. This is the subject of the final section of the chapter.

Academic Life: The Occupational Structure

Pursuit of an academic discipline in modern society is part of a career, undertaken for financial and other gains; to most of its practitioners, the career is a professional one, complete with entry rules and behavioural norms. In the initial development of almost all of the academic disciplines studied today, some of the innovators were amateurs, perhaps financing their activities from individual wealth. There are virtually no such amateurs now; very few of the academic publications in human geography are by other than either a professional academic with a training in the discipline or a member of a related discipline. The profession is not geography, however. Rather geography is the discipline professed by the individual academics who probably state their profession as university teacher or some similar term. Indeed, the great majority of academic geographers are teachers in universities or comparable institutions of higher education. (Recent years have seen the invention of new types of higher education institution. University is used here as a generic term, therefore.) Academic geographers are distinguished from other geographers (many of whom are also teachers) by their commitment to all three of the basic canons of a university; to propagate, protect, and advance knowledge. It is the advancement of knowledge – through the conduct of fundamental research and the publication of its original findings – which identifies an academic discipline; the nature of its teaching follows from the nature of its research.

The academic career structure

Members of university staffs – hereafter termed academics – follow their chosen occupation within a well-defined career structure. Two variants of this structure are relevant here: the *British model* and the *American model*. Entry to both is by the same route. The individual must have been a successful student as an undergraduate and, more especially, as a postgraduate. The latter involves pursuing original research, guided by one or more supervisors who are expert in the relevant specialized field. The results of this research are almost invariably presented as a thesis for a research degree (usually the PhD), which is examined by relevant experts. The PhD is an almost obligatory entrance ticket for both models.

   While undertaking the research degree, most postgraduate students will obtain experience in teaching undergraduates, most particularly in practical and tutorial classes: some universities, notably those operating the American model, finance many of their research students through their teaching activities. The individual may then proceed to further research experience, or may gain appointment to a limited-tenure teaching post in a university. This appointment may be for a limited period only, offering an 'apprenticeship' in the teaching aspects of the profession whilst either the research degree is completed or the individual's research expertise is consolidated.

   Beyond these limited-tenure positions lie the permanent teaching posts, and it is here that the British and American models deviate (Figure 1.1). In the *British model*, the first level of the career structure is the lectureship. For the first years of that appointment (usually three) the lecturer is on probation: annual reports are made on progress as teacher, researcher and administrator,

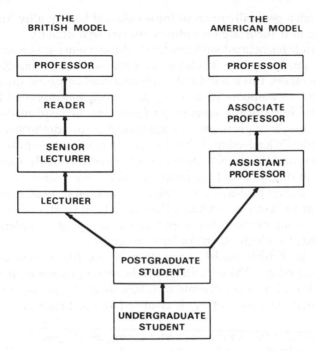

Fig 1.1   The academic career ladder. Note that whereas in the American model it is very unusual not to progress up through the stages in an orderly sequence, in the British model missing steps is quite common (i.e. some lecturers move direct to readerships, even to professorsips, without first being senior lecturers – there are no senior lecturers in the 'Oxbridge' universities and a few others – and many professors are recruited from the senior lecturer rather than the reader grade).

and advice is offered on adaptation to the demands of the profession. At the end of the probationary years, the appointment is either terminated or confirmed.

Appointment in this model is almost always to the staff of a department; most departments are named for the discipline which the individual staff member pursues. The prescribed duties involve the undertaking of research and such teaching and administration as directed by the head of the department. The lecturers are on a salary scale, and receive an annual increment; accelerated promotion may be possible. In the United Kingdom there is an 'efficiency bar' after a certain number of years' service; 'crossing the bar' involves a promotion, and is determined by an assessment of the lecturer's research, teaching and administrative activities.

Beyond the lectureship are further grades into which the individual can be promoted. The first of these is the senior lectureship for which there is no allocation to departments; entry to it is based again on an assessment of the lecturer's conduct in the three main areas of academic life, and is based on open competition across the whole university. The next level is the readership, a position which is generally reserved for scholars of high quality; the criteria for promotion to it focus almost entirely on research activity.

The final grade (associated with academic departments as against administration of the university as a whole) is the professorship. Although superior in status to the others, this is not simply a promotional category: until recently most professors were appointed from open competition preceded by public advertisements. Initially the posts of professor and of head of department were synonymous, so a professor was appointed as an administrative head, to provide academic leadership. With the growth in department size in recent years, however, and the development of specialized sub-fields within disciplines, each requiring its own leadership, it has become common for departments to have several professors. In some, the position of head remains with a single appointee; in others, probably the majority, it rotates among the professors; in a growing number, the headship is now a position independent of the professoriat, to which other grades may aspire.

Finally in the British model, promotion is possible to non-advertised, personal professorships. These positions are becoming increasingly common, as the possibilities for appointments to established 'chairs' are reduced. In most cases, a personal professorship is awarded for excellence in research and scholarship.

The system under the *American model* is simpler (Figure 1.1). There are three permanent staff categories: assistant professor, associate professor, and professor. The first contains two sub-categories – those staff on probation who do not have 'tenure' and those with security of tenure. Each category has its own salary scale but not automatic annual increments. (In the United States, these scales vary from university to university – according to prestige, state etc.) Salary adjustments are the result of personal bargaining, on the basis of academic activity in the three areas already listed, and as a result it is possible for the salary scales of the categories to overlap in the same department. Movement from one category to another is promotional, and is a recognition of academic excellence. Professorships are simply the highest promotional grade and do not carry obligatory major administrative tasks. Heads of departments in the American model are separately appointed, usually for a limited period only, and they need not be professors (usually referred to as 'full professors').

Status, rewards and promotion prospects

The rewards of the academic profession are the salary levels, plus the general status of the profession, the particular status of its individual promotional categories, and the relative independence and flexibility of the working conditions. The tangible rewards – the payments – are determined by the academic's position within the career structure. Promotion must be 'earned'. How?

Academic work has three main components – research, teaching and administration. Entrants to the profession have little or no experience of academic administration and their only teaching has probably been as assistants to others. Thus it is very largely on proven research ability that the potential of the aspirant for an academic career is judged. To some degree, research ability can be equated with probable teaching and administrative competence, since all require the same personal qualities – enthusiasm, orderliness, incisive thinking, and ability to communicate orally and in writing; to a considerable extent, however, academics are appointed to their first position on faith, hence the usual probationary periods before tenure is granted.

Once admitted to the profession, the academic will have to undertake all three types of work, so that promotional prospects can be more widely assessed. In effect, teaching and administration probably carry less weight with those responsible for promotions than does research. This is partly because of preceived difficulties in assessing performance in the first two, and partly because of a general academic ethos which gives prime place to research activity in the evaluation of peers.

Although not necessarily progressive in terms of increasing level of difficulty, administrative tasks tend to be more complex and demanding of political and personal judgement and skills as the academic becomes more senior. As made clear by the 'Peter Principle' (Peter and Hull, 1969), a person's ability to undertake a certain task can often only be fully assessed after promotion to the relevant position. Promotion must frequently be based on perceived potential, and although it is possible to point to somebody whose administrative skills are insubstantial it is not always easy to assess who will be able to cope with the more demanding tasks.

It has long been argued that assessment of teaching ability is difficult (although clear inability is often very apparent). Student and peer evaluations are possible and useful, as is scrutiny of the work done by the students taught. But criteria for judging teaching performance at university level are ill-defined, and what is expected from a lecturer/tutor/seminar leader often varies quite considerably within even a small group of students. Thus the majority of teachers are usually accepted as competent and undistinguished, and their performance is neither help nor hindrance to their promotion prospects.

And so the main criterion for promotion is usually research performance, although a relatively undistinguished record in this area can be compensated by excellence elsewhere. How then is research ability judged? Details of how research is undertaken are considered in the next section; here the concern is with its assessment rather than with stimulus and substance.

Successful research involves making an original contribution to a field of knowledge, in a variety of ways. It may involve the collection, presentation, and analysis of new information, within an accepted framework; it may be the development of new ways of collecting, analysing and presenting facts; it may comprise the development of a new way of ordering facts – a new theory or hypothesis; or it may be some combination of all three. The originality of a contribution is judged through its acceptance, or validation, by those of proven expertise in the particular field. The generally accepted validation procedure is publication, hence adages such as 'unpublished research isn't research' and 'publish or perish'.

The main outlets for the publication of research findings are the scholarly journals, which operate fairly standard procedures for the scrutiny of submitted contributions. (There is general belief that the journals published by academic societies tend to have higher standards than those published by commercial companies, but the validity of this is difficult to assess.) Manuscripts are submitted to the editor, who seeks the advice of qualified academics on the merits of the contribution; these referees will recommend either publication, rejection, or revision and resubmission. When accepted, a manuscript will enter the publication queue, which in some cases may be up to two years long, depending on the academic reputation of the journal.

Although widely accepted, this procedure has certain inbuilt flaws, largely because it is operated by human decision-makers. The opinions of both editor (on the manuscript, and on the choice of referees) and referees may be biased in some way, so that a paper can be rejected by one journal but accepted by another, without alteration. In most disciplines there is an informal ranking of journals in terms of their prestige, and it is considered more desirable to publish in some rather than others. (This prestige ranking is sometimes taken into consideration by appointment and promotion committees.)

Some research results are published in book form, rather than as journal articles. Most academic books in geography are texts, however, published by commercial companies whose main interest is marketability among the large student population. The textbook may be innovative in the way that it orders and presents material, and can be beneficial to its author's reputation (as well as bank balance), but it is not usually a vehicle for demonstrating research ability. Many companies, including the university presses, do publish research monographs, however, to present the results of major research projects to relatively small academic markets. Their decisions on whether to publish are made on academic as well as commercial grounds, usually with the aid of academic referees, and their output is validated through the book review columns of the journals.

Processes of promotion and appointment: patronage

Whatever the weighting given by the relevant committees to the three main academic activities (there are others pursued by some, such as consulting for outside bodies and contributions to the work of learned societies), there is still a major question of how such committees make their assessments. The only 'objective' information which can be presented to them is lists of publications, most of which have been validated by academic journals. But how is such information to be evaluated?

Two modes of assessment are widely used and relied upon: the written opinion of a third party (a referee) and the interview, sometimes associated with presentation of lecture or seminar. In the British model, considerable weight is placed on the former. An applicant for a position must supply a list of referees who will provide an opinion on the candidate's suitability for the post; fairly clearly, people are likely to ask those whom they have worked with, and who are favourably inclined towards them, to act in this capacity. As appointment committees tend to be swayed very much by these reports, especially in their preparation of a shortlist of candidates to be interviewed, the opinions of well respected members of the discipline who act as referees are often crucial. Thus certain leaders in a subject often find it easier to get their candidates appointed to posts than do others: there is a considerable element of patronage involved in obtaining a university post, especially a first university post.

Promotions under the British model are frequently based on the opinion of one person, the head of the candidate's department. Reports must be made on each lecturer: annually during the probation period, and then at the confirmation stage after probation, on reaching the 'efficiency bar', and for either accelerated promotion within the lecturer scale or promotion to senior lecturer. Again, therefore, there is a strong element of patronage, although constraints are built into the committee system to try and ensure fairness to all, including the right either to present one's own case or to appeal against a decision. Some universities use outside referees to provide extra evidence for cases of promotion to senior lecturer, and promotions to readerships and professorships always involve the use of external referees, usually nominated by the head of department concerned.

Referees and interviews are also used in the appointment of professors. Two sets of referees are used. The first contains those nominated by the candidates as being prepared to provide a confidential report on their potential for the job in question; the second is a group of assessors nominated by the university, usually senior academics in the relevant field. The latter not only comment on the list of candidates who have applied for established chairs but also suggest other worthy candidates who might be approached: their potential patronage power is great.

Procedures are slightly different under the American model. More weight is usually given to an enlarged interview, often involving candidates in giving seminars to the department and meeting with various groups of staff. (Such procedures are increasingly used in British universities.) The reference is still important, however, especially for aspirants to first teaching positions, and a letter from a respected leader in a field can be very influential in gaining appointment for a former student. In general, the individual candidate is more active in this system, however, perhaps canvassing for interviews during the annual conferences of scholarly societies, for example. For promotions and for salary rises there is considerable bargaining between individual, department chair, and university administrators: external referees' opinions may be sought when tenure is being confirmed, or promotion to full professor proposed.

In all of these procedures the applicants depend to a considerable extent on the opinions of senior academic colleagues in the evaluation of their prospects. Some opinions carry more weight than others, and so it is important when developing a career to identify potentially influential individuals, to keep them informed of your work, and to enlist their support for your advancement. Because of the lack of truly objective criteria for measuring research, teaching and administrative ability, such patronage is crucial.

Other rewards and the sources of status

The tangible rewards of an academic career are the salary and the life style, plus the occasional extra earnings that are possible – for examining, writing, lecturing and consulting. In addition the hours are flexible; the possibilities for travel are considerable; and the constraints on when, where and how work is done are relatively few, compared to most other professions. And there are other, less tangible rewards. Involvement with the intellectual development of students is a considerable reward for many, and brings much satisfaction. There is also the charisma associated with recognized excellent teachers, and even more so for leading researchers, whose publications are widely read, whose invitations to give outside lectures are many, and whose opinions as examiners, referees and reviewers are widely canvassed. And the conduct of research brings its own rewards, apart from the charisma; the satisfaction of having identified and solved a significant problem is often considerable, and a major reward for the dedicated researcher.

One reward common to social systems exists in the academic community too: power. Patronage is power, as is any work as examiner, referee, or reviewer. The careers of others are being affected, and exercise of this power can bring with it the loyalty and respect of those who benefit. Because the academic system is so dependent on the opinions of individuals, because the opinions of some individuals are more valued than are those of others, and because power over others is a 'commodity' widely desired in most societies, many academics seek positions of influence.

Among the most influential positions within an academic discipline are the administrative headships of departments. Holders of these positions can instruct other staff members (usually after consultation) in their teaching and administrative duties; they are frequently used by staff and students as referees for job and other (such as research grant) applications; and their reports are crucial in the promotions procedure. The departmental organiza-tion of universities is a bureaucratic device which makes for relative ease in administering what is often a very large institution. (It also tends to fossilize disciplinary boundaries, as will be discussed later.) Departmental heads not only have power over members of their own discipline's staff, they also par-ticipate in the administration of the university as a whole, and they treat within the university committee system for departmental resources. As in all bureaucracies, there is a tendency for the status and power of the various departmental heads to be a function of the size of their 'empires' (Tullock, 1976). Heads of large departments, especially large and growing departments (growth being generally considered as a 'good thing') and those attracting large numbers of students and research grants/contracts, are very often the most important individuals in a bureaucracy. Thus they have the incentive, whether or not they are permanent occupants of the headship, to build up their departments, which usually means increasing student numbers, since universities tend to allocate resources to departments according to the numbers taught. This brings power and prestige, both within the university and beyond; it is an added reward for the academic bureaucrat, and the power over resources which it involves is usually of benefit to the whole department.

Finally, the academic bureaucrat, whether or not a head of department, can gain power beyond the home university through, for example, obtaining positions on committees. These may be concerned with the subject through professional bodies, with the allocation of research moneys by public or private foundations, or with a wide range of public duties. Again, the status and power obtained can spill over to others, since patronage is important in all of those roles.

The Academic Working Environment

The continuing goal of an academic discipline is the advancement of knowledge. Each discipline pursues that goal with regard to particular areas of study. Its individual members contribute by conducting research and reporting their findings, by integrating material into the disciplinary corpus, and by pedagogical activities aimed at informing about, promoting and reproducing the discipline: in addition, they may argue the discipline's 'relevance' to society at large. But there is no fixed set of disciplines, nor any one correct division of academia according to subject matter. Those disciplines currently in existence are contained within boundaries established by earlier communities of scholars. The boundaries are porous, so that disciplines interact. Occasionally the boundaries are changed, usually through the establishment of a new discipline that occupies an enclave within the pre-existing division of academic space. (The boundaries are not necessarily the same in all comparable institutions.)

Just as there is no immutable set of disciplinary boundaries so there is also no right way of undertaking research nor, in many cases, any exact criteria for determining whether research findings, and even more their interpretations, are correct. The 'right' and 'wrong' ways of doing research, the 'correct' and 'incorrect' interpretations of research findings, and the 'proper' ways of presenting knowledge and training students are all the product of decisions by academics themselves. Thus, not surprisingly, there is considerable debate within disciplines over these issues. At any one time, there may be consensus within a disciplinary community regarding both its subject matter and its research methods. But controversy is just as likely, as academics discuss the relevance of particular research findings, the validity of certain research methodologies, and so on. Indeed, there is controversy over the definition of knowledge itself.

The study of the controversies and consensuses that characterize academic disciplines is the function of historians of science. (Science is used here as a very broad term to encompass the entire range of academic disciplines in the natural and social sciences.) To the outsider, the workings of a science are generally mysterious – especially regarding disciplines that require a great degree of prior training before original research is undertaken and whose literature is virtually impenetrable to the untrained. It is generally believed, however, that science is an objective activity undertaken within very strict rules, and involves the continuous excitement of the search for new discoveries. Indeed, scientists frequently present themselves in this light. A certain set of values, it is suggested, is universally subscribed to within academia. The main five (according to Mulkay, 1975, p. 510) are:

1   The norm of originality; academics strive to advance knowledge, and they conduct original research designed to discover and account for aspects of the world as yet not fully understood;
2   The norm of communality; all information is shared within the academic community – it is transferred through accepted channels (notably the research journals) and its provenance is always recognized when it is being used;
3   The norm of disinterestedness; academics are devoted to their subject, and their main reward is the satisfaction of participating in the advancement of knowledge – a reward that may bring with it charisma and promotion;
4   The norm of universalism; judgements are made on entirely impartial criteria, which take into account the academic merits of work only and make no reference to the personalities of the researchers; and
5   The norm of organized skepticism; knowledge is furthered by a continuing process of constructive criticism, by which academics are always reconsidering both their own work and that of others.

According to these five norms, therefore, academic work is carried out in a neutral fashion; there is a complete lack of partiality, self-seeking, secrecy and intellectual prejudice. The existence of objective criteria for assessment is assumed, as are high levels of ability and humility on the part of members of the academic community.

Against this ideal view of science and scientists, one which many of the latter seek to promote, are the results of studies in the history of science (most of which refer to the physical sciences: Mulkay 1975; Mulkay, Gilbert and Woolgar, 1975). These show that the procedures adopted are frequently by no means objective and neutral, and the picture they present is of disciplines that grow 'by gathering more detail in areas already investigated, and by stumbling across new sets of facts in areas of experience never previously investigated' (Barnes, 1974, p. 5). Science as a whole is a culture, and each discipline within it is one (or more) subculture(s). It has its own rules and procedures which, like those in other cultures and subcultures, are open to change as a result of internal decision-making. Furthermore (as will be suggested in more detail below), scientific cultures are parts of wider cultures, and although to some extent scientists – because of their (self-imposed) expert status – can impose their own views of themselves on their host societies, they are subject to external influences (see Barnes, 1974).

Each scientific discipline is a separate academic community, therefore; many are groupings of several related communities. The goal is the advancement of knowledge, but the definitions of advancement and of knowledge itself are influenced, if not determined, by the members of the community. Thus the study of the history of a discipline is not simply a chronology of its successes. It is an investigation of the sociology of a community, of its debates, deliberations and decisions as well as of its findings. (See Watson, 1968, for an example of this; for a fictional account, see Cooper, 1952.) Such investigations may take one of two general forms. The first is the empiricist which seeks to portray history as it happened. In this, each community is treated separately and is the subject of a specific history. The other seeks to generalize, to understand how sciences progress. This involves either an inductive approach – studying individual histories and identifying their common themes – or a deductive framework that provides a model of scientific progress against which events in a particular discipline are compared. Most of the models currently available have been developed for, and tested on, the physical sciences. Their relevance to human geography has been suggested, however (e.g. Haggett and Chorley, 1967; Harvey, 1973) and they are presented here as a backcloth for a later evaluation of the substantive material arranged in Chapters 2–8.

Kuhn, normal science, and revolutions

The framework for studying the history of science that has received most attention (indeed, the book is one of the most frequently cited by social scientists) is T. S. Kuhn's (1962, 1970a) *The Structure of Scientific Revolutions*. As Kuhn himself (see Kuhn, 1970b) and many commentators have pointed out, this work is a study in the sociology of science. It is a positive interpretation – a presentation of what scientists do – rather than a normative programme – an argument for what scientists *ought* to do. And it seeks to make generalizations, to identify common elements in the histories of scientific disciplines, although these generalizations are not the basis for a predictive methodology. Kuhn's goal is to identify 'what science, scientific research as it is actually practised, is really like' (Barnes, 1982, p. 1).

According to Kuhn, scientists work in communities, groups of researchers and teachers who share a common approach to their work. They operate within an agreed philosophy, concur on the theoretical focus of their work and use accepted methodological procedures. Their research involves using the procedures to solve problems identified within the theoretical framework, thereby adding to knowledge (the store of problems solved) and extending the range of their theory. The framework, its procedures, and its empirical substance are codified in their textbooks. What they share is termed a *paradigm* by Kuhn; 'a scientific community consists of men who share a paradigm' (Kuhn, 1970a, p. 176). What this means, as Popper (1959) expresses it, is that once scientists are socialized into a research field they can proceed directly to its unsolved problems. The existing framework defines these problems, providing a context for the research, and a methodology is available with which they can be tackled. The researcher does not set out to tackle a problem *de novo*, therefore, but on the basis of what is already known in the chosen field. Thus a paradigm is 'an accepted problem-solution' (Barnes, 1982, p. xiv), which by its very solution poses the next problem. Progress in science is achieved by problem-solving.

To be able to undertake research within a paradigm requires an understanding and acceptance of its philosophy and methodology. This is provided by a period of training, during which the potential new researcher is socialized into the paradigmatic culture, its way of thinking about its scientific problems. The key to this training is the paradigm's textbooks, the summaries of its literature which define what is known and how more knowledge can be obtained. The purpose of this training is preparation for work within an accepted mould: 'Scientific training is dogmatic and authoritarian . . . [it] does not generate or encourage traits such as creativity or logical rigour; rather it equips scientists so that it is possible for them to be creative, or rigorous, or whatever else, in the context of a specific form of culture' (Barnes, 1982, pp. 16–17.)

Having been integrated into the paradigm through a period of training, the scientist joins a research community. Such communities, sometimes termed 'invisible colleges', operate through close interaction involving attendance at specialized conferences and the private circulation of research papers in pre-publication form, and reflected in citations to each other's work (Crane, 1972). Within such communities, individuals receive recognition for the value of their work and attract the patronage of leaders who may assist in their career advancement; some communities have only a few patrons, perhaps even one, and may be identified as a particular school of thought.

The nature of research within a paradigm involves filling in the gaps; the researcher 'has to make the unknown into an instance of the known, into another routine case' (Barnes, 1982, p. 49). The paradigm provides the resources for this task – guidance but not direction. Success, which brings the rewards of recognition, patronage and status, involves conforming to the paradigmatic norms (Mulkay, 1975, p. 515):

> It is clear that the quality or significance of a scientist's work is judged in relation to the existing set of scientific assumptions and expectations. Thus, whereas radical departures from a well defined framework are unlikely to be granted recognition early under normal circumstances, original contributions which confirm to established preconceptions will be quickly rewarded.

Thus the dominant norm of academic life is not one of the five listed above (p. 10), but rather conformity. Science is not the constant search for novel discoveries but rather the careful application of agreed procedures to the solution of problems in order to extend existing well-structured bodies of knowledge. Judgements are being made all of the time, but within an academic environment carefully structured by the training process. Science progresses through filling the gaps in a pre-defined framework.

This operation of a paradigm is known as *normal science* (Kuhn, 1962, pp. 35.6):

> Perhaps the most striking feature of the normal research problems . . . is how little they aim to produce major novelties, conceptual or phenomenal. Sometimes . . . everything but the most esoteric detail of the result is known in advance . . . the range of anticipated, and thus assimilable, results is always small compared with the range that imaginations can conceive . . . the aim of normal science is not major substantive novelties . . . the results gained in normal research are significant because they add to the scope and precision with which the paradigm can be applied. . . . Though its outcome can be anticipated, often in detail so great that what remains to be known is itself uninteresting, the way to achieve that outcome remains very much in doubt. . . . The man who succeeds proves himself an expert problemsolver.

Within normal science, therefore, the researcher has available:

1 an accepted body of knowledge, ordered and interpreted in a particular way;
2 an indication of the puzzles that remain to be solved; and
3 a set of procedures for puzzle-solving.

Training within a paradigm places the researcher in a fairly deep rut, and provides the tools for extending the paradigmatic body of knowledge (deepening the rut). The result is 'conventional, routinised practice' (Barnes, 1982, p. 11). This does not imply, however, that normal scientific activity is one of 'long periods of dreary conformity' (p. 13) because extending and developing knowledge is not simply 'a matter of following instructions or rules. Rather, normal science is a test of ingenuity and imagination, with paradigms figuring largely among the cultural resources of the scientist' (p. 13). Solving problems is rarely easy; Kuhn uses chess-playing as an example, arguing that much ingenuity as well as existing knowledge (practice) must be brought to bear if many of the problems that it sets are to be solved (Kuhn, 1970c, pp. 36–39).

Scientists are not omniscient. They do not understand everything – even within a particular paradigm – so that occasionally their predictions prove to be inaccurate. While the process of normal science continues, therefore, slowly accumulating extra knowledge as problems are solved, it sometimes throws up anomalies, findings that are not in accord with the paradigm's assumptions. These must be accounted for (Barnes, 1982, p. 53):

> Puzzle-solving activity frequently attempts to show that what is *prima facie* anomalous is either the spurious product of bad equipment or technique, or a familiar phenomenon in disguise. And most anomalies are successfully assimilated in this way.

Either the work was badly done or the researcher interpreted the results wrongly. Minor adaptation of the paradigm may be needed, but the general process of normal science continues.

Some anomalies cannot readily be accounted for, however, and they continue to worry a few scientists. Their persistence leads to work on alternative paradigms, potential new frameworks that structure knowledge so that there are no anomalies. This is 'extraordinary research', conducted outside the bounds of the accepted paradigm. When it is successful, a 'revolutionary episode' is in progress. Regarding such research, Kuhn (1962, pp. 89–90) notes that:

> Almost always the men who achieve these fundamental inventions of a new paradigm have been either very young or very new to the field whose paradigm they change . . . obviously these are the men who, being little committed by prior practice to the traditional rules of normal science, are particularly likely to see that those rules no longer define a playable game and to conceive another set that can replace them.

The result is an alternative paradigm, which is presented to the adherents of the current normal science. These are asked to make a judgement, a major choice between two competing views of their chosen subject. A preference must be expressed. Either the accepted mode of working is to be maintained, despite the anomalies, or a new subculture is to be adopted. The invitation is to discard existing authorities and habits and to take up new ones, which claim to be superior – because they are better predictors of that aspect of the world being studied. If the need for change is accepted, then a revolution in scientific practice occurs; one paradigm is replaced by another. That choice between competing paradigms is an extremely difficult one because of their incommensurability; there are no common standards against which both can be compared. As Kuhn (1970a) points out

> the proponents of competing paradigms will often disagree about the list of problems that any candidate for paradigm must resolve. Their standards or their definitions of science are not the same (p. 148).

Further, the new paradigm will almost certainly use some of the language and procedures of that it is seeking to replace, but in slightly different ways, giving rise to considerable misunderstanding in discussions between the rival paradigms' antagonists. More importantly, however, the two groups of scientists may be looking at the world in very different ways

> Both are looking at the world, and what they look at has not changed. But in some areas they see different things, and they see them in different relations one to the other. That is why a law that cannot even be demonstrated to one group of scientists may occasionally seem intuitively obvious to another (p. 150).

Thus the switch from one paradigm to another, if it is made, is not forced simply by logic. It is what Kuhn calls a 'gestalt switch', a decision to abandon one way of viewing the world and replace it by another on intuitive grounds, rather than through the application of strict scientific criteria, that one is better than the other. Of course, not all scientists may come to the same intuitive decision, so that some continue to work in the context of a paradigm that others have discredited.

Kuhn's representation of scientific activity, therefore, is that researchers are trained to employ a proven mode of looking at their subject matter and to use an accepted methodology for solving the problems that they identify. Their problem-solving proceeds in a steady, cumulative manner, adding to the store of knowledge: small modifications may be needed to accommodate minor anomalies that they discover. Very occasionally, anomalies are encountered which cannot be either explained away or accommodated. Some researchers may decide to focus on these, and to develop new paradigms that will account for them, as well as everything else that was already known. When this is achieved, the new paradigm is presented to the research community for approval. A revolution is invited, for the alternative paradigms are incommensurable and only one can be right: the community is asked to accept a new direction to its work. In a sentence, therefore, science proceeds in a steady fashion, along well-trodden paths, with occasional major breaks in its continuity marked by important changes in the organization of its material, in the definition of its problems, and in its techniques for problem-solving.

Criticisms of Kuhn's approach, and his response

Kuhn's work stimulated a great deal of debate among philosophers of science, because it challenged orthodox views of scientific progress and implied, especially in the concept of revolutions, that some scientific decision-making was 'irrational' (see Watkins, 1970, on Kuhn's analogy between scientific and religious communities). Indeed, it was the introduction and treatment of the concept of the revolutionary episode that attracted much of the attention (see Stegmuller, 1978). This was because most of the views of science that Kuhn was challenging were normative rather than positive; they prescribed what science *should be* like whereas he described what it was *actually* like.

A major problem that many commentators had with Kuhn's original presentation was that the term paradigm was used in a variety of ways. Masterman (1970) identified no less than twenty-one different usages, which 'makes paradigm elucidation genuinely difficult for the superficial reader' (p. 61). From these, she was able to distil three main groups of definitions, as follows.

1   The *metaparadigms* (or metaphysical paradigms), which can be equated with 'world views', or general organizing principles;
2   The *sociological paradigms*, which are the concrete scientific achievements of a community which define the working habits; and
3   The *artefact* or *construct paradigms*, the classic works that provide the tools for future work.

It is the second of these which provides the structure within which individual scientists work, whereas the third provides the means for puzzle-solving within that structure.

Kuhn accepted the force of Masterman's case, and in later writings clarified his views. In doing so, he focused almost entirely on the second and third of Masterman's definitions. First, however, he indicated that were he to rewrite the original book, he would give primacy not to paradigms but to scientific communities (Kuhn, 1970a), because it is as members of communities that scientists work. Such communities operate at a variety of scales: the global community of natural scientists, for example; the main professional groups (physicists, chemists etc.); and intra-professional groups working on particular empirical problems. The last are the focus of his attention

> Communities of this sort are the units that this book has presented as the producers and validators of scientific knowledge. Paradigms are something shared by members of such groups (p. 178).

With regard to the use of the term paradigm in this context, Kuhn (1977) suggests a twofold definition, with the second fitting within the first.

> One sense of 'paradigm' is global, embracing all the shared commitments of a scientific group; the other isolates a particularly important sort of commitment and is thus a subset of the first (p. 460).

The first definition, the sociological, is of what he terms a *disciplinary matrix*: 'what the members of a scientific community, and they alone, share' (p. 460). Such a matrix comprises (Kuhn, 1970c, pp. 152 ff): the accepted generalizations; shared commitments to particular models, guiding frameworks for the construction and validation of theories (elsewhere – Kuhn, 1977, p. 501 – he equates the disciplinary matrix with a theory); and shared values as to the procedures to be applied. It also contains a fourth element, which provides the second, and subsidiary, definition of paradigms, and which he claimed (Kuhn, 1977, p. xx) was the originally intended meaning. This is the set of *exemplars* (the construct or artefact paradigms in Masterman's classification), which are

> the concrete problem-solutions that students encounter from the start of their scientific education, whether in laboratories, in examinations, or at the ends of chapters in science texts. To these shared examples should, however, be added at least some of the technical problem-solutions found in the periodical literature that scientists encounter during their post-educational research careers and that also show them by example how their job is to be done (p. 187).

The solution of a problem involves scientists in recourse to these exemplars; they search for analogies, classic works that will suggest how the current problem should be approached. Thus students learn about the exemplars, and apply them in their own training, in order to appreciate the empirical content of their disciplinary matrix. This provides a way of working for scientists:

> One of the fundamental techniques by which the members of a group, whether an entire culture or a specialists' sub-community within it, learn to see the same things when confronted with the same stimuli is by being shown examples of situations that their predecessors in the group have already learned to see as like each other and as different from other sorts of situations (pp. 193–4).

Revolutions, then, can involve the replacement of one exemplar by another, the modification of the existing set of exemplars to accommodate new material, or the replacement of the disciplinary matrix. The last, a revolution in the sociological paradigm, is presumably a major event in the history of a science; the first and second can occur without affecting the bases of the disciplinary matrix.

The usual interpretation of Kuhn's work is that scientific communities are operating within one paradigm, according to the normal science model, whereas according to Masterman (1970) and others it is possible to have long periods of non-paradigm, multi-paradigm, or dual-paradigm activity. This possibility is addressed in an alternative view of the history of sciences presented by Lakatos (1978a). With Kuhn, Lakatos accepts that no theory (or paradigm) is falsified until a better theory is available, but he posits long debates between competing theories. Central to the debates are what he calls *research programmes* (which are similar to Kuhn's paradigms as disciplinary matrices). Each programme has a hard core, an irrefutable central set of beliefs (Lakatos calls it the *modus tollens*). The methodological rules of the programme include a negative heuristic which directs attention away from the hard core. It also includes a positive heuristic, which directs researchers towards the solution of problems in the 'protective belt' that surrounds the core. Anomalies are solved in this protective belt, by the development of auxiliary hypotheses which can account for the observed deviations and so protect the programme's core. Thus progress within a research programme depends on the ingenuity of the scientists in devising hypotheses that are consistent with the core and which can account for anomalies. Success 'hardens' the core, and is measured by the number of 'verifications' or successful predictions, not by failures ('refutations'). The content of the core itself is never in doubt. (The core, according to Lakatos, 1978b, is conventionally accepted and 'irrefutable', defining the problems within a preconceived plan: p. 110.) Research programmes may falter, however. Their positive heuristic may fail to produce successful predictions. When this happens, the programme falls into a degenerative phase, and it is thus ripe for replacement by a new programme which is still in the progressive phase of expanding its content substantially. A programme shift takes place because the new is able to demonstrate its superiority over the old, in much the same way as Kuhn's paradigm shifts, except that the shift usually takes a considerable time. Change is not instantaneous, Lakatos claims (despite its presentation as such in 'scientific folklore': p. 85). Nor are there crucial experiments, the results of which convince a community that one programme is right and the other wrong. (With hindsight, crucial experiments may be identified, but these are not recognized as such at the time when they are reported. There is a danger, Lakatos and others claim, of rewriting history as a series of crucial experiments.) Thus much of the history of a discipline may involve two or more competing research programmes coexisting (Lakatos, 1978a, p. 69):

> The history of science has been and should be a history of competing research programmes (or, if you wish, 'paradigms'), but it has not been and must not become a succession of periods of normal science: the sooner competition starts the better for progress.

Lakatos not only recognizes but requires theoretical pluralism (which leads to criticism from Barnes, 1982, that his is a normative view of science, not a positive one like Kuhn's), and within this pluralist situation (Lakatos, 1978a, p. 92):

> Criticism of a programme is a long and often frustrating process and one must treat budding programmes leniently.

Although Lakatos denies Kuhn's concept of normal science as one of paradigm dominance within a discipline, he accepts that progressive research programmes comprise relatively routine extensions to knowledge through the testing of new hypotheses derived from the positive heuristic. Refutations are rare; the aim is verification and progress. Popper has argued against this, however, claiming that 'science is essentially critical' (Popper, 1970, p. 55), being characterized not by normal science but by extraordinary research. To him, the normal scientist is really an applied scientist (Popper, 1970, pp. 52–3):

> 'Normal' science . . . is the activity of the non-revolutionary, or more precisely, the not-too-critical professional: of the science student who accepts the ruling dogma of the day; who does not wish to challenge it; and who accepts a new revolutionary theory only if almost everybody else is ready to accept it —if it becomes fashionable by a kind of bandwagon effect. To resist a new fashion

needs perhaps as much courage as was needed to bring it about . . . The success of the 'normal' scientist consists, entirely, in showing that the ruling theory can be properly and satisfactorily applied in order to reach a solution of the puzzle in question.

Science, to Popper, consists of bold conjectures and the conduct of experiments designed to refute them. (In his view of science – see p. 72 – hypotheses can never be verified, only falsified, so that disciplines are in constant revolution as researchers seek to prove that each others' theories are wrong.

Popper's concept of a 'revolution in permanence' has been criticized by Barnes (1982) as normative and not descriptive of science as it is actually practised. Kuhn's (1970, p. 243) response is that:

> [Popper] and his group argue that the scientist should try at all times to be a critic and a proliferator of alternate theories. I urge the desirability of an alternate strategy which reserves such behaviour for special occasions.

According to this alternative strategy, most scientists are 'normal scientists' working routinely rather than critically. This view is supported by Eilon (1975), who has classified management scientists into:

1 Chroniclers, whose role is to describe reality within the constraints of a particular paradigm;
2 Dialecticians, who stimulate debate and progress – a dialectician 'believes it is necessary to debate and argue issues in order to elicit the facts . . . challenging stated views or records, in order to uncover what otherwise may remain hidden from an innocent observer' (Eilon, 1975, p. 361);
3 Puzzle-solvers, who advance the empirical content of the accepted paradigm;
4 Empiricists, who are like chroniclers in their focus on description;
5 Classifiers, who take information generated by empiricists and chroniclers and order it within the paradigm framework;
6 Iconoclasts, who destroy cherished beliefs, the assumptions on which they are built, the deductions, conclusions and interpretations, and expose the incompatibilities between theory and practice, between predicted and observed worlds – such iconoclasts may be destructive only, or they may be constructive in their presentation of alternative theories, in which case they are the agents of paradigm change; and
7 Change-agents, who are the applied scientists concerned not so much with the establishment of theories and facts but rather with the use of existing knowledge to create a better world.

Individual workers may occupy (not necessarily contemporaneously) more than one of these archetypes. If Kuhn and Lakatos are correct, however, most will be chroniclers, puzzle-solvers, empiricists and classifers (Mercer, 1977).

The change-agents, too, are conformists, since they seek to apply the accepted normal science, not to challenge it. Popper, then, focuses on a few key scientists, and seeks to characterize the whole of science as if they were typical. (Note, however, that in defending this view, Magee (1975, p. 41) claims that the work of normal scientists can be studied in Popperian terms. They may 'take for granted, in order to solve problems at a lower level, theories which only a few of their colleagues are questioning', but they should be seeking intra-paradigm progress by using the methodology of conjecture and refutation. Note also Barnes', 1982, contention that much 'normal science' research involves refuting conjectures.)

Popper's arguments have been taken much further by Feyerabend (1975). He claims that history is a series of accidents, and that this is how it should be. Similarly science should be allowed to evolve as a series of accidents, since this is the best way of ensuring progress. In the past, the main discoveries have been made by individuals who either deliberately or unwittingly flouted the rules, but modern scientific education seeks to prevent this by constraining its practitioners into myopic paradigms. Feyerabend claims that the only rule in science should be 'anything goes', in a scientific anarchy, like a political anarchy whose hallmark is (Feyerabend, 1975, p. 187):

> its opposition to the established order of things: to the state; its institutions, the ideologies that support and glorify those institutions.

Like Popper, however, Feyerabend presents a normative model, one that is concerned with major scientific developments and not with their everyday extensions. With regard to these latter, if Lakatos is correct, and not Kuhn – if revolutions take a long time – then this suggests that a discipline need not be characterized by consensus over much of its history. Is it likely that a body of scholars (especially a large body) will agree on ends and means and will not differ at all, except very occasionally and then only for short periods, on fundamental interpretations? From his research on radio astronomy, Mulkay (1978, p. 11) concludes that 'Scientific consensus . . . in a given area of interest is seldom complete'. A discipline may contain several branches (Mulkay, 1975, p. 520):

> In science, new problem areas are regularly created and associated social networks formed . . . The onset of growth in a new area typically follows the perception, by scientists already at work in one or more existing areas, of unresolved problems, unexpected observations or unusual technical advances, the pursuit of which lies outside their present field. Thus the exploitation of a new area is usually set in motion by a process of scientific migration.

This does not involve a paradigm shift, nor even a degenerating research programme. Rather it indicates the establishment of a new paradigm-exemplar (in Lakatosian terms, a shift to another area of the positive heuristic or protective aureole). A new branch may be identified either by its focus on methods and techniques, or by its attention to, as-yet, relatively ignored subject matter.

The branching process suggested by Mulkay allows for debate and movement within a paradigm/research programme without substantial conflict,
since the disciplinary matrix/hard core is not being attacked, let alone the
'world view' (see p. 16). Kuhn (1977, p. 462) accepts this, noting that 'Individual scientists, particularly the ablest, will belong to several such [branches]
. . ., either simultaneously or in succession', and Suppe (1977b, p. 498) notes
that inter-branch consensus is usual:

> to account for normal science all [one] has to assume is that scientists in a parti-
> cular scientific community are in sufficient agreement on what theory to
> employ, what counts as good and bad science, what the relevant questions are,
> what sort of work to take as exemplary, and so forth.

It is the disciplinary matrix/hard core that is central to the paradigm/research
programme, not the exemplars and the type of problem that is attacked.

Training in its disciplinary matrix allows researchers to move among
branches of a scientific community, therefore. Such branches may eventually
break away, establishing new communities – if not new disciplinary
matrices – by what may be termed 'quiet revolutions'. Such breaks are not
usually in the interests of the parent community, on political grounds, for they
are likely to be against the interests of the disciplinary bureaucracy; separate
communities competing for students and research funds, yet covering similar
subject-matter, are not favoured. Thus communities may be prepared to contain dissenting groups, even potential revolutionaries, rather than risk break-
away success. But such dissent is often contained, and may even be repressed
(see Lichtenberger, 1984). Toulmin (1970, p. 45) notes that the conflict is frequently intergenerational:

> perhaps every new generation of scientists having any original ideas or 'slant'
> of its own finds itself, at certain points and in certain respects, at cross-purposes
> with the immediately preceding generation.

Its seniors may decide to accommodate the differences, 'for the good of the
subject'. But (Mulkay, 1978, p. 116):

> there are now several well documented studies of instances where demonstrably
> competent scientists have been excluded from a field of study as their ideas have
> come to diverge from those in the majority.

Thus in some cases the competition between paradigms/research programmes
is contained within a discipline. In others, it results in the establishment of
separate disciplines, usually after a stage in which the nascent discipline
operates as a separate community within the parent body.

Kuhn and the social sciences

These critiques of Kuhn's ideas collectively focus on most of the elements of
his thesis. Thus Lakatos questions whether revolutions are achieved in short
periods, Popper doubts the existence of normal science, and Mulkay suggests

that several paradigms (as exemplars) can coexist within a discipline which is not characterized by consensus. In all cases, there is no questioning the basic world-view, which (implicitly) is that science is the study of an empirical world, in which subject and object can be separated, and that scientific progress is measured by the volume of successful predictions. This assumes a certain philosophy of knowledge, as made clear below (p. 30).

This last assumption raises doubts about the validity of Kuhn's thesis — plus those of Lakatos, Popper and Mulkay — to the social sciences. It has not prevented social scientists seeking to fit the Kuhnian model to their disciplines, however, an exercise which Kuhn himself thought to be nonviable (because of the great variety of incommensurable writings: Kuhn, 1970a, p. 165) and which has drawn scathing criticism (Barnes, 1982, p. 120):

> The popularity of debates about whether sociology has a paradigm, or whether there have been scientific revolutions in economics or in psychology, attests more to the prevalence of intellectual laziness than to the significance of Kuhn's thinking. He himself . . . has stressed that a case for their utility has only been made in the context of the history of the natural sciences.

Kuhn's model of how sciences operate is not positivist, but his conception of science is, in that he talks of paradigms (especially exemplars) being assessed according to their predictive ability (1970c, p. 185). This is not a valid approach according to some social scientists, as parts of this book will show. Particular paradigms/research programmes may be assessed on the criterion of predictive accuracy, with degenerative phases following poor predictions (as Blaug, 1975, suggests for economics), but how does one assess different world-views, basic conceptions of the nature of science?(This is Masterman's 1970, first definition of a paradigm, which Kuhn did not respond to: see also Gutting, 1980, and Hacking, 1983.) A switch from one world-view to another, from one conception of science to another, clearly should fit Kuhn's model in that the two conceptions are incommensurable and the decision must involve an 'act of faith' rather than one compelled by defined criteria logically applied. But Kuhn's work does not address such a switch, since all of his examples come from the natural sciences (as Kuhn, 1979, himself stresses; he does not claim relevance to the social sciences for his model).

One potential framework for the analysis of a social science discipline that is not confined to the particular world-view of Kuhn and his critics has been outlined in Foucault's (1972) *The Archaeology of Knowledge*. This aims to provide a method for the 'pure description' of discourses, which are unified systems of statements (however expressed) that can only be understood within their context (Foucault, 1972, p. 97):

> One cannot say a sentence, one cannot transform it into a statement, unless a collateral space is brought into operation.

Anything that is said or written can only be understood by those privy to the context of the discourse; as with a language, one can only comprehend the words, and the sequence in which they are used, because one understands the rules that govern their use.

According to this view, the history of ideas is the history of discourses, of systems (somewhat akin to languages) used for the discussion of subjects that are defined within the discourses. (There is, for example, no fixed definition of madness; each discourse that discusses it has its own definition and any discussion of madness is particular to that definition and the discourse in which it is set.) The nature of a discourse is deposited in an archive, and it is the function of archaeology to reconstitute the discourse from the archive, to describe what was being done in a particular configuration (Foucault, 1972, pp. 138–40, 157–65). It describes the nature of the discourse without imposing a prescribed framework upon it. As Foucault (1972, pp. 33–4) describes nineteenth-century medical science:

> [it] was characterized not so much by its objects or concepts as by a certain *style*, a certain constant manner of statement . . . medicine no longer consisted of a group of traditions, observations and heterogeneous practices, but of a corpus of knowledge that presupposed the same way of looking at things . . . [in addition it was] a group of hypotheses about life and death, of ethical choices, of therapeutic decisions, of institutional regulations, of teaching models, as a group of descriptions . . . if there is a unity, its principle is not therefore a determined form of statements; is it not rather the group of rules, which, simultaneously or in turn, have made possible purely perceptual descriptions . . .? What one must characterize and individualize is the coexistence of these dispersed and heterogeneous statements; the system that governs their division, the degree to which they depend upon one another, the way in which they interlock or exclude one another, the transformation that they undergo, and the play of their location, arrangement, and replacement. . . .

Discourses, therefore, are sets of mutually agreed rules which govern description and discussion among the members who agree those rules, and in that sense they are similar to the scientific communities given central place in Kuhn's (1970a) later statements. They are not independent of wider conditions, however. Archaeology may identify separate discursive formations, but these must be related to what Foucault calls the *episteme*, defined as (Foucault, 1972, p. 19):

> something like a world-view, a slice of history common to all branches of knowledge, which imposes on each one the same norms and postulates, a general stage of reason, a certain structure of thought that the men of a particular period cannot escape.

In this concept, he appears to suggest that in any period a particular world-view (macro-paradigm?) predominates and influences (controls?) the contents of individual discourses. Presumably, too, there must be periods of competition between *epistemes* (which may suggest a similar process to that outlined by Lakatos). Foucault does not outline how such change occurs, however. One is left with the concept of discourses set in a societal matrix, but with little indication of how the nature of the matrix changes, presumably in part through its interactions with those discourses.

Foucault's ideas set the study of scientific disciplines more firmly in the context of the wider environment in which (and for which) they are practised than is the case with the other approaches discussed here, all of which very largely abstract the study of science from its social milieu. (As Berdoulay, 1971, expresses it: 'little interest is paid to historical contexts or intellectual climates since the focus is placed on the internal evolution of each science' – p. 9.) Such abstraction is especially unfortunate for the social sciences, the disciplines that investigate and interact with their milieux and whose contents, in the broadest sense if not in detail, are likely to be strongly influenced by that context. Just how social science and society interact remains to be mapped out in detail (as, of course, does the interaction between natural science and society because the contents of the former, too, are clearly influenced by the environmental constraints), and whether Foucault's proposal of a single dominating *episteme* at any time is valid is open to doubt. That human geography should be studied in its social context appears an irrefutable claim, however. The remainder of this chapter outlines that context.

The External Environment

The discussion so far in this chapter has suggested that scientific disciplines (and/or discourses) are communities, small societies that are microcosms of those within which they are contained. As such, the proper study of how they operate is sociological, although philosophy may provide a normative framework for such investigation.

Sociological studies of contemporary societies accept that communities are not autonomous. Their members are not cut off from the world. (Some of the earliest, monastic scientific communities were, of course.) They need the support of the wider society in order to exist, for society employs academics. And while in part scientists may be able to impose their own priorities over what type of work is done, they are strongly influenced by external factors (Barnes, 1972, pp. 102–3):

> Social, technical and economic determinants routinely affect the rate and direction of scientific growth. . . . It is true that much scientific change occurs despite, rather than because of, external direction or financial control. . . . Progress in the disinterested study [of certain] . . . areas has probably occurred just that bit more rapidly because of their relevance to other matters.

Thus the study of a discipline must be set in its societal context. It must not necessarily be assumed, however, that members of academic communities fully accept the social context and the directives and impulses that it issues. They may wish to counter it, and use their academic base as a focus for their discontent. But the (potential) limits to that discontent are substantial. Most academic communities are located in universities, many of which are dependent for their existence on public funds disbursed by governments which may use their financial power to influence, if not direct, what is taught and researched. And some universities are dependent on private sources of finance, so they must convince their sponsors that their work is relevant to current societal concerns (as Taylor, 1985c, suggests). What, then, have those concerns been in the period covered by this book?

World War II is more than a convenient period from which to commence this history of human geography; it marked a major watershed in the development of the societies which are the prime focus of the book – the United Kingdom and the United States. It cannot be considered in isolation, however. Just as important for the present discussion are the world-wide economic depression which preceded it and the Cold War, the economic boom, and then the recession and restructuring which followed.

For the first time a major international conflict was not determined solely by the sacrifices of men in battles on land and sea, although there were many such sacrifices during World War II. And the extra dimensions of this war did not just involve the development of air space as a further arena for conflict. The war was fought not only between military forces with guns, but also between scientists, and victory was hastened, if not ensured, by the scientific superiority of the Allied Powers, most obviously at Hiroshima and Nagasaki. It marked the 'coming-of-age' of science and technology. For long these had been major elements in the developing industrialization of the western world, but their dominance was established during the years of conflict, and there was to be no retreat from the many technological advances made by the researchers who assisted in the military effort. Thus the war heralded the era of the dominance of the machine.

Associated with this growth in scientific activity, and also its prestige (with governments and with society at large), was a parallel development of what has become known as social engineering. The major economic depression of the 1930s, finally triggered by the Wall Street crash of 1929, had a massive impact on the nature of government activity and led to the initiation of many measures aimed at the relief of poverty and deprivation and the assuaging of the liberal conscience. In the United States, this was represented by the New Deal legislation of President Roosevelt's governments, which aimed at relief and encouragement to industry and, through the Social Security Act, public support for those who, by no fault of their own, were indigent. Similar measures were introduced by the National Government in Britain; more were foreshadowed by the plans of the war years, such as those promoted in the Beveridge Report on social security, and the landslide victory of the Labour Party in 1945 heralded the introduction of many social democratic policies aimed at giving government a much greater peacetime role in the organization of the economy and society than previously envisaged.

This development of social engineering was associated with a rising status for the social sciences, and a great expansion in their activities. Economics was the first to achieve prestige, through the contributions of Keynes and others to the solution of the problems of the depression, the organization of economies during wartime, and participation in the planning of a new world economic order after the war. Others followed. Social psychological research was widely used in the evaluation of personnel by the armed forces and after the war opinion surveys proved valuable to politicians and related groups while market research was increasingly used by industry (along with psychology in its advertising efforts). All of these fields adopted the 'scientific methods' of the more prestigious hard sciences, and their successes were emulated by other disciplines, such as sociology, social administration and, later, geography. To be scientific was to be respectable and useful.

The war years saw the end of the economic deprivations of the depression, as manufacturing output was boosted to provide the machinery of war. During the cold-war period that followed, military production remained considerable and kept many people in work. Further, there were many years of doing-without to be compensated for, and with full employment, government direction of, and increasing involvement in, economic affairs, plus the need to re-equip industries, the two decades following the war were characterized by an economic boom in the western world. Apart from the greater government involvement, this era in industrial development was marked by another major new characteristic, the development of the giant firm, including the multi-national. The concentration and centralization of capital proceeded rapidly; the average size of firms and factories increased and the economy of the world became dominated by a relatively small number of concerns, encouraged in their activities by governments.

Rebuilding the ravaged war arenas of Europe also placed new demands on societies, and the planning profession emerged from earlier obscurity to take on a major role in preparing the blueprint for a new social order. The need for such action had been realized during the war years in the United Kingdom with the preparation of a series of reports concerned with future land-use patterns, and with the spatial distribution of economic activity, at local and regional scales. Cities were to be rebuilt; New Towns were to be constructed; a more balanced inter-regional distribution of industry and employment was to be ensured; agricultural land was to be protected; and residential environments were to be improved: all of this made great demands on social scientists, as well as engineers. The greater degree of commitment to the private ownership of land in the United States led to a slightly slower acceptance of the need for spatial planning there, but its heyday came with the rapid growth of problems involved in catering for the upsurge of ownership and use of the automobile: transport planning and engineering soon became growth industries, allied with the automobile industry and the companies which constructed the major highways.

For all of these tasks – economic growth and planning; spatial planning; social administration; technological change; management, etc. – there was a need for educated personnel, and the universities received unprecedented demands for their graduates to serve the new needs of society. Education expanded rapidly. The existing universities and colleges grew and many more were founded. Science and social science departments expanded to meet the need for more students. The extra staff were involved in research, which increased the tempo of paradigm development and questioning, and the products of the research were wanted by governments and businesses to assist in the achievement of their aims. Rather than the places where a small elite were educated and a few privileged individuals followed their research interests, the universities became centres of society's development – the 'white-hot technological revolution' which Harold Wilson promised the British in the early 1960s. Research projects became bigger, supported by large grants from outside bodies and carried out by specially employed graduates, and the rate and volume of publication increased exponentially.

The years from 1945 to about 1965 were a period of scientific and technological dominance, therefore. The problems of production had been solved, it was claimed, in that enough goods and services could be provided to satisfy all. The problems of distribution were still being solved, for as yet there was inequality of provision at all spatial scales. But these could be handled, it was argued, and the prospect of a prosperous and healthy life for all was widely canvassed. Academic disciplines were contributing substantially to this problem-solving, by their own scientific progress. Advances in the natural sciences and technologies were solving the problems of production – of food, housing, and consumer goods – as well as of ill-health. And advances in the social sciences were aiding in the management of success. Investment in education was thus investment in social progress (as well as an investment in the life chances of the individuals involved).

Despite the successes of this initial post-war period, doubts persisted. By the mid-1960s they were growing, and by the early 1970s they were having a major impact on the world scene. The seeds of the doubt were many. Initially they were focused, especially in the United States, on the problems of nuclear weapon development and of war, particularly the increasingly unpopular conflict in Vietnam and surrounding countries where technology was not carrying all before it against strong popular resistance and the casualty rates were more and more deplored. Beneath the humanitarian concerns were doubts about the inequalities that continued, both at a world scale and within the 'successful' capitalist societies. Poverty was not being alleviated; if anything the disparities between rich and poor were being extended, and absolute standards of living remained appallingly low in many parts of the world, condemning the majority of the population to short lives of continuous deprivation. The prospects for solving these problems were much less rosy than they had been a few years earlier.

Within the successful societies, it was increasingly realized that success was being bought at considerable cost. Scientific and technological advancement required the dominance of the machine and the large factory. Work for large proportions of the labour force was being made more repetitive and boring, as skilled tasks were taken over by automated production and assembly lines. Alienation of the individual from society was increased. And within society, particular groups suffered more than others, as the results of prejudice and discrimination. Ethnic minority groups were the main sufferers, along with women in most societies, and they were the focus of civil rights movements. Finally, interest was kindled in the growing despoliation of the environment to fuel the production goals of advanced capitalist societies.

The problems of the dignity of the individual, the repression of minorities, the quality of life and the depletion of environmental resources were not new in the late 1960s. Nor were they first realized then. What was realized was that the form of social 'progress' advanced during the previous decades was in many cases exacerbating and not solving such problems. As the realization grew, so the proposed solutions varied. To some, the problems could be solved by greater state involvement, at an international and national scale. Human and civil rights must be protected; greater equality must be achieved through the redistribution of wealth; the environment must be conserved, and where necessary preserved. In the language of the previous section, the research programme is maintained, but major efforts are made within its positive heuristic to solve the many anomalies. To others, this solution was insufficient. It would only lead to new anomalies because, according to the developing critique of capitalist systems, these are necessary to social 'progress': capitalism, it was argued, only survives on inequalities, on alienation, and on the rape of the environment. Only a new research programme could change society for the better.

Within society, the educational institutions were the centres for much of this developing concern. There were major confrontations between students and other elements of society in the late 1960s, for example, in particular at Berkeley, Chicago, London and Paris. The student body was in the forefront of the anti-war movements. In addition to these explicit statements of concern, there was academic consideration of the problems, notably in the social sciences which were concerned with the 'managerial' issues, considered more crucial than the 'production' issues covered by the natural sciences and technologies. A threefold division developed. In one, the need for social scientists to become more active in developing solutions to the problems of distribution and environmental depletion was advanced: social science must become more 'relevant', more 'policy-oriented', within the constraints of the proposed societal 'research programme'. A second argued for greater concentration on the problem of the alienation of the individual, who should be released from the overbearing dominance of the machine and the big organization and should be encouraged to take a much greater part in creating her/his own life. The individual was to be protected against the increasingly distrusted expert. Finally, a third group developed a critique of capitalist society, seeking to show that while specific problems may be soluble this would merely lead to others, while the general problems would remain because they are endemic to that mode of social organization. The call was for major social reform – to some, revolution – as the only long-term solution to the problems of human dignity and inequality.

The force of these arguments can be identified in a variety of ways, not least the declining popularity of scientific and technological subjects among students and the growing demand for places in the social sciences and humanities. Soon, however, a further major problem arose, because the capitalist world spent much of the 1970s in economic recession. To some, this was brought about by the decision of the Arab countries during the 1973 Yom Kippur war to use oil as an economic weapon. The price of this vital raw material was increased many-fold in a few years, with major impacts on all economies. But to others, the recession had already set in – as illustrated by Britain's problems in the late 1960s – and the Arab decision was just a major additional stimulus. To an increasing number of analysts, the recession reflected the failure of state policies of demand management following Keynesian principles. The search for an alternative saw a growing divergence between the political parties. In Britain, for example, the relatively high degree of consensus over demand management broke down after 1970, with the Conservative party promoting a greater emphasis on free markets and a reduction in the role of the state, whereas the Labour party, shifting to the left, promoted the opposite. This growing polarization added to Britain's problems, some claim, because of the uncertainty it engendered about the future; a change of government would bring in major shift in policy.

To some social theorists, recession and its major impacts (notably unemployment) should accelerate the demands for reform and revolution. In the countries studied in this book, at the end of the 1970s both the United Kingdom and the United States elected right-wing governments dedicated to radical programmes of economic regeneration by a reduction in public expenditure and a liberalization of those capitalist forces that produce the inequalities so widely condemned only a decade earlier. Education has been subject to significant policy changes throughout the 1970s and 1980s because of this shift. For the first time for more than two decades, expenditure on higher education in Britain was to be cut, and the numbers of students taking undergraduate degrees and post-graduate training were reduced. The cuts were selective with relative protection for science and technology – growth in which was seen as necessary for economic progress – and substantial reductions in the social sciences, believed by many to be the homes of left-wing radicals and the fomenters of discontent. Research funds were similarly cut and redistributed. The reaction to these policies has been in part an attempt to defend academic freedom and independence and the need for a 'critical conscience' within society but there has also been a desire to reorient work within disciplines to make them more 'relevant' to current societal concerns.

The educational system within which the research components of academic disciplines are located has been closely involved in economic, social and political change during the last forty years. It benefited from the boom years of the first two decades. Expansion was rapid and academic activity was considerable. In the later years, it has been cut back, as – to some decision-makers at least – expansion, especially expansion in certain areas such as arts and social sciences (excluding business studies and management), was seen to have been a luxury that could be ill afforded. Economic progress did not require large numbers of students and potential researchers being trained in disciplines with little relevance to perceived societal needs and working on topics that were critical of societal structure. Education was to be cut back, and investment programmes more closely geared to those perceived needs. Disciplines and scholars were to prove their relevance and to sell their skills in the market-place. Academic freedom was not entirely removed, but was to be curtailed, simply by denying it resources if it was felt that freedom was being abused. The result is that after participating gleefully in the booms of the 1950s and 1960s, academia went into deep depression, suffering internal and external crises of confidence and subject to considerable political direction.

Towards the end of the 1980s, there was a reversal in political attitudes towards higher education, if not also in the funding provided. In the United Kingdom, for example, there was a growing realization that national competition in the restructured global economy required developing human resources to their full potential, through a substantial increase in the participation rate of the 18–25 year-olds and an expansion of continuing education for older people. Thus despite a demographic downturn (which particularly affected the size of the teenage population in the socio-economic classes from which few traditionally moved into higher education), universities, polytechnics and colleges were expected to expand their provision and numbers. But, in line with the economic ideology of the governing party, they were expected to become more efficient in doing their teaching (i.e. to take more students without additional resources), and to obtain more income (especially for research and for continuing education) from sources other than the state. Further, there was an increased emphasis on the 'customer pays' principle (for long the norm in North America), which was expected to lead to students being more concerned with getting 'value for money' and to increased popularity for courses with a clear vocational orientation. Departments of geography had to respond to these political, institutional and potential market changes, and to restructure their course and research offerings accordingly.

Three Types of Science

So far in this chapter, little has been said about various conceptions of the nature of scientific activity, except for the material on different paradigms as 'world views'. It has been implicit in much that has been said that geographers share a world view, and that the only differences in what they have done, and still do, reflect adherence to separate sociological paradigms and to different exemplars (see p. 17): changes in the relative importance of such paradigms and exemplars reflect responses by geographers, both individually and collectively, to changes in their external environment. But is this the case? Is there just one 'world view' which all human geographers have shared during the period under review? Or are there different conceptions of the discipline?

In outline form, three separate conceptions of the nature of a scientific discipline such as human geography can be identified. Each has its own world view, its beliefs regarding both the nature of knowledge (its epistemology, which answers such questions as 'What can be known?', and 'How can we know it?') and the means of obtaining knowledge. From this, each has its own beliefs in the use to which knowledge can be put. What the remainder of this book will illustrate is the relative importance of those three conceptions within Anglo-American human geography since 1945 and the debates among the protagonists of the various positions. The present section provides a brief introductory outline of the three world views. (The classification is drawn directly from Habermas, 1972, and draws on the presentation in Johnston, 1986a, and 1989a.)

1) *The empirical (or analytic) sciences* are based on an empiricist world view, according to which knowledge comes from direct experience and is thus based on the senses, especially visual observation. Its methodology calls for accurate observation and reportage. To some, this is a neutral, value-free position, in which the 'facts speak for themselves', but this view has been countered by those who argue that all observation is theoretically based – what is recorded as present in a place reflects what was being sought and what is deemed to be important, and its classification reflects a prior selection of categories. Thus empiricist work is not the presentation of unordered material, but the recording of information within an agreed and approved conceptual framework; as will be illustrated below (p. 42), for geographers in the decades prior to 1945 this involved the collection and recording of material within a framework which identified the physical environment as the major determinant of the pattern of human activity on the earth's surface.

A particular form of empirical science is generally known as *positivism*, and is the approach which is most frequently assumed to be characteristic of all science. Its goal is not only to describe (in a geographical context, to show what is where), but also to explain (to say why it is there). Such explanation is provided by presenting individual occurrences as examples of general laws (of the form 'if A then B': if A is present in a place, it is because B is there also, for example). Thus the goal of positivist science is to identify laws, thereby providing not only an explanatory device – the distribution of A can be accounted for by the distribution of B in the above example – but also a predictive device – the presence of further occurrences of B can be used to predict future occurrences of A.

Empirical science involves the collection and reporting of information; positivist empirical science involves the use of that information to produce a particular form of explanation. The individual event is thus presented as an example of the operation of one or more general laws. The predictive content of those laws can be used in processes of technical control; the presence of A in a place can be ensured (if it is desired) by putting B there, or its absence (if wished) can be guaranteed by preventing the occurrence of B there. Thus successful positivist physical science can be used to manipulate and control the environment through the application of known physical laws; successful positive social science can be used to manipulate and control society through the application of known social laws.

2) *The hermeneutic sciences* deny the existence of a separate empirical world which exists outside the individual observing it. Any observation and description cannot be neutral, it is argued, but involves the interpretation of the world as it is perceived through a system of meanings, which are human constructs developed by each individual through a continuous process of socialization and resocialization in contact with others. Thus as a human I am more than a combination of living cells; I have powers of reason and emotional traits. I share many characteristics with others, some (such as age and gender) based on biological criteria, but others (such as religious beliefs and class position) based on human constructs that are far from universal – my interpretation of my class position may differ from that of others, who may also disagree among themselves. All of these characteristics influence how I act, because I draw on them, and my interpretation of what they mean (what I think a person in 'my class' should do, for example): thus the only way to understand what I do is to understand me. I observe the world and ascribe meanings to what I see, and I then act in accordance with those meanings, which may differ from the meanings that an empirical scientist observing me may choose to use. According to a hermeneutic scientist, the meanings that matter are mine, since they are the foundations for my behaviour.

In the hermeneutic sciences, therefore, general laws of human behaviour cannot be developed because humans, with their powers of memory and reason, cannot be treated as equivalent to machines, which will always respond in the same way to an identical stimulus (which is what the positivist sciences proclaim). Thus hermeneutic science does not offer explanations, but rather understandings. Its goal is to appreciate what people believe, how those beliefs develop within societies, and how they are drawn upon as the bases for actions. Such appreciation helps one to understand the past and the present, and may provide a guide to the future, but it is in no way predictive: it cannot say, 'if A, then B'.

Empirical sciences, especially positivist sciences, are applicable in strategies for control of environments and societies, as described above. Hermeneutic sciences are not. This does not mean that they cannot be used within society, however; far from it. The understanding that is gained from hermeneutic appreciation can be used to promote mutual understanding, thereby enriching societies by making people better aware both of others and of themselves.

3) *Critical sciences* differ from both of the other two, in that they accept neither the implicit determinism of the positivist nor the voluntarism of the hermeneutic: the former implies that people ultimately have no control over their lives whereas the latter implies that they have complete control. According to critical sciences, people live within societies which are complex organizations created by them as ways of ensuring both individual, day-to-day and collective, generational survival. Those organizations are built on rules which must be operated if the society is to continue. At the most fundamental level, they must ensure there is sufficient food for all, for example, but in different types of society that is done in different ways: in capitalist societies, for example, food is only produced if it can be sold for a profit; in socialist societies it is produced according to collectively-agreed plans.

Within societies, people are free to interpret the rules in a variety of ways; in capitalist societies, for example, the rules require the production of food for sale at a profit but do not determine what foods will and will not be profitable – that is decided by individuals, both separately and collectively, and over time the types of food produced may change. Thus there are hermeneutic processes involved, because the operation of a society depends on how people interpret its rules; further, conditions change (with environmental variations, both temporary and secular, for example) and these changes must be interpreted and responded to. In the critical sciences, therefore, it is necessary to appreciate the basic rules by which a society operates in order to get a fundamental understanding; to gain an understanding of what happens in an individual society in particular circumstances, it is necessary to appreciate how the people operating the rules interpret them. (All sports have basic rules. Participants interpret those rules, and plan courses of action within them. To understand the sport, you must know the rules; to appreciate a particular game, you must understand how the participants have decided to operate within those rules.)

Like the other two, critical science is applicable, but in a different way. Its goal is to ensure that people understand the rules by which a society operates (which may be hidden and unwritten, and can only be determined through abstraction from the many different interpretations of the rules that lead to the empirical world of appearances). Once they understand the rules, then they understand the fundamentals of the society – in technical terms, they are emancipated. They are then freed from any constraints to their understanding, and are able, if they wish, to become involved in the transformation of society, to change the rules to a set which they find more acceptable.

These, then, are three very different conceptions of science, of what it is, how it is done, and what its purpose is. Clearly, if people disagree as to the relative merits of the different views, then debate will follow, as adherents to the various causes (and perhaps to variants within each) promote their own view. Within any one discipline, therefore, it is possible for competition over the relative merits of each approach, as well as for competition within each as to the proper way for that particular form of science to be practised. One can thus have a hierarchy of debates within a discipline such as human geography: at the highest, and most fundamental, level, there is debate over the relevant world view; lower down, there can be debate within each world view over the conduct of research; and at the lowest there can be debate over the details of procedure, as set out by different exemplars.

Human geography is not alone among the social sciences in having experienced all three levels of debate in recent decades. In general terms, the initial debates were within the empirical/analytic world view, and these were followed by the introduction, in turn, of cases for each of the other world views, as well as debates within each regarding procedures and exemplars. Thus the task of charting the history of Anglo-American human geography over the last four and a half decades involves identifying the major features of these various debates. That is the role of the next seven chapters; the last evaluates those debates, not in terms of trying to reconcile the various positions but rather by setting them in context and seeking to appreciate why and when they occurred, and were settled (to the extent that they were).

Conclusions

The thesis of this chapter is that the history of an academic discipline must be set in a context comprising three elements: the occupational structure; the organizational framework for research; and the societal environment. These three interact in a variety of ways. The occupational structure is very much constrained by the societal environment, for example, as indicated by the negligible promotional opportunities in British universities in the later 1970s/early 1980s because of the cuts in educational funding. Similarly, the framework for research, although established by and for academics, is subject to societal support. Some frameworks are much more acceptable than others, and so are much more likely to receive the needed public finance.

In the following chapters, the content of human geography in Britain and North America since World War II is reviewed, within the context set by the discussion here. The emphasis is on 'extraordinary research' rather than the cumulative achievements of 'normal science', stressing the debates over the need for change in how research is done in human geography. No attempt is made to test the models outlined in the section above on 'The academic working environment', although the ideas outlined there have clearly influenced the organization of the book. The main purpose is to present a reasoned chronology of debates in human geography (the discipline being defined as comprising that which is claimed as human geography), based entirely on the published record. The relationship between this chronology and the models of scientific progress only resurfaces in the final chapter, where an attempt is made to evaluate and structure the chronology.

2

Foundations

Although this book is about human geography since 1945, the discussion of that period requires a brief outline of the nature of the discipline in the previous decades. Such a foundation is needed for a variety of reasons. The first is that although 1945 was something of a watershed year in many aspects of the social, economic and intellectual life of the countries being considered here, it did not mark a major divide in the views on geographical philosophy and methodology. Not surprisingly, the war years were not a major period of intra-disciplinary academic debate. Most academics spent much of the war either on active service or in associated intelligence activities (some of those involved in the latter retained their teaching commitments); the everyday activities of teaching, pure research, and administration were replaced by commitment to the war effort. It took a few years for academic life to return to something like normality, to assimilate the large numbers of new staff needed to replace the losses of the war years and to teach the backlog of students, and to react to the new social and economic environments.

A second reason for surveying the period preceding that being studied relates to the processes of change in academic work. New paradigms are created as reactions to those currently in favour, and not as inventions in an intellectual vacuum. Thus the post-Second World War changes were reactions to the philosophies and methodologies which had been developed and taught in the preceding decades; the nature of the reactions cannot be studied without some knowledge of what went before.

Finally, change is not instantaneous in academic life. A new research programme usually takes years to mature, while experimentation with alternatives takes place, the programmatic statements are written, and the converts are won over by the prophets of the new approach. Meanwhile the current paradigm continues (or paradigms, if there are several with considerable support). Its adherents continue to work in their accepted ways, conducting research, publishing, and teaching generations of undergraduates according to the conventional wisdom. Even when a new paradigm has been crystallized, it may be that it must coexist for several years with its predecessors, as a competitor for the support of academics and students. This may be especially characteristic of the social sciences, in which interpretations of data are frequently more subjective than is the case with the physical sciences; it is quite feasible for two or more separate world views to find adherents at the same time, quite possibly in the same academic department.

Geography in the Modern Period

The hallmark of an academic discipline, according to one of geography's chroniclers (James, 1972), is that it has an educational organization which provides a specialist training in the subject. James dates the beginning of such an organization for geography at around 1874, when the first university geography departments were established in Germany (see also Taylor, 1985c): Britain and the United States followed a little later, with the main developments coming in the twentieth century. Before 1874, geography was a subject investigated either by amateurs or by scientists trained in other fields. With its own specialized institutional training, geography left its classical age and entered what James terms its modern period, which lasted for about eighty years, being superseded after 1945 by what James calls its contemporary period.

James's modern period is virtually co-extensive with the decades surveyed by Freeman (1961) in his *A Hundred Years of Geography* which, with James's book, is one of the few relatively attempts to provide a history of the discipline (see also Freeman, 1980a; Stoddart, 1986; Gaile and Willmott, 1989). Freeman identified six main trends in the geographical literature.

1. *The encyclopaedic trend*, associated with the collection of new information about the world, particularly areas little known to the residents of western Europe and North America. Although the great age of discovery was over, and by the late nineteenth century much of the world had been visited by Anglo-Saxon explorers, there were still vast tracts, notably in Africa, which if not *terra incognita* were extremely empty on contemporary maps. Indeed, at the beginning of geography's modern period much of the North American continent itself remained to be settled by permanent farms.
2. *The educational trend*, which, as James stresses, characterizes an academic discipline needing to propagate its knowledge, establish its relevance, and ensure its reproduction. Much work was undertaken to achieve a solid foundation of geographical work in schools, colleges and universities, involving both proselytizers and the architects of curricula (Freeman, 1980a, 1980b; Stoddart, 1986).
3. *The colonial trend* reflects a major environmental preoccupation during the early decades of the modern period, especially in Britain whose empire was being consolidated and developed into a spatial division of labour based on its metropolitan hub and covering a considerable

proportion of the earth's surface. Organization of the commercial world required a great deal of information about the various countries concerned, the provision of which became a major task of geographical research whilst its propagation was the keystone of geographical education.

4   *The generalizing trend* describes the use to which data collected in the encyclopaedic and colonial traditions were increasingly employed. Academic study involved more than the collection and collation of facts: these had to be interpreted, and the methods and aims of such interpretation defined the early paradigms of the discipline's development.

5   *The political trend* was reflected in the contemporary uses made of geographical expertise. Isaiah Bowman was a chief adviser to Woodrow Wilson at the conferences which re-drew the map of the world after the First World War, for example, and the work of geopoliticians such as Haushofer was influential on the *lebensraum* ideology of Nazi Germany (James and Martin, 1981; Parker, 1985).

6   *The specialization trend* was a reaction to the growth of knowledge and the inability of any one individual to master it all, even within the single discipline of geography. Prior to the modern period, it was possible for scientists and other academics to be extremely catholic in their interests and expertise, but as the volume of research literature increased and the techniques of investigation demanded longer and more rigorous training so it became necessary for the individual to specialize, first as a geographer and then within geography, focusing either on one substantive area or on a particular region of the earth's surface.

Some of these trends represent philosophies, some methodologies, and some ideologies with regard to the purpose of academic geography. From them it is possible to identify three paradigms (disciplinary matrices) which characterized the modern period, both of human geography as a whole and of its component parts, such as urban geography (Herbert and Johnston, 1978). Discussion of these three occupies the remainder of this chapter.

Exploration

The first of the approaches was carried over into the modern period from the classical, for exploration was the major activity recognized as geography through most of the nineteenth century. The collection and classification of information about 'unknown' parts of the earth (unknown, that is, to western Europeans and North Americans) was undertaken by geographers. Many of their expeditions were financed through the geographical societies which were founded during that century (Freeman, 1961, 1980b); these, in turn, obtained money from commercial as well as philanthropical sources, for the information gathered was of great value to the mercantile world. As well as supporting and sponsoring exploratory expeditions, the geographical societies also undertook major educational roles. Their lecture meetings provided opportunities for the general public to see and hear of the new discoveries, and their officers worked hard to establish the teaching of geography in schools and universities: the Royal Geographical Society of London (RGS), for example, was involved in discussions which led to the establishment of geography teaching at England's two oldest universities, Oxford and Cambridge (Stoddart, 1975a; Freeman, 1980b; Cameron, 1980).

The importance of exploration declined as geography matured in its new academic-discipline status during the early twentieth century, although in 1899 Halford Mackinder felt it necessary to establish his credentials as a geographer by becoming the first recorded person to climb Mt Kenya. There was still much *terra incognita*, however, and the geographical societies maintained their interest in and sponsorship of expeditions. Indeed, the RGS still acts as a major sponsor of scientific expeditions and its major publication – the *Geographical Journal* – reports their findings. The nature of the work undertaken is very different from that of a century ago in most cases, reflecting developments in scientific technology and the available store of knowledge, but basic activities such as accurate map-making are still crucial to many successful expeditions. Many of the Society's meetings still present, in words and pictures, the results of expeditions and travels to all parts of the world, meetings which remain very popular with its large membership that is dominated by non-academics.

The American Geographical Society (AGS) in New York is the American counterpart of the RGS. It has probably retreated a little further from the exploration role on which it too focused early in the modern period, and it now sponsors research in many other areas of geography, while still providing major support for investigations of relatively unstudied parts of the globe, such as the Arctic. The exploration tradition is maintained in the United States by the National Geographical Society and its popular journal, the *National Geographical Magazine*. (A journal launched in 1984 – *National Geographic Research* – seeks to bridge the gap between academic research and a wider audience.) Other societies have been established to take over some of the other professional roles: there are separate academic bodies in both the United States and the United Kingdom (the Association of American Geographers and the Institute of British Geographers) as well as those which concentrate on geographical education (the National Council for Geographical Education and the Geographical Association respectively).

Although most of it was not strictly exploration, the work summarized by Freeman under the colonial trend can also be included here, since its aims were the collection, collation and dissemination of information. Much of the material was about commercial activities and infrastructure, as in volumes such as Chisholm's *Handbook of Commercial Geography* (first edition, 1899) and *Gazetteer of the World* (1895), which were aimed at the world of commerce, with companion volumes for schools (Wise, 1975). Their content comprised statistics and descriptions of production and trade, and a training in this type of geography was boring to many with its focus on the assimilation of large bodies of factual knowledge ('capes and bays' geography). But the existence of this geographical expertise was widely recognized, and was called on at the end of the modern period when geographers were made responsible for the preparation of intelligence reports about areas in which allied troops were likely to be engaged, work characterized by the set of British Admiralty Handbooks.

Environmental Determinism and Possibilism

These two competing approaches represent the first attempts at generalization by geographers of the modern period. Instead of merely presenting information in an organized manner, either topically or by area, geographers began to seek explanations for the patterns of human occupation of the earth's surface. The major initial source of their explanations was the physical environment, and a theoretical position was established around the belief that the nature of human activity was controlled by the parameters of the physical world within which it was set.

The origins of this environmental determinism lie in the work of Charles Darwin, whose seminal book *On the Origin of Species* (first published in 1859) influenced many scientists. His notions regarding evolution were taken up by the American geographer William Morris Davis in his famous cycle-of-erosion model of landform development. Ideas of natural selection and adaptation formed the basis of statements regarding environmental determinism, including one by Davis (1906) whose programmatic paper identified the core of geography as the relationship between the physical environment, as the control, and human behaviour as the response (Stoddart, 1966; Martin, 1981; see also Campbell and Livingstone, 1983, and Livingstone, 1984 on the influence of Lamarckism in the development of geography, and Peet, 1985a, on a similar theme).

Chief among the early nineteenth-century environmental determinists was the German geographer Ratzel, whose American disciple Ellen Churchill Semple opened her book *Influences of Geographic Environment* (1911) with the statement that 'Man is the product of the earth's surface'. In some hands, the environmental influences adduced were gross, and with hindsight it is hard to believe that they could have been written and taken seriously; a brief survey by Tatham (1953), for example, illustrates the extent to which authors were prepared to credit all aspects of human behaviour with an environmental cause.

Reaction to the extreme generalizations of the environmental determinists led to the development of a counter-thesis, that of possibilism, in which the individual was presented as an active rather than a passive agent. Led by

French geographers, followers of the historian Lucien Febvre, possibilists presented a model of people perceiving the range of alternative uses to which they could put an environment and selecting that which best fitted their cultural dispositions. Taken to extremes, this approach could be as ludicrous as that which it opposed, but in general the possibilists recognized the limits to action which environments set, and avoided the great generalizations which characterized their antagonists.

Debate over environmental determinism and possibilism continued into the 1960s (Lewthwaite, 1966: Spate, 1957, for example, proposed a middle ground with the concept of 'probabilism'.) The determinist cause was continued in the period between the world wars by writers such as Ellsworth Huntington, who advanced theories relating the course of civilization to climate and climatic change. Perhaps the most doughty of all advocates was the Australian Griffith Taylor, whose views so angered politicians interested in the settlement of outback Australia that he was virtually hounded out of his homeland (Powell, 1980a). Taylor's reaction to Tatham's (1953, p. 150) statement that when industrialists decide where to locate a new factory 'Geographical controls are rarely mentioned' was, 'Surely this definitely illustrates the stupidity of the owner!'. His case was that the possibilists had developed their arguments in temperate environments such as that of northwestern Europe, which do indeed offer several viable alternative forms of human occupance. But such environments are rare: in most of the world – as in Australia – the environment is much more extreme and its control over human activity that much greater accordingly. He coined the phrase 'stop-and-go' determinism to describe his views. In the short term, people might attempt whatever they wished with regard to their environment, but in the long term, nature's plan would ensure that the environment won the battle and forced a compromise out of its human occupants.

Many debates begin as two opposing, extreme positions, and end as a compromise accepted by all but the most fervent devotees of either polar position. Thus the lengthy discussion among geographers about whether people are free agents in their use of the earth or whether there is a 'nature's plan' slowly dissolved as the antagonists realized the existence of merits in each case. (And some geographers proceeded independently to study people-environment interactions outside the confines of these debates: see Fleure, 1919.) But while environmental determinism was a view strongly held and widely preached by geographers, respect for the discipline declined somewhat in the eyes of the academic community at large, which rejected the approach. As a consequence, geography's next focus, which nevertheless had strong roots in environmental determinism, was very much an introspective and conservative one.

The Region and Regional Geography

This third approach dominated British and American geography for much of the first half of the present century. Like environmental determinism, it too was an attempt at generalization, but at generalization without structured explanation, and thus of a very different type from the increasingly discredited law-making attempts of the previous writings. Much of the early development took place in Britain, and involved work at two scales (Freeman, 1961, p. 84; Johnston, 1984d). At the large scale were efforts, such as Herbertson's (1905), to divide the earth into major natural regions, usually on the basis of climatic parameters and thus having some links with the earlier determinism. At the smaller scale, the aim was to identify individual areas with particular characters:

> The fundamental idea was that the small area would legitimately be expected to show some distinct individuality, if not necessarily entire homogeneity, through a study of *all* its geographical features – structure, climate, soils, vegetation, agriculture, mineral and industrial resources, communications, settlement and distribution of population. All these, it has often been said, are united in the visible landscape, linked into one whole and dependent one on another. And more, every area, save those few never occupied by man, has been influenced, developed and altered by human activity, and therefore the landscape is an end-product, moulded to its present aspect by successive generations of people. The practice has therefore been to take an evolutionary view and . . . to attempt to reconstruct the landscape as it was a hundred, or a thousand years ago (Freeman, 1961, p. 85).

Some of this work, exemplified by Herbertson's (1905), was the precursor of the ecosystem concept.

Hartshorne and the American view

The ideas and methods of regional geography were taken up a little later in the United States. In the late 1930s, two non-geographers published a major survey of American regionalism (Odum and Moore, 1938) and in 1939 the Association of American Geographers published a monograph – Richard Hartshorne's *The Nature of Geography: A Critical Survey of Current Thought in the Light of the Past* – which rapidly established itself as the definitive statement of the current orthodoxy (see Stoddart, 1990). As Hartshorne (1948, 1979) later made clear, there was much debate among American geographers during the 1930s (most of it apparently unpublished) about the nature of their discipline. Hartshorne was concerned about both tone and content of the debate, and in 1938 submitted a paper to the *Annals*, as a contribution to the philosophical discussions. He then proceeded to Europe for fieldwork on boundary problems, as part of his ongoing research into political geography. This work was frustrated by the political situation, and so he spent his time reading European, mainly German, work on the nature of geography. He used this to extend his 1938 paper, adding the sub-title; the result was a 'paper' of 491 pages (some 230,000 words) which became the major philosophical and methodological contribution to the literature of geography in English then available.

A synopsis of Hartshorne's scholarship, and his interpretations of the scholarship of others, notably Hettner, is not possible in a few paragraphs, and only the main conclusions can be stressed here. Hartshorne argued force-fully that the focus of geography is areal differentiation, the mosaic of separate landscapes on the earth's surface (see Agnew, 1990, on the represen-tation of Hartshorne's focus as 'areal variation' rather than 'areal differen-tiation'). Thus the discipline is:

> a science that interprets the realities of areal differentiation of the world as they are found, not only in terms of the differences in certain things from place to place, but also in terms of the total combination of phenomena in each place, different from those at every other place (p. 462)

so that

> geography is concerned to provide accurate, orderly and rational description and interpretation of the variable character of the earth surface (p. 21)

and it

> seeks to acquire a complete knowledge of the areal differentiation of the world, and therefore discriminates among the phenomena that vary in different parts of the world only in terms of their geographic significance − i.e. their relation to the total differentiation of areas. Phenomena significant to areal differentia-tion have areal expression − not necessarily in terms of physical extent over the ground, but as a characteristic of an area of more or less definite extent (p. 463).

According to this view, the principal purpose of geographical scholarship is synthesis, an integration of relevant characteristics to provide a total descrip-tion of a place − a region − which is identifiable by its peculiar combination of those characteristics. There is then, according to Hartshorne, a close analogy between geography and history; the latter provides a synthesis for 'temporal sections of reality' whereas the former performs a similar task for 'spatial sections of the earth's surface' (p. 460).

Hartshorne also indicated the methodology to be used for this integrating science aimed at orderly description of the earth's surface. To him, 'the ultimate purpose of geography, the study of areal differentiation of the world, is most clearly expressed in regional geography' and accepted procedures were necessary for regional identification. Regions are characterized by their homogeneity on prescribed characteristics, selected for their salience in high-lighting areal differences. Two types of region were identified; the *formal region* (or uniform region) in which the whole of the area is homogeneous with regard to the phenomenon or phenomena under review, and the nodal or *functional region* in which the unity is imparted by organization around a common node, which may be the core area of a state or a town at the centre of a trade area. Identification of such regions

> depends first and fundamentally on the comparison of maps depicting the areal expression of individual phenomena, or of interrelated phenomena . . . geography is represented in the world of knowledge primarily by its technique of map use (pp. 462–4).

Hartshorne placed his emphasis on map *use*. Although it is valuable for geographers to know something about the preparation and construction of maps, the sciences of surveying and map projections are of only secondary interest to them; the prime task of the geographer is the interpretation of maps, and increasingly, from about 1940 on, of various forms of aerial photograph. Much of this information to be interpreted may have been placed on the maps by geographers during their fieldwork, and the role and nature of fieldwork were of considerable interest to American geographers during the period when Hartshorne was developing his ideas.

Preparation for a regional synthesis required materials both from other sciences specializing in certain phenomena (though usually not their areal patterning) and from the topical systematic specialisms within geography which complemented, but which were eventually subsidiary to, regional geography. Physical, economic, historical and political were the main systematic subdivisions recognized within geography at the time Hartshorne wrote, although a later survey, set firmly within the regional paradigm, identified many other 'adjectival geographies', including population, settlement, urban, resources, marketing, recreation, agricultural, mineral production, manufacturing, transportation, soils, plant, animal, medical, and military, plus climatology and geomorphology (James and Jones, 1954). A number of these were of only minor importance, however, so that despite the apparent diversity of interests among geographers of the time, the 'classic' regional study usually followed a sequence comprising physical features, climate, vegetation, agriculture, industries, population and the like (Freeman, 1961, p. 142) and was summarized by a synthesis of the individual maps to produce a set of formal regions.

To most geographers of the period spanning World War II, and notably those who contributed to the survey edited by James and Jones (1954), regional geography was at the forefront of their discipline's scholarship and systematic studies were the providers of information for that enterprise: thus to James, 'Regional geography in the traditional sense seeks to bring together in an areal setting various matters which are treated separately in topical geography' (1954, p. 9). Urban geographers studied towns because they 'constitute distinctive areas' (Mayer, 1954, p. 143), in line with the regional concept; political geographers studied the functions and structures of an area 'as a region homogeneous in political organization, heterogeneous in other respects' (Hartshorne, 1954, p. 174); and in defining the 'new' field of social geography, Watson (1953, p. 482) saw it 'as the identification of different regions of the earth's surface according to associations of social phenomena related to the total environment'. Each of these topical specialisms produced its own regionalizations (notable in this was the work of agricultural geographers, especially O. E. Baker, in a series of papers published in *Economic Geography* during the 1920s and 1930s outlining the agricultural regions of various parts of the world), and each had its links with the relevant systematic sciences – social geography with sociology, for example. The key differentiating factor between the two was the geographer's focus on the region, both the specialist's single-attribute region and the synthesiser's multi-attribute region.

Given this focus on the region, it is not surprising that the literature contained many contributions discussing the nature and delimitation of such homogeneous areas, for virtually every region was in effect a generalization, complete homogeneity being very rare over more than a small area. As already indicated, British geographers were active early in the definition of large-scale regions, usually based on climatic parameters. Much effort was made to develop methods to define multi-attribute regions; in agricultural geography, for example, it culminated in the statistical procedure developed by Weaver (1954). But at the small scale it was widely accepted that regional delimitation should be based on personal interpretation of landscape assemblages. For this, the model was the work by the French geographer Paul Vidal de la Blache and his followers on the *pays* of their homeland, small regional units with distinct physical characteristics, notably in soils and drainage, and associated agricultural specialisms (Buttimer, 1971, 1978a).

One systematic specialism which stood slightly apart from the others was historical geography, the study of which was based on the argument that investigations of genesis were needed in order to comprehend the regional patterns of the present. Two approaches to historical geography can be recognized from the 1920s on. The first, often thought of as the British approach and closely associated with the work of H. C. Darby, involved the detailed study of past geographies (Perry, 1969). This was done in a series of cross-sections, whose locations in time were almost always determined by the available source material, such as the Domesday Book of c.1086 which was analysed in great depth by Darby and his associates (culminating in Darby, 1977; Perry, 1979). These cross-sectional analyses, complete with their regionalizations in many cases, were linked together by a narrative outlining the changes between the periods studied: most emphasis was placed on the cross-sections, however, for which data allowed analysis rather than interpretation (see Darby, 1973, 1983a).

The second approach was largely American in its provenance, and centred upon the works of C. O. Sauer and his associates. (on the differences between Hartshorne and Sauer, see Lukermann, 1990, and Butzer, 1990.) Their focus was the study of processes leading to landscape change up to, and including, the present and beginning at the prehuman stage of occupance (Mikesell,

1969): most of the work was conducted either outside the United States itself (particularly in Latin America) or in the less industrialized parts of that country. Sauer's (1925) first methodological statement constrained geographical endeavour closely to the generic study of landscapes, with emphasis on their cultural features (although work was also done on the borderlands between geography and botany); there was no glorification of the region, however. In his later 'sermons' – as he called his methodological and philosophical statements – Sauer (1941, 1956) encouraged research over a much wider field, but emphasized the study of cultural landscapes and the links which he had forged with anthropology, to produce a creative art-form whose hallmark was that it was not prescribed by pattern or method: the human geographer is obliged 'to make cultural processes the base of his thinking and observation' (Sauer, 1941, p. 24). The work, as undertaken by Sauer and his students, involved neither detailed reconstruction of past geographies nor close consideration of regional boundaries: instead it led to a catholic historical geography whose rationale (Clark, 1954, p. 95) was that:

> through its study we may be able to find more complete and better answers to the problems of interpretation of the world both as it is now and as it has been at different times in the past.

Not all American historical geographers followed this lead – Brown (1943), for example, worked on detailed reconstructions of past periods – but the 'Berkeley School' which Sauer founded and led for almost five decades had many followers and a particular point of view, focused on a single iconoclast (Hooson, 1981). Sauer's influence was carried on by his students, notably Leighly, Parsons, and Clark (Bushong, 1981).

The major statement of the approach engendered by Sauer was the symposium on 'Man's role in changing the face of the earth' which was conceived by Thomas (see Glacken, 1983) and resulted in a substantial publication (52 chapters plus discussions: 1193 pages in all) which had a very substantial impact. The range of material included was vast. Its theme was identified by Sauer (1956a) as

> the capacity of man to alter his natural environment, the manner of his so doing, and the virtue of his actions. It is concerned with historically cumulative effects, with the physical and biologic processes that man sets in motion, inhibits, or deflects, and with the differences in cultural conduct that distinguish one human group from another (p. 49).

It presented no grand methodology or set of general findings – indeed, in his closing statement Sauer (1956b) criticized the tendency of American authors who 'have an inclination to universalize ourselves' (p. 1133). Diversity in response to environments, and in impacts on them, a diversity reflecting cultural differences, was rather stressed. Indeed, the conclusion reached by Mumford (1956) is very similar to that advanced in the 1980s by adherents of structuration theory (see p. 237): 'the future is not a blank page; and neither is it an open book' (p. 1142).

One of the contributors to Thomas's symposium, and also a member of the Berkeley school, was Glacken (1956), who focused on various conceptions of nature that have been current in Western thought at some times and places. This was a forerunner to his magnum opus, *Traces on the Rhodian Shore* (Glacken, 1967), which was a major survey of various interpretations of nature, and in which he demonstrates 'how all-pervading teleology has been in the history of Western interpretation of nature' (Glacken, 1983, p. 32). Like the Thomas symposium before it, this book is widely recognized as a classic on society–nature inter-relationships. But it was published at a time when that topic was receiving a rapidly diminishing amount of attention, and its impact was consequently less than might otherwise have occurred.

The British view

British geographers seem to have been less concerned with philosophical and methodological debate than their American counterparts during the 1920s, 1930s, and 1940s (though see the exchange in the *Scottish Geographical Magazine* during the late 1930s, initiated by Crowe, 1938). They were apparently more pragmatic in their work, less prone to contemplate the nature of their subject and more prepared, perhaps, to adopt the well used adage that 'Geography is what geographers do'. But they too accepted that the *raison d'être* of geography was synthesis, the integration of the findings of various systematic studies with a strong emphasis on genesis, as in the studies of geomorphology and historical geography (Darby, 1953). According to Wooldridge and East (1958):

> geography . . . fuses the results, if not the methods, of a host of other subjects . . . [it] is not a science but merely an aggregate of sciences (p. 14)
> its *raison d'être* and intellectual attraction arise in large part from the shortcomings of the uncoordinated intellectual world bequeathed us by the specialists (pp. 25–6)
> in its simplest essence the geographical problem is how and why does one part of the earth's surface differ from another (p. 28).

All of these statements indicate a strong trans-Atlantic common body of opinion (see Stoddart, 1990, on Hartshorne's influence on Woodridge), although, despite a statement that 'The purpose of regional geography is simply the better understanding of a complex whole by the study of its constituent parts' (p. 159), the British writers did not elevate the regional doctrine as much as did their American counterparts. (Nor were they carried to excesses of environmental determinism in earlier decades.) Nevertheless, Wooldridge (1956, p. 53) wrote in 1951 that

> the aim of regional geography . . . is to gather up the disparate strands of the systematic studies, the geographical aspects of other disciplines, into a coherent and focused unity, to see nature and nurture, physique and personality as closely related and interdependent elements in specific regions

and argued that in any department of geography each staff member should be committed to the study of a major region (p. 64).

One major difference between British and American geography by the 1950s was in attitude to physical geography, the study of the land surface, the atmosphere and the oceans, and their faunal and floral inhabitants. Both countries had strong traditions of work on these topics, and many geographers had academic roots in the associated field of geology. But in North America (the United States much more than Canada) this tradition had slowly dissolved and interest in the physical environment, and particularly its understanding as against its description, waned. This may have been a consequence of the excesses of environmental determinism, and a subsequent desire to remove all traces of that connection and to see society as the formative agent of landscape patterns and change: associated with this was probably the attempt to redefine geography in the 1920s as the study of human ecology, in which people are seen as reacting and adjusting to environments while at the same time attempting to adjust the environment to their own needs (Barrows, 1923). Thus with regard to geomorphology – the science of landform genesis – Peltier (1954, p. 375) wrote:

> the geographer needs precise, factual information about particular places. What landforms actually exist in a given area? How do they differ? Where are they? What are their distribution patterns? The geomorphologist may concern himself with questions of structure, process, and stage, but the geographer wants specific answers to the questions: what? where? and how much?

What geographers were interested in, according to this view, was the geography of landforms: geomorphology, the genetic study of landforms, was a part of geology and, unlike historical geography, was deemed irrelevant to the geographical enterprise. Similar reactions saw the wholesale removal of climatology and biogeography from American geographical curricula, and their replacement by introductory courses in physical geography which described landforms, climates, and plant assemblages – usually in a regional context – but paid little or no attention to their origins. (On later trends involving a substantial revival of physical geography, see Marcus, 1979 and the essays in Gaile and Willmott, 1989.)

This American trend was not repeated in Britain where, according to Wooldridge and East (1958, p. 47):

> To treat geography too literally as an affair of the 'quasistatic present' is to make both it and its students seem foolish and superficial. It is true that our primary aim is to describe the present landscape; but it is also to interpret it.
> . . . Our study has therefore always to be evolutionary. . . . It is unscholarly to take either landforms or human societies as 'given' and static facts, though we must not let temporal sequences obscure spatial patterns.

Thus geography students at British universities in the 1950s rarely specialized, except perhaps in the final year of their course, in either physical or human geography. Both were considered essential parts of a geographical education, as contributions to the genetic study of regional landscapes which was the integrating focus of geographical scholarship (see Johnston and Gregory, 1984; Cosgrove, 1989a). As researchers, most British geographers specialized in either physical or human geography (though rarely exclusively so), but almost all had a regional specialism as well, in which they 'integrated' studies from 'both sides' of their subject, as widely illustrated in the regional textbooks of the period; the 'Dogma of regional synthesis' (Darby, 1983b, p. 25) was being softened, however, and geographers were increasingly turning their attention from regions to problems.

Conclusions

This chapter has presented an extremely brief outline of geography during its 'modern period', since the focus of the book is on the ensuing 'contemporary period'. Three approaches have been identified, although deeper analysis may well indicate more coexisting during any one time (see Taylor, 1937). All three lasted into the contemporary period, although one, the regional, dominated in the years before and just after the Second World War. Its main focus was on areal differentiation, on the varying character of the earth's surface (basically, the inhabited parts of the earth's surface), and its picture of that variation was built up out of parallel topical studies of different aspects of the physical and human patterns observed. By the 1950s, initially in America and then in Britain too, disillusionment with the empiricist philosophy of regional geography was growing. (Though see defences by, for example, Paterson, 1974 and Hart, 1982. Chapter 8 below discusses attempts in the later 1980s to promote a new form of regional geography.) Slowly the topical specialisms came to greater dominance and the regional synthesis was ignored.

3

Growth of Systematic Studies and the Adoption of 'Scientific Method'

Dating the origin of a change in the orientation of a discipline, or even a part of it, is difficult. Several pieces which contain the kernel of the new ideas can usually be found in its literature, but often these are derivative of the earlier teachings of others, whose views are never published. Further, it is possible for a change to emanate contemporaneously from several separate though usually not entirely independent nodes, as various iconoclasts introduce stimuli to change. An attempt to locate the first stirrings against regional geography would be a futile exercise, therefore. Instead, the present chapter isolates what appear to have been the most important and influential statements published by geographers, and traces their impact on the geographical community of scholars.

As pointed out in Chapter 1, change within a discipline involves both dissatisfaction with existing approaches and the preparation of an acceptable alternative, a new disciplinary matrix (if not world-view). The existence of the former was spelled out by Freeman (1961), who noted that 'disapointment with the work of regional geographers has led many to wonder if the regional approach can ever be academically satisfying and to turn to specialization or some systematic branch of the subject' (p. 141). He suggested three reasons for such disappointment. The first was that so much regional classification was naive, particularly at the large scale, where generalizations, such as Herbertson's world climatic regions, were found on detailed investigation to contain too many discrepancies. The second, and perhaps most important to many people, was the 'weary succession' of physical and human activity 'facts' which characterized so much regional writing (though not all, as exemplified by James's, 1942, *Latin America*): 'The trouble has perhaps been that many regional geographers have tried to include too much' (p. 143). Thirdly, he claimed that the model of regional writing, derived from work on the French *pays*, suggested that the whole of the earth's surface could be divided into such clear regions, each with its own character: that this proved to be not so was reflected by many pedestrian studies of areas lacking such personality.

Whereas Freeman focused on the failings of regional geography as practised, a case made in the United States during the late 1940s and early 1950s was that the insistence on the primacy of regional geography was undermining the associated systematic studies. This was put forcefully by Ackerman (1945) in a paper reporting on his experience of working in the wartime intelligence services. He identified two major failings of professional geographers there: their inability to handle foreign languages, and the weakness of their topical specialisms. Regarding the latter, he criticized much of the geographical work of the preceding quarter of a century as having been conducted by scholars who were 'more or less amateurs in the subject on which they published' (p. 124), so that when they were called upon to provide intelligence material for wartime interpretation what the geographers produced was extremely thin in its content. Regional geographers could provide no more than a superficial analysis, and the division of labour within the discipline whereby people specialized on different areas of the earth was both inefficient and ineffective. (Gould, 1979, p. 140, calls the geography of the fifty years prior to 1950 'bumbling amateurism and antiquarianism'.)

Ackerman suggested that rectification of this major deficiency in geographical work required much more research and training in the systematic specialisms: this would not be contrary to the philosophy of the subject which gave primacy to the regional synthesis, he claimed, since more detailed systematic studies would lead to greater depth in regional interpretations. There is little evidence that his paper had an immediate impact, however, and the publications of American geographers over the next few years, including the abstracts of the papers presented at the annual conferences of the Association of American Geographers, indicated no major shift in the orientation of academic work with the return to post-war 'normality': two of the few exceptions are the abstracts of papers presented by Garrison and McCarty at Cleveland in 1953, which were clearly based on a different methodology to that widely used (see below, p. 60). The systematic fields had undoubtedly been gaining in importance prior to Ackerman's statement, and continued to do so, as indicated by the extent of their treatment in the review volume edited by James and Jones (1954). But it was not until the mid-1950s that this volumetric change in the substance of geographical research was matched by any widespread changes in its methodology and philosophy.

Schaefer's Paper and the Response

As it was in the United States that Hartshorne published his major statement of the regional paradigm, and as it was there, rather than in Britain, that philosophy and methodology were apparently debated most earnestly, it is perhaps not surprising that the revolution against the regional paradigm originated on that side of Atlantic. One of the first shots was a paper by Schaefer (1953) – which was published posthumously – that is often referred to by those who seek the origins of the 'quantitative and theoretical revolutions'. Schaefer was originally an economist: he joined the group of geographers teaching in the economics department at the University of Iowa after his escape from Nazi Germany (Bunge, 1979).

Schaefer claimed that his paper was the first to challenge Hartshorne's presentation and interpretation of the works of Hettner and others, and it was published fourteen years after Hartshorne's monograph. His intent was to criticize the 'exceptionalist' claims made for regional geography, and to present the case for geography adopting the philosophy and methods of the positivist school of science (see Martin, 1990, 72). His first task, then, was to outline the nature of a science and to define the peculiar characteristics of geography as a social science. He argued that to claim that geography was the integrating science which put together the findings of the individual systematic sciences was arrogant, and that in any case its products were 'somewhat lacking in . . . startlingly new and deeper insights' (p. 227). A science is characterized by its explanations, and explanations require laws:

> To explain the phenomena one has described means always to recognize them as instances of laws (p. 227).

In geography, according to Schaefer, the major regularities which are described refer to spatial patterns:

> Hence geography has to be conceived as the science concerned with the formulation of the laws governing the spatial distribution of certain features on the surface of the earth (p. 227)

and it is these spatial arrangements of phenomena, and not the phenomena themselves, about which geographers should be seeking to make law-like statements. Geographical procedures would then not differ from those employed in the other sciences, both natural and social: observation would lead to a hypothesis – about the interrelationship between two spatial patterns, for example – and this would be tested against large numbers of cases, to provide the material for a law if it were thereby verified.

The argument against this definition of geography as the science of spatial arrangements Schaefer termed *exceptionalist*. It claims that geography does not share the methodology of other sciences because of the peculiar nature of its subject matter – the study of unique places, or regions. Using analogies from physics and economics, Schaefer argued that geography is not peculiar in its focus on unique phenomena; all sciences deal with unique events which can only be accounted for by an integration of laws from various systematic sciences, but this does not prevent – although it undoubtedly makes more difficult – the development of those laws.

It is, therefore, absurd to maintain that the geographers are distinguished among the scientists through the integration of heterogeneous phenomena which they achieve. There is nothing extraordinary about geography in that respect (p. 231).

In the second part of his paper, Schaefer traced the exceptionalist view in geography back to an analogy drawn by Kant (1724–1804) between geography and history, an analogy repeated by Hettner and by Hartshorne (see above, p. 43). He quoted (p. 233) from Kant's *Physiche Geographie* (Vol. I, p. 8) that 'Geography and history together fill up the entire area of our perception: geography that of space and history that of time'. But when Kant was working, Schaefer claims, history and geography were cosmologies, not sciences, and a cosmology is 'not rational science but at best thoughtful contemplation of the universe' (p. 332). Hettner, however, followed Kant's views and developed geography as a cosmology, arguing that both history and geography deal with the unique, and thus do not apply the methods of science. Schaefer argued that this is a false position, for in explaining what happened at a certain time period historians must employ the laws of the social sciences. Time periods, like places, are undoubtedly unique assemblages of phenomena, but this does not preclude the use of laws in unravelling and explaining them. History and geography can both be sciences for

> What scientists do is . . . *They apply to each concrete situation jointly all the laws that involve the variables they have reason to believe are relevant* (p. 239).

According to Schaefer, Hartshorne disregarded one aspect of Hettner's writing which was nomothetic in its orientation, however, and in doing this he to some extent misled American geographers. (Muller-Wille, 1978, p. 55, claims that Hettner predated Christaller in the development of ideas regarding central place theory; Hartshorne made no reference to the paper by Hettner cited by Muller-Wille. On the same point, see Butzer, 1990, and Smith, 1990.)

The final part of Schaefer's paper reviews some of the problems of applying his nomothetic (law-producing) philosophy to geography as a spatial, social science. He recognizes the problems of experimentation and of quantification, for example, and suggests a methodology based on cartographic correlations. A major point concerns the difference between laws produced in geography and those from other, 'maturer' social sciences. The former are morphological, the latter are process: in order fully to comprehend the assemblages of the phenomena described in geographers' morphological laws, therefore, it is necessary to derive process laws from other social sciences, a procedure which requires team work (the last point was made also by Ackerman). Geography according to Schaefer, then, is the source of the laws on location, which may be used to differentiate the regions of the earth's surface.

Hartshorne's response

Schaefer's paper did not produce much direct reaction in print, despite later claims that it was a major stimulus to work in the genre which he proposed (Bunge, 1962). It did, however, draw considerable response from Hartshorne, in the form first of a letter to the editor of the *Annals* (Hartshorne, 1954b) and later three substantive pieces (Hartshorne, 1955, 1958, 1959): the last of the latter was another major book which, although probably not as influential as the 1939 volume, showed the continued importance of Hartshorne to American geographers as an interpreter of their subject's methodology and philosophy.

The purpose of Hartshorne's first (1955) paper (which subsumed the earlier letter) was to indicate the many flaws which he identified in Schaefer's scholarship (see also Gregory, 1978a, p. 31). He begins with a further discussion of the *mores* of methodological debate (Hartshorne, 1948): most of the paper was organized to illustrate that Schaefer was limited in his references, drew unsupportable conclusions, and misrepresented the views of others, so that 'In every paragraph, in nearly every sentence of this third section, there is serious falsification, either by commission or by omission, of the views of the writer discussed' (p. 236). (It should be noted that this statement refers to the third part of Schaefer's paper, which focused on the work of Hettner.) In more general terms Hartshorne claimed that Schaefer's paper 'ignores the normal standards of critical scholarship and in effect offers nothing more than personal opinion, thinly disguised as literary and historical analysis' (p. 244). Since Hartshorne himself (1959, p. 8) was a strong believer that 'geography is what geographers have made it', to him all methodological and philosophical statements should be based on a close and careful analysis of the published works of others.

Although most of this paper is concerned to examine the nature of Schaefer's 'evidence', in the final section Hartshorne turned to an examination of the anti-exceptionalist argument. He pointed out (p. 237) that in coming to the conclusion that geography should take process laws from the systematic sciences and use them to produce morphological laws, Schaefer came very close in effect to preaching the sort of exceptionalist claim that he sought to destroy. It could be argued, therefore, that Schaefer's critique 'is a total fraud' (p. 237). Schaefer's position is summed up as 'geography must be a science, science is the search for laws, and all phenomena of nature and human life are subject to such laws and completely determinable by them' (p. 242). Such scientific determinism is opposed to the summary of what geographers do as set out in *The Nature of Geography*, which has in any case been treated in a most cavalier way by Schaefer.

In his second paper, Hartshorne (1958) addressed Schaefer's claim that Kant was the source of the exceptionalist view. Literary analysis suggests that both Humbolt and Hettner reached the same view independently, being unaware of Kant's views when they were writing. May (1970, p. 9) suggests

that both Hartshorne and Schaefer could have misunderstood Kant's conception of a science, however, and of the role of geography as a science, although
he confirms Hartshorne's dismissal of Schaefer's interpretation of the source
of Kant's ideas (see the later exchange between Hartshorne, 1972 and May,
1972).

The third and most substantial piece in Hartshorne's rebuttal of Schaefer's
argument was a monograph (Hartshorne, 1959) entitled *Perspective on the
Nature of Geography*, the production of which was stimulated by Schaefer —
and by requests from colleagues that he respond in detail to Schaefer's argument — but which was also used as a vehicle for a discussion of a wide range
of other issues raised during the two decades since the publication of his
original statement (Hartshorne, 1939). He organized the discussion in a
framework of ten separate questions/topics: the aim was to provide a methodology by which geography could meet its need for 'new conceptual
approaches and more effective ways of measuring the interrelationships of
phenomena' (p. 9), which could only develop out of an understanding and
acceptance of the subject's 'essential character'.

The first set of questions was concerned with the meaning of areal differentiation, with the definition of the earth's surface, with a discussion of the
peculiar geographical interest in the integration of phenomena in 'the total
reality [that] is there for study, and geography is the name of the section of
empirical knowledge which has always been called upon to study that reality'
(p. 33), and with the determination of what is significant for geographical
study; it led Hartshorne to the definition that 'geography is that discipline that
seeks *to describe and interpret the variable character from place to place of
the earth as the world of man'* (p. 47). He considered that human and natural
factors do not have to be identified separately — any prior insistence on this
was a function of the arguments of environmental determinists — and that a
division into human and physical geography is unfortunate, because it limits
the range of possible integrations in the study of reality.

Turning to temporal processes, Hartshorne argued that geographers need
only study proximate genesis, since it is classification by form of appearance
rather than by provenance which is important for the geographical investigation of areal differentiation: as most landforms are stable, or virtually so, from
the point of view of human occupance, for example, the study of their change
is irrelevant to the aims of geography. According to this argument (see also
p. 48 above), geomorphology, insofar as it is the study of landform genesis,
is not part of geography; the study of landforms is. With regard to cultural
features in the landscape, Hartshorne made an important distinction between
expository description and explanatory description:

> geography is primarily concerned to describe . . . the variable character of areas
> as formed by existing features in interrelationships . . . explanatory description
> of features in the past must be kept subordinate to the primary purpose (p. 99).

Thus historical geography should be the expository description of the historical present 'but the purpose of such dips into the past is not to trace developments or seek origins but to facilitate comprehension of the present' (p. 106); studies of causal development and genesis are the prerogative of the systematic sciences.

In attempting an answer to the question 'Is geography divided between systematic and regional geography?' Hartshorne developed a position different from that in *The Nature of Geography*. Thus in 1959 he accepted that studies of interrelationships could be arranged along a continuum 'from those which analyse the most elementary complexes in areal variation over the world to those which analyse the most complex integrations in areal variation within small areas' (p. 121). The former are called topical studies and the latter regional studies, but whereas

> every truly geographical study involves the use of both the topical and the regional approach (p. 122)

there is no argument that one is superior over the other, as being that to which all geographers should aspire. In this presentation, therefore, Hartshorne somewhat downgraded the regional synthesis from its earlier centrality, in his view, in the geographical enterprise.

With regard to the important question raised by Schaefer's paper – 'Does geography seek to formulate scientific laws or to describe individual cases?' – Hartshorne argued for the latter, largely by pointing out the difficulties of establishing such laws through geographical investigations though he did not argue that geographers should not seek and use general laws, for the understanding of individual cases – it is an 'erroneous presumption that to focus on studies of individual places and to focus on generic concepts are opposing alternatives mutually exclusive' (Hartshorne, 1984, p. 429). Scientific laws must be based on large numbers of cases, but geographers study complex integrations in unique places; scientific laws can best be established in laboratory experiments which allow only a few independent variables to vary, but such work is rarely possible in geography; interpretation requires skills in the systematic sciences which are beyond the capability of geographers; scientific laws suggest some kind of determinism, but this is inappropriate to the human motivations which are in part the causes of landscape variations: for all these reasons, the search for laws is irrelevant to geography. But laws are not the only means to the scientific end of comprehending reality in any case: instead

> Geography seeks (1) on the basis of empirical observation as independent as possible of the person of the observer, to describe phenomena with the maximum degree of accuracy and certainty; (2) on this basis, to classify the phenomena, as far as reality permits, in terms of generic concepts or universals; (3) through rational consideration of the facts thus secured and by logical processes of analysis and synthesis, including the construction and use wherever possible of general principles or laws of generic relationships, to attain the maximum comprehension of the scientific interrelationships of phenomena; and (4) to arrange

these findings in orderly systems so that what is known leads directly to the
margin of the unknown (pp. 169–70),

which, he says, is a perfectly respectable scientific goal. (It is very similar to
the overall goal of positivist work – p. 31 – and is the reason why several
commentators see very little difference in ends, if not means, between
Hartshorne's work and that of the spatial scientists.)

Finally, in discussing geography's position within the classification of
sciences, Hartshorne returned to the Hettnerian analogy of geography as a
chorological science with history as a chronological science. This is valid, he
argues, because it describes the way in which geographers have worked, on
both topical and regional subjects, with reference to interrelationships and
integrations within areas. (This view was revived by Harris, 1971.)

Reconciliations?

The major basis of the methodological and philosophical difference between
the two was that Hartshorne's was a positive view of geography – geography
is what geographers have made it – whereas Schaefer's view, on the other
hand, was a normative one, of what geography should be, irrespective of what
it had been. Over the next decade after Hartshorne published his *Perspective*
it was Schaefer's view which came to prevail, on both sides of the Atlantic,
although the extent of Schaefer's personal influence based on his 1953 paper
was probably very slight and the real iconoclasts of the 'revolution' were those
discussed in the next section. (Indeed in Britain, although Hartshorne's two
books were clearly widely read and referenced, Schaefer's paper was not. It
receives no mention in Freeman's (1961; 1980a) books, none in Chorley and
Haggett's (1965b) trail-blazing *Frontiers in Geographical Teaching*, and only
one in their major (Chorley and Haggett, 1967) *Models in Geography* – in
the chapter by Stoddart. See, however, Stoddart, 1990.) Thus it is not surprising that relatively little attention has been paid elsewhere in the geographical literature to the Schaefer/Hartshorne debate (Gregory, 1978a, p. 32.
Schaefer is not in the index of authors referred to in the encyclopedic *Geography in America* – Gaile and Willmott, 1989).

An attempt to suggest that they were not so antagonistic in their views as
they themselves suggested has been provided by Guelke (1977a, 1978; see also
Gregory, 1978a, p. 31 and Entrikin, 1981, 1990). He shows that in general
terms Hartshorne was very much a supporter of the scientific method as
defined by the positivists, but that he created his own problems regarding the
application of this method in geography because of his view on uniqueness.
Schaefer, on the other hand, accepted the full positivist position, and showed
that uniqueness was a general problem of science, and not a peculiar characteristic of geography. Thus

> In extending the idea of uniqueness to everything, Schaefer effectively removed
> a major logical objection to the possibility of a law-seeking geography and
> demonstrated that Hartshorne's view of uniqueness as a special problem was

untenable for anyone who accepted the scientific model of explanation (Guelke, 1977a, p. 380),

and Hartshorne's distinction between idiographic and nomothetic approaches was misleading. Both Hartshorne and Schaefer ignored the possibility of geographers being major 'law-consumers', however; to Hartshorne, the alternatives were either law-making or the description of unique places, whilst to Schaefer geographers had to develop morphological laws, and ignore the interest in process laws which characterizes the systematic sciences.

According to Guelke (1977a, p. 348), when Schaefer insisted on the need for geographers to develop laws 'he created a major crisis within the discipline'. Whether Schaefer himself was responsible for the crisis is doubtful, as the next section suggests. There is no doubt, however, that within about a decade of Schaefer's paper being published many human geographers, especially members of the youngest generation currently within the profession, had adopted at least part of his manifesto, with the growing concern for quantification and law-making. They were presented with a choice between such activity and the sort of contemplation of the unique advocated by Hartshorne. As Guelke (1977a, p. 385) points out, 'Not surprisingly, most geographers opted for geography as a law-seeking science' because (Guelke, 1978, p. 45) by then:

> Universities were expected to produce problem-solvers or social-technologists to run increasingly complex economies, and geographers were not slow in adopting new positions appropriate to the new conditions. Statistics and models were ideal tools for monitoring and planning in complex industrial societies. The work of the new geographers, however, often lacked a truly intellectual dimension. Many geographers were asking: 'Are our methods rigorous?', 'What are the planning implications of this model?', and not 'How much insight does this study give us?', 'Is my understanding of this phenomenon enhanced?', 'Does this study contribute to geography?'. The last-mentioned question was considered of little consequence. Yet it should have been asked, because one of the weaknesses of the new geography was a lack of coherence.

Developments in Systematic Geography in the United States

Whether because of, or independently of, the statements of Ackerman (1945), Schaefer (1953), and Ullman (1953), it is clear that during the 1950s systematic studies became much more important in the research and teaching of American geographers. (On Hartshorne's influence on systematic studies, see Butzer, 1990). This did not mean a departure from Hartshorne's views, since by 1959 he no longer gave primacy to regional studies, but the trend towards the scientific method proposed by Schaefer did mark a break with the Hartshornian tradition.

The growing popularity of topical specialisms is shown by the review chapters in the collection edited by James and Jones (1954) and by the journal literature of the 1950s. Very few of the investigations reported were aimed at the generation of laws in any sense, however: indeed some could almost be categorized under the exploration paradigm, in that their major purpose seemed to be the provision of new factual material: such work is best described an empiricist – it lets 'the facts' speak for themselves.

Fundamental to the progress of science in the positivist mould espoused by Schaefer is the development of theory. Several of the reviews in the James and Jones (1954) volume refer to what is in one place termed location theory (Harris, 1954, p. 299), but very few examples are cited of empirical investigations related to that body of theory. The chapter on urban geography, for example, cites all of the seminal pieces on central place theory, such as Ullman's (1941) original paper, and devotes two pages (Mayer, 1954, pp. 152–63) to the three 'models' of intra-urban spatial patterns which had been reviewed a decade previously by Harris and Ullman (1945), but there is not a single reference to any work done by geographers since in the context of those models. Thus although there were some precedents in the literature, in general very little work had been done by geographers, prior to the mid-1950s, which followed the dictates of the 'scientific approach'.

Once a new idea gains circulation through the professional journals it is available to be taken up by all. Nevertheless, development of the idea is usually concentrated in a few places only, where the pioneer teachers encourage their students to conduct research within the new framework. Thus most of the methodological changes in systematic studies in geography during the 1950s can be traced back to a few centres in the United States, and it is the work conducted at those centres which is discussed here. It should be stressed at the outset that the changes to be outlined were largely concerned with method, and that their scientific underpinning was stressed very little, although law-seeking was the clear goal. Certainly it was methods which dominated the literature, of both the pros and cons; many of the early contributions of the former groups were in relatively fugitive, departmental publications, presumably because of difficulties in getting such 'new' material accepted by the journals.

The Iowa school

Although Schaefer was at Iowa until his death in 1953, he was not the major influence on the developments which occurred there among the geographers who were, for a number of years, part of the economics department and thus open to the views and approaches of their peers in that more 'mature' social science. The leader of this group was Harold McCarty, author of a major text on American economic geography (McCarty, 1940). Associated with him were J. C. Hook, D. S. Knos, H. A. Stafford, and, later, J. B. Lindberg, E. N. Thomas and L. J. King (McCarty, 1979; King, 1979a).

The intent of McCarty and his co-workers was to establish the degree of

correspondence between two or more geographical patterns, akin to the morphological laws of accordance discussed by Schaefer. (Interestingly, none of
their publications refers to Schaefer's paper, although they do refer to the
works of, and assistance given by, Gustav Bergmann, a positivist of the
Vienna School who also strongly influenced Schaefer and read the proofs of
his 1953 paper: Davies, 1972, p. 134; King, 1979a; Golledge, 1983. See also
Martin, 1990.) These laws were to be embedded in a theory; thus (McCarty,
1954, p. 96):

> If we are to accept the idea that economic geography is becoming the branch
> of human knowledge whose function is to account for the location of economic
> activities on the various portions of the earth's surface, it seems reasonable to
> expect the discipline to develop a body of theory to facilitate the performance
> of this task.

Such a theory could be either topically or areally focused, and in its early
stages of development would probably be restricted both in its areal coverage
and in the topics whose spatial interrelationships it considered.

The purpose of theory is to provide explanations, and McCarty recognized
two sorts of explanation. The first is based on a search for the cause of observed
locational patterns, but:

> the search for causes can never produce an adequate body of theory for use in
> economic geography. . . . Variables became so numerous that they were not
> manageable, and, in consequence, solutions to locational problems were not
> obtainable (p. 96).

The second, and preferred, type focuses on associations:

> Its proponents take the pragmatic view that if one knew that two phenomena
> always appear together in space and never appear independently, the needs of
> geographic science would be satisfied, and there would be scant additional
> virtue in knowing that the location of one phenomenon caused the location of
> another (p. 97).

Such laws of association are built up in a series of stages, which begins with
a statement of the problem and of the necessary operational definitions, and
proceeds through the measurement of the phenomena (with attendant
problems of sampling in time and space) to a statement of the findings, in
tabular or graphical form. These three descriptive stages precede analysis
which seeks out correlations between the distributions of phenomena:

> the nub of the problem of research procedure seems to lie in finding the best
> techniques for discovering a, b and c in the 'where a, b, c, there x' hypothesis
> in order to give direction to the analysis. But where shall we search for its com-
> ponents? . . . One source of . . . clues lies in the findings of the systematic
> sciences. The other source lies in the observations of trained workers in the field
> or in the library (p. 100).

Thus geography, in its search for morphological laws, is to a considerable

extent a consumer of the laws of other disciplines. These laws may be theoretically rather than empirically derived. According to the causal or process
approach to explanation:

> Models may be created showing optimal locations for any type of economic
> activity for which adequate cost data may be obtained. These models may then
> be used (as hypotheses) for the comparison of hypothetical locations with actual
> locations. Divergences of pattern may then be noted and the hypothesis altered
> to allow for them (often by inclusion of factors not ordinarily associated with
> monetary costs). Ultimately the hypothesis becomes generally applicable and
> thus takes on the status of a principle (McCarty, 1953, p. 184).

This statement, although not referenced as such, very faithfully reflects the
views of positivists, and also of Popper and Lakatos, as to how science progresses by the continual modification of its hypotheses, so as better to represent
reality.

   In their major demonstration of this procedure in operation, McCarty *et
al.* (1956) discussed several statistical procedures for measuring spatial
association and adopted the now well-known technique of multiple regression
and correlation which had been used previously, among geographers, by Rose
(1936) and Weaver (1943) – both apparently as a product of contacts with
agricultural economists. Their empirical context was similarity in the location
patterns of certain manufacturing industries in the United States and in
Japan: other studies by the group included Hook's (1955) on rural population
densities, Knos's (1968) on intra-urban land-value patterns, and King's (1961)
on the spacing of urban settlements. Thomas (1960) had used similar procedures in his study of population growth in suburban Chicago, presented as
a PhD thesis to Northwestern University (where he was a contemporary of
Garrison), and he extended the methodology with a paper on the use of residuals from regression for both identifying where the putative laws of association do not apply fully and suggesting further hypotheses for areal
associations. (This last paper developed on an earlier one by McCarty (1952)
which was not widely circulated.) Later, McCarty (1958) expressed some
doubts about the statistical validity of the procedure, but the method that he
and his associates pioneered, with its focus on the testing of simple hypotheses
derived either from observation or from theoretical deductions, became the
model for much research in the ensuing decades.

Wisconsin

The Department of Geography at the University of Wisconsin, Madison, has
a long tradition of research with a quantitative bent. Notable among its early
products was the PhD thesis of John Weaver on the geography of American
barley production, which included a major section (published in his 1943
paper with no supporting methodological argument) using multiple correlation and regression to identify the influences of climatic variables on
barley yields. (Weaver later taught at the University of Minnesota, where he

developed a widely adopted statistical procedure (Weaver, 1954) for the definition of agricultural regions.) Other work at Madison focused on the quantitative description of population patterns (e.g. Alexander and Zahorchak, 1943). A combination of these two interests was furthered by a group led by A. H. Robinson, whose main interests were in cartography, and cartographic correlations were apparently introduced to him by his research supervisor at Ohio State University, Guy Harold Smith (Brown, 1978); Robinson worked with R. A. Bryson, of the Department of Meteorology, who was a source of statistical ideas and expertise. (Cartographic work was for a long time called 'mathematical geography' by some. It also developed statistical interests: see Blumenstock, 1953.)

Robinson's concern was to develop statistical methods of map comparison, as indicated by the title of an early paper – 'A method for describing quantitatively the correspondence of geographical distributions' (Robinson and Bryson, 1957). As with the work done at Iowa, the lead of Rose and of Weaver was followed with the adoption of correlation and regression procedures. Particular attention was paid to the problems of representing areal data by points (Robinson et al., 1961) and of using correlation methods in the comparison of isarithmic maps (Robinson, 1962). Like McCarty (1958), Robinson was aware of difficulties in applying classical statistical procedures to areal data, and he proposed a procedure to circumvent one of these (Robinson, 1956): Thomas and Anderson (1965) later found this proposal wanting, as it dealt with a special case only and not with the more general problems. Interestingly, though, the main early work on this topic was published by a group of sociologists, under the title of *Statistical Geography* (Duncan, Cuzzort and Duncan, 1961: perhaps even more interestingly, this work was virtually ignored by geographers).

W. L. Garrison and the Washington school

By far the largest volume of work in the spirit of Schaefer's and McCarty's proposals that was published during the 1950s came from the University of Washington, Seattle. The leader of the group of workers there was W. L. Garrison, whose PhD was from Northwestern University, where he was associated with Thomas (the two returned to Northwestern in the early 1960s; Taaffe, 1979), and who, according to Bunge (1966, p. ix), was influenced by Schaefer's paper, although the dates of his earliest publications indicate that he was involved in applying the positivist method to systematic studies in human geography before 1953. Also involved was E. L. Ullman, who moved to Seattle in 1951 (Harris, 1977), and who had already done pioneering research into urban location patterns and transport geography. (see Morrill, 1984). A large group of graduate students worked with Garrison and several became leaders in the new methodology during the subsequent decade, including B. J. L. Berry, W. Bunge, M. F. Dacey, A. Getis, D. F. Marble, R. L. Morrill, J. D. Nystuen, and W. R. Tobler (Garrison, 1979). The group also benefited from a visit to Seattle by the Swedish geographer, Torsten Hägerstrand, who was developing methods of generalizing spatial patterns and processes (see below, p. 143), and from Garrison's contacts with the Business School and the Engineering Department at Seattle (Halvorson and Stave, 1978).

Garrison and his co-workers had catholic interests in urban and economic geography. Much of their work was grounded in theory which they gleaned from other disciplines – notably economics – and they directed their efforts towards both testing those theories and applying them to problems of planning. In developing testable theoretical statements they displayed a much stronger mathematical base than was the case at Iowa and Madison. They also searched widely for statistical tests which were relevant to their investigation of point and line patterns – the biological sciences provided several of those which they adopted, such as nearest-neighbour analysis of point patterns (Dacey, 1962), and others, used for grouping and classifying, were derived from psychology (Berry, 1968). Garrison's (1956a, p. 429) view was that 'there is ample evidence that present tools are adequate to our present state of development. No type of problem has been proposed that could not be treated with available tools', which was in contradiction to an earlier claim by Reynolds (1956), although he was critical of how some standard techniques had been used (Garrison, 1956b). The dominant thrust of the group's work therefore involved the derivation from other systematic sciences of relevant normative theories, mathematical methods and statistical procedures with which to develop morphological laws.

The wealth of the work done at Seattle is best illustrated by a few of their major publications. Garrison (1959a, 1959b, 1960) contributed an important three-part review article on the state of location theory, for example. The first part comprised a review of six recent books – none of them by geographers – devoted to the question 'What determines the spatial arrangement (structure, pattern, or location) of economic activity?' (Garrison, 1959a, p. 232). Each incorporated locational considerations into traditional economic analysis, and Garrison concluded that this offered valuable economic insights to traditional geographical problems.

Central place theory was the dominant location theory on which the group worked. This had several independent origins, as Ullman (1941) had indicated (see also Harris, 1977, and Freeman, 1961, p. 201, who notes that findings akin to those in central place theory were reported by the 1851 Census Commissioners of Great Britain). It was Christaller's (1966) thesis which attracted most attention, however (see Muller-Wille, 1978). Working in Germany in the 1930s, Christaller developed ideas regarding the ideal distribution of settlements of different sizes acting as the marketing centres of functional regions, within the constraints of assumptions relating to the physical environment and the goals of both entrepreneurs and customers: a translation became available in the late 1950s, and was published in 1966. Studies of functional regions were not novel, of course (see above, p. 44), and geographers had already attempted to test Christaller's notions regarding a hierarchical organization of settlements distributed on a hexagonal lattice (e.g. Brush, 1953); related work, on a more inductive base, on 'principles of areal organization' was reported by Philbrick (1957). Dacey was concerned to make the analysis of these spatial hierarchies more rigorous (Dacey, 1962) whereas Berry's research focused on the central place aspects of the settlement pattern north of Seattle and on the retail centres in the city of Spokane (Berry and Garrison, 1958a, 1958b; Berry, 1959a).

The second part of Garrison's (1959b) review article dealt with possible geographical applications of the mathematical procedures of linear programming, which produce the optimal solutions to problems of resource allocation in constrained situations. He illustrated how the procedures of neoclassical economic analysis could be adapted in order to investigate ideal solutions to the problems of where to locate economic activities and how to organize flows of goods. Six such problems which could be treated by linear programming were identified:

1   the transportation problem, which takes a set of points, some with a given supply of a good and some with a given demand for it, plus costs of movement, and determines the most efficient flow pattern of the good from supply to demand points which minimizes the expenditure on transport;

2   the spatial price-equilibrium problem, which takes the same information as the transportation problem, but determines prices as well as flows;

3   the warehouse-location problem, which determines the best location for a set of supply points, given a geography of demand;

4   the industrial-location problem, which determines the optimum location for factories from knowledge of the sources of their raw materials and the destinations for their products;

5   the interdependencies problem, which locates linked plants so as to maximize their joint profits; and

6   the boundary-drawing problem, which determines the most efficient set of boundaries (i.e. that which minimizes total expenditure on transport) for, for example, school catchment areas.

The purpose of these analyses, if they are being used to investigate actual patterns and not as the bases for future plans, is, as Lösch (1954) put it, to see whether reality is rational, whether decision-makers have acted in ways that would produce the most efficient solutions, with efficiency defined as cost-minimization, particularly transport-cost minimization. Investigations by the Washington group in this context included studies of interregional trade (Morrill and Garrison, 1960) and the optimal location, by regions, of agricultural activities in the United States (Garrison and Marble, 1957).

In the final part of his review article, Garrison (1960a) dealt with four further books on locational analysis, which were empirical in orientation and shared a common interest in the agglomeration economies reaped by industrial clusters. Several topics and techniques were discussed, such as the use of input-output matrices to represent industrial systems, and Garrison concluded by stressing the need for geographers to investigate location patterns as systems of interrelated activities.

The empirical work with a planning orientation undertaken by the Seattle group is illustrated by one of the outputs of Garrison's large study of the impact of highway developments on land use and other spatial patterns (Garrison *et al.*, 1959). This book includes four studies: Berry's on the spatial pattern of central places within urban areas; Marble's on the residential pattern of the city (as indexed by property values) and relationships between household characteristics – including location – and their movement patterns; Nystuen's on movements by customers to central places; and Morrill's on the locations of physicians' offices, both actual and the most efficient. In addition, Garrison himself worked on the accessibility impacts of highway improvements, and devised indices of accessibility based on graph theory (Garrison, 1960b: the work was continued by Kansky, 1963, after Garrison and Berry moved to work in the Chicago area). He also used the simulation procedures that had been developed by Hägerstrand (1968) to investigate urban growth processes (Garrison, 1962), a topic taken much further by Morrill (1965). Berry (1958) extended his work on central places with a piece on planned shopping centres.

Somewhat separate from the work of the others in the group, although aligned with their general purpose, was Bunge's thesis, *Theoretical Geography* (1962, reprinted in enlarged form, 1966). This too displays a catholic view of geography, together with an acknowledged debt to Schaefer (Bunge worked at Iowa for a short period, and also at Madison). It is an extremely difficult book to summarize, but the basic theme is very clear: geography is the science of spatial relations and interrelations; geometry is the mathematics of space; hence geometry is the language of geography. Thus the early chapters are concerned with establishing geography's scientific credentials, in a debate with Hartshorne's published statements, especially those concerning uniqueness and predictability. As Lewis (1965) and others have also argued, Bunge claimed that Hartshorne confused uniqueness and singularity: he opposed Hartshorne's claim that geography cannot formulate laws because of its paucity of cases by arguing for even more general laws, and countered the argument that geographical phenomena are not predictable with the claim that science 'does not strive for complete accuracy but compromises its accuracy for generality' (p. 12).

Having established geography's scientific credibility to his satisfaction, Bunge then investigated its language. An intriguing discussion of cartography led him to conclude that descriptive mathematics is preferable to cartography as a more precise language. The remainder of the book looked at aspects of the substantive content of the science of geography, beginning with 'a general theory of movement' and then a chapter on central place theory:

> If it were not for the existence of central place theory, it would not be possible
> to be so emphatic about the existence of a theoretical geography . . . central
> place theory is geography's finest intellectual product (p. 133).

Problems of testing the theory were then discussed, showing, as did Getis
(1963), the need for map transformations, and in the final chapter of the first
edition the links between geography and geometry were made clear:

> Now that the science of space is maturing so rapidly, the mathematics of
> space — geometry — should be utilized with an efficiency never achieved by
> other sciences (p. 201).

The richness of the work done by this group during the mid and late 1950s
continued in various locations after it broke up (only Ullman remained,
although Morrill later joined the staff at Seattle). Most prolific and seminal
has been Berry, not only in his original field of central place theory (Berry,
1967) but also over a very wide range of other topics in economic and social
geography. Berry's work has always had a very strong empirical and utilitarian base, whereas Dacey continued to work on the mathematical representation of spatial, especially point, patterns (e.g. Dacey, 1973). In total, the work
of this significant group of scholars influenced the research and teaching of
a whole generation of human geographers, throughout the world.

The social physics school

The work of this group was initiated and developed independently from that
of any of the other three — its early publications preceded Schaefer's paper
by more than a decade. The leader was J. Q. Stewart, an astronomer at
Princeton University, who traced the origins of social physics in the work
of a number of natural scientists who applied their methods to social data
(Stewart, 1950). His own work apparently began when he noted certain
regularities in various aspects of population distributions, regularities which
were akin to the laws of physics, such as a tendency for the number of students
attending a particular university to decline with increasing distance of their
home addresses from its campus. From these observations he developed his
ideas on social physics, which he defined (Stewart, 1956, p. 245) as:

> . . . that the dimensions of society are analogous to the physical dimensions and
> include numbers of people, distance, and time. Social physics deals with obser-
> vations, processes and relations in these terms. The distinction between it and
> mathematical statistics is no more difficult to draw than for certain other phases
> of physics. The distinction between social physics and sociology is the avoidance
> of subjective descriptions in the former.

and he established a laboratory at Princeton to investigate the wide range of
regularities which could be analysed in this context. (Note Warntz's, 1984,
remark that he was introduced to Stewart's ideas via a book on *Coasts, Waves
and Weather* — Stewart, 1944 — which was 'prepared primarily to explain to

marine and air navigators the physical environment . . . Stewart could not resist the temptation to include an exotic chapter describing potential of population and its sociological importance'.)

Stewart's ideas were introduced to geographers by a paper in the *Geographical Review* (Stewart, 1947). Four empirical rules were adduced: the first, the rank-size rule for cities, showed that in the United States the population of a city multiplied by its rank (from 1 for the largest to n for the smallest), and standardized by a constant, equalled the population of the largest city, New York (Carroll, 1982); the second indicated that at various dates the number of cities in the country with populations exceeding 2500 was very closely related to the proportion of the population living in such places; the third showed that the distribution of a population could be described by the population potential at a series of points, in the same manner as the potential in a magnetic field is described in Newtonian physics; and the fourth illustrated a close relationship between this population potential and the density of rural population in the United States. From these regularities, Stewart claimed that

> There is no longer any excuse for anyone to ignore the fact that human beings, on the average and at least in certain circumstances, obey mathematical rules resembling in a general way some of the primitive 'laws' of physics (p. 485).

No reasons were given why this should be so (Curry, 1967b, p. 285, called this a 'deliberate shunning of plausible argument'): the rules were presented as empirical regularities which had some similarity to the basic laws of physics. Causal hypotheses were not even postulated, let alone tested.

One of Stewart's collaborators was William Warntz, a graduate of the University of Pennsylvania who was later employed by the American Geographical Society as a research associate, working on what he termed 'the investigation of distance as one of the basic dimensions of society' (Warntz, 1959b, p. 449; see also Warntz, 1984). The wide range of empirical regularities which they observed (see Stewart and Warntz, 1958, 1959) was used to develop their concept of macrogeography (Warntz, 1959b, 1959c). Geographical work, Warntz claimed, was dominated by micro-studies:

> The tendency of American geographers to be preoccupied with the unique, the exceptional, the immediate, the microscopic, the demonstrably utilitarian, and often the obvious is at once a strength and a weakness (Warntz, 1959b, p. 447)

but

> the assembly of more and more area studies involving an increase in the quantity of detail does not mean *per se* a shift from the microscopic to the macroscopic (p. 449).

Thus geographers were in danger of being unable to perceive general patterns within their welter of local detail. To counter this, Stewart and Warntz suggested the search for 'regularities in the aggregate'. Stewart's concept of population potential was used to describe general distributions, and was shown to be related to a large number of other patterns in the economic and social geography of the United States. These findings, it was realized, were only empirical regularities, but they could be used as the basis for theory development (Stewart and Warntz, 1958, p. 172), for geography's need was theory which 'has as its aim the establishment and coordination of areal relations among observed phenomena. General laws are sought that will serve to unify the individual, apparently unique, isolated facts so laboriously collected' (Warntz, 1959b, p. 58). The approach to theory, was inductive (see Figure 3.1) rather than deductive, although there was a clear underlying belief in the importance of distance and accessibility as influences on individual behaviour. To Warntz, as to Garrison, Ullman and others, the ideas of Christaller were seminal (see Bunge, 1968).

These macroscopic measures, particularly that of population potential, were used in a variety of contexts, as in Warntz's (1959a) *Towards a Geography of Price*, which established strong relationships between the prices of agricultural commodities in the USA and measures of supply and demand potential; Harris (1954b) and Pred (1965a) also used the potential measure in their studies of industrial-location patterns. The 'macrogeographers' also did much work on various distance-decay functions (see Chapter 4) and developed the early work of a Russian group on centrographic measures (Sviatlovsky and Eels, 1937; Neft, 1966), both at the American Geographical Society and later, under Warntz, at the Graduate School of Design's Laboratory for Computer Graphics and Spatial Analysis at Harvard University.

These lines of work contrasted markedly with that of the other three groups reviewed here, in a variety of ways. First was the topic of scale; Stewart and Warntz perhaps conformed more than any others to Bunge's call for a scientific approach which aimed at a high level of generality. Second there was the nature of the approach to theory, for macrogeography was inductive in its search for regularity rather than testing deductive hypotheses. Finally, the analogies sought for human geography were in a natural science — physics — and not in the other social sciences.

Summary

The developments outlined in this section marked the beginning of major changes in the field of human geography, changes which were rapidly taken up by others, within and beyond the United States. Although the focus was on theory and measurement, and the development of 'geographical laws', in line with the general ethos of academia in the immediate post-war decades, to some extent the work did not deviate too far from Hartshorne's expanded definition of the nature of geography (see above, p. 56). The main difference between the new work, with its focus in the systematic studies, and its regional predecessor was the greater faith of geographers in their ability to produce laws, to work within the canons of accepted scientific method, and to move out of their self-imposed academic isolation (Ackerman, 1945, 1963).

Scientific Method in Human Geography

Whether or not the changes just described initiated a 'Kuhnian revolution' in human geography it is clear that they involved at least a major reorientation in the nature of geographical research. Perhaps surprisingly, this reorientation was focused on no programmatic statement. There was no published paper or book which provided a detailed outline of how research should be conducted in this new framework: Schaefer's paper said nothing about how geographical laws were to be stated and derived, and although McCarty and his co-workers discussed methods in both general (McCarty, 1954) and specific (McCarty et al., 1956) contexts, they did not provide an overall programme. As Gregory (1978a, p. 47) puts it, 'geography has (with some notable exceptions) paid scant attention to its epistemological foundations'.

One piece was not central to the initial efforts, because it post-dated many of them, but it was widely quoted in the 1960s as the new ideas spread. Ackerman's (1958) essay on *Geography as a Fundamental Research Discipline* was an analysis of research organization. He indicated that the ultimate goal was integration to provide a full comprehension of reality, and that with regard to current developments, 'If any one theme may be used to characterize this period, that theme would be one of illuminating covariant relations among earth features' (p. 7). As a science, even one which is eventually an idiographic science since it deals with unique places, geography, according to Ackerman, needed to strive for 'an increasingly nomothetic component'. Its fundamental research

> need not necessarily be law-giving. . . . Much fundamental research in geography has not been law-giving in the strict sense but it has been concerned with a high level of generalization, and it has given meaning to other research efforts which succeeded it. In this sense it has a block-building characteristic (p. 17).

Such fundamental research 'is likely to rest on quantification . . . accurate study depends on quantification' (p. 30) and should 'furnish a theoretical framework with capacity to illuminate actually observed distributional patterns and space relations' (p. 28).

Ackerman's essay was a clarion call for the development of theory, for the application of quantitative methods, and for a focus on laws and generalizations to form the building-blocks for further nomothetic research. But there was no detailed discussion of how such research should be undertaken: it was a clarion call without reference to detail. Seven years later, the report of a National Academy of Sciences-National Research Council (1965) committee on *The Science of Geography* discussed 'Geography's problem and method' with the statement that

> Geographers believe that correlations of spatial distributions, considered both statistically and dynamically, may be the most ready keys to understanding existing or developing life systems, social systems, or environmental changes. In

the past . . . progress was gradual, however, because geographers were few, rigorous methods for analysing multivariate problems and systems concepts were developed only recently (p. 9).

Again, a general statement on orientation of research provided no detail on how research was to be conducted. And yet, in a paper published in 1963, Burton claimed that an intellectual revolution – the quantitative and theoretical revolution – had occurred in geography: 'The revolution is over, in that once-revolutionary ideas are now conventional' (p. 156). Something had become conventional, but nobody had written a full formulation for the discipline of what that something was!

Scientific method

There is no suggestion here that the groups of researchers who proposed changes in the nature of human geography lacked a clear rationale for their work; indeed, those involved were undoubtedly very clear as to both means and ends (though this may not be the case with some of their disciples), but they did not discuss these in detail in print. Nor, if their citations in the published works are any lead, did they research deeply into the philosophy that they were adopting: the exceptions to this are the references to Bergmann in the Iowa group's papers (see Golledge, 1983) and in Bunge's thesis. Texts on statistical and mathematical procedures were widely quoted and several were produced by and for geographers (eg Gregory, 1963; King, 1969), but the first major work on the philosophy of the 'new geography' was not published until 1969, in a book which received wide acclaim (Harvey, 1969a: a parallel, but briefer statement is Moss, 1970: note that Harvey was trained in Britain and his book was published there).

There are two routes to explanation, according to Harvey (Figure 3.1). The first, occasionally known as the 'Baconian' or inductive route, derives its generalizations out of observations: a pattern is observed and an explanation developed from and for it. This involves a dangerous form of generalizing from the particular case, however, because, as Moss (1970) argues, acceptance of the interpretations depends too much on the charisma of the scholar involved and on the unproven representativeness of the case(s) discussed. So the preferred method is the second route in Figure 3.1 (though see Bennett, 1985b). This also begins with observers perceiving patterns in the world; they then formulate experiments, or some other kind of test, to prove the veracity of the explanations which had been offered for those patterns. Only when ideas have been tested successfully against data other than those from which they were derived can a generalization be produced.

Scientific knowledge, obtained via the second route, is 'a kind of controlled speculation' (Harvey, 1969a, p. 35), and it is such a procedure that an increasing number of human geographers sought to apply during the 1950s. Its philosophy, known as positivism, was developed by a group of philosophers working in Vienna during the 1920s and 1930s (Guelke, 1978). It is based on

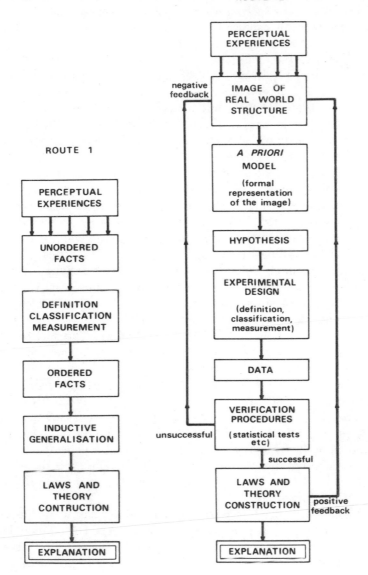

Fig 3.1 Two routes to scientific explanation
Source: Harvey (1969a, p. 34)

a conception of an objective world in which there is order waiting to be discovered. Because that order – the spatial patterns of variation and covariation in the case of geography – exists, it cannot be contaminated by the observer. A neutral observer, on the basis of either observations or reading of the research of others, will derive a hypothesis (a speculative law) about some aspect of reality and then test that hypothesis: verification of the hypothesis translates the speculative law into an accepted one.

A key tenet of this philosophy is that laws must be proven through objective procedures, and not accepted simply because they seem plausible: as Bunge (1962, p. 3) puts it, 'the plausibility or intuitive reality of a theory is *not* a valid basis for judging a theory'. A valid law must predict certain patterns in the world, so that having developed an idea about those patterns, the researcher must formulate them into a testable *hypothesis* – 'a proposition whose truth or falsity is capable of being asserted' (Harvey, 1969a, p. 100). An experiment is then designed to test the hypothesis, data are collected, and the validity of the predictions evaluated.

If the results of the test do not match the predictions, then either the observations on which the hypothesis was based or the deductions from the works of others are thrown into doubt. There is thus negative feedback (Figure 3.1) and the image of the world has to be revised, creating a new hypothesis. This in fact is the Popperian view that any hypothesis is found wanting by a single falsification. Harvey (1969a, p. 39) gives only eight lines to this view, however, preferring the more general one that only 'severe failure' – which he does not define – discredits an hypothesis totally (see, however, Moss, 1977; Bird, 1975; Petch and Haines-Young, 1979; Haines-Young and Petch, 1985). Hay (1985a) and Marshall (1985) present cases for adopting the Popperian approach of critical rationalism in human geography. The goal of critical rationalism is the same as that of positivism – the development of comprehensive theories which allow predictions to be made with high degrees of certainty. The two differ on means, not ends, because critical rationalists believe that hypotheses can never be comprehensively verified, only falsified. Clearly, if the researcher is a good observer and a logical thinker, such falsification of hypotheses should be rare. If the test is successful, on the other hand, then the speculation of the hypothesis becomes an acceptable generalization. One successful test will not turn it into a law. Replication on other data sets will be needed since a law is supposed to be universal; and there is always the possibility of a falsification.

Bird (1989) has extended his case for critical rationalism, with a procedure that he entitles PAME – an acronym for Pragmatic Analytical Methodology-Epistemology. He places pragmatic first in the sequence to stress the importance of external validation of conjectures against the 'real world' (p. 236), and it is followed by analytical because Bird adopts a hypothetico-deductive approach rather than 'a methodology which uses consideration of individual cases *inductively*, in the Micawberish hope that something will turn up to confirm the over-arching structures already in place' (p. 237). By methodology, he implies the use of paradigms as exemplars (see p. 17), and this is hyphenated with epistemology because the development of a theory of knowledge requires a workable, pragmatic set of procedures. With the whole (pp. 238–9):

The one stable element is the hypothetico-deductive nature of the methods of inquiry. And because the method is pragmatically warranted by successful correspondence to the thing in the real world, all else in the methodological-epistemological structure can be changed as experience dictates.

This, to him, is an open-ended procedure, which should be employed, not in the search for 'ultimate truths' but rather for the stimulating comparison of 'ideas that we hold, always on probation' (p. 246).

According to Harvey (1969a, p. 105):

A scientific law may be interpreted as a generalization which is empirically universally true, and one which is also an integral part of a theoretical system in which we have supreme confidence. Such a rigid interpretation would probably mean that scientific laws would be non-existent in all of the sciences. Scientists therefore relax their criteria to some degree in their practical application of the term.

After sufficient (undefined) successful tests, therefore, a hypothesis may be accorded law-like status, and is fed into a body of *theory*, which comprises a series of related laws. There are two types of statement within a full theory: the *axioms*, or givens, which are statements taken to be true, such as laws; and the deductions, or *theorems*, from those initial conditions, which are derived consequences from agreed facts – the next round of hypotheses. There is a positive feedback from the theory stage to the world view, therefore (Figure 3.1), so that the whole scientific enterprise, aimed at total explanation as Ackerman argued, is a circular procedure whereby the successes of one set of experiments become the building blocks for thinking about the next.

One stage in Figure 3.1 so far ignored is the *model*, a widely used term which has been given a variety of meanings (Chorley, 1964). There are two basic functions of a model: as a *representation of the real world*, such as a scale model, a map, a series of equations, and some other analogue (Morgan, 1967); and as an *ideal type*, a representation of the world under certain constrained conditions. Both are used in the positivist method to operationalize a theory, as a guide to the derivation of testable hypotheses.

Quantification has a central function in this scientific method. Mathematics are particularly useful in the development of models, as in the linear programming procedures adopted by Garrison. Relatively few geographers have strong backgrounds in mathematics, however (this was especially true in the 1950s), and so little work was done which involved representation of the real world as sets of equations. Instead the central role was given to statistics, used in hypothesis-testing. Two types of statistics are available: *descriptive statistics* can be used to represent a pattern or relationship; *inductive statistics* are used to make generalizations about a carefully defined population from a properly selected random sample of that population. (They use the same procedures.) Many geographical researchers confused the two. Inductive statistics employ significance tests to show whether what has been observed in the sample probably also occurs in the parent population, so that if the data analysed are not a sample, such tests are irrelevant (some disagreement was expressed over 'what is a sample?': see Meyer, 1972 and Court, 1972). Many geographers have used inductive methods in a descriptive manner, however, using the significance tests as measures of the validity of their findings (as argued for in Hay, 1985b).

The main attraction of statistics to many of the early adherents of the 'new geography' was their precision and lack of ambiguity – compared to the English language – in description. This was expressed by Cole (1969), who annotated a quotation from a well-known text (Stamp and Beaver, 1947, pp. 164–5): in this the text is Stamp and Beaver's and the annotations in parentheses, to shown the ambiguities, are Cole's:

> The present distribution of wheat cultivation in the British Isles (space) raises the conception of two different types of limit. Broadly speaking (vague), it may be said that the possible (vague) limits (limit) of cultivation of any crop are determined by geographical (vague), primarily by climatic conditions. The limits so determined (how?) may be described (definition) as the ultimate (vague) or the geographical (vague) limits . . . (Cole, 1969, p. 160).

The full quotation (only part is reproduced here), according to Cole, is so full of ambiguities that it could refer to about one million million possible combinations of some forty counties and it is impossible to reconstruct a map from that description:

> the correlations suggested are so tentative and imprecise that they leave the reader still wondering why wheat is grown where it is. The application of a standard correlation procedure . . . in itself would give a more precise appreciation of the relationship (p. 162).

Similar views became widely held during the 1950s and 1960s, and quantification became the *sine qua non* of training in the new methods (LaValle, McConnell, and Brown, 1967).

The scientific method increasingly adopted by geographers was a procedure for testing ideas, therefore, but a highly formalized one, about which there has been a great deal of debate among philosophers of science and others (Harvey, 1969a). Although many aspects of the method were used by geographers, their citations indicate relatively little exploration in depth into the full philosophy of positivism. (Positivism, as used here, refers to what is often known as 'scientific method'. It is embraced by the philosophy of logical positivism, which claims that only scientifically obtained knowledge is valid knowledge: Johnston, 1986a, 1986b.)

Reactions to scientific method

Despite (or perhaps because of) the lack of a clear programmatic statement of the 'new Theology' (Stamp, 1966, p. 18) until Harvey's (1969a) book, reactions to the developments were many and varied. (James, 1965, p. 35, called the debate 'continued, bitter and uncompromising warfare'.) Two related issues were the main foci of contention: whether quantification was sensible in geographical research, and whether law-making was possible. As Taylor (1976) points out, to some extent the debate was inter-generational, of the type discussed in Chapter 1 (p. 14): to some of the 'old guard' what was being proposed was just not geography and should be banished to some other corner of academia.

The quantification issue was the less important, and few spoke out against it in its entirety, although its extent was criticized. Thus Spate (1960a, p. 387) recognized that quantification is 'an essential element' and

> This is, like it or not, the Quantified Age. The stance of King Canute is not very helpful or realistic; better to ride the waves, if one has sufficient finesse, than to strike attitudes of humanistic defiance and end, in Toynbee's phrase, in the dustbin of history (p. 391).

He found three dangers in the development, however. The first was a confusion of ends and means. Quantifiers wanted to quantify everything (after Lord Kelvin − 'when you cannot express it in numbers, your knowledge is of a meagre and unsatisfactory kind': Spate, 1960b), but some things, like the positions of Madrid and Barcelona in Spanish thought, cannot be treated in that way. Secondly, there was the dogged analysis of trivia, producing platitudinous findings, a fault which Spate recognized as part of all academia, and especially its revolutions: 'Quantified or not, the trivial we will always have with us' (Spate, 1960a, p. 389), and the problem is usually the extreme positions taken up by the protagonists − Robinson's (1961) perks (the hyperquantifiers) and pokes (the hypoquantifiers). Finally, there was the vaunting ambition of the quantifiers, the belief that solution of the world's problems lay just around the corner.

Spate was not the only critic, and he was more generous than many. Burton (1963) identified five types of critic:

1 those who felt geography was being led in the wrong direction;
2 those who felt geographers should stick with their proven tool − the map;
3 those who felt that quantification was suitable for certain tasks only;
4 those who felt that means were being elevated over ends, and there was too much research on methods for methods' sake; and
5 those who objected not to quantification but to the quantifiers' attitudes.

He believed, however, that quantification had been proven to be more than a fad or fashion and that geography would develop out of a stage of testing relatively trivial hypotheses with its new tools so that 'The development of theoretical, model-building geography is likely to be the major consequence of the quantitative revolution' (p. 156).

More critical to many geographers than quantification was the issue of theory, and in particular the question of the role of laws in geography. For some, this continued the debate over environmental determinism, which was still active in Britain (Clark, 1950; Martin, 1951; Montefiore and Williams, 1955; Jones, 1956). Jones, for example, carried this debate over to the topic of scientific determinism, and its implications with regard to human free will. Martin (1951) had argued that possibilism is 'not merely wrong but is mischievous' (p. 6) because all human actions are determined in some way, so that in human geography:

> Unless we can assume the existence of laws or necessary conditions similar in stringency to those of physical science, there can be no human geography nor social sciences worth the name, but only a series of unexplainable statements of bare events . . . such laws cannot differ, except in respect of . . . far greater complication, from those of physical science (pp. 9–10).

Jones (1956) pointed out the impossibility of discovering universal laws about human behaviour and indicated the existence of two types of law in physics: the determinate laws of classical physics, which apply macroscopically; and the probabilistic quantum laws which refer to the behaviour of individual particles. Use of the latter would allow for the exercise of free will within prescribed constraints, and would at least allow answers to be offered to the question 'how?' if not to 'why?'. But the question of causality clearly worried many, as indicated by Lewis's (1965) counterargument that 'it is erroneously assumed that causes compel their effects in some way in which effects do not compel their causes' (p. 26).

Golledge and Amedeo (1968) addressed this same problem, by pointing out that critics of law-seeking in human geography applied a definition of a law as a universal postulate which brooked of no exception. They indicated that science recognizes several types of law, and also that the veracity of a law-like statement can never be finally proven, since it cannot be tested against all instances, at all times and in all places. They indicated four types of law which have relevance for human geographers. *Cross-sectional laws* describe functional relationships (as between two maps) but show no causal connection, although they may suggest one. *Equilibrium laws* state what will be observed if certain criteria are met, whereas *dynamic laws* incorporate notions of change, with the alteration in one variable being followed by (and perhaps causing) an alteration in another. Dynamic laws may be *historical*, showing that B would have been preceded by A and followed by C, or *developmental*, in which B would be followed by C, D, E etc. Finally, there are *statistical laws* which are probability statements of B happening, given that A exists: all laws of the other three categories may be either deterministic or statistical, with the latter almost certainly the case with phenomena studied by geographers.

None of the papers just discussed was part of an ongoing debate on quantification and theory-building; they appear to have been reactions to attitudes rather than to published critiques (in Britain there were none for several years: Taylor, 1976). There was one debate, however, in the American literature. It was initiated by Lukermann (1958), who was reacting to the views of

Warntz on macrogeography (see above, p. 67) and to a paper by Ballabon (1957). The latter had claimed that economic geography was lacking general principles and was 'short on theory and long on facts' (p. 218). McCarty had shown how to conduct research, but Ballabon stressed the need to use location theory being developed by economists as a source for hypotheses. Lukermann's response was that the main problem in the proposals of Ballabon and Warntz lay in the assumptions behind their hypotheses (Warntz's analogies with physics and Ballabon's with economics) which did not conform to his view of geography as an empirical science. Statistical regularities and isomorphisms with other subject matter do not provide explanations, so that hypotheses derived from such models test only the models themselves (see also Moss, 1970): 'the hypotheses to be tested are neither statistically nor rationally derived; that is, they are derived neither from empirical observation nor from deductions of previous knowledge in the social, economic or geographic fields' (p. 9).

Lukermann was countered by Berry (1959b), who argued that models, for all their simplifications and unreal assumptions, can offer insights towards understanding the real world: 'A theory or model, when tested and validated, provides a miniature of reality and therefore a key to many descriptions. There is a single master-key instead of the loaded key ring' (p. 12). Lukermann (1960a) was not convinced that models based on assumptions of perfect knowledge and competition, for example, could help in understanding if they were not empirically derived: 'the crucial problem is the construction of hypotheses from the empirical realities of economic geography . . . more light is shed and less truth is sophisticated through inventory than through hunches' (p. 2). King (1960) then entered the debate, pointing out that all laws are really only hypotheses, and that deviations of observed from expected in their testing indicates where the assumptions are invalid. Lukermann responded three times. In the first paper, he showed the lack of consensus in 'explanations' of the geography of cement production in the United States (Lukermann, 1960b) because economic analyses ignored 'Historical inertia, geographical momentum, and the human condition' (p. 5). His second paper (1961), in response to King, presaged some of the arguments developed later by Sack, who worked with him at Minnesota (see below, p. 111), and pointed out that much of the theory being introduced to economic geography (such as Lösch's) was not based on providing understanding of, and explanation for, reality. Finally, he presented a longer paper (Lukermann, 1965) which discussed several aspects of the debate, concluding with the statement that

> Thus, we see scientific explanation as far removed from the context within which the macroscopic geographers would have us put it — the end product of geographic research. Science does not explain reality, it explains the consequences of its hypotheses (p. 194),

and a further call for explanations in geography to be based on observations of reality and not the import of analogies which cannot offer explanations, but only unreal assumptions. Lukermann's basic point, never fully tackled by his critics, was that tests showing conformity between empirical reality and a model were tests of the model only, and could not indicate how empirical reality was created.

The clear difference of opinion between Lukermann and his antagonists over the way in which geographers should seek explanations (which was not about the positivist scientific method itself, but about the inputs to the images of the real-world structure – Figure 3.1) suggests the sort of generation gap discussed in Chapter 1. It is doubtful whether papers such as those of Jones, of Lewis, and of Golledge and Amedeo quieted the fears of those unconvinced by the arguments of the 'quantifiers', any more than Berry and King convinced Lukermann. But the differences soon became a non-issue, at least in the published papers resulting from the research activities of geographers in many topical specialisms. As Burton claimed, by the mid-1960s the changes seen to have been widely accepted, and the regional approach had certainly been ousted from its prime position in the publications of human geographers, Increasingly, quantitative and theoretical material came to dominate not only the more obvious journals, such as *Economic Geography* and *Geographical Analysis* (a 'journal of theoretical geography' founded in 1969), but also the prestigious general journals, notably the *Annals of the Association of American Geographers*. (The *Geographical Review* was an early partial 'convert' through the American Geographical Society's sponsorship of the macrogeographers although Berry states that it rejected his early papers with Garrison as 'not geography': Halvorson and Stave, 1978.) Most of the work contributed little to theory, however. It was quantitative testing of theory- or model-derived hypotheses in some cases, but with little indication of how good the results were. In others cases, it was quantitative description that could inform theory and model development, but in many instances was merely a series of 'factual reports'. By the 1970s, textbooks were being published which began with discussions of scientific method and quantification before proceeding to the substantive content of the 'empirical science' (Abler, Adams and Gould, 1971; Amedeo and Golledge, 1975).

Spread of Scientific Method

Within human geography in the United States, the initial development of systematic studies using the positivist scientific method was very largely focused on economic geography and the associated economic aspects of urban geography. This undoubtedly reflects the relative sophistication of economics within the social sciences, providing a model for geographers to copy, not only to advance their discipline but also to promote its cause in the search for utility to the world of business and government. The long tradition of empirical work in human geography meant, however, that with few exceptions research in the systematic areas mainly comprised the statistical testing of relatively simple hypotheses, with little mathematical modelling or writing of formal theory.

Contemporaneous with these developments in human geography, and an important stimulus for them, was the emergence of a new discipline in the United States – regional science. This was very much the product of one iconoclast scholar – Walter Isard – an economist who built spatial components into his models, in part to provide a stronger theoretical basis for urban and regional planning than had existed previously. In general terms, regional science is economics with a spatial emphasis, as illustrated by Isard's (1956a, 1960) two early texts, but the Regional Science Association attracted relatively more practising geographers than economists. To some, regional science and economic geography are hard to distinguish: the former can be separately characterized by its greater focus on mathematical modelling and economic theorizing, however, whereas geographical work has remained more empirical and less dependent on formal languages. (Initially Isard, 1956b, saw geographers as doing the empirical tests of the regional scientists' models.) Over time, the interests of regional scientists have broadened (Isard, 1975), but the strong theoretical base has remained.

The emphasis on statistical methods in so much of the new work in American human geography led to its partial rapprochement with physical geography. (One of the leading 'quantitative geographers' of the 1960s, Leslie Curry, trained as a climatologist.) More physical geography papers were published in the leading journals, more physical geographers were appointed to university departments, geologists such as Krumbein, Leopold, Schumm and Wolman were major sources of quantitative ideas, and there was a common interest in the training of graduate students (LaValle et al., 1967). This common interest in procedures was illustrated by the papers given at a conference held in 1960 on Quantitative Geography, which led to the publication of two volumes (Garrison and Marble, 1967a, 1967b) on the development of methods, one for human geography and the other for physical geography. In the former, for example, Berry introduced the family of factor analysis methods as a way of collapsing and ordering large data matrices; Dacey investigated line patterns and Beckmann the optimal location of routes; Robinson continued his work on the statistical comparison of maps; Mayfield and Thomas extended the analysis of central place patterns; Marble, Morrill, and Nystuen looked at patterns of movement; and Warntz continued the work on macrogeography. Other conferences and summer schools to train geographers in quantitative techniques were held at this time (on their impact, see Gould, 1969; Taaffe, 1979), and American geographers were to the forefront in launching an International Geographical Union Commission on Quantitative Methods.

Expansion within American geography

The launching of Burton's 'quantitative and theoretical revolutions' took place in a few topical specialisms within American human geography, so one of the first tasks for the established 'revolutionaries' was to spread their 'new Theology' wider through the discipline, by convincing others of the benefits which quantification and the associated scientific method could bring to their specialisms. One of the major pieces of advocacy was an NAS/NRC report (1965) on *The Science of Geography* which was prepared in order to chart research priorities within the discipline. The case was presented for more 'theoretical-deductive' work to balance the earlier emphasis on 'empirical-inductive analysis', the detailed argument being based on four premises:

> (a) Scientific progress and social progress are closely correlated, if not equated. (b) Full understanding of the world-wide system comprising man and his natural environment is one of the four or five great overriding problems in all science. (c) The social need for knowledge of space relations of man and natural environment rises, not declines, as the world becomes more settled and more complex, and may reach a crisis stage in the near future. Last, (d) progress in any branch of science concerns all branches, because science as a whole is epigenetic.
>
> The social need for knowledge of space relations means an imminent practical need. As the population density rises and the land-use intensity increases, the need for efficient management of space will become even more urgent (p. 10).

And since, to the members of the committee (E. A. Ackerman, B. J. L. Berry, R. A. Bryson, S. B. Cohen, E. J. Taaffe, W. L. Thomas Jr, and M. G. Wolman), geography 'involves the study of spatial distributions on the earth's surface' (p. 8) then it followed that 'Geographic studies will be irreplaceable components of the scientific support for efficient space management' (p. 10). The positivist scientific method was being sold to geographers and geography was being sold to the scientific establishment, in the search for financial research support.

The committee chose four problem areas within geography to illustrate the subject's potentials as a 'useful science'. The first of these was physical geography. The second was cultural geography, which studies 'differences from place to place in the ways of life of human communities and their creation of man-made or modified features' (p. 23). A major focus in this area, it was noted, was on landscape development and the diffusion over space and time of specific cultural features: 'applying modern techniques to studying the nature and rate of diffusion of key cultural elements and establishing the evolving spatial patterns of culture complexes' (p. 24) was seen as an avenue for development. The third problem area was political geography, and the committee proposed work on boundaries and resource management. Finally, the committee recognized location theory studies, an amalgam of work in economic, urban and transport geography in which the 'dialogue' between the empirical and the theoretical had gone furthest, 'revealing the potential power of a balanced approach when applied to other geographical problem areas' (p. 44). Location theory involved work on spatial patterns, the links and flows between places in such patterns, the dynamics of the patterns, and the preparation of alternative patterns through model-building exercises which identify efficient solutions.

In the development of the science of geography,

> A major opportunity seen by workers in the location theory problem area is that of integrating their work more closely with other geographers as they begin to deal with spatial systems of political, cultural, and physical phenomena. . . . This could be achieved . . . by the accelerated diffusion of techniques and concepts to other geographers, and communication on the definition of research problems. The result would be to hasten the confrontation of empirical-inductive studies by theoretical-deductive approaches throughout geography. . . . Testing the theory in a variety of empirical contexts should aid in the overall development and refinement of viable theories. It should also serve to connect geographic progress to local problems more rapidly and more effectively (pp. 50–1).

The deductive-theoretical scientific methodology was central to their blueprint for the advancement of geographical research, therefore. All geographers would have a role to play in this movement forward, for:

> Geographers have one other asset that should be capitalized on. Those who have been interested in the study of a specific part of the earth (regional geography) develop competences for interpreting the physical-cultural complexes of the regions that they study. Students of the way a particular part of the earth has evolved (historical geography) have other competences for interpreting the historical development and modification of a region. These two groups have students that are particularly qualified to undertake the field observation and field study of problems recognized in a more systematic way and to conduct field tests of generalizations arrived at through systematic study. . . .
>
> The regional or historical geography specialist who has mastered the technique of field observation and historical study thoroughly . . . can make himself indispensable if he understands the direction in which the generalizing clusters are headed and relates his work closely to their growing edges (p. 61).

A clear division of labour was being suggested, comprising theoretical-deductive 'thinkers' and empirical-inductive 'workers', a division which was apparently unequal in status and was resented by some as such (James, 1965; Thoman, 1965).

A somewhat similar report, prepared for the Committee on Science and Public Policy of the National Academy of Sciences and the Problems and Policy Committee of the Social Science Research Council, was published five years later (Taaffe, 1970). Also the product of a committee (E.J. Taaffe, I. Burton, N. Ginsburg, P.R. Gould, F. Lukermann, P.L. Wagner), this stressed human geography as 'the study of spatial organization expressed as patterns and processes' (pp. 5–6), incorporating people-environment relationships and cultural landscapes and stressing relevance to planning and other policy issues. Much of the report is constructed to illustrate the nature of human geography. The case is

> that there are many opportunities for the expansion and improvement of geographic research. If geography is to have a strong and beneficial impact on the constantly changing patterns of spatial organization of American society, it will be necessary to continue this development (p. 131)

which led to six conclusions: (1) greater collaboration among the social sciences; (2) alleviation of geography's manpower shortage; (3) establishment of centres for cartographic training and research; (4) development of remote sensing and related data bases; (5) greater support for foreign area study; and (6) programmes established 'to strengthen the mathematical training of geographers'. Human geography was presented as a relevant component of the social sciences, increasingly sophisticated in its analytical tools, focusing on spatial organization, and offering particular skills in mapping and data acquisition.

One of the systematic areas of geography that was colonized early by the new methods was that part of urban geography which dealt with the internal spatial structure of cities. Until the 1960s, little work had been done on this topic except with regard to commercial land uses (particularly the Central Business District and the relationship of the pattern of suburban shopping centres to the postulates of central place theory): almost no attention was paid to the human content of residential areas, perhaps because geography was seen to be the science of places, not of people. Recognition that 'people live in cities' (Johnston, 1969) led to a growth of interest in residential areas, which gained much stimulus from the work of the urban ecology school of sociologists at Chicago (some of their works had been introduced to geographers earlier – Harris and Ullman, 1945; Dickinson, 1947 – but with little success). The methods of social area analysis gained in popularity, using the techniques being applied elsewhere (Berry, 1964a): a new form of urban geography was initiated which adopted its norms from the functionalist schools of sociology. Society is made up of socio-economic classes, the nature and composition of which are widely accepted, and these classes come to consensual agreements about the allocation of land among competing groups (Johnston, 1971). This type of urban geography in effect became a separate systematic branch of the discipline; few people did research in it as well as in other aspects of urban geography.

The argument being advanced by those who sought to spread the new methodology more widely was focused on a common set of procedures to tackle geographical problems. This was described by Berry (1964b), who argued that the geographer's viewpoint emphasizes space, with regard to distributions, integration, interactions, organization and processes. All of its data can be categorized by a single matrix (Figure 3.2) in which places form the rows and characteristics the columns: each cell defines a geographic fact. Berry then suggested that five different types of geographical study can be recognized by focusing on different elements of this matrix: study of a single

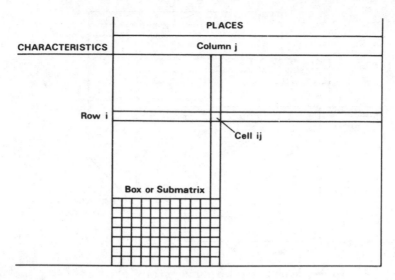

Fig 3.2   The geographic matrix: each cell — ij — contains a 'geographic fact' — the value assumed by characteristic i at place j
Source: Berry (1964b, p. 6)

row (a place) or column (a characteristic); comparison of two or more rows (places) or columns (characteristics); or study of rows and columns together. Adding further matrices, one for each time-period (Figure 3.3.), allows for five further types of study, based on the earlier five but concentrating on changes over time. Thus, he concluded, systematic and regional geography are part of the same enterprise — a repetition of Hartshorne's (1959) arguments — with neither sufficient in itself.

Berry's matrices referred only to the characteristics of places, and further matrices could be introduced (Figure 3.4) which show the flows between places, with one matrix for each flow category in each time-period (Clark, Davies and Johnston, 1974). Berry used this extension himself, though he did not formalize it, in his attempt to fuse the procedures for formal and functional regionalization (see above, p. 43) to produce a general theory of spatial behaviour — Berry's (1968) field theory, which he applied in a large study of the spatial organization of India (Berry, 1966). The techniques which he used in this work became widely used in the 1960s, as access to high-speed computers for the handling of very large data matrices became very easy, if not universal, for university academics. They were given the umbrella term of factorial ecology (Berry, 1971), and were widely applied in many aspects of geography, resulting in a methodological unity which was previously unknown across the various systematic specialisms.

The developments of the 1950s in the United States spread into several of the discipline's topical specialisms, and by the mid-1960s use of statistical methods to test hypotheses was common. It was indeed the methods which

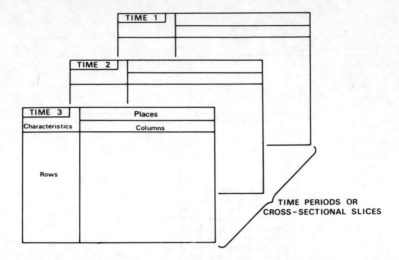

Fig 3.3   A third dimension to the geographic matrix
Source: Berry (1964b, p. 7)

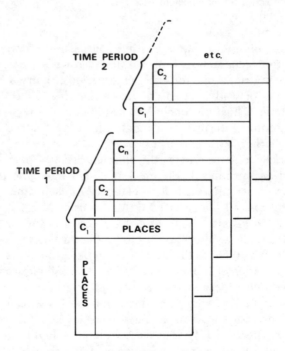

Fig 3.4   Geographic flow matrices, one per commodity, for each time period
Source: after Clark, Davies and Johnston (1974)

gave unity to these specialisms, which in terms of substance remained very separate, identifiable branches within the geographical enterprise. The decline of interest in work which aimed to integrate the findings of the specialisms into regional syntheses, despite the efforts of Berry and a few others (see also Taaffe, 1974), meant that human geography experienced a centrifugal trend with regard to substance contemporaneously with a centripetal one with regard to procedures. Since positivist scientific method, and the statistical techniques, were used much more widely than in human geography alone, it seems that the former of these trends was probably the most important.

Transatlantic Translation

By the early 1960s the quantitative and theoretical revolutions were having considerable impact beyond the United States, as the result of two agencies. The first was the publication of the work of the American iconoclasts in the major journals. Secondly, and probably more importantly, during the 1950s and 1960s a number of British geographers went to the United States, either as postgraduate students or as visiting staff members. Some returned with the new ideas, which they disseminated among their students and, via the Study Group in Quantitative Methods of the Institute of British Geographers (Gregory, 1976), their fellow academics. (Others stayed in North America: Brian Berry was one.) There was also a local base, mainly in physical geography and arising out of the early use of statistics by climatologists (e.g. Crowe, 1936): as a result, and perhaps somewhat surprisingly, the first undergraduate text in statistics for geographers was written by an English academic (Gregory, 1963. Note that the positivist methodology is entirely implicit in Gregory's book. His Preface speaks only of the geographer's raw material 'becoming progressively more of a quantitative nature' and 'the need to present both data and conclusions in sound quantitative terms' – pp. xiii–xiv. The use of statistical techniques is thus required, but their use in hypothesis testing is not spelled out – see p. 72). In addition, there was some interest in location theory – at University College, London, in the early 1950s, for example (Halvorson and Stave, 1978), and in work on both settlement patterns (Dickinson, 1933; Smailes, 1946) and industrial location (Smith, 1949; Rawstron, 1958).

Although statistics courses were introduced in several British university departments of geography by the mid-1960s, and aspects of the scientific methodology were taught by at least a few staff members (Whitehand, 1970), the main focus for the introduction of the 'new geography' to Britain during the early years of the decade was the University of Cambridge. The leaders were R. J. Chorley (a geomorphologist, who had spent some time studying in the United States) and P. Haggett (a Cambridge-trained human geographer, although his early published work was in biogeography, who had also visited the United States and experienced the development there: Haggett, 1965c, p. vi: see also Haggett and Chorley, 1989). Their impact on British geography was considerable, through innovative research and teaching (Gregory, S., 1976). They worked on the adaptation of certain statistical techniques to geographical (both physical and human) problems (Chorley and Haggett, 1965a; Haggett, 1964: Haggett and Chorley, 1969), but their most lasting contribution was probably in editing two collections of papers which resulted from courses that they directed, aimed at introducing the 'new geography' to teachers.

The first of these books – *Frontiers in Geographical Teaching* (Chorley and Haggett, 1965b) – was based on a course given in 1963 which was designed 'to bring teachers and like persons into the University, there to encounter and discuss recent developments and advances in their subjects' (p. xi). In it Wrigley (1965), for example, discussed the changing philosophy of geography and saw the increasing use of statistical techniques as the contemporary development 'of singular importance' (p. 15). He pointed out that techniques of themselves do not form a methodology and that 'Geography writing and research work has in recent years lacked any general accepted, overall view of the subject even though techniques have proliferated' (p. 17). He offered no outline of such a view, however, arguing that eclecticism in mode of analysis was likely to be most productive and that 'the best sign of health is the production of good research work rather than the manufacture of general methodologies' (p. 17). Many of the other chapters interpret geography as if the 'revolutions' had not occurred in the United States, however: Smith's (1965) on historical geography, for example, is an excellent British companion to the American statement published a decade earlier (Clark, 1954).

Elsewhere in the book, Pahl (1965) introduced the models of the Chicago school of urban sociologists and suggested a social geography in which the prime factor is distance (p. 95), but it was only the chapters by Haggett and by Timms which introduced much of the transatlantic turmoil. Haggett (1965a) wrote on the use of models in economic geography, both those based on simple views of the world, such as developments on von Thunen's (Chisholm, 1962), and those derived from observations of particular cases (e.g. Taaffe, Morrill, and Gould, 1963). He noted that

> Perhaps the biggest barrier that model builders in economic geography will have to face in the immediate future is an emotional one. It is difficult to accept without some justifiable scepticism that the complexities of a mobile, infinitely variable landscape system will ever be reduced to the most sophisticated model, but still more difficult to accept that as individuals we suffer the indignity of following mathematical patterns in our behaviour (p. 109),

and as a consequence introduced the notion of indeterminacy at the individual level and showed how random variables must be introduced to operational models. His chapter on scale problems (Haggett, 1965b) illustrated methods of sampling and of map generalization from samples. Timms (1965) demonstrated the use of certain statistical techniques for the analysis of social patterns within cities (based on Shevky and Bell's social area analysis, and thus developed independently of Berry's work on this topic – see above, p. 82), pointing out that

> The sciences concerned with the study of social variation have as yet produced few models which can stand comparison with the observed patterns or which can be used to predict those patterns. . . . Prediction rests on accurate know-ledge of the degree and direction of the interrelationships between phenomena. This can only be attained by the use of techniques of description and analysis which are amenable to statistical comparison and manipulation. If the goal of geographical studies be accepted as the formulation of laws of areal arrange-ment and of prediction based on those laws, then it is inevitable that their tech-niques must become considerably more objective and more quantitative than heretofore (p. 262).

If the majority of the contributors to *Frontiers in Geographical Teaching* were not as committed to the 'new geography' as was Timms (later to become a professor of sociology, as was Pahl), this cannot be said of the editors, who used their epilogue (Haggett and Chorley, 1965) to present a strong case for the 'theoretical revolution':

> We cannot but recognize the importance of the construction of theoretical models, wherein aspects of 'geographic reality' are presented together in some organic structural relationship, the juxtaposition of which leads one to compre-hend, at least, more than might appear from the information presented piecemeal and, at most, to apprehend general principles which may have much wider application than merely to the information from which they were derived. Geographical teaching has been remarkably barren of such models. . . . This reticence stems largely, one suspects, from a misconception of the nature of model thinking. . . . Models are subjective frameworks . . . like discardable cartons, very important and productive receptacles for advan-tageously presenting selected aspects of reality (pp. 360–1).

This view was the dominant one in their next, and substantially more influen-tial, volume (Chorley and Haggett, 1967).

Models in Geography presented a synthesis of most of the work completed before the mid-1960s by adherents to the 'quantitative and theoretical revolu-tions'. Individual authors had been asked 'to discuss the role of model-building within their own special fields of research' (Haggett and Chorley, 1967, p. 19), which resulted in a series of substantive review essays, some dealing with particular topical specialisms (urban geography and settlement location; industrial location; agricultural activity – there were similar reviews for physical geography), some with particular themes ranging across several specialisms (economic development; regions; maps; organisms and eco-systems; the evolution of spatial patterns), and some with methods and approaches (demographic models; sociological models; network models). A catholic use of the term model was allowed, allowing it as a synonym for a theory, a law, a hypothesis, or any other form of structured idea (see Moss, 1970). The approach was strongly nomothetic, however: as Harvey (1967a, p. 551) expressed it,

> the student of history and geography is faced with two alternatives. He can either bury his head, ostrich-like, in the sand grains of an idiographic human history, conducted over unique geographic space, scowl upon broad generalization, and produce a masterly descriptive thesis on what happened when, where. Or he can become a scientist and attempt, by the normal procedures of scientific investigation, to verify, reject, or modify, the stimulating and exciting ideas which his predecessors presented him with.

All the contributors to the book had clearly chosen the latter course: their focus is on models – on generalization of reality – and methods are very much secondary.

The orientation of this significant volume is given by the editors' introduction. (The significance lay in its two uses: first, as a synthesis and argument, the volume was widely read and used by researchers and teachers as a guide; secondly, as a series of major reviews, when republished as a series of paperback volumes, the book was extensively employed as an undergraduate text.) Haggett and Chorley (1967, p. 24) presented the model as:

> a bridge between the observational and theoretical levels . . . concerned with simplification, reduction, concretization, experimentation, action, extension, globalization, theory formation and explanation (p. 24).

It can be descriptive or normative, static or dynamic, experimental or theoretical (see also Chorley, 1964). It forms the basis for a paradigm, which made no attempt 'to alter the basic Hartshorne definition of Geography's prime task' (p. 38) but offered much greater progress:

> the new paradigm . . . is based on faith in the new rather than its proven ability. . . . There is good reason to think that those subjects which have modelled their forms on mathematics and physics . . . have climbed considerably more rapidly than those which have attempted to build internal or idiographic structures (p. 38).

Models in Geography stands as a statement of that faith, and as a major illustration of the expanding use of scientific methods in the systematic fields of human geography.

Although the editors and contributors to *Models in Geography* represented most of the early active participants in the move to change British geography towards a 'more scientific' approach, there were others who are not represented, directly, in that book. Notable amongst them was a group who graduated at the University of Cambridge in the 1950s (Haggett was among them), having been tutored by A. A. L. Caesar (Chisholm and Manners, 1973, p. xi, credit his role, one which continued until the end of the 1970s with a steady stream of productive research workers from St Catherine's College, Cambridge). It included Michael Chisholm, Peter Hall and Gerald Manners as well as Haggett, the only one who worked within the 'quantitative revolution'. Chisholm, for example, worked with theoretical developments within systematic fields (e.g. Chisholm, 1962, 1966, 1971a) but with relatively little concern for detailed quantitative analysis (though see Chisholm and O'Sullivan, 1973). Both Hall and Manners were more concerned, as was Caesar it seems, with geographical analysis of contemporary issues, although in some cases the analyses led to attempts at theory-derivation (Hall, 1981a).

Chorley and Haggett's editing, and their joint work on technical developments – such as trend surface analysis (Chorley and Haggett, 1965a) and network analysis (Haggett and Chorley, 1969) – represented a belief in the unity of physical and human geography. This was based on an assumption that a shared interest in methods and techniques could unite the two – Haggett (1967, p. 664) writes with

> the basic proposition that a wide range of different geographical networks may be usefully analysed in terms of their common geometrical characteristics.

As in North America, while the focus of geographical analysis remained geometry, then physical and human geographers could find common cause (Woldenberg and Berry, 1967). Explanation of the geometry required the study of very different processes, however.

The Relatively Untouched

The NAS/NRC (1965) report (see above, p. 80) indicated that the two main systematic specialisms within human geography relatively untouched by the developments were cultural and historical geography (see also Darby, 1983a): in addition, despite Berry's attempt to reframe it (Berry, 1964b), regional geography remained largely separate from the changes in methodological emphasis. Not all cultural, historical and regional geographers ignored the changes occurring elsewhere, of course: some, indeed, were in the vanguard of the 'revolution' – two of the chapters in *Models in Geography*, for example, were written by individuals (David Grigg and David Harvey) who had done empirical research (eg Harvey, 1985c) on historical topics. But in general terms the NAS/NRC report was undoubtedly correct; there is not much evidence of success in winning cultural, historical and regional geographers over to the new methodology.

Of the three groups listed in the previous paragraph, the *historical geographers* were probably most concerned about their apparent isolation within the discipline. This concern was summarized by Baker (1972) in terms of the approaches which historical geographers need to consider in greater detail:

> An assumption is necessary here: that methodologically the main advances can be expected from an increased awareness of developments in other disciplines, from a greater use of statistical methods, from the development, application and

testing of theory, and from exploitation of behavioural approaches and sources. . . .

Rethinking becomes necessary because orthodox doctrines have ceased to carry conviction. As far as historical geography is concerned, this involves a questioning of the adequacy of its traditional methods and techniques (p. 13).

All of these would have to be followed with care, and the potentials of the methodological developments assessed with caution, but Baker clearly believed there was considerable scope for change, as had already been shown in economic and in social history, and perhaps even more so in archaeology (see Renfrew, 1981). Particular areas of historical geography, including those relating to urban settlements (e.g. Ward, 1971; see also Johnston and Herbert, 1978, p. 20), are perhaps more open to such changes than are others, if for no other reason than the better quality, as well as quantity, of available data, and increasing amounts of such work were reported (e.g. Whitehand and Patten, 1977; Johnson and Pooley, 1982; Dennis, 1985). There are possible implications in such work, however: as Baker notes,

Studies in, for example, 'historical agricultural geography', 'historical urban geography' and 'historical economic geography' seem to offer possibilities of fundamental development, particularly in terms of a better understanding of the processes by which geographical change through time may take place. Such an organization of the subject would view historical geography as a means towards an end rather than as an end it itself (p. 28).

In the early discussions of the relationships between historical geography and the 'theoretical and quantitative revolutions', most attention focused on quantification rather than on theory. As Vance (1978) has pointed out, however, the development of theory does not have to involve 'quantitative abstraction', as work by himself (Vance, 1970), Pred (1977b), Conzen (1971) and others has shown. If available, data can be manipulated to test theories regarding past spatial patterns (e.g. Goheen, 1970), but, as Radford (1981, p. 257) makes clear, theory is the more important:

In the cities of the nineteenth-century United States, a set of principles . . . was taken to something approaching a logical conclusion.

Such a view assumes that theory is possible in historical geography. As illustrated in Chapter 6, some dispute this — for geography as a whole as well as for historical geography. The positivist method implies objectivity, but the geographer in describing a landscape is subjective:

In describing a landscape, is he not committed by his past training and his past experiences — by his prejudices, if you will? Just as the portrait an artist paints will tell you much about the artist as well as his sitter, so the description of a countryside will tell you a great deal about the writer (Darby, 1962, p. 4).

Thus to Darby geography is both science and art. It

is a science in the sense that what facts we perceive must be examined, and perhaps measured, with care and accuracy. It is an art in that any presentation (let alone any perception) of those facts must be selective, and so involve choice, and taste, and judgement (p. 6).

Such a position clearly separated those wedded to an implicitly idealist view of historical geography (see p. 169) from those advancing the cause of a more scientific approach, whether or not it was quantitative, though some would argue that the first quote above from Darby could equally well apply to positivist work (positivistic training introduces subjectivity in choice of subject matter and approach too).

Cultural geographers would appear to have been less concerned about their apparent drift away from the mainstream of geographical activity than were historical geographers, perhaps because of the lack of any parallel developments to those in geography in anthropology, the discipline with which many cultural geographers probably had most contact (see Mikesell, 1967, for a general comparison). (This is a generalization, of course. Anthropological work has experienced major paradigmatic threats, if not changes, notably in the structural work of Claude Lévi-Strauss; see Leach, 1974.) The increasing general interest of geographers in diffusion, stimulated by Hägerstrand's (1968) work and extended into other contexts led to contact between the spatial analysis and cultural analysis schools of thought, however (Clarkson, 1970). Nevertheless, as Mikesell (1978, p. 1) expressed it, 'Stubborn individualism and a seeming indifference to academic fashion are well-known characteristics' of cultural geographers, whose preferences are for: a historical orientation; a focus on the role of human agency in environmental change, on material culture, and on rural areas; links with anthropology; an individualistic perspective; and field work. (These are all illustrated in a book of essays on *Geography as Human Ecology*: Eyre and Jones, 1966.) Similarly, Porter (1978, pp. 30–31) concludes his review of 'geography as human ecology' with:

> in the past 25 years those interested in the mutual relations of people and environment have taken an interesting journey in search of a satisfactory replacement of environmental determinism. Along the way they have been offered, but generally have declined to use, the shiny wares of gravity and . . . [other] models. . . . They have been impressed by, and at times been perhaps a bit envious of, the accomplishments of their colleagues in the analysis of spatial organization. . . . [But as the] impulse [in human ecology] is cosmographical, holistic and synthetic, it tends to reject the analytical methods of normal science.

Cultural geography has very largely been a preoccupation within North American human geography, and very few British practitioners have called themselves cultural geographers. Within North America, the Berkeley 'school', founded and led for several decades by Carl Sauer, was the main centre of the work, with a focus on the morphology of landscape (Sauer, 1926) and particular reference to human intervention in the evolution of landscapes through

plant and animal domestication, the use of fire, the diffusion of ideas and artifacts, and the creation of settlements, for example (all themes reviewed in
Thomas, 1956). Sauer's approach was ecological and was clearly opposed to
the determinism of other workers; Duncan (1980) argues that in general
members of the school tended to reify culture, however, promoting a form
of 'cultural determinism' rather than seeing culture as a human creation that
enables and constrains human agency in the recreation, and modification, of
that resource.

Another criticism of this dominant view of cultural geography is that it very
largely ignores certain social relations, those elements of culture that are
directly related to the production of goods and services, so that cultural
geographers had little to offer the growing number of spatial scientists
interested in economic and urban geography, and also those promoting social
geography with its major interest in the concept of social class. Thus in their
introductory textbook on the subject, Spencer and Thomas (1973) provided
the following definitions:

> *Culture* is the sum total of human learned behavior and ways of doing things.
> Culture is invented, carried on, and slowly modified by people living and
> working in groups as each group occupies a particular region of the earth and
> develops its own special and distinctive system of culture. Related single *culture*
> *traits* that go together in practice form a *culture complex*; a large assemblage
> of culture complexes fit together into a *culture system*. A culture system followed
> by a population inhabiting a specific area of the earth forms a *culture region*.
> A group of related culture regions is termed a *culture world* (p. 6).

But the contents of their book concentrate on artifacts and certain aspects of
social organization (religion and language) only, and nothing is said about
many of the salient aspects of 'the sum total of human learned behavior'.
Zelinsky's (1973b) *The Cultural Geography of the United States* is similarly
partial, though it introduces more material on the political content of societal
organization. And this focus is sustained in a later compilation that is
presented as *An Atlas of United States and Canadian Society and Cultures*
(Rooney, Zelinsky and Louder, 1982).

This particular subdiscipline of geography has been criticized on a number
of grounds. Cosgrove (1983) claims that because it ignored the dialectic
between nature and culture

> it dissolved into either the idealist reification of culture as an agent of change
> or a semi-determinism dignified by the name 'possibilism' . . . This has left
> cultural geography theoretically impoverished, many of its studies existing in
> a theoretical vacuum (p. 3)

and he identified it as

> so diffuse that one is tempted to characterize cultural geography more by its
> refusal to adopt economic or social theory as its guiding principle than by any
> unity of aim or method (p. 3).

The economic and social theories that Cosgrove promotes are those discussed in Chapter 8 of this book, and not those of spatial science. But spatial scientists, too, found cultural geography atheoretical and empiricist in explicit orientation yet often, as Duncan (1980) indicates, implicitly determinist. The links between the two developed hardly at all.

Finally, the situation with regard to *regional geography* has been surveyed by Paterson (1974), whose essay comprises two main sections – 'On the problems of writing regional geography' and 'Is progress possible in regional geography?'. Within the first of the major sections he investigates six problems, which include the growing shortage of subordinate materials (micro-regional studies), and the increasing submergence of regional distinctiveness, though

> only a certain amount of innovation is possible if the regional geographer is to perform his appointed task, which is to convey to his reader the essentials of his region; to illuminate the landscape with analytical light. Landforms and climate are common to all terrestrial landscapes, and human activities to most of them: how shall repetition be avoided? (p. 8).
>
> So long as contrasts between region and region [remain], and no matter to what they are attributable, there is work for the geographer to do (p. 16).

He does not conclude, despite the constraints, that there is no possibility of progress: regional geography, he argues, can advance with regard to two criteria – content and insight. Reference to Zelinsky's (1973b) book illustrated the increased range of content currently being introduced; discussion of Meinig's work (e.g. Meinig, 1972) showed the ability of regional geographers to produce fresh spatial insights, although Paterson has to conclude that 'Adventurousness is not a quality that most of us associate with regional geography' (p. 9). Thus:

> The way is open for regional studies which are less bound by old formulae; less obliged to tell all about the region; more experimental and, in a proper sense of the word, more imaginative than in the past, and covering a broader range of perceptions, either popular or specialist (p. 23).
>
> Regional Geography['s] . . . goals are general rather than specific; it is not primarily problem-orientated but concerned to provide balanced coverage, and its aims are popular and educational rather than practical or narrowly professional. Such relevance as it possesses it gains by its appeal . . . to the two universal human responses of wonder and concern. . . . One may recall Medawar's assertion that in science we are being progressively relieved of the burden of singular instances, the tyranny of the particular, and in turn assert that there is a frame of mind on which the particular exercises no tyranny, but a strong fascination (p. 21).

Mead (1980, p. 297) has presented a strong defence of geographers who 'adopt other lands, . . . share other cultures, . . . [and] make a contribution to the store of knowledge about them' and Hart (1982, p. 29) argues that an important element in the 'highest form of the geographers' art' requires them to 'adopt a region, to immerse themselves in its culture, to acquire a specialist understanding of it'.

The implication to be drawn from the preceding paragraphs is that there was a difference between, on the one hand, many historical geographers and, on the other, most cultural and regional geographers with regard to the degree to which they have felt 'left behind' or 'relatively untouched' by the changes that occurred during the 1950s and 1960s in other branches of human geography. Certainly the former seem to have been impelled at least to consider the possibility of making methodological changes whereas the latter have continued to work within their established tradition (see also Mikesell, 1973). Not all historical geographers would agree with Baker's analogy from systems theory that simply 'Historical geography has a long relaxation time' (p. 11), however, and Chapter 6 indicates the degree to which they have mounted an attack against the positivist approach.

Conclusions

Reaction to the regional approach began to take shape in the United States during the mid-1950s. To a large extent, the aims of research in human geography were not debated, and relatively traditional definitions of the field were observed: the main issues concerned means and methods. The innovations of the period involved the strengthening of the systematic and topical geographies, and their release from a largely subservient relationship to regional geography, by attempts to develop laws and theories of spatial patterns, using models of various kinds for illumination, and by applying mathematical and, especially, statistical procedures to facilitate the search for generalizations. Whereas the regionalists saw geography as, at most, law-consuming, those of the new persuasion aimed at the production of their own laws, which could be used to explain particular regional outcomes.

These changed means to the geographic end were rapidly accepted in many branches of human geography, particularly in those topical specialisms dealing with economic aspects of contemporary life. They were soon accepted in the growing field which focuses on contemporary social geography, but were relatively ignored in historical geography and almost completely shunned in cultural and regional investigations, which, it was claimed, still focus on unique characteristics of unique places. They also spread into the corresponding fields of study across the Atlantic (and across the Pacific, too), and within little more than a decade British geographers produced a major review volume containing 816 pages of testimony to the enthusiasm of the innovators and the links which they had established with other sciences. But methods are insufficient to sustain an academic revolution unless they can be applied to a coherent substantive core. It is to the search for such a core that the next chapter turns.

4

The Search for a Focus

As shown in the previous chapter, the changes in human geography which emanated from several centres in the United States during the 1950s were very much concerned with methods of investigation. The ultimate aim of geographical study – as stated in Hartshorne's revised definition (p. 56) – remained the same: indeed, one could argue, from the definitions offered by Ackerman (1963) and the NAS/NRC committee (1965–see above, p. 80), that human geographers had become even more ambitious in their hopes of explaining 'the world-wide system comprising man and his natural environment'. But within this general ethos, the proximate aims of geographical investigation were not always clear. Systematic studies were in the ascendant, and the implicit intent was to develop valid laws and theories within the implicit positivist framework, but what the exact content of those laws and theories should be was not immediately apparent.

In furthering their analyses, human geographers increasingly sought a clear identity of their own within the social sciences. (Adoption of the positivist philosophy requires that disciplines be identified by their content not their methods, although use of particular procedures – e.g. maps – might be confined to certain disciplines.) They required their discipline to provide a particular viewpoint and contribution to the overall goal of the group of disciplines with which they made common cause. For them, geography required a new focus as well as a new methodology. This new focus was developed around the spatial variable and the study of spatial systems.

Spatial Variables and Spatial Systems

Geography is a discipline in distance, according to the inaugural lecture given by a Scottish professor (Watson, 1955), and its central theme is the relative location of people and places. The importance of relative location within society, and therefore to geography, is seen by Cox (1976) to result from alterations in societal structure consequent upon technical change. In primitive societies, the main interactions are between relatively isolated groups of individuals and their physical environments, so that a natural early focus for geographical work was the relationships between societies and 'a spatially differentiated nature' (p. 192). With technological advancement, however, the main links are among individuals. Interdependence within and between societies increases as a consequence of the more complex differentiation between places which reflects the division of labour, so that the most important facts in modern human existence relate to spatially differentiated societies, not to a spatially differentiated nature. It is this interdependence between groups living in different places which creates the patterns of human occupance on the surface of the earth, and provides the basic subject matter for human geographers.

The focus on spatial arrangements or spatial structures – the areal differentiation in human activities and the spatial interactions which this produces – and the role of distance as a variable influencing the nature of those arrangements can be identified in the textbooks of the 1960s and 1970s which summarized the contemporary activities of human geographers for the next generation of students. A pioneer among such texts was Haggett's (1965c), whose depiction of pattern and order in spatial structures was phrased within a decomposition of nodal regions into five geometrical elements; a sixth element was added in the second edition of the book (Haggett, Cliff and Frey, 1977).

The geometrical elements in Haggett's schema (Figure 4.1) assume a spatially differentiated society within which there is a desire for interaction; people in place X want to trade with those in place Y, for example, whereas those in place Z want goods and services which they themselves cannot provide. This results in patterns of *movement* – of goods, of people, of money, of ideas, and so on – between places, and so the first element in the analysis of nodal regions involves the representation of the patterns of movement. Some movement is unimpeded – aircraft can move in all directions – but most is channelled along particular route corridors. Thus the second element in the analysis involves characterization of the movement *channels* or networks. Networks comprise edges and vertices; in a transport system, many of the latter are the *nodes*, the organizational nexus. Their spatial arrangement forms the third element in the decomposition of the nodal region, whereas the fourth investigates their organization into *hierarchies*, which define the importance of places within the framework of settlements. Finally, in the original scheme, there are the *surfaces*, the areas of land within the skeleton of nodes (settlements) and networks (routes) which are occupied by land uses of various types and intensities.

Patterns in the human occupation of the earth's surface change frequently in many societies, and the spatial order to such changes forms the sixth element in Haggett's revised schema. Change does not take place uniformly over space in most circumstances: usually it originates at one or a few localities from whence it spreads to others, along the movement channels, through the

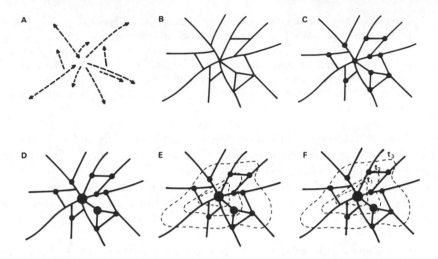

Fig 4.1   The elements in Haggett's schema for studying spatial systems:
A movement; B channels; C nodes; D hierarchies; E surfaces; and F diffusion
Source: Haggett, Cliff and Frey (1977, p. 7)

nodes, across the surfaces, and down the hierarchies. The processes of change
over space and time thus involve spatial *diffusion*.

Haggett and his associates stress that geography is a science of distributions,
and their emphasis is on the regularities in various elements of these distributions. (The first volume of the text was very reliant on work in other disciplines. The second illustrates the volume of work done by geographers in a short
time: this work has strongly influenced recent developments in aspects of
archaeology; Renfrew, 1981.) Other texts have taken a similar general view
of the study of what have been termed spatial systems, although perhaps
emphasizing different aspects of those systems. Morrill (1970a), for example,
chose a title – *The Spatial Organization of Society* – which clearly emphasizes his view of the role of geographical analysis in the larger task of the social
sciences, 'understanding society'. According to him, the core elements of
human geography are:

> Space, space relations, and change in space – how physical space is structured,
> how men relate through space, how man has organized his society in space, and
> how our conception and use of space change (p. 3).

In this context, space has five qualities relevant to the understanding of human
behaviour: (1) distance, the spatial dimension of separation; (2) accessibility;
(3) agglomeration; (4) size; and (5) relative location. Put together, these can
be used to build theories, such as those on which Garrison based his work.

> Virtually all theory of spatial organization assumes that the structure of space
> is based on the principles of minimizing distance and maximizing the utility of
> points and areas within the structure, without taking the environment, or

variable content of space, into account. Although the differential quality of area is interesting and its effect on location and interaction is great, most of the observable regularity of structure in space results from the principles of efficiently using territory of uniform character. The theoretical structures for agricultural location, location of urban centres, and the internal patterns of the city are all derived from the principle of minimizing distance on a uniform plane (p. 15).

According to this view, all location decisions and decisions about the use of land are taken in order to minimize the costs of movement. The spatial approach to understanding society assumes a world in which one variable is predominant as an influence on human behaviour – distance – and it seeks to account for observed spatial patterns within this framework. And so in Morrill's book:

> the explanation of spatial structure proceeds from the deductive – what would occur under the simplest conditions – to the inductive – how local factors distort this 'pure' structure. To begin with, all the local variation may introduce is a risk of missing the underlying structure. Most theory of location therefore stresses the spatial factors – above all, distance – which interact to bring about the regular and repetitive patterns (p. 20).

Morrill's book suggests an organizing framework for geographical scholarship centred on the single variable of distance. His summarizing 'theory' of spatial structures proceeds as follows:

1 Societies operate to achieve two spatial efficiency goals:
   (i)   to use every piece of land to the greatest profit and utility; and
   (ii) to achieve the highest possible interaction at the least possible cost.
2 Pursuit of these goals involves four types of location decisions:
   (i)   the substitution of land for transport costs when seeking accessibility;
   (ii) substituting production costs at sites for transport costs when seeking markets;
   (iii) substituting agglomeration benefits for transport costs; and
   (iv) substituting self-sufficiency (higher production costs) and trade (higher transport costs).
3 The spatial structures resulting from these decisions include:
   (i)   spatial land-use gradients; and
   (ii) a spatial hierarchy of regions.
   These are somewhat distorted by environmental variations to produce:
   (iii) more irregular but predictable patterns of location.
   Whereas over time distortion may result from:
   (iv) non-optimal location decisions; and
   (v)   change through processes of spatial diffusion.

Like Haggett, therefore, Morrill stresses the geometry of human organization of activities on the earth's surface, but whereas Haggett emphasizes pattern and geometry Morrill pays more attention to the decision-making processes which would produce the most 'efficient' pattern, as an underlying basis for the imperfect examples of that pattern which are observed in the 'real world'. Other texts (such as Abler, Adams and Gould, 1971, which has a stronger focus on positivist methodology: see also Gould, 1977, 1978) have followed Morrill's lead. (In the third edition of the book – Morrill and Dormitzer, 1979 – the importance of the spatial variable is less dominant; location theory is presented as providing 'fairly simple models that permit us to highlight some essential principles and factors of human location. The real world, of course, does not correspond very closely to the patterns projected by location theory because the human landscape is the complex product of many different forces – historical, physical, cultural, political, and behavioral, as well as economic (spatial)'. Later, however, in identifying 'Some important geographical questions' Morrill, 1985, returned to a strong focus on spatial variables.)

These textbooks illustrate the centrality of space or distance as the major focus of geographical interest in the 1960s. The emphasis on pattern, evident especially in Haggett's book, was noted by King (1969) in a major review of 'The geographer's approach to the analysis of spatial form . . . the mathematics which are used and the geometrical frameworks which are favored' (p. 574). His focus was descriptive mathematics which represent 'what is' rather than 'what should be'. He realized that 'when they are pursued to their extremes in very formal terms these studies run the risk of appearing as seemingly sterile exercises in pure geometry' (p. 593; see also King, 1976, 1979b) but felt that geographers had not proceeded very far in providing process theories which would account for observed spatial patterns. The school of thought which he was reviewing involved working backwards, finding what order there was to explain rather than deducing what the world should be like from knowledge of human behaviour.

Spatial Theory

Just as the methodological developments reviewed in the previous chapter proceeded without any clear guidelines in terms of a programmatic statement, so the growth of the spatial viewpoint similarly lacked any manifesto. (Watson's paper of 1955, mentioned above, was not widely referenced.) The only attempt to provide such a lead – apart from general statements about geography and geometry, such as Bunge's (1962) – was provided by Nystuen (1963), in a paper which was not widely read until its reprinting in 1968.

Nystuen's objective was 'to consider how many independent concepts constitute a basis for the spatial point of view, that is, the geographical point of view' (p. 35 – all page references are to the 1968 reprint) so that rather than look at the 'real world', with its many distorting tendencies, he sought clarity in considering abstract geographies. To illustrate his deduced basic concepts he used the analogy of a mosque completely lacking furniture (i.e. an isotropic plain) in which a teacher chooses a location at random. His students then distribute themselves so that they can see and hear him; their likely arrangement is in semi-circular, staggered rows facing him, with a greater density close to him. This arrangement has three characteristic features:

1   Directional orientation – they all face the teacher, the better to hear his words and to perceive his expressions;
2   Distance – they cluster around him, because the effectiveness of his voice diminishes with distance; and
3   Connectiveness – they arrange themselves in rows, so organized that each person has a direct line of sight to the teacher.

The third of these, connectiveness, is in part a function of distance and direction, but not entirely so. As Nystuen expresses it:

A map of the United States may be stretched and twisted, but so long as each state remains connected with its neighbors, relative position does not change. Connectiveness is independent of distance and direction – all these properties are needed to establish a complete geographical point of view (p. 39).

In addition

Connections need not be adjacent boundaries or physical links. They may be defined as functional associations. Functional associations of spatially separate elements are best revealed by the exchanges which take place between the elements. The exchanges may often be measured by the flows of people, goods, or communications (p. 39).

In the mosque, therefore, the connectivity between teacher and student involves not only a direct line of sight between them but also a flow from one to the other, in this case of ideas.

These three concepts – direction, distance and connectiveness – are the necessary and sufficient ones for the construction of Nystuen's abstract geography, which is grounded in the study of sites (abstract places) rather than of locations (real places).

The terms which seem to me to contain the concepts of a geographical point of view are *direction or orientation*, *distance*, and *connection or relative position*. Operational definitions of these words are the axioms of the spatial point of view. Other words, such as pattern, accessibility, neighbourhood, circulation, etc., are compounds of the basic terms. For abstract models, the existence of these elements and their properties must be specified (p. 41).

Nystuen was unsure whether these three comprised the full set of necessary and sufficient concepts for a geographical argument; boundary, he felt, might be a primitive concept and not a derivative of the basic three (see also

Papageorgiou, 1969). But his general case was that arguments in human geography could be based on a small number of such concepts, a case that was implicitly accepted by much of the work in 'the spatial tradition', but which was rarely explicitly referred to.

An alternative approach to the writing of theory in human geography was adopted by Haynes (1975), based on the mathematical procedures of dimensional analysis. Five basic dimensions are defined – mass, length, time, population size, and value – and these are manipulated to indicate the validity of functional relationships, such as distance-decay equations (see p. 103), by checking their internal consistency. This approach is defended by the statement that:

> Although most quantitative geographers would probably claim to be engaged in the discovery of relationships, it appears that geography has not passed the first stage [in the development of a science] with any degree of rigor. . . . With no clear idea of which variables are relevant and which particular characteristics in a system should be isolated, it is pragmatic to define our measurement scales with regard to a particular set of observations rather than the other way round. The method of physical science . . . is a superior system, as measurements can be interpreted exactly, different results compared, and experiments replicated (p. 66).

This is clearly a deductive approach to research. It is not as closely tied to a 'spatial view' as Nystuen's but has the same end in view – the derivation of a set of fundamental concepts which can form the basis for the writing of geographical theory, to be tested in the 'real world' (see also Haynes, 1977, 1982).

These attempts at isolating human geography's primary concepts differ from most contemporary efforts at producing geographic theory which, according to Harvey (1967b, p. 212), were 'either very poorly formulated or else derivative'. Central place theory, for example, was based entirely on postulates from economics about how people behave as 'rational economic actors', to which the basic geographic concept of distance was added, producing a theory about the size and spacing of settlements. The attraction of central place theory to many was indeed that geographers could apparently contribute their own basic concept to the development of theory, and need not be totally dependent on other disciplines for concepts, as the regional approach had perhaps suggested that they should be. For Harvey (1970) geography has a group of such concepts – location, nearness, distance, pattern, morphology; most of them are compounds of Nystuen's basic terms – which could form indigenous elements in theory-building, allowing development of integrated social science theories drawing concepts of equal status from all component disciplines.

An example of the development of theory involving both derivative and indigenous concepts is the field of diffusion research, which received considerable attention in the late 1960s (Brown, 1968). The basic behavioural postulate, taken from sociological research findings, was that the most effective form of communication about innovations is by word of mouth. Geographers expanded on this by introducing the effect of distance: most inter-personal communication is between neighbours, so that information about innovations should spread outwards in an orderly fashion from the locations of the initial adopters. Pioneer work on this hypothesis had been carried out in Sweden by Hägerstrand, who introduced it to the Washington school in the 1950s, where it was taken up by Morrill (1968): Hägerstrand's own major work was made available in English translation in 1968. Much work has since been done, both on the process of diffusion and, even more, on patterns of spatial spread which, it is assumed, result from diffusion processes (see Abler, Adams and Gould, 1971, Chapter 11). An extended review of this literature is provided by Brown (1981), who has introduced a more behavioural perspective into the processes involved (see p. 153).

Social physics and spatial science

Of the three basic concepts identified by Nystuen, two – distance and connectivity – received most attention from those advocating geography as a spatial science. Direction was relatively ignored, except for some work on migration patterns (Wolpert, 1967) which included a seminal statement by Adams (1969). (Direction is used here in cardinal terms. To some extent, any discussion of movement patterns which identified destinations more precisely than in terms of distance from origins involved directional analysis.)

By far the greatest volume of work on spatial science followed the lines of research established by the social physics school (p. 66). The relationship between distance and a variety of types of interaction – migrations, information flows, movements of goods, etc. – had been identified by several workers in the nineteenth century, such as Carey (1858), Ravenstein (1885; Grigg, 1977), and Spencer (1892). The impact of these early writings is not clear. McKinney (1968), for example, has suggested that Stewart and others were unaware of the seeds of the 'gravity model' and 'population potential' ideas in the works of Carey and Spencer, and claimed that 'current geographers could learn much' (p. 105) from their publications. Warntz (1968) retorted that Stewart was well aware of such writings, although McKinney in a rebuttal pointed out that Stewart referred to them in his 1950s papers, but not in those of the 1940s. Ravenstein's papers, on the other hand, were clearly influential on later generations of researchers into migration patterns. (It is of interest that the pioneering work on distance-decay and the gravity model, as with much of the rest of spatial science, was done outside geography: as Tocalis, 1978, p. 124 expresses it, 'geographers' contributions to the theoretical evolution of the gravity concept were minor', although one major contributor – Alan Wilson – 'became a geographer'.)

Apart from Stewart, whose pioneering efforts were referred to in the previous chapter, the most influential figure on social physics after World

War II was probably Zipf, who devised a 'principle of least effort'. According to this, individuals organize their lives so as to minimize the amount of work which they must undertake (Zipf, 1949). Movement involves work, and so the minimization of movement is part of the general principle of least effort. To explain this, Zipf expanded on Stewart's finding that with increasing distance from Princeton, fewer students from each state attended that university. Two aspects of work are involved in going to university: (1) the work involved in acquiring information about the university; and (2) the work involved in actually travelling there. Thus the greater the distance between any potential student's home and Princeton, the less that is likely to be known about the university and the less prepared they will be to travel there. The validity of this distance-decay argument was tested against many other data sets: material on the contents of newspapers and on their circulation, for example, illustrated the expected distance bias in flows of information, and data on movements between places showed that the greater the distance separating them, the smaller the volume of inter-place contact.

Zipf called the regularity which he had identified the P_1P_2/D relationship, and Stewart noted the analogy between this and the Newtonian gravity formula

$$F_{ij} = k \frac{M_i M_j}{d_{ij}^2}$$

where M_i and M_j represent the mass at places i and j respectively; d_{ij} is the distance separating i and j; k is a coefficient of proportionality (a scaling coefficient); and F_{ij} is the gravitational force between places i and j. For interaction patterns, this was rewritten as

$$I_{ij} = k \frac{P_i P_j}{d_{ij}^2}$$

where P_i and P_j are the populations of places i and j respectively, k and d are as in the previous equation, and I_{ij} is the amount of interaction between places i and j. Much work was done which involved fitting this equation to flow data, as shown in the reviews by Carrothers (1956) and Olsson (1965). In order to achieve reasonable statistical fits, the various elements of the equation had to be weighted, in the form

$$I_{ij} = f (P_i^a P_j^b d_{ij}^c)$$

where a, b, and c are weights estimated from the data set being analysed. Because different values of a, b and c were produced in almost all studies, it was claimed that the so-called gravity model of interaction was 'an empirical regularity to which it has not yet been possible to furnish any theoretical explanation' (Olsson, 1965, p. 48: such an explanation, in statistical terms, was offered by Wilson, 1967). In effect, the influence of distance apparently varies from place to place, from population to population, and from context to context, in the use of the model to represent migration flows. The influence, as shown by the established connectivities, would seem to be virtually universal; what no theory has been able to account for is the variability in the strength of its impact.

It was not only in social physics, and the work of Stewart, Zipf and others, that distance was receiving attention as an important variable in the years after the Second World War. As Pooler (1977) has indicated, both economists and sociologists were becoming increasingly aware of its influence on behaviour, the former in the location theories of Weber, Hoover, Lösch and others, which stimulated the work of Garrison and his associates (p. 62), and also of Isard, and the latter in the studies of the Chicago school, out of which developed a large literature on urban residential patterns (Johnston, 1971, 1980b). And so, according to Pooler:

> a number of geographers became aware of the spatial enquiries that were being undertaken in a social science context outside their own discipline and, upon realizing their relevance to geography, proceeded to emulate them. The appearance of the spatial tradition was prompted, not by discoveries from within geography, but by an awareness and acceptance of investigations external to the discipline. The space-centred scientific enquiries of other social sciences became paradigms for geographers, simply because those enquiries, being spatial, were seen to be of relevance by some practitioners (p. 69)

thereby fitting in with both the philosophical framework outlined by Schaefer and the 'quantitative revolution'. In their adoption of spatial viewpoints pioneered in other disciplines, human geographers were frequently selective in what they imported from the various sources. Thus the work on urban residential patterns concentrated on certain aspects of the urban sociology of the Chicago school, for example. Robert Park's dictum relating social distance to spatial distance stimulated much work on the measurement of residential separation (Peach and Smith, 1981), but the social Darwinism and ecological theory underlying this dictum was largely ignored (though see Robson, 1969; Entrikin, 1980) and the humanistic concerns in Park's work have only recently been identified (Jackson and Smith, 1981; 1984).

In their distance-based analyses, various social scientists looked not only at the influence of distance itself but also at the meaning and measurement of that concept. Stouffer (1940), for example, established a relationship in which migration between X and Y was accounted for not so much by the distance between them but rather by the number of intervening opportunities. In effect, he was measuring distance in terms of opportunities; the greater the number of opportunities available locally, the less work that has to be expended in moving to one. Others took up this flexible approach to measurement of the basic variable. Ullman (1956), for example, developed a schema for analysing commodity flows in which the amount of movement between two places was related to three factors:

1   complementarity – the degree to which there is a supply of a com-
    modity at one place and a demand for it at the other;
2   intervening opportunity – the degree to which either the potential desti-
    nation can obtain similar commodities from a nearer, and presumably
    cheaper, source or the potential source can sell its commodities to a
    nearer market; and
3   transferability – for complementarity to be capitalized it is neces-
    sary for the movement to be feasible, given channel, time and cost
    constraints.

This schema was not as easily fitted statistically as the 'gravity model', but
its relationship to that is clear (Hay, 1979b). Fitting such models also requires
accepting that the influence of distance, as time and cost, varies from place
to place and from time to time, as shown by Abler (1971), Forer (1974), and
Janelle (1968, 1969).

All of this work on the analysis of various movement patterns was stimulated not only by its obvious relevance to the spatial science focus within geography, and its use in the development of location theories, but also by its
clear applicability in forecasting contexts. The planning of land-use patterns
and transport systems (especially road systems) became increasingly sophisticated, in a technical sense, during the 1950s and 1960s, first in the United
States and then in Britain. Initially, data were collected to show both the
traffic-generating power of various land uses and the patterns of interaction
between different parts of an urban area, with the gravity model being used
to describe the latter. Future land-use configurations were then designed,
their traffic-generating potential derived, and the gravity model used to
predict the patterns of flows and the needed road systems. Later models, most
of them based on one initiated by Ira Lowry, were able to assess different configurations in terms of traffic flows, thereby suggesting the 'best' directions
for future urban growth (see Batty, 1978).

The demands for sophisticated planning devices stimulated much research
based on the gravity and Lowry models. American economists initiated this,
but it was later taken up by British workers, led by, *inter alia*, Alan Wilson,
who in 1970 was appointed to a professorship of geography at the University
of Leeds, thereby becoming a professional geographer, although he had no
training in the discipline. He derived the gravity model mathematically,
thereby giving it a stronger theoretical base (Wilson, 1967), and developed
the Lowry model into a more general set of models concerned with location,
allocation and movement in space (see below, p. 125).

Much of this work involved collaboration between academic geographers
and practising planners, and led to developments which paralleled those in
regional science in the United States. Two new British journals catered for
these and related research areas – *Regional Studies* and *Environment and
Planning* – both of which attract contributions and readers from other social
sciences. Thus the new geographical methodology was proving of considerable

applied value. Careers as planners became extremely popular among geography graduates for a few years, notably in the late 1960s and early 1970s, and the growing desire of academic geographers for their discipline to equal that of other social sciences in its policy-making relevance seemed well on the way to fulfilment.

Spatial science and spatial statistics

The developments just outlined were characterized by a large volume of technical research within human geography, concerned not only with fitting the gravity model but also with a range of problems associated with the description of spatial patterns and connectivities (for example, Haggett and Chorley, 1969). Although Bunge (1962), Harvey (1969a) and others argued that the language for the analysis of spatial form is geometry, much of this work in fact concentrated on the application of descriptive and inferential statistics to spatial problems, in line with the strong empirical tradition in geographical work.

Most researchers, including Garrison (1956a), accepted that statistical procedures developed for other fields of enquiry could be adopted for geographical investigations without difficulty. For some, it was necessary to introduce modifications – as in spatial sampling (Berry and Baker, 1968) – but, despite the early work of Robinson (1956; see p. 62), it was generally assumed that there were no technical problems involved in the application of standard procedures to spatial data sets. A number of student texts appeared, especially in the late 1960s, and these made little or no reference to any peculiarities of geographical data; they differed from the texts produced by other social scientists only in the nature of their examples. (Even in the 1980s, few contributors to a book on *Recent Developments in Spatial Data Analysis* – Bahrenberg *et al.*, 1984 – discussed spatial data per se; most of their work referred to the use of standard statistical procedures in geographical applications.)

During the late 1960s, however, a group of researchers at the University of Bristol began to question the widespread assumption about the relevance of most statistical procedures in geographical investigations. For some time, statisticians had been aware of difficulties in applying the general linear model – notably in its regression and correlation form – to the time-series data used in economic analysis and forecasting. The major issue for geographers was that of autocorrelation. One of the assumptions of the model is that all observations are independent of each other; the magnitude of one reading on a variable should in no way influence that of any other. Such autocorrelation clearly exists in most time series: the value of the retail price index at one date, for example, has a very strong influence on what the value will be at nearby later dates, and is itself influenced by the value at earlier times. (This issue was first made clear to geographers in the discussion in Chisholm, Frey and Haggett, 1971, p. 465.) Because of such interdependence between adjacent observations, conventional regression methods could not be used: autocorrelation led to biased regression coefficients and therefore cast doubt on the validity of any forecasts.

The Bristol group argued that this autocorrelation problem also existed with spatial data sets, and further that it was much less tractable than was so with temporal series. Time progresses in one direction only, but space is two-dimensional, and the independence requirement can be violated in all directions around a single point. Spatial autocorrelation can therefore involve all neighbours influencing all others with regard to the values of a particular variable, as recognized by some statisticians (e.g. Geary, 1954) and hinted at by geographers such as Dacey (1968) whose work stimulated the Bristol investigations. The group expended considerable effort over a number of years on this problem (Cliff and Ord, 1973, 1981), and the research was extended over a wide range of spatial applications, including the well-known gravity model (Curry, 1972; Johnston, 1976a; Sheppard, 1980; Fotheringham, 1981).

Recognition of the spatial autocorrelation problem indicated severe constraints on the application of conventional statistical procedures to geographical analyses, since the argument was that application of regression methods, and others based on the general linear model such as principal components and factor analyses, was invalid with spatial data sets (Haining, 1980). As Harvey (1969a) put it:

> The choice of the product-moment correlation coefficient for regionalization problems appears singularly inappropriate, since one of the technical requirements of this statistic is independence in the observations. Since the aim of such regionalization is to produce contiguous regions which are internally relatively homogeneous, it seems almost certain that this condition of independence in the observations will be violated (p. 347).

The general tenor of the argument was obvious for, as Gould (1970a) noted, spatial autocorrelation was the order that geographers were seeking to establish with their laws and theories. On realizing the force of the case, some accepted that conventional statistical procedures could not be applied in their work (e.g. Berry, 1973b) and the Bristol group omitted them from their rewrite of Haggett's major text (Haggett, Cliff and Frey, 1977). Most continued to apply the methods, however, either in ignorance of the autocorrelation case or on the grounds that the biased-coefficients problem refers only to the use of the general linear model in forecasting and prediction, and does not affect use of the procedures for description (see Johnston, 1978a) and for certain types of ecological analysis (Johnston, 1982d, 1984f).

The forecasting and prediction issue was basic to the work of the Bristol group, however, since their activities were focused on what they termed spatial forecasting, which involved development of procedures for estimating how trends — in the spread of a disease, for example, and in prices and unemployment — would proceed through time and over space (Haggett, 1973; Cliff *et al.*, 1975). They organized a major symposium on this (Chisholm, Frey and

Haggett, 1971) and stimulated a considerable volume of work, much of it technical, on the problems of identifying and forecasting spatio-temporal trends (e.g. Bennett, 1978b). Hägerstrand's work on diffusion patterns is the natural base for much of this research, which focuses on the patterns of spread rather than on their generating processes. There is now a large literature on the technial aspects of forecasting (e.g. Bennett, 1979), and on deducing 'spatial processes' from mapped patterns (Haining, 1981, 1990).

The nature of such spatial forecasting has been reviewed by Hay (1978), who challenges what he sees as its fundamental assumption, that phenomena behave coherently in both time and space. He questions the assumed stability of inter-place interrelationships over time present in analyses such as that of Martin and Oeppen (1975) on market-price variations, and argues instead for consideration of the value of catastrophe theory. In this, small changes in the control variable(s) can lead to major changes in the dependent variable being studied (such major changes are the catastrophes). If catastrophes occur, then the linear extrapolations typical of the work of the Bristol group have clear limitations as forecasting procedures; as yet, relatively little work has been done by geographers on the application of this relatively new area of mathematics to their problems (Wilson, 1976a, 1981a: it has received more attention among physical geographers – Thornes, 1989a, 1989b).

Technical advances in the modelling and analysis of geographical data continue to be made, in a variety of ways. The spatial peculiarities of geographical data have been stressed by some, in arguments – developed from the work on spatial autocorrelation – that particular geographical procedures are needed as a consequence (see Gaile and Willmott, 1984). One of those peculiarities refers to the linked issues of aggregation and scale. Openshaw (1984a, 1984b) has shown in a number of important papers how different spatial aggregations of the same data set (counties into regions, perhaps, or census enumeration districts into social areas) can produce very different results in terms of the correlation between two variables; indeed, his simulations suggest that with many data sets any correlation between $+1.0$ and -1.0 might be obtained, so that the particular aggregation employed needs careful justification. Others have sought to ensure proper use of the standard statistical procedures (e.g. Jones, 1985; Wrigley, 1984), with the use of statistical significance tests forming the basis of further debate (Summerfield, 1983; Hay, 1985b) and the merits of exploratory data analysis being extolled (Cox and Jones, 1981). Better ways of testing hypotheses have also been expounded, notably with regard to the use of categorical (or nominal) data (e.g. Fingleton, 1984; Wrigley, 1985) but also in terms of pattern analysis (Upton and Fingleton, 1984) and representing relationships through structural models (e.g. Cadwallader, 1985). Much of this work has been criticized for its reliance on methods that impose structures on data rather than 'letting the data speak for themselves' (Gould, 1981); the mathematics of q-analysis has been proposed to meet the latter criterion (Gould, 1980; Beaumont and Gatrell, 1982; Gatrell, 1983: see also the essays edited by Macgill, 1984.)

In terms of more formal modelling, various aspects of spatial interaction continue to be a focus of attention, with continued application, for example, to the study of spatial diffusion of diseases (Cliff *et al.*, 1987). Recent presentations (Bennett and Haining, 1985; Bennett, Haining and Wilson, 1985) have placed such work at the forefront of developments. Much of it has been summarized by Wilson and Bennett (1985) in a volume that is part of a *Handbook of Applicable Mathematics* series; the inclusion there of a book on *Mathematical Methods in Human Geography and Planning* is testimony to the substantial achievements in the field of spatial analysis.

These technical developments have been aided, and indeed stimulated, by developments in data-handling capacity with high-speed computers (Rhind, 1989). Traditional data sources, such as censuses and surveys, have been added to by a wide range of others collected by traditional means (such as market research) and those made available by new collection methods such as remote sensing from satellites and other airborne devices. More recently, the analysis of these data has been advanced by the development of Geographical Information Systems (GIS: Curran, 1984; Green *et al.*, 1985; Chrisman et al, 1989), which bring together rapid advances in computer cartography and data collection in dedicated machines (comprising both hardware and customized software) for the analysis of the three main types of spatial data: those referring to points (such as mapped locations), to areas (such as towns and fields), and to lines (transport routes, for example). Increasingly data are geocoded (i.e. given unique spatial references which facilitate spatial analysis), and technological advances are leading to the introduction of computers with which it is possible to gather, store, display and analyse spatial data.

Rapid development of this technology in the United Kingdom was promoted by a major project initiated to mark the nine hundredth anniversary of the Domesday Book census in 1086. A GIS to provide a modern equivalent was produced, and marketed as a teaching aid for schools and other education institutions (Goddard and Armstrong, 1986); it provides a massive data base which can be used not only to display a wide range of maps (including the Ordnance Survey 1:50 000 series for the whole of Great Britain) and pictures, but which can also be analysed interactively (Openshaw *et al.*, 1986).

GIS provide a major research tool which allow many problems to be addressed that previously could not be afforded in terms of the time and resources necessary for data collection, analysis and display: they are the basis for much applied research work (see p. 214). Within less than a decade, the British Economic and Social Research Council had established a network of Regional Research Laboratories to conduct research into both their potential and their advancement as research tools (see the October 1988 issue of the *ESRC Newsletter*, which is devoted to the topic 'Working with geographical information systems') and the United States National Science Foundation had invested 5.5 million dollars into a National Center for Geographic Information and Analysis, based at three sites (see the announcements in the

Association of American Geographers' *Newsletter* for August 1987 and October 1988 and Fotheringham and MacKinnon, 1989). Their use was already being promoted in teaching (Maguire, 1989; Fisher, 1989a), an Association for Geographic Information had been established in the United Kingdom, following a major report by a House of Lords Select Committee for which a geographer (Rhind) acted as scientific advisor (Rhind, 1986; Rhind and Mounsey, 1989), a specialist journal had been launched (*International Journal of Geographical Information Systems*), and a bibliography of over 1000 items was published in early 1990 (Bracken *et al.*, 1990).

In his 1989 Presidential address to the Canadian Association of Geographers, Roger Tomlinson (1989), a pioneer in the development of GIS from the 1960s on, referred to their growing use in the following terms (p. 298):

> Geographers have a crucial role to play in integrating a wide variety of technologies into new forms of 'earth description' which will act as a foundation for geographical methodology and open the way to richer forms of spatial analysis and geographical understanding.

To him, spatial problems will multiply and become more complex in the future, and geographers' ability to handle and analyse large bodies of data in the search for solutions, using GIS, should demonstrate the strength of their 'integrating science', as part of a 'data are good ethic' (p. 292: see also p. 214 below).

For Dobson (1983a), dealing with these massive data sets will require the development of what he terms *automated geography*, an

> integrated systems approach to geographic problem solving in which the problem is defined, the appropriate methods are chosen, and the tools are selected from a broad repertoire of automated and manual techniques (p. 136).

Such an approach would be highly dependent on computer hardware and software developments – sufficient of which are already available (though see Cowen, 1983) – and would facilitate participation in public policy research at a large scale. Most commentators on Dobson's paper (in the August 1983 issue of *The Professional Geographer*) argued that automated geography was a misnomer, since the main benefits of the hardware and software that he described related to the scale and speed of data manipulation only. They preferred less emotive terms such as 'computer-assisted geography' or 'computer-assisted geographic systems', and some, like Poiker (1983), argued that the case was no more than one for another set of tools, just as the case for quantification turned out to be decades earlier: '. . . our tool seems to attract an inappropriate number of prophets' (p. 349). Dobson (1983b) disagreed, however, arguing that

> what I am talking about is not a system or collection of systems. It is a *discipline* which uses human and electronic cybernetic systems to further understanding of physical and social systems (p. 351)

with some decisions (e.g. with regard to how data are displayed) taken by the computers, not by people. Thus computers should be programmed so that they incorporate 'the character of *our* discipline', presenting the results of geographical analysis without the detailed intervention of geographers (see Couclelis, 1986b; Fisher, 1989b; Haines-Young, 1989).

These technological developments have not, according to some, been associated with parallel developments in substantive geographic theories, although there have been advances in the use of existing theories, many of which predate the 'quantitative and theoretical revolutions'. The 'traditional' models associated with the developments of the 1950s/1960s (see p. 64) have provided the basic underpinning, focusing on optimum distributions of points and lines and on flows between those points along the lines. Wilson (1984) has argued that mathematical development enables us to build some new models by combining old problems (for example von Thunen's and Weber's) with new methods, claiming that comprehensive models can now be built combining macropopulation backcloth, macroeconomic backcloth, spatial interaction, the location of population activities, the location of economic activities, and the development of economic infrastructure into representations of spatial pattern or settlement structure. This claim has been exemplified in two papers (Birkin and Wilson, 1986) which 'demonstrate the ability of models of spatial interaction and structure to reproduce the results of classical industrial location theory' (p. 305). Few other workers show much interest in such modelling, however, preferring the behavioural approaches detailed in the next chapter.

Countering the Spatial Separatist Theme

Opposition to the presentation of human geography as a spatial science developed largely as a counter to the claims for separate status for such a discipline. Some, such as Crowe (1970), saw the use of the spatial variable in nomothetic studies as a naive spatial determinism which paralleled the earlier environmental determinism. Others based their criticisms on the implicit divisibility of the social sciences in the spatial claims, and it is these criticisms which form the subject of the present section.

The most sustained argument against geography as a spatial science — what he calls the 'spatial separatist' theme — has been presented in a series of papers by Sack, a former associate of Lukermann at the University of Minnesota (see p. 77). There are three dimensions of reality — space, time and matter — and geography, according to the spatial separatist view, is the science of the first of these. But according to Sack, space, time and matter cannot be separated analytically in an empirical science which is concerned to provide explanations. Thus in his first paper he argued that geometry is not an acceptable language for such a science (Sack, 1972). Geometry is a branch of pure mathematics which is not concerned with empirical facts; its laws are static laws, with no reference to time, and they are not derivable from any dynamic or process laws. Geographic facts have geometric properties (locations) but if, as Schaefer proposed, geographical laws are concerned only with the geometries of facts, then they will provide only incomplete explanations of these facts. (To illustrate this contention, Sack used an analogy of chopping wood. If the answer to the question 'why are you chopping wood?' is 'because the force of the axe on impact splits the wood' then it is a static, geometric law, but if the answer is 'to provide fuel to produce heat' then it is an instance of a process law, which incorporates the geometric law. In this analogy, a process law is equated with the intention behind an action.) The laws of geometry, according to Sack, are sufficient to explain and to predict geometries, so that if geography aimed only to analyse points and lines on maps it could be an independent science using geometry as its language. But 'We do not accept the description of the changes of its shape as an explanation of the growth of a city' (p. 72) so that 'Geometry alone, then, cannot answer geographic questions' (p. 72) leading to the conclusion that:

> To explain requires laws and laws (if they are valid) explain events. Since the definition of an event implies the delimitation of some geometric properties (all events occur in space), the explanation of any event is in principle an explanation of some geometric properties of events (p. 77).

Thus geography is closely allied with geometry in its emphasis on the spatial aspects of events (the instances of laws), but geometry alone is insufficient as a basis for explanation and prediction since no processes are involved in the derivation of geometries.

Bunge (1973a) responded to this statement, claiming that spatial prediction was quite possible with reference to the geometry alone, as instanced by central place theory and Thunian analysis. Such geometries provide 'classic beauty', and 'purging geometry from geography reduces our trade to no apparent gain' (p. 568). Sack's (1973a) reply was that the static laws espoused by Bunge are only special cases of dynamic laws having antecedent and consequent conditions, and that:

> Although the laws of geometry are unequivocally static, purely spatial, nondeducible from dynamic laws, and explain and predict physical geometric properties of events, they do not answer the questions about the geometric properties of events that geographers raise and they do not make statements about process (p. 569).

Sack did not argue, as Bunge supposed, that geometry should be purged from geography, but only that space should not be considered independently from time and matter. He developed this theme (Sack, 1973b) with the contention that:

> for a concept of physical space to conform to the rules of concept formation and be useful in a science of geography every instance of the geometric or spatial

terms must be connected or related to one or more instances of non-geometric terms (to be called substance terms) (p. 17).

Thus physical distance is not a concept in itself: it is necessary to know the terrain which a road crosses, for example, in order to assess the significance of its length in a gravity model – geometry alone is not enough (hence the considerations of the meaning of distance referred to above – p. 104 – and the work of Mackay (1958) on the influence of boundaries on movement patterns). Since there is no such thing as empty physical space so there are no frictions of distance per se. There are frictions which demand work in crossing a substance, but it is the substance itself and the context in which it is being crossed which create the frictions, not simply the distance: 'There are frictions and there are distances, but there is no friction of distance' (p. 22). Geography, according to Sack, is concerned to explain events and so it requires substantive laws: such laws may contain geometric terms, such as the frictions of crossing a certain substance, but these terms of themselves are insufficient to provide explanations.

The spatial separatist approach proposes an independent position for geography within the social sciences based on its use of geometry, but Sack (1974b) contends that 'The spatial position's aim of prying apart a subject matter from the systematic sciences by arguing for spatial questions and spatial laws does not seem viable' (p. 446). Instead, two types of law relevant to geographical work must be identified (Sack, 1974a). *Congruent substance laws* are independent of location: statements of 'if A then B' are universals which require no spatial referent. *Overlapping substance laws*, on the other hand, involve spatial terms: 'if A then B' in such cases contains some specific reference to location. Both types are relevant and necessary in providing the answers to geographical questions, so no case can be made for a necessary 'spatialness' to the substance laws of human geography. Further, it is necessary to realize that 'Space is an essential framework of all modes of thought' but that 'geographic space is seen and evaluated in different ways at different times and in different cultures' (Sack, 1980, pp. 3–4). His book illustrates this through an examination of different approaches to the study of space: that of the social scientist concerned with objective meanings of space; that of the social scientist concerned with subjective meanings; the practical view of people who live in and learn about space (e.g. children); the mythical and magical views of space; and the societal conceptions, in which organizations and institutions structure and use space. Only the first of these is the concern of 'spatial separatists', whose approach takes space out of its relational context, a consequence of which is that 'Ignoring spatial relations or conceiving them non-relationally will hinder the discovery and confirmation of social science generalisations' (p. 85).

May (1970) has also argued against Schaefer's claim that geography is the study of spatial relations:

If we extend Schaefer's argument to include time, and assign the study of temporal sequences or relations to the historian, then the only conclusion respecting this matter that can be drawn is that economic, social, political, and other relations must be non-spatial and non-temporal. Hence economics, sociology, political science, etc. are non-spatial, non-temporal sciences. But this is absurd . . . insofar as economics qualifies as a science possessing empirical warranty, then its generalizations must apply to given spatio-temporal situations (p. 188).

If, then, all sciences have a spatial content, what is there left with which to define a separate discipline of geography? May lists five possibilities.

1   Geography is a 'super-science' of spatial relations, 'a generalizing science of spatial relations, interactions and distributions' (p. 194) drawing on the findings of other sciences. This would leave the latter truncated and their studies unfinished. In any case such an approach has been unsuccessful; 'the issue of the conception of geography as a generalizing or law-finding science that somehow stands above the social sciences and history is not even appropriately debatable' (p. 195).

2   Geography is a lower-level science of spatial relations, applying in empirical contexts the laws of higher-level, generally more abstract sciences. (This may be a description of much of the geography of the 1960s.) This again seems to truncate the latter sciences and raises the question 'what differentiates economic geography from economics, and vice versa?'.

3   Geography is the study of geographical spatial relations. This implies that there are spatial phenomena not studied in the other social science disciplines and which can therefore be claimed as geography's: May can conceive of no objects which are purely geographical (or, in the parallel argument, purely historical either).

4   Geography is the study of 'things in reality' spatially. Yet again, this abstracts from other sciences, although May does admit that there are certain 'bits and pieces' which are not studied elsewhere; these, however, do not make a satisfactory empirical foundation for a separate discipline.

5   'Geography is not a generalizing or law-finding science of spatial relations' (p. 203).

The first four of these possibilities indicate that, because of the analytical indissolubility of time, space and matter, all social sciences are concerned with spatial relations. For May, as for Sack, therefore, geography cannot claim an independent status on the basis of the spatial variable, in the way claimed by those called 'spatial separatists' by Sack, with their emphasis on the geometrical aspects of space alone. Moss (1970) reached a similar conclusion at about the same time:

geometrical relationships must be assigned economic, social, physical, or biological meaning before they can in any sense become explanatory . . . though

> geometries may be important tools in geographical study and research, they
> cannot be a source of theory since their analogy with geographical phenomena
> is simply through particular logical structures, and not through explanatory
> deduction . . . such an application implies that space, area, distance, etc., are
> important in and of themselves, quite independently of any implications they
> may have in terms of diffusion, of cost, of time, or of process. This is manifestly
> false (p. 27).

Gregory (1978b, 1980), too, has criticized the extremely narrow, even superficial, view of spatial processes which he perceives in the work of many spatial
scientists. Their view, he claims, is an instrumentalist one involving theories
which cannot be validated conclusively but which can only be evaluated pragmatically against the real world. Bennett (1974), for example, accepts that
his models do not mirror actual processes, but makes assumptions that they
do allow policy formulation (and therefore produce self-fulfilling prophecies):
because they can postdict the world as it presently is, it is assumed that they
explain it, and so can be used to predict the future.

Sack did not reject a 'spatial viewpoint' for geography as a consequence of
his arguments against the 'spatial separatist' theme, however, and in later
works (Sack, 1983, 1986) he developed a theory of territoriality as a basis for
understanding certain aspects of human behaviour. Territoriality was defined
as 'a human strategy to affect, influence and control' (1986, p. 2) and he
showed how 'under certain conditions territoriality is a more effective means
of establishing differential access to people, or resources, than thus readily
communicated; and it can be used to displace personal relationships, between
controlled and controller, by relationships between people and 'the law of the
place'. He exemplifies this with a number of case studies, and concludes that
(1986, p. 215):

> it is clear that territoriality alone cannot alter social relations to the point of
> changing the complexion of an entire society, but it can, through its own internal
> dynamics, set in motion heretofore unforeseen, and often undesirable, social
> consequences. This was true with ancient civilizations. It was true with the
> Catholic Church. It was the case with the American territorial system and the
> work place. By all accounts it is true in socialist countries and one can expect
> it will be true in attempts at establishing more utopian communal organizations.
> Territoriality's effects are multiple, important, and must be reckoned with.

Thus Sack replaces the 'spatial separatist' theme with a theory in which space
is used by people, individually and collectively, to promote social goals, an
argument taken up by others. (See Johnston, 1991, for an extension of Sack's
work. Wolch and Dear's, 1989, book *The Power of Geography* is subtitled
How Territory Shapes Social Life, but territoriality as defined here is not
widely discussed therein, and the focus is largely on what is discussed
below – p. 240 – as locality research. Cox's, 1989, is relevant to the territoriality theme, however, emphasising what he terms 'the politics of turf'.)

The arguments reviewed in the present section are highly critical of much of the work undertaken by geographers in the fashion which dominated the 1960s, impelled by the 'Victorian myth of the supremacy of the natural sciences' (Gregory, 1978a, p. 21). The alternatives to such work are discussed in the next chapter. Nevertheless, the case for spatial analysis continues to be argued. Gatrell (1983), for example, counters Sack's critique of spatial science – while accepting his case that the separation of space from substance is untenable. He does not confine spatial analysis to a positivist philosophy, however, stating that

> My response to both structuralists and humanists is that, since they too deal with *relations* (among individuals or social groups, or between man and his environment), they cannot avoid the notion of space, since any relation defines a space. Moreover, because every relation has a geometry associated with it . . . they cannot avoid the fact that geometry underlies much of what they deal with. Structures . . . *are* intrinsically spatial, but not in any simple geographical sense (p. 5).

His definition of space is clearly much broader than simple distance, therefore, and he promotes spatial analysis not as a separate paradigm of geography but as an arsenal of tools to be used in all empirical research: much of that research, he argues elsewhere (Gatrell, 1985, p. 191), involves portrayal of objects arranged in space, investigating the role of distance as a constraint on human spatial organization, and the need to achieve efficiency in locational arrangements.

Systems

The study of systems, as currently understood, was first introduced to the geographical literature by Chorley in 1962 although Foote and Greer-Wootten (1968) claimed that systems analysis was promoted in Sauer's (1925) programmatic statement *The Morphology of Landscape* with the words 'objects which exist together in the landscape exist in interrelation': Garrison's (1960a) review paper made a similar point. To some extent, the adoption of a systems approach involved putting 'old wine into new bottles', although the holistic approach currently espoused differs very much in format from that used by Sauer. More generally, the notion of a system has a long history, as Bennett and Chorley (1978, pp. 11–14) point out: teleological traditions, for example, postulate the world as 'a vast system of signs through which God teaches man how to behave' (p. 12), whereas functionalism links observed phenomena together as 'instances of repeatable and predictable regularities' of form.

The keystone of the study of systems is connectivity. As Harvey (1969a, p. 448) points out, reality is infinitely complex in its links between variables, but systems analysis provides a convenient abstraction of that complexity in a form which maintains the major connections. A system comprises three components (p. 451):

1   a set of elements;
2   a set of links (relationships) between those elements; and
3   a set of links between the system and its environment.

The last component may be non-existent, in which case the system is termed a closed one. Closed systems are extremely rare in reality, but are frequently created, either experimentally or, more usually in human geography, by imposing artificial boundaries, in order to isolate the salient features of a system. Thus, just as an internal-combustion engine comprises a set of linked elements which receives energy from its environment and returns spent fuel to that environment, so a set of settlements linked by communications networks forms a spatial system, with links to settlements outside the defined area of the system being the contacts with the environment. In a system, the elements have volumetric qualities whereas material flows along the links. As the system operates, so the various quantities may change.

The use of systems terminology to describe a spatial assemblage was widely adopted by human geographers in the 1960s, and it formed the basis, for example, of Haggett's (1965c) pioneering text. Not all applications of the terminology involved the study of explicitly spatial systems. In many cases, the elements were phenomena whose spatial locations were not studied, and the links between the phenomena were functional relationships. In such contexts, geographical study of causal systems was identical to the study of similarly structured problems in other disciplines, but because the phenomena occupied locations and because the links involved crossing space this suggested the need for an extra, geographical dimension which led to investigations of causal, spatial systems.

The early literature on systems analysis in geography was programmatic rather than applied; it suggested how the terminology might be applied in a research and teaching context, often reinterpreting old material (McDaniel and Eliot Hurst, 1968). Relatively few applications were reported, and more than a decade later much of the literature assessed in a major review was written by other scientists (Bennett and Chorley, 1978). Nevertheless, Harvey (1969a) wrote that:

> If we abandon the concept of the system we abandon one of the most powerful devices yet invented for deriving satisfactory answers to questions that we pose regarding the complex world that surrounds us. The question is not, therefore, whether or not we should use systems analysis or systems concepts in geography, but rather one of examining how we can use such concepts and such modes of analysis to our maximum advantage (p. 479).

In the search for answers to this question, two variants on the systems theme have been employed. The first is *systems analysis*; the second is *general systems theory*, which is an attempt to provide a more unified science than current disciplinary boundaries allow. The two are sometimes confused, but will be treated separately here.

Systems analysis

Having defined a system of geographical interest, with all the attendant difficulties that this entails (Harvey, 1969a, pp. 445–9), how might it be studied?
Several typologies of systems and systems analyses have been suggested.

Chorley and Kennedy (1971) identify four types of system (Figure 4.2).
Morphological systems are statements of static relationships – of links
between elements: they may be maps showing places joined by roads, or they
may be equations describing the functional relationships between variables.
Much of the spatial analysis described earlier in this chapter outlined such
morphological systems. *Cascading systems* contain links along which energy
passes from one element to another: factories can be portrayed as cascading
systems, in that the output of one factory is in many cases the input for
another. Each element may itself be a system (linked departments within a
factory, for example), so a nesting hierarchy of cascading systems can be
described, as with Haggett's (1965c) nodal regions and the input-output
matrix representation of an economy (Isard, 1960): Berry (1966) has linked
these two examples of cascading systems together in his inter-regional input-
output study of the Indian economy. Within each element in a cascading
system, the material flowing through is manipulated in some way (the
industrial process in a factory, for example). The nature of the manipulative
process may be ignored entirely in the investigation, with focus on the inputs
and outputs only: in such a case the representation of the element is termed
a black box. White-box studies investigate the transformation process,
whereas grey-box analyses make a partial attempt at their description.

Process-response systems are characterized by studies of the effects of linked
elements on each other. Instead of focusing on form, as in the first two types,
these are studies of processes, of causal interrelationships. In systems terms
these may involve, for example, the effects of a variable, X, on another, Y;
in the analysis of spatial systems they could involve the effect of variable X
in place a on variable Y in place b, as with the effect of inflation in the United
States on unemployment in the United Kingdom at some later date, perhaps,
or with the transmission of a disease from one area of a country to another
(Cliff *et al.*, 1975). Finally, there are *control systems*, which are special cases
of process-response systems, having the additional characteristic of one or
more key elements (valves) which regulate the system's operation and may be
used to control it.

Attention has focused on the last two types. Langton (1972), for example,
has suggested that process-response systems provide an excellent framework
for the study of change in human geography. He identifies two sub-types.
Simple-action systems are unidirectional in their nature: a stimulus in X
produces a response in Y, which in turn may act as a stimulus to a further
variable, Z. Such a causal chain is merely a reformulation of 'the characteristic cause-and-effect relation with which traditional science has dealt'
(Harvey, 1969a, p. 455); in another language it is a process law.

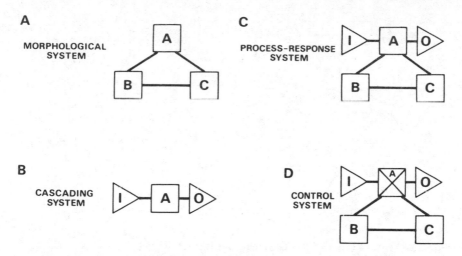

Fig 4.2 Types of system. In the diagrams, A, B and C indicate elements in the system, I = input, O = output, and in the control system, A is a valve
Source: Chorley and Kennedy (1971, p. 4)

More important, and relatively novel to human geography, is the second sub-type, *feedback systems*. According to Chorley and Kennedy (1971):

> Feedback is the property of a system or sub-system such that, when change is introduced via one of the system variables, its transmission through the structure leads the effect of the change back to the initial variable, to give a circularity of action (pp. 13–14).

Feedback may be either direct – A influences B which in turn influences A (Figure 4.3A) – or it may be indirect, with the impulse from A returning to it via a chain of other variables (Figure 4.3B). With *negative feedback* the system is maintained in a steady state by a process of self-regulation known as homeostatic or morphostatic: 'A classic example is provided by the process of competition in space which leads to a progressive reduction in excess profits until the spatial system is in equilibrium' (Harvey, 1969a, p. 460). But with *positive feedback* the system is characterized as morphogenetic, changing its characteristics as the effect of B on C leads to further changes in B, via D (Figure 4.3D).

The concept of feedback, with the associated notions of homeostasis and morphogenesis, provides 'the nuclei of the systems theory of change' (Langton, 1972, p. 145): as a consequence, Langton argues that the nature of feedback should be the focus of geographical study. In many spatial systems, feedback may be uncontrolled, but others may include a regulator, such as a planning policy (Bennett and Chorley, 1978). There are few geographical studies of such feedback processes, however. For homeostatic systems, Langton cites investigations of central place dynamics in which the pattern of service centres is adjusted as the population distribution changes,

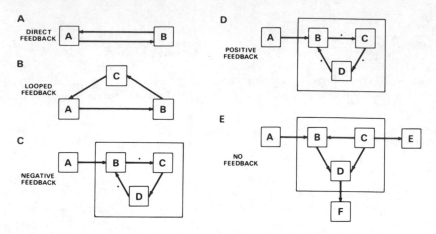

Fig 4.3   Various types of feedback relationship within systems
Source: Chorley and Kennedy (1971, p. 14)

to reproduce the previous balance between supply and demand factors (e.g. Badcock, 1970). Morphogenetic systems are illustrated by Pred's (1965b) model of the process of urban growth, in which expansion in a sector generates, via a series of links, further expansion there, as in Myrdal's (1957) more general theory of cumulative causation: such systems modelling has been used to predict urban futures (Forrester, 1969). But in most of these studies the input from systems theory is slight, leading Langton (1972) to the paradoxical conclusions that:

> *First*, there is little correlation between the extent of the penetration of the ter-minology of systems theory and the rigorous application of its concepts. The 'empty' use of terminology, which is typified by the use of the term feedback as an explanatory device rather than as a description of a fundamental research problem, must be counter-productive in a situation in which the terms themselves may be given many subtle different shades of meaning. . . .
> *Second*, somewhat paradoxically, many of the concepts of systems theory are already used in geography without the attendant jargon and without apparently drawing direct inspiration from the literature of systems theory (pp. 159–60).

This second conclusion suggests that a discipline should develop the necessary conceptual framework itself without the introduction of relevant concepts from related disciplines, but Langton disputes this, arguing that systems theory clarifies questions in established theories, focuses directly on the processes of change, and forces careful analytical study.

One of the most substantial attempts to apply systems theory to a problem in human geography is the work of Bennett (1975) on the dynamics of location and growth in northwest England. Having represented the system – its elements, links, and feedback relationships – he estimated the influence of various external (i.e. national) events on the system's parameters, isolated the effects of government policy (Industrial Development Certificates) on the system's structure, and produced forecasts of the region's future spatio-temporal morphology. He has developed the forecasting aspects of this methodology in later papers (Bennett, 1978a, 1979), has suggested how an optimal distribution of government grants can be achieved (Bennett, 1981b), and has outlined the likely spatial variation in the impact of a new tax (the 'poll tax': Bennett, 1989b).

One type of study which has firmly adopted the systems approach covers the border area between human and physical geography. The *ecosystem* is a process-response system concerned with the flows of energy through biological environments, most of which include, or are affected by, people. It is also a control system in that the living components act as regulators of the energy flows: 'they further represent a major point at which human control systems must intersect with the natural world' (Chorley and Kennedy, 1971, p. 330). Most naturally occurring ecosystems are, for much of the time, homeostatic (see Chapman, 1977, Chapter 7), but human entry often transforms them into morphogenetic systems, with potentially catastrophic effects (Johnston, 1989b).

Stoddart (1965, 1967b) has argued that the ecosystem should be employed as a basic geographical principle, but despite other programmatic statements (e.g. Clarkson, 1970), including two based on the associated concept of community (Morgan and Moss, 1965; Moss and Morgan, 1967), Langton's conclusion about relatively little substantive research would appear to be valid (see Grossman, 1977). Similar attempts, but involving less consideration of the biotic environment, have been made in allied disciplines, and have occasionally been imported into the geographical literature. The human ecosystem models of sociologists (e.g. Duncan, 1959; Duncan and Schnore, 1959) have been used as frameworks for the investigation of migration (Urlich, 1972) and of urbanization (Urlich Cloher, 1975), for example, and the operational research techniques of economists, with their important feedback mechanisms, have stimulated some work in transport geography (e.g. Sinclair and Kissling, 1971).

The most comprehensive attempt to forge a systems approach to geographical study has been provided by Bennett and Chorley (1978). The intention of their book is to provide 'a unified multi-disciplinary approach to the interfacing of "man" with "nature" ' (p. 21), with three major aims:

> First, it is desired to explore the capacity of the systems approach to provide an inter-disciplinary focus on environmental structures and techniques. Secondly, we wish to examine the manner in which a systems approach aids in developing the interfacing of social and economic theory, on the one hand, with physical and biological theory, on the other. A third aim is to explore the implications of this interfacing in relation to the response of man to his current environmental dilemmas. . . . It is hoped to show that the systems approach provides a powerful vehicle for the statement of environmental situations of ever-growing temporal and spatial magnitude, and for reducing the areas of uncertainty in our increasingly complex decision-making arenas (p. 21).

This mammoth task (undertaken in a mammoth book of 624 pages!) involves elucidation of not only the 'hard systems' of physical and biological sciences but also the 'soft systems' characteristic of the social sciences. With regard to the latter, they cover a very large and fertile literature concerned, first, with the cognitive systems describing people as thinking beings and the decision-making systems used by humans, as individuals and in groups, and, secondly, with the socio-economic systems made up of very many of these interacting individuals and groups. They then attempt to interface the two types, because:

> in large-scale man-environment systems the symbiosis of man as part of the environment of the system he wishes to control introduces all the indetermin-acies of socio-economic control objectives. . . . In particular, we need to ask what are the political and social implications of control, and for whom and by whom is control intended? (p. 539).

Not surprisingly, they end their essay into the field with a discussion of the very many substantial problems involved in such interfacing, although many of these are firmly tackled in the text (which was written after the widespread introduction to the literature of many of the criticisms discussed in the following chapters in this book).

This use of systems analysis is based on the assumption (usually implicit) underlying much positivist work in human geography, that valid analogies can be drawn between human societies on the one hand and both natural phenomena-complexes and machines on the other. Individual elements in a system have predetermined roles, and can act and change in certain ways only − depending on the structure of the system and its interrelationships with the environment. As a descriptive device, this analogy allows the structure and operation of society and its components to be portrayed and analysed, and it provides a source of ideas from which hypotheses can be generated (see Coffey, 1981). And once a system has been defined and modelled, systems analysis can be used as a predictive tool, to indicate the nature of the elements and links following certain environmental changes (such as the introduction of new elements and/or links, as in the classic Lowry model used to predict the impact of new land-use configurations on traffic flows: Batty, 1978).

The potential fertility of this analogy has been examined by several authors. Wilson (1981b), for example, has discussed methods of analysing environ-mental systems in which he defines environment as 'natural, man-nature, and manufactured 'systems of interest' ' (p. xi), in all of which

> the main concern is with *complicated* systems whose components exhibit high degrees of interdependence. The behaviour of the 'whole' system is then usually something very much more than the sum of the parts (p. 3).

His case is that moorland ecosystems, water resource systems, and cities (his three initial examples) can all be studied in the same way and his book investi-gates the methods for this; a further book (Wilson, 1981a) presents the mathematics for studying systems in which the rates and directions of change suddenly alter. Huggett (1980) similarly argues that systems analysis has wide applications in both human and physical geography, plus the interface where people and environment interact, and his book illustrates the methods of systems analysis (see also Huggett and Thomas, 1980). And once the system has been successfully modelled, it can then be manipulated using control theory which:

> is a *dynamic* optimization technique . . . [which] permits optimal allocation over long time horizons . . . [and] shifts emphasis from mere model construction to model use (Chorley and Bennett, 1981, p. 219).

Such a combination of models describing systems with a theory of system control has a wide range of potential applications, according to Chorley and Bennett, in such fields as pollution control, catchment management, inter-area resource allocation and urban planning. It suggests a commonality of interest, focused on methods, between applied physical and applied human geography.

Systems theory, information, and entropy

The definition of a system presented so far in this chapter is of a series of linked elements interacting to form an operational whole. This has been challenged by Chapman (1977) who opens his book with the statement:

> I do not think that the concept of a system will have any great operational consequences in geography for a long time yet. It represents an ideal that the real world does not fully approach. On the other hand, in conceptual terms I think the concept is extremely important and useful, and that it has a great and immediate role to play for those who are about to plan the strategy of their research. As a framework for analysis, it has no current peers (p. 6).

For Chapman, a system comprises a series of elements which can take alternative states, and his definition – following Rothstein (1958) – is

> A system is a set of objects where each object is associated with a set of feasible alternative states: and where the actual state of any object selected from this set is dependent in part or completely upon its membership of the system. An object that has no alternative states is not a functioning part but a static cog (p. 80).

An example of such a system is a number of farms, each comprising a series of fields: every farmer has to decide how to use each of the fields. In part, each decision will reflect the general operations of the farm and the uses to which all other fields are put; in part, it will be a function of the external market and the decisions made by other farmers regarding their own fields. Thus there is a large number of possible states for the system of fields – different configurations of land uses. According to Chapman, systems analysis should involve investigation of these configurations and the placing of the observed pattern within the context of the alternatives:

to theorize merely about what does exist is not very useful. If we restrict ourselves to that alone, all explanation will be merely historical accidental. At all stages it is most important to include consideration of what else could have been. The definition of organization in a system even explicitly requires the assessment of what else could have been (pp. 120–1).

Taylor and Gudgin (1976) have argued in the same way in a particular research context: instead of simply asking 'is there a bias in the electoral districting of a borough?' they ask 'what is the likelihood of a bias occurring, given the constraints of the system?', and they have set the study of electoral districting, the aggregation of spatial units into constituencies and its consequences, on a strong statistical footing (Gudgin and Taylor, 1979).

Such analyses focus on one configuration of the system as a sample from a set of possible configurations, and among their key concepts is *entropy*. In general terms, the entropy of a system is an index of uncertainty. (In the second law of thermodynamics an increase in system entropy is an increase in system uncertainty. A good example of this is the introduction of a layer of hot water onto a body of cold water. Initially, the two types are separate, and one can be completely certain about the location of the hot molecules, for example. But with no external influence the two slowly mix, until all are at the same temperature. As the mixing proceeds, so the entropy increases.)

Social scientists have drawn their usage of entropy from two separate, though linked, definitions. Thermodynamic entropy relates to the most probable configuration of the elements, within the constraints of the system's operations. In information theory, entropy refers to the distribution of the elements across a set of possible states, and is an index of element dispersion. One can be completely certain about a distribution, in terms of predicting where one element will be, if all elements are in the same state; conversely, one will be most uncertain when elements are equally distributed through all possible states, so that prediction of the location of any one element is most difficult. (An example of this use is in Johnston's, 1976a, work on the pattern of international trading partners; see also Webber, 1977, and Thomas, 1982 on the relationship between entropy and uncertainty.)

Used in its simplest form, the information-theory measure of entropy is another descriptive index, but it can be developed in a variety of ways. Chapman (1977) illustrates three uses:

1   as a series of indices of variations in population distributions;
2   as an index of redundancy in a landscape, where redundancy is defined as relating to a regular sequence so that it is possible to predict the land use at place a, for example, from knowledge of the land uses at neighbouring places; and
3   as a series of measures of reactions to situations in states of uncertainty.

In general terms, although not in detailed methodology, these continue the tradition of Stewart and Warntz's macrogeography (p. 67): the aim is to describe a pattern rather than to explain it, although the nature of the constraints used to derive the entropy measures provides an input to explanatory modes of analysis (Webber, 1977).

The use of entropy as developed in statistical mechanics rather than in information theory was introduced to the geographical literature by Wilson (1970): his initial example was a flow matrix. The number of trips originating in a series of residential areas is known, as is the number ending in each of a series of workplace areas, but the entries in the cells of the matrix – which people move from which residential area to which workplace area – are unknown. What is the most likely flow pattern? Even with only a few areas and relatively small numbers of commuters, the number of alternatives is very large. Wilson defines three states of the system. The first is the macro-state, comprising the number of commuters at each origin and the numbers of jobs at each destination. The second is the meso-state, comprising a particular flow pattern: five people may go from zone A to zone X, for example, and three from the same origin to zone Y, but it is not known which five are in the first category and which three in the second. A micro-state, on the other hand, is a particular example of a flow pattern – one of the many possible con-figurations of eight people moving from zone A, five to X and three to Y. Entropy-maximizing procedures find that meso-state with the largest number of micro-states associated with it; in other words it is the meso-state about which the analyst is least certain of which configuration produces the pattern. Such a procedure shows that

> the most probable distribution is that with the greatest number of micro-states giving rise to it. Thus the distribution corresponds to the position where we are most uncertain about the micro-state of the system, as there are the largest possible number of such states and we have no grounds for choosing between them (p. 6).

This, too, follows the macrogeography tradition. It is not an attempt at explanation. Rather Wilson sees his work as illustrating

> the application of the concept of entropy in urban and regional modelling, that is, in *hypothesis development*, or theory building. ('Model' and 'hypothesis' are used synonymously, and a theory is a well tested hypothesis.) . . . the entropy-maximizing procedure enables us to handle extremely complex situations in a consistent way (pp. 10–11).

The hypothesis that the entries in the flow matrix conform to the most likely distribution can be tested against 'real' data. If it is falsified, either entirely or in part, it can be refined by building in more constraints. Wilson does this with his intra-urban transport models, for example, by introducing travel-cost constraints, different types of commuters (class, age, etc.), different types of jobs, and so on. The aim is to describe the most likely system structure from a given amount of information, which is incomplete.

Wilson has developed both the theory of his modelling and the substantive applications (see Wilson, 1981b). His general text (Wilson, 1974) contains a whole family of models that can be used to represent, and then to forecast, the various components of a complex spatial system such as an urban region. Some of these models have been expanded (e.g. Rees and Wilson, 1977, on demographic accounts) and they have all been applied, with varying success, to the West Yorkshire region (Wilson, Rees and Leigh, 1977).

Wilson's work has been applied and developed by others (see Batty, 1976, 1978, for example): it has been extended to other areas of study in, for example, Johnston's (1985b) estimation of spatial variations in voting behaviour within England. In reviewing Wilson's 1970 presentation, Gould (1972) termed it 'the most difficult I have ever read in geography' but continued 'he has planted a number of those rare and deep concepts whose understanding provides a fresh and sharply different view of the world' (p. 689). Webber (1977) has extended Wilson's argument that the purpose of entropy-maximizing models is to draw conclusions from a data set which are 'natural' in that they are functions of that data set alone and contain no interpreter bias. For him, they provide a convenient way of organizing processes of thinking about a complex world, and he identifies an 'entropy-maximizing paradigm' (p. 262) which focuses on location models (the probability of an individual being in a particular place at a particular time), on interaction models (the probability of a particular trip occurring at a particular time), and on joint location/interaction models. And at Leeds, Wilson's work on the entropy-maximizing approach has been extended into the fields of micro-simulation (Birkin and Clarke, 1988, 1989; Clarke and Holm, 1988) which produces statistically reliable estimates of micro-level characteristic within population (the number of people aged 25–34 with cancer, for example) from macro-data (the number of people in each age group and, separately, the number with cancer).

In emphasizing aggregate patterns, this work is macrogeographic: according to Webber (1977) 'The entropy-maximizing paradigm asserts . . . that, though the study of individual behavior may be of interest, it is not necessary for the study of aggregate social relations' (p. 265). The patterns predicted by the models are functions of the constraints (which are the information provided at the meso-state), so that knowledge of these means that 'the entropy-maximizing paradigm is capable of yielding meaningful answers to short-run operational problems' (p. 266) and thus is of immense value for immediate planning purposes. But:

> in the longer run, much of the economic system is variable: the constraints and the spatial form of the urban region may change . . . the research task facing entropists is (1) to identify the constraints which operate upon urban systems, which is partly an economic problem; (2) to deduce some facets of the economic relations among the individuals within the system from the use of the formalism; and (3) to construct a theory which explains the origins of the constraints. Only when the third task has been attempted may the paradigm be adequately judged (p. 266).

Thus the entropy-maximizing model acts not only as a 'black box' forecasting device (p. 118) but also as a hypothesis: if the operation of the systems described is to be understood, the axioms – the constraints – must themselves be explained. Given the nature of the constraints (in Wilson's initial example, why people live where they do, why people work where they do, and why they spend a certain amount of time, money and energy on transport) the task is a major one: entropy-maximizing models aim to clarify it and indicate the most fruitful avenues for investigation.

The study of systems allows dynamic processes to be incorporated within geographical analyses, instead of focusing on static patterns which are the outcomes of such processes. Thus much of the mathematical development reviewed above (p. 106) has been concerned with the study of such processes, in order to advance understanding of change and the ability to forecast change. (On the use of the term process in this context, see the critique by Hay and Johnston, 1983.) Dynamical systems theory and analysis has been the focus of a major research programme conducted at the University of Leeds by Alan Wilson and his associates since the mid 1970s, for example, during which a number of major advances have been made in the analysis of change; in particular, attention has been directed away from the relatively straight-forward linear modelling to complex representations in which change is presented as discontinuous and not necessarily unidirectional (see Wilson, 1981a).

Many geographical analyses of dynamical systems have focused on static spatial patterns or structures, representing these as equilibrium or steady-state situations within the ongoing dynamic processes. Change is then handled, as Clarke and Wilson (1985, p. 429) describe it

> by forecasting (in some other theory or model) the independent variables associated with a system and then calculating the new equilibrium or steady state.

However, their applications of dynamical systems analysis suggests that this approach is not tenable because in complex systems

> There are too many possibilities of transition to different kinds of equilibrium or non-equilibrium states (p. 431)

which thereby doubts the validity of the traditional approach to forecasting and hence the contribution of geographical modelling to planning. The nature of that contribution must be rethought, therefore, because conditional forecasting is of little value – 'there are simply too many possible futures for this to be useful' (p. 446). The new contributions, they argue, could involve

> First, it may often be possible to recognize the 'nearness' of some instability or structural shift to an undesirable state. Policy can then be focused on conservation. Secondly, it may be possible to see how to bring about a shift to a new *desired* state by changing policy in order to move a parameter through some critical value. Thirdly, both the ideas of dynamical analysis and the capabilities

of modern computer technology lend themselves to the construction of planning systems focused on information retrieval . . . and monitoring; so that at least planners and policy makers are in a position to respond more rapidly when difficulties are identified (p. 446).

As such geographers come more to terms with the inherent complexity, and hence unpredictability, of the world, so they are reassessing their contribution to its management (Clark and Wilson, 1984, 1987).

The theory of systems and general systems theory

Like regional science and the impact of Walter Isard, the development of General Systems Theory (GST) has been very much tied up with the academic career of one man − in this case Ludwig von Bertalanffy (see von Bertalanffy, 1950). It reflects an attempt to unify science via perspectivism instead of the more usual division of science through reductionism. Its focus is on isomorphisms, the common features among the systems studied in different disciplines, and 'Its subject matter is the formulation and derivation of those principles which are common for systems in general' (Walmsley, 1972, p. 23). The goal is a metatheory with rules that apply in a variety of contexts; application (which might be termed the theory of systems rather than GST) is usually by analogy from one discipline in order to advance understanding in another (as in Chappell and Webber's, 1970, use of an electrical analogue of spatial diffusion processes and in much recent work an artificial intelligence using computer modelling: Couclelis, 1986a). For geography, GST offers an organizing framework; GST itself is an empirical exercise using inductive procedures to fashion general theories out of the findings of particular disciplines (see Coffey, 1981).

It has been claimed that there have been no advances in either the theoretical base or the empirical application of GST (Greer-Wootten, 1972). It has been employed by some geographers, however: Woldenberg and Berry (1967) drew analogies between the hierarchical organization of rivers and of central-place systems, for example; Berry (1964a) argued that cities are open systems in a steady-state, as exemplified by the stability of their behaviour-describing equations; and several authors (e.g. Ray, Villeneuve and Roberge, 1974) have applied the concept of allometry − that the growth rate of a component of an organism is proportional to the growth of the whole − in several contexts.

According to its proponents, the advantages of GST to human geography lie in its interdisciplinary approach, its high level of generalization, and its concept of the steady-state of an open system (Greer-Wootten, 1972; Walmsley, 1972), but they also contend that geography's strong empirical tradition means that it has more to contribute than to take from GST. But one critic has claimed that 'General systems theory seems to be an irrelevant distraction' (Chisholm, 1967, p. 51), an argument based largely on a paper by Chorley (1962) referring to the Davisian system of landscape development. Chisholm summarizes the case for GST as:

1 there is a need to study systems rather than isolated phenomena;
2 there is a need to identify the basic principles governing systems;
3 there is value in arguing from analogies with other subject matter; and
4 there is a need for general principles to cover various systems.

In his view, however, something as grand as a metatheory is unnecessary in order to convince people of the need to understand what they study, of the value of interdisciplinary contact, and of the potential fertility of arguing by analogy.

Moving Forward

Much of the remainder of this book is concerned with alternative approaches to human geography to those outlined here; most of those alternatives are based on critiques of 'positivist spatial science'. Nobody has expressed these criticisms more pungently than Harvey (1989b), who, in reviewing the twenty years that had elapsed since the publication of *Models in Geography* (Chorley and Haggett, 1967), claimed that (pp. 212–3):

> Those who have stuck with modelling since those heady days have largely been able to do so, I suspect, by restricting the nature of the questions they ask. I accept that we can now model spatial behaviours like journey-to-work, retail activity, the spread of measles epidemics, the atmospheric dispersion of pollutants, and the like, with much greater security and precision than once was the case. And I accept that this represents no mean achievement. But what can we say about the sudden explosion of third world debt in the 1970s, the remarkable push into new and seemingly quite different modes of flexible accumulation, the rise of geopolitical tensions, even the definition of key ecological problems? What more do we know about major historical-geographical transformations (the rise of capitalism, world wars, socialist, revolutions, and the like)? Furthermore, pursuit of knowledge by the positivist route did not necessarily generate usable configurations of concepts and theories. There must be thousands of hypotheses proven correct at some appropriate level of significance in the geographic literature by now, and I am left with the impression that *in toto* this adds up to little more than the proverbial hill of beans.

This was the second time in which he had made such a claim regarding the irrelevance of much geographical work in the spatial science mould (the first was made in 1973, and is set out in more detail on p. 196). It provoked many responses at the conference where it was first delivered, as indicated by Macmillan's (1989b) rejoinder.

   If the paradigm model discussed in Chapter 1 (p. 11) were relevant to geography, then interest in the approaches set out in the present chapter should have waned in the 1970s and 1980s, if not disappeared totally. In relative terms there has undoubtedly been some decline, as the alternative world-views on offer (and discussed later in this book) have attracted substantial attention. But a considerable amount of work is still being done which is firmly based within the world-view described here. Some of the adherents have sought to accommodate to the critiques (e.g. Wilson, 1989a) but others have counterattacked and argued for the validity and vitality of their point of view. There is a general consensus among the counterattackers that modelling is a viable approach to human geography, though there is considerable variability in emphasis as to the way forwards.

Recent reviews suggest that modelling within human geography has led to 'dramatic advances' within the discipline (Wilson, 1989b, p. 29), and that it has 'a substantial contribution to make in the long term' (Clarke and Wilson, 1989, p. 30). Wilson (1989b, p. 30) accepts the limitations of the approach – models 'have relatively little to offer in relation to individual behaviour directly', but are important tools which can 'help to handle complexity in a variety of situations'. His review focuses on work (much of it his own) which has sought to develop the 'classics' of location theory (those of von Thunen, Weber, Burgess and Hoyt, and Reilly: see also Clarke and Wilson, 1985), and which he considers to have provided, through its mathematical sophistication, substantial advances in understanding. (Wilson, 1989b, claims that the use of mathematics to model complexity distances his work from positivism: statistics are needed to calibrate and test models, but 'a purely statistical approach to theory and model-building is limited in scope and is also more directly connected to positivism', p. 41.)

The achievements of modelling are similarly lauded by Macmillan (1989a, 1989b), who equates it with 'quantitative theory construction'; theories, to him, are empirically testable statements of 'universal empirical propositions, law-like generalizations' (1989a, p. 93), so that modelling involves the development of theories which contain 'quantifiable propositions' that can be tested. It has already 'helped geography to achieve widespread and significant advances' (1989b, p. 292), and the feelings within the modelling community are of 'frustrated optimism rather than pessimism' (p. 291). He argues against a return to focusing on the uniqueness of places (see Chapter 8), arguing, for example, that (p. 305):

> if we want to understand famines, we must look at famine processes wherever they occur and test our theories about them accordingly.

Several authors have argued for a shift in emphasis within the approach, however, as a consequence of recent developments in information technology and data availability. Macmillan (1989b) identifies three separate areas of modelling activity: statistical; mathematical; and data-based, which is largely inductive in orientation. The case for the last is forcefully argued by Openshaw (1989) who terms 'the application of a mathematical tool kit to urban and regional systems modelling within a hypothetico-deductive framework', as in Wilson's work, 'noble objectives' (p. 71). He claims that the available models have not been much used, however (see also Batty, 1989), leading to the situation whereby 'so much of the intellectual capital of quantitative human geography [is] encapsulated in theoretical models that seemingly serve no useful purpose outside of geography itself' (p. 72). The deductive route to understanding, and eventually to applied work, 'has been taken too far and has not been particularly successful' (p. 73):

> There is no doubt about either the quality of the work or of the utility of the mathematical methods; rather, criticism is focused on the lack of applied relevancy, the lack of attention to empirical study, and the absence of explicit geography.

Since the beginning of that work, there has been an explosion of data collection, and the provision of that information in machine-readable form. (Though see Openshaw and Goddard, 1987, on the problems of much of that data being held in the private sector as commodities.) Openshaw's proposal is to capitalize on that wealth of data with a type of work which he defines as 'Data-driven computer modelling in an information economy'.

According to Openshaw, the prime concern of the owners of data (including those in the public sector who are increasingly required to justify the costs of data collection by its sale to users) is to 'add value' to their information, by analyses which make it more readily usable, and hence saleable. Theory is much less relevant than the ability to conduct spatial analysis of data, which relies much more on inductive approaches rather than deductive, a situation which he accepts is pragmatic but which he proposes as a means of ensuring the discipline's short-term survival (p. 81). As he expresses it:

> never before in human history has so much information about so many people and their spatial behaviour patterns been stored in computers and therefore, theoretically speaking, accessible for analysis. Yet it appears that if geographers want access to such rich data sources as now exist they will in future either have to pay or join the data-keepers in providing information services (pp.81–2).

The latter is his chosen way forward, using the analytical skills of geographers, including those of GIS (p. 109), not to advance theoretical understanding but rather to improve business and predictive efficiency by inductively seeking methods that work – as with answers to questions such as 'given the population profile of an area, what pattern of spending can be expected there?' and 'Can house prices in that area be predicted with accuracy?'. Thus data bases should be explored, in order to identify patterns that provide useful, and hence saleable, information. In this context, he has developed what he calls a Geographical Analysis Machine (Openshaw, Charlton, Wymer and Craft, 1988), which has been used to identify clusters of disease outbreaks and to suggest hypotheses regarding their causes (Openshaw, Charlton, Craft and Birch, 1988), and he has used GIS technology to explore issues regarding the potential impact of nuclear attacks within Great Britain (Openshaw, Steadman and Greene, 1983), the siting of nuclear power stations (Openshaw, 1986), and the disposal of nuclear waste (Openshaw, Carver and Fernie, 1989).

Openshaw's call for a return to inductive methods as a way of adding value to data, and thereby to prove the utility of geography within modern society, is backed by others, who identify technical ability with quantitative methods as one of geographers' strongest selling points (e.g. Beaumont, 1987). Thus Rhind (1989) argues that geographers should develop as 'gatekeepers' to usable information, as a way of staying 'central to the action' (p. 189). These are clearly calls for more applied geography (which are discussed in more detail below: p. 188), and sit uneasily alongside the technical arguments of Haining (1989) for more sophisticated analytical work, though applications such as those of Cliff and Haggett (1989; see also Smallman-Raynor and Cliff, 1990) on the spread of diseases indicate how sophisticated spatial analysis based on deductive modelling can be put to use.

The division between the inductive 'number-crunchers' and the 'deductive modellers' suggests a growing split within the body of human geographers concerned with quantitative analysis: on the one hand, there are those who take well-known, usually relatively straightforward and easily applied methods, and promote their widespread application, and on the other there are those who advance the development of sophisticated procedures, whose use demands considerable technical expertise. Cox (1989) argues that the latter have had a very limited impact on geography as a whole, because: they have shown that spatial data are 'messy', requiring special analytical procedures that are not generally available, and so set 'intellectual and practical difficulties [which] have limited widespread understanding and application of the more correct procedures that have been produced' (p. 206); and second, with few exceptions (such as Cliff and Haggett's work) the procedures have not been applied to problems that are in the mainstream of attempts at geographical understanding, have little basis in known 'human processes or behaviour', and so are peripheral to most geographers' interests. Thus much quantitative analysis has been marginalized within geography, whereas the adherents to Openshaw's approach and the use of GIS have been able to promote more readily appreciated expertise which is saleable (p. 207):

> It is clear that geographers specializing in geographical information systems will survive only by combining considerable technical expertise with a taste and talent for the *Realpolitik* of grants, contracts, committees, administrators, and entrepreneurs. A canny awareness of commercial and political realities will be as necessary as any particular intellectual qualities.

This carries, for him, the danger that 'preoccupation with data will omit imagination and creativity' (p. 208) but, as the later section on applied geography shows, it is seen by many as a major way of protecting a discipline in a context where utility and saleability are the crucial indicators of the worth of its work.

While a small number of geographers continue to promote the development of analytical methods within geography, and some at least see this development linked to not only better explanatory procedures and predictive methods that will lead to a wider applicability and application of geographers' skills, many more are relatively unconcerned with either the sophistication of method or the search for grand generalizations. As Flowerdew (1976) force-fully pointed out, their work is very largely empiricist in orientation, having as its goal the portrayal of the 'objective' world as they perceive it, and of the salient elements of it which they identify as needing research. A great deal of it is concerned with describing the changing geography of the world, and the amount and rapidity of change has called forth a great volume of pub-lished work. At the global scale, for example, major changes in the geography of productive activity have been recorded (as in Dicken, 1986; Knox and Agnew, 1988; Wallace, 1989); more locally, changes in the geography of individual countries have been the subject of substantial attention (as with the United Kingdom – Johnston and Doornkamp, 1982; Johnston and Gardiner, 1990: Lewis and Townsend, 1989 – and the United States – Knox *et al.*, 1988 – to give but a few examples). Similarly, changes in the structure of society and their geographical ramifications, have been a major focus, as with the growth of service industries (Daniels, 1982, 1985; Price and Blair, 1989).

This work is not entirely atheoretical – as critics of the empiricist and positivist positions on value-freedom and neutrality point out, the choice of what to study (i.e. what is significant) and how to study it must be theoret-ically informed, however implicitly – nor is it undertaken in isolation from the theoretical and methodological debates and developments taking place elsewhere in the discipline. A large number of geographers prefer not to get embroiled in those, however, but rather to draw on them, as they see fit, to inform their own work which in its orientation is close to Hartshorne's well-known call 'to describe and interpret the variable character from place to place of the earth as the world of man'. The debates and developments charted in this book have engaged directly only a minority of practising geographers, certainly to more than a passing degree, but they have all been directly or indirectly influenced by them as they follow their personal bents within the world of geography.

Conclusions

As stressed in the previous chapter, much of the force of the developments in human geography during the 1950s and 1960s related to methodology and the approach to traditional geographical questions. In addition, however, attempts were made to inaugurate and press a particular geographical point of view; the two main themes advanced have been reviewed here. The first – the spatial-science viewpoint – was fairly widely and rapidly accepted and many geographers placed the spatial variable at the centre of their research efforts: as will be indicated in the next chapter, their work came under increasing attack in the mid 1960s. The second – the systems approach – has received much less detailed attention, despite frequent gestures of approval towards it. Compared with the spatial-science view, which could be rapidly assimilated within the developing statistical method-ology (although note the critique discussed on p. 66), the systems approach was technically much more demanding, and perhaps for that reason attracted fewer active researchers (though see the defence in Coffey, 1981). These have remained the source of fertile ideas, however, and have continued to publish major works throughout the 1970s, paralleling, and in some cases (e.g. Bennett and Chorley, 1978) responding to, the academic movements outlined in the following chapters.

Human geography as spatial science was inaugurated in North America in the 1950s. By the end of the 1960s it was dominating the journals published there and in the rest of the English-speaking world. Most research was positivist in its tone, if not its detail, seeking to describe patterns of spatial organization and to account for these as consequences of the influence of distance on human behaviour. A great deal of that work was quantitative, and it contributed to bodies of theory, either about spatial organization in general or certain aspects of it in particular (as with industrial location: Smith, 1981). And, as illustrated here, it has influenced other academic dis-ciplines and the planning profession.

Since the 1970s, positivist spatial science has been under considerable attack among Anglo-American human geographers, as discussed in the next two chapters. But this attack has had little effect on the volume of work done in this paradigm, as illustrated by a major review of *Quantitative Geography* by British workers (Wrigley and Bennett, 1981); this work has been stimulated and aided by advances in data handling technology and display (Rhind, 1981). At the same time, the approach has been fostered outside the Anglo-American realm, especially in Western Europe where the reaction to quantification has been stronger than in Britain and North America (see Bennett, 1981c).

This great volume of work suggests that there has been 'progress' within the positivist approach. Whether this is so is not easy to assess. Certainly, as suggested here, there have been substantial advances in the development and adaptation of sophisticated modelling and analytical techniques (on the former, see Papageorgiou, 1976), although to some these advances, although 'scholarship of the highest order', may reflect 'a misdirection of effort' (King, 1979b, p. 157) because they have not illuminated spatial organization as much as they might. But new techniques continue to be advanced. Empirical work in the spatial science context has very much taken the form of case studies set in a general theoretical context, and – despite the efforts of some general surveys (e.g. Haggett, Cliff and Frey, 1977) – it is not clear whether such *case studies* have provided any more *general* understanding than has been provided by historical and cultural geography, which continued to operate quietly through individual investigations throughout the period under discussion here. What is without doubt, however, is the volumetric impact of spatial science on human geography.

One of the most salient features of this conception of human geography is its focus on space, especially distance as a component of space, as the central element of geographical study. As such, it presents a particular view of the spatial variable, as Sack (1980) has clearly indicated. This conception of human geography, of a discipline concerned with the laws of spatial behaviour, was soon challenged, as the next chapters indicate.

5

Behavioural Geography

The changes outlined in the previous chapter had achieved a substantial impact on the practice of human geography by the middle of the 1960s (as Burton's, 1963, coverage of 'the quantitative revolution and theoretical geography' implied), not only in the United States, Canada and the United Kingdom but also in other countries whose academic traditions and life are closely tied to one or more of those North Atlantic states. The changes were resisted by some geographers, as already documented, who defended the (usually implicit) philosophies and methodologies within which they had been academically socialized but, as suggested in the previous chapter, the 'new' very largely prevailed over the 'old'. By the end of the decade, those defences had been joined by other critiques of 'quantitative and theoretical geography' which were based not on the split between the 'old' and the 'new' but rather on the latter's perceived failures to provide viable paths to understanding. A considerable number of those critiques involved proposals for yet other philosophies and methodologies, some of them linked (weakly in a few cases) to previous approaches within human geography and others promoting more radical views: they are discussed in detail in Chapters 6 and 8. There was also a substantial critique from within the general spatial science approach, however, from those who had tried the 'new', were attracted to many of its tenets but were disappointed by their 'accomplishments'.

The outcome of the proposed modifications to the spatial science approach was the growth of an activity that became known as 'behavioural geography', whose birth was announced in a seminal book of essays (Cox and Golledge, 1969) and whose maturity was reviewed twelve years later in a companion volume (Cox and Golledge, 1981). Its essential ingredients, as set out by Golledge and Timmermans (1990), are:

(a) a search for models of humanity which were alternatives to the economically and spatially rational beings of normative location theory;
(b) a search to define environments other than objective physical reality as the milieux in which human decision making and action took place;

(c) an emphasis on processural rather than structural explanations of human acitivity and the physical environment;

(d) an interest in unpacking the spatial dimensions of psychological, social, and other theories of human decision-making and behaviour;

(e) a change in emphasis from aggregate populations to the disaggregate scale of individuals and small groups;

(f) a need to develop new data sources other than the generalised mass-produced aggregate statistics of government agencies which obscured and over-generalised decision making processes and consequent behaviour;

(g) a search for methods other than those of traditional mathematics and inferential statistics that could aid in uncovering latent structure in data, and which could handle data sets that were less powerful than the traditionally used interval and ratio data; and

(h) a desire to merge geographic research into the ever broadening stream of cross-disciplinary investigation into theory building and problem solving.

This chapter reviews the field as they define it. (For a commentary from practitioners in the related field of psychology, see Spencer and Blades, 1986.)

Towards a More Positive, Behaviouristic Spatial Science

The main ground for disillusion within the positivist camp was a growing realization that the models being propounded and tested were not very good descriptions of reality, so that progress towards the development of geographical theory was painfully slow and its predictive powers consequently weak. Thus the large body of work based on central place theory, for example, was built on certain axioms regarding human behaviour, with regard to choice between spatial alternatives, and from these axioms a settlement pattern was deduced. But the deductions were often only vaguely reflected in settlement morphologies, which suggested that the axioms on which they were based provided a weak foundation for understanding this aspect of the spatial organ-ization of society. The theory suggested how the world would look under certain circumstances of economic rationality in decision-making; that those circumstances did not prevail suggested that the world should be looked at in other ways in order to understand how people do behave and structure their spatial organization. As Brookfield (1964) put it, with regard to the whole family of models then popular:

> We may thus feel that we have proceeded far enough in answering our questions when, by examination of a sufficient number of cases, we can make assertions such as the following: population density diminishes regularly away from metro-politan centres in all directions; crop yields diminish beyond a certain walking distance from the centres of habitation; air-traffic centres lying in the shadow of major centres do not command the traffic that their populations would lead us to expect. . . . Such answers, which represent the mean result of large numbers of observations whether statistically controlled or otherwise, are valuable in themselves, and sufficient for many purposes. But each is also an

observation demanding explanations which may seem self-evident, or which may in fact be very elusive. Furthermore, there will be exceptions to each generalization, and in many cases there are also limits to the range of territory over which they hold true. Both the exceptions and the limits demand explanation (p. 285).

The issues being raised, therefore, were concerned not with the basic goal of positivist work – the establishment of generalizations and theories – but rather with the particular route being taken to that goal. The criticisms focused on the models being used, and their axioms regarding rational economic behaviour on the basis of perfect information. The hypotheses derived from these models were, at best, being only weakly verified in empirical studies. The need was for better models, and the search for these took a more inductive route than that previously followed. Rather than base hypotheses on assumptions about behaviour, behaviour was to be investigated inductively, to provide inputs to a superior range of models. (This involved creating a new 'image of real world structure': Figure 3.1.)

Rationality in land-use decisions

One of the first attempts by geographers to explore behaviour inductively, and thus to provide inputs for later modelling, was the series of investigations into human responses to environmental hazards, initially floods, which was organized at the University of Chicago during the late 1950s and early 1960s. Its director was Gilbert White, whose own thesis on human adjustment to floods was published in 1945. His associates developed a behaviourist approach for studying reactions to the hazards, basing this on Herbert Simon's (1957) theories of decision-making. Thus Roder (1961), for example, categorized Topeka residents according to their attitudes to the probability of future floods there, concluding that:

> Flood danger is only one of the variables affecting the choices of the flood-plain dweller, and many considerations operate to discourage a resident from leaving the flood plain, even when he is aware of the exact hazard of remaining (p. 83).

Such behaviour, it seemed, did not fit easily into the notions of profit-maximizing decision-making on which geographical theories were currently being built.

A major exponent of the behaviouristic approach was Kates (1962), who began his study of flood-plain management with the statement that 'The way men view the risks and opportunities of their uncertain environments plays a significant role in their decisions as to resource management' (p. 1). In studying such decision-making, Kates developed a schema which he claimed was relevant to a wide range of behaviours. It was based on four assumptions.

1   People are rational when making decisions. Such an assumption may be either prescriptive – describing how people should behave – or descriptive of actual behaviour. The latter seems to be the most fruitful, both for understanding past decisions and for predicting those yet to be

made. Kates suggested adoption of Simon's concept of bounded rationality as a basis for such study. According to this, decisions are made on
a rational basis, but in relation to the environment as it is perceived by
the decision-maker, which may be quite different from either 'objective
reality' or the world as seen by the researcher.

In this model, men bounded by inherent computational disabilities, products
of their time and place, seek to wrest from their environments those elements
that might make a more satisfactory life for themselves and their fellows (p. 16).

Rational decision-making is constrained, therefore, and is not necessarily the same as the maximum rationality assumed in the neo-classical
normative models discussed in earlier chapters of this book; people make
decisions in the context of the world as they observe and interpret it,
which may differ from their perceptions (including those of geographers
studying them).

2 People make choices. Many decisions are either trivial or are habitual
   so that they are accorded little or no thought immediately before they
   are made. Some major decisions regarding the environment and its use
   may also be habitual, but such behaviour usually only develops after a
   series of conscious choices has been made, which leads to a stereotyped
   response to similar situations in the future.

3 Choices are made on the basis of knowledge. Only very rarely can
   decision-makers bring together all of the information relevant to their
   task, and frequently they are unable to assimilate and use all that they
   have.

Thus, a descriptive theory of choice must deal with the well informed and the
poorly informed and the choices that men make under certainty, risk or uncertainty . . . such a theory must deal with the eventuality that not only do the
conditions of knowledge vary, but the personal perception of the same information differs (p. 19).

4 Information is evaluated according to predetermined criteria. In
   habitual choice the criterion is what was done before, but in conscious
   choice the information must be weighed according to certain rules.
   Some normative theory prescribes maximizing criteria (of profits, for
   example); descriptive theory may use Simon's notion of satisficing
   behaviour, involving decision-makers who seek a satisfactory outcome
   (a given level of profit, perhaps) only.

The results of decision-making which do not match the predictions from
the sorts of theories being used by spatial scientists do not necessarily imply
irrational behaviour, therefore. Instead, most decisions are made rationally
on the basis of a, probably non-random, selection of information, are
intended to satisfy some goal which is not to make a perfect decision, and are
based on criteria which vary somewhat from individual to individual. Having
learned a satisfactory solution to a given class of problems, decision-makers

will then continue to apply it every time such a problem occurs, unless changed circumstances require a re-evaluation.

Kates's study aimed to understand why people choose to live in areas which are prone to flooding. Their information was based on their knowledge and experience, and they could be categorized according to the certainty of their perceptions regarding further floods. In justifying their decisions, most were boundedly rational, and had made conscious choices in order to satisfy certain objectives. Similar work was reported by a number of others associated with White's leadership, and, as he points out, their findings had some impact on public policy formulation in the United States (White, 1973). The work was extended to cover a wide range of environmental hazards, providing inputs for both national policies and programmes of inter-national cooperation (Burton, Kates and White, 1978). Their initial impact on the wider geographical enterprise was not great, however, especially in the early years of their work. This was perhaps because they were operating on the boundaries between human and physical geography, which few American researchers approached, and it was probably the later work of others which brought Simon's ideas more forcefully before the geographical audience.

It is perhaps in this area of research, more than any other, in recent years that the subdisciplines of human and physical geography have come closest together. To some, such as Cooke (1985a), this is desirable not only because of the importance of such topics as human response to hazards (as in Hewitt, 1983) and society-induced modifications of the physical environment (Goudie, 1986; Cooke, 1985b), but also because of the integrating role that geographers are believed to play between the physical and the social sciences. Little of the work on these important topics does integrate the two types of science, however (Johnston, 1983a, 1986a), and though Cooke (1985a) argues that

> some extremists . . . In writing the post-war history of geography . . . will be tempted to ignore or underplay, for example, those geographers who have contributed most influentially to studies of the relations between communities, cultures and the physical environment. The names of Carl Sauer and Gilbert White, and their numerous students, will not figure prominently in their reviews (p. 146)

and it is difficult to find anything in the writings of Sauer and White that could be categorized as physical geography and reviewed as such (e.g. in K. Gregory, 1985).

The researches of Sauer, White (see Kates and Burton, 1985) and of Cooke (1985b) himself, throw a great deal of light on the interpretation and use of the natural environment by societies (Blaikie, 1985, sets it in a realist framework – see p. 223 below), and that of others explores their impact on the environment (e.g. Goudie, 1986). Such interactions have long been of interest to geographers, and a strong case has been made for retaining them as a major focus of geographical teaching (Pepper, 1987); Douglas (1983) has illustrated their importance in the urban context. But such study of the interactions, it is argued, does not integrate the study of physical and human processes (for an exploration of the semantics of this argument, see Johnston, 1986b; see also Graham, 1986): nor is such integration needed, according to Sayer (1983) –

> in human geography . . . we may be interested in the causes of flooding and this will often include 'social' as well as 'natural' events. But although floods may be the effects of social actions this does not make the floods social . . . Understanding the social character of the actions which caused the floods . . . would not be essential for understanding the latter (pp. 55–6).

The work of White and his students, of Cooke, and of many others demonstrates that people act according to 'manufactured' views of environmental resources in their conflict 'over who should benefit from the exploitation of the natural resource base' (Rees, 1985, p. xv). Geographers may well, as Pepper (1987) argues, seek to alter those views. This may eventually produce an interesting outcome in terms of future behaviour, but at present there is virtually no research that perceives the need to provide an understanding of physical processes in order to advance an appreciation of human behaviour. (Flowerdew, 1986, contends that 'basically . . . most human geography is essentially irrelevant to physical geography and *vice versa*', p. 263: Johnston, 1989b, provides an introduction to the social science literature necessary for an appreciation of how people respond to and use environments.)

Wolpert and the decision process in a spatial context

For many human geographers, it was probably a paper published by Julian Wolpert in the *Annals of the Association of American Geographers* for 1964 which introduced them to the behaviourist alternative to the normative approaches then popular. (Wolpert's paper was based on his PhD thesis submitted to the University of Wisconsin, and is further testament to the innovative qualities of the geographers there, and of their contacts with other social scientists, including agricultural economists. His research was conducted in Sweden.) The normative theory espoused by many geographers at that time assumed a rational economic decision-maker who, according to Wolpert (1964),

> is free from the multiplicity of goals and imperfect knowledge which introduce complexity into our own decision behaviour. Economic Man has a single profit goal, omniscient powers of perception, reasoning, and computation, and is blessed with perfect predictive abilities . . . the outcome of his actions can be known with perfect surety (p. 537).

In the study of spatial patterns, however,

> Allowance must be made for man's finite abilities to perceive and store information, to compute optimal solutions, and to predict the outcome and future events, even if profit were his only goal (p. 537).

Thus farmers face an uncertain environment – both physical and economic – when they make their individual land-use decisions, which in aggregate comprise the land-use map. Wolpert suggested that differences between these decisions and those that would be made by 'economic man' should reflect aspects of the farmers' economic and social environments.

Comparing the labour productivity of farms in an area of Sweden with what could have been achieved under optimizing decision-making, Wolpert decided that the farmers were probably satisficers, although such a hypothesis is difficult to verify without detailed knowledge of aspiration levels. How they acted was undoubtedly contingent upon their available information, and clear spatial variations in the levels of potential productivity achieved suggested parallel spatial variations of knowledge. Only conspicuous alternatives are considered, it was suggested, and the result is rational behaviour, adapted to an uncertain environment.

Wolpert (1965) continued this theme with studies of migration, aiming to model the decision-making which lies behind the patterns of migration reported in census volumes and assiduously analysed by spatial scientists. To him, the gravity model is inadequate as a representation of such flow patterns; indeed 'Plots of migration distances defy the persistence of the most tenacious of curve fitters' (p. 159). Boundedly rational individuals make sequential decisions, first, whether to move, and secondly, where to, and do so on the basis of place utilities, their evaluations of the degree to which each location, including that which is currently occupied, meets defined needs. Not only is the information on which these utilities are based far from complete; for many places people have none. Thus each individual has an action space – 'the set of place utilities which the individual perceives and to which he responds' (p. 163) – whose contents may deviate considerably from that portion of the 'real world' which it purports to represent. Once the first decision – to migrate – has been made, then the action space may be changed as the potential mover searches through it for potential satisfactory destinations and, if necessary, extends the space if no suitable solution to the search can be found (see Brown and Moore, 1970).

Wolpert's papers heralded – certainly in timing and to some extent in influence too – the development of what was termed behavioural geography (Cox and Golledge, 1969) 'united by a concern for the building of geographic theory on the basis of postulates regarding human behaviour . . . upon social and psychological mechanisms which have explicit spatial correlates and/or spatial structural implications' (pp. 1–3). This behavioural approach has focused on topics related to decision-making in spatial contexts. Golledge (1969, 1970), for example, looked at models of learning about space and of habitual behaviour, and with Brown investigated methods of spatial search (Golledge and Brown, 1967). Others researched into the information flows, on which decisions are based, indicating the influence of local context on behaviour (Cox, 1969), and Brown and Moore (1970) extended Wolpert's place utility and action space concepts for the study of intra-urban migration.

The aim in behavioural geography, according to a review by Golledge, Brown and Williamson (1972), has been to derive alternative theories to those based on 'economic man', 'more concerned with understanding why certain activities take place rather than what patterns they produce in space' (p. 59), which involves 'the researcher using the real world from a perspective of those individuals whose decisions affect locational or distributional patterns, and . . . trying to derive sets of empirically and theoretically sound statements about individual, small group, or mass behaviours' (p. 59): the individual is an active decision-maker, not a reactor to particular institutionally–created stimuli (Cox and Golledge, 1981; Thrift, 1981). In their evaluation of such behaviouristic endeavours, Golledge, Brown and Williamson indicate the seminal influence of Hägerstrand (1968), who used the concept of the mean information field (analogous to the action space of a place's residents) to model migration flows and the adoption of innovations. The initial interest in resource management decisions, as outlined above, was followed by an extension from environmental perception and decision-making into aspects of attitudes and motivation. These were applied to studies of migration, the diffusion of innovations, political behaviour (especially voting), perception, choice behaviour, and spatial search and learning. By studying behavioural processes in these contexts, the aspiration was to increase geographers' understanding of how spatial patterns evolve, thereby complementing their existing ability to describe such patterns. Morphological laws and systems are insufficient of themselves for understanding; the amalgamation of concepts about decision-making taken from other social sciences with geography's spatial variable would allow development of process theories that could account for the morphologies observed.

Further developments included another series of pioneering papers by Wolpert and his associates, this time relating to political decision-making. Regarding the distribution of certain artefacts in the landscape, Wolpert (1970) pointed out that the location of, for example, a public facility in an urban area frequently is the product of policy compromise:

> Sometimes the location finally chosen for a new development, or the site chosen for a relocation of an existing facility, comes out to be the site around which the least protest can be generated by those displaced. Rather than being an optimal, a rational, or even a satisfactory locational decision produced by the resolution of conflicting judgements, the decision is perhaps merely the expression of rejection by elements powerful enough to enforce their decision that another location must not be used . . . These artefacts are rarely 'the most efficient solutions', and frequently not even satisfactory neither for those responsible for their creation nor for their users (p. 220).

(This argument avoids considering any definition of optimal, in either economic or political terms.) Such decisions involve what Wolpert terms maladaptive behaviour. The work of Kates and others had suggested that decisions are adaptively rational, within the constraints of uncertainty, utility, and problem-solving ability. Coping strategies under the mutual exchange of threats between interested parties, however, can lead to decision-making which does not involve the careful and methodical investigation of alternatives until a satisfactory solution is found. Instead decisions are the consequences of conflict between groups with different attitudes and motivations, and are not the result of joint application of criteria on whose relevance there is a consensus.

> This formulation then lays the framework for the interpretation of locational decisions which appear to be more the product of stress responses than the end result of a dispassionate and considered selection of alternatives posited by the classical normative approaches or even the Simon scheme of bounded rationality (p. 224).

Wolpert and his associates have applied this formulation in a variety of contexts, such as the routes for intra-urban freeways and the siting of community mental-health facilities (Wolpert, Dear and Crawford, 1975).

Mental maps

One aspect of behavioural analysis enthusiastically adopted by a number of workers was the concept of mental map of the environment which guides the deliberations of decision-makers. The term mental map was not new to the geographical literature, having been used by Wooldridge (1956) in his descriptions of the perceived environments within which farmers make their land-use decisions. The seminal paper which revived it was published by Gould in 1966; his guiding belief was that

> If we grant that spatial behavior is our concern, then the mental images that men hold of the space around them may provide a key to some of the structures, patterns and processes of Man's work on the face of the earth (p. 182 — reference to 1973 reprint).

Increasingly, he argued, location decisions are being taken with regard to perceived environmental quality, so it is necessary to know how people evaluate their environments, and whether their views are shared by their contemporaries. To investigate such questions, Gould required respondents in various countries to rank-order places according to their preferences for them as places in which to live, and these rankings were analysed to identify their common elements — the group mental maps (Gould and White, 1974, 1986). Such maps, it was argued, are useful not only in the analysis of spatial behaviour but also in the planning of social investment — such as differential salaries to attract people to less desirable areas.

Those who followed Gould's lead investigated a range of methods for identifying and analysing spatial preferences (Pocock and Hudson, 1978). The results obtained provided little input to theoretical development, however, and Downs (1970) wrote that

> Even the most fervent proponent of the current view (that human spatial behaviour patterns can partially be explained by a study of perception) would

admit that the resultant investigations have not *yet* made a significant contribution to the development of geographic theory (p. 67).

Apart from Gould's rank-ordering procedures, Downs identified two other major approaches to the study of environmental images: the structural approach, which inquires into the nature of the spatial information stored in people's minds and which they use in their everyday lives – Lynch's (1960) book was a model for such work – and the evaluative approach, in which 'The question is, what factors do people consider important about their environment, and how, having estimated the relative importance of these factors, do they employ them in their decision-making activities' (Downs, 1970, p. 80). With this evaluative approach geographers moved into the wider field of cognitive mapping – 'a construct which encompasses those cognitive processes which enable people to acquire, code, store, recall and manipulate information about the nature of their spatial environment' (Downs and Stea, 1973, p. xiv). In this they worked alongside both psychologists, who were becoming increasingly interested in the individual's relationship to a wider area than the proximate environment and in the development of relevant non-experimental research techniques, and designers concerned with the creation of more 'liveable' environments. The journal *Environment and Behavior* was launched in 1969 to cater for this interdisciplinary market, but despite some interest (e.g. Tuan, 1975a; Downs and Stea, 1977; Pocock and Hudson, 1978; Porteous, 1977) the general field has not made a major impact within human geography. (On the links and contrasts between human geography and psychology, see Spencer and Blades, 1986.)

The concept of 'mental map' and the associated process of 'cognitive mapping' – that 'seems to imply the evocation of visual images which possess the kinds of structural properties that we are familiar with in "real" cartographic maps' (Boyle and Robinson, 1979, p. 60) – became the centre of considerable debte both among behavioural geographers and between them and outside critics. Gould's initial work, and that which it stimulated, has been criticized as the study of space preferences only (Golledge, 1981a; see also Golledge, 1980, 1981b; Guelke, 1981; Robinson, 1982). But, as Downs and Meyer (1978) make clear, 'perceptual geography' – 'the belief that human behaviour is, in large part, a function of the perceived world' (p. 60) – extends much further than the elicitation and mapping of space preferences. The fundamental argument of behavioural geography is that: (i) environmental images exist; (ii) these images can be identified accurately (as in the evaluation of landscapes: Penning-Rowsell, 1981); and (iii) 'there is a strong relationship between environmental images and actual behaviour' (Saarinen, 1979, p. 465). The nature of these images – whether they are maps in the understood sense of that word and whether they can be apprehended by researchers – remains a problem: the concept of a 'mental map' may be a red herring but, to behavioural geographers, the argument on which it is based is not. (For a review of research into cognitive mapping, see Golledge and Rushton, 1984.)

Time geography

One area of work that is sometimes identified as behavioural, but which extends into the humanistic and realist philosophies discussed in later chapters, was developed by Hägerstrand from the late 1960s on and introduced to a wider audience by Pred (1973). As interpreted by Carlstein *et al.* (1978), time and space are presented as resources that constrain activity. Any behaviour that requires movement involves individuals tracing a path simultaneously through space and time, as depicted in Figure 5.1 where movements along the horizontal axis indicate spatial traverses and those along the vertical signify the passage of time. Any journey, or lifeline, involves movement along both and thus is displayed by a line that is neither vertical nor horizontal: vertical lines indicate remaining in one place; horizontal lines are not possible for people, though they are (or virtually so) for the transmission of messages.

Movement in space and time is constrained in three ways, according to Hägerstrand. First, there are capability constraints: over time, these include the biological need for about eight hours sleep in every twenty-four; movement across space is constrained by the available means of transport. Secondly, coupling constraints require certain individuals and groups to be in particular places at stated times (teachers and pupils in schools, for example) and thus limit the range of mobility during 'free time'. Finally, authority constraints may preclude individuals from being in stated places at defined times. Together, these three define the time-space prism (Figure 5.1) which contains all of the possible lifelines available to an individual who starts at a particular location and has to return there by a given time.

Pred (1977) claims that time geography 'has the potential for shedding new light on some of the very different kinds of questions customarily posed by 'old-fashioned' regional and historical geographers, as well as 'modern' human geographers' (p. 207) because

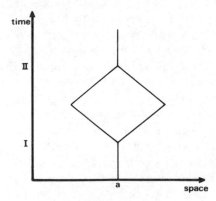

Fig 5.1   The time-space prism. In this simple example a person starts at point a: he cannot leave this point until time I and he must return to it by time II: the prism between those times indicates his maximum available spatial range.

It is . . . a great challenge . . . to cease taking distance itself so seriously . . .
to accept that space and time are universally and inseparably wed to one
another; to realize that questions pertaining to human organization of the
earth's surface, human ecology, and landscape evolution cannot divorce the fini-
tudes of space and time . . . It is a challenge to turn to the 'choreography' of
individual and collective existence — to reject the excesses of inter- and intra-
disciplinary specialization for a concern with collateral processes (p. 218).

It was, then, in part a critique of spatial analysis as the dominant concern
of human geographers. But to Hägerstrand it was much more, for the problems that he wished to address were concerned with the quality-of-life implications of packing people together in space and time. This is made clear in
some of his later writings: for example (Hägerstrand, 1984), we are enabled to

see existing together what we otherwise have chosen to see apart. Neighbour
meets neighbour in some sort of association. My concern now will be with how
their presence together has come about, how they go along together and what
is going to happen ahead in time (p. 375).

For this exploration of what Pred (1977, p. 213) calls the 'principle of
togetherness', Hägerstrand employs three concepts — path, project, and
diorama. A path (or lifeline in the earlier terminology) is very simply a 'succession of situations' (Hägerstrand, 1982, p. 323) traced by an individual. To
study paths alone is just to map outcomes (in the same way that other behavioural geographers map migrations or shopping trips), but that tells nothing
about the

living body subject, endowed with memories, feelings, knowledge, imagination
and goals — in other words capabilities too rich for any conceivable kind of
symbolic representation but decisive for the direction of paths (p. 324).

Paths are created by people pursuing projects towards goals — which may be
mere survival. Studying paths alone may divulge very little about the 'purpose
and meaning' behind the events that they incorporate. Projects, then, produce
paths and the intersections of those paths produce situations, particular
moments in the flow of history in particular places. For geographers, study
of such situations has traditionally involved the concept of landscape, devised
to represent 'the momentary thereness and relative location of all continuants'
(p. 325). To Hägerstrand, however, this concept insufficiently incorporates

the human body subjects, the keepers of memories, feelings, thoughts and intentions and initiators of projects (p. 320).

He prefers the concept of diorama, normally used to denote museum displays
which depict (statically) people and animals in their usual environments. To
Hägerstrand, the concept implies that

All sorts of entities are in touch with each other in a mixture produced by history,
whether visible or not . . . [we] appreciate how situations evolve as an aggregate
outcome quite apart from the specific intentions actors might have had when
they conceived and launched projects out of their different positions (p. 320).

He illustrates this with a description of his childhood home, using it to demonstrate the importance of coupling and authority, as well as capability, constraints on the flow of daily life and the dioramas (particular situations) that resulted. The study of paths alone is insufficient if time geography is adequately to portray the 'real life of real people' (p. 338), and autobiographical material is promoted (as in Buttimer, 1983; Billinge, Gregory and Martin, 1984) as an important source on projects and dioramas because

> Only one's own experience is able to provide the kind of intimate detail which can bring the study of project and situation into any real depth. He is after all an expert on his own networks of meanings (p. 338).

Hägerstrand's initial work, and its interpretation by others, focused on the study of paths, and thus to many was set in the positivist mould of other behavioural geography enterprises. Indeed, it was this aspect only of time geography that was presented in an introductory review by Thrift (1977) who emphasized that a ' "physicalist" approach is the backbone' (p. 4). With it, for example, Parkes and Thrift (1980) sought 'to place time firmly in the minds of human geographers' (p. xi) in an approach that they termed chrono-geographical, arguing that 'Together, territories, societies and times are the principal components of urban and social geography' (p. 34).

The concept of diorama, and the 'togetherness' of a situation that it denotes, was absent from these early presentations, apart from passing vague references such as Thrift's (1977, p. 7) quoting of Hägerstrand (1975) that 'every situation is inevitably rooted in past situations'. Projects are mentioned too – as in Thrift's (1977) statement that 'All human beings have *goals*. To attain these they must have projects, series of *tasks* which act as a vehicle for goal attainment and which, when added up, form a *project*' (p. 7), but it is implicit that those projects can be treated in the same sort of aggregate data analysis and policy prescription (see Palm and Pred, 1978) that characterizes most behavioural geography. Van Paassen (1981), however, argued that Hägerstrand's work is essentially humanistic, aiming 'to provide insight into what is specifically human in man's nature and . . . [to] elucidate the specific human situation' (p. 18), an argument accepted by Hägerstrand (1982) in his reference to human intentions. More recently, the concept of diorama has led authors to associate Hägerstrand's work not so much with the humanistic approaches outlined later in this chapter but rather with the realist proposals discussed in Chapter 8. The social theorist Giddens (1984), for example, draws heavily on Hägerstrand in his arguments for a structurationist approach (see below p. 236), though he too stresses the physicalist and behavioural elements when noting that

> Hägerstrand's approach is based mainly upon identifying sources of constraint over human activity given by the nature of the body and the physical contexts in which activity occurs (p. 111).

(Note, however, Gregson's, 1986, critique of Giddens's attempts to incorporate time geography into structuration theory.)

Criticisms of time geography have, not surprisingly, focused on the physicalist description of paths. Thus Baker (1979) argued that

> While space and time may usefully be considered as resources whose competitive allocation gives rise to patterns of use which may be observed empirically and modelled theoretically, the nature of that human struggle to control and structure time and space — the process underlying the form — should be of paramount concern rather than descriptions of temporal or spatial organization (p. 563).

As with other aspects of spatial science, description of the outcomes, however sophisticated, cannot elucidate the processes involved in their production. (Processes here are defined as mechanisms, the products of human agency, and not just sequences: see Boots and Getis, 1978; Haining, 1981; Hay and Johnston, 1983.) The response to Baker from Thrift and Pred (1981) denied his physicalist interpretation; to them

> time-geography is much more than that. It is a discipline-transcending and still evolving perspective on the everyday workings of society and the biographies of individuals. It is a highly flexible and growing language, a way of thinking about the world at large as well as the events and experiences, or content, of one's own life (p. 277).

They argued that time geographers are necessarily concerned with underlying processes, with the ideological uses of time and space as devices to channel individual paths, and with the crucial role of human agency in the production of particular situations. Thus they tie time geography into Giddens's ideas on structuration and with developing marxist humanism. They conclude that

> Some see the graphs used in time-geography as just neat pieces of art but others, in turn, are able to internalize the perspective represented by the graphs and use the path and project language as a way of thinking about themselves and the world. This will we believe be *the* lasting legacy of time-geography (p. 284).

Baker's (1981) response was largely positive, accepting that time geography could be of value in a reorientation of geographical work:

> we should be examining the social organization of space and time, not the spatial and temporal organization of society for this is to put the cart before the horse (p. 440).

Gregory (1985a) is more cautious, however, arguing that Hägerstrand too readily focuses on paths rather than on the people whose projects fashion those paths, thereby failing to explore the meanings that are hidden beneath the tasks that define the biographies.

Methods in behavioural geography

Whereas the theory- and model-builders of the spatial-science school of human geographers received much of their stimulus from neo-classical economics, in some cases via regional science, the alliance for behavioural geography was largely with the social sciences having a major empirical content, notably psychology and sociology. The behaviouristic approach is an inductive one, with the aim being to build general statements out of observations of ongoing processes. The areas studied were very much determined by the work in the spatial science school. As Brookfield's statement quoted at the beginning of the next chapter suggests, the models and theories of the latter, such as central place theory, raised many of the queries which the behaviourists, stimulated by their observations of the failings of such theories when matched against the 'real world', sought to follow up. In terms of the accepted route to scientific explanation (Figure 3.1), therefore, behavioural geography involved moving outside the accepted cyclic procedure to input new sets of observations on which superior theories might be based. In doing this, the behaviourists did not really move far from the spatial-science ethos. Indeed, many of their methods were those of their predecessors; Gould's mental map studies, for example, used the same technical apparatus as the factorial ecologies (p. 82).

Somewhat away from this general orientation of behavioural work, Pred (1967, 1969) presented an ambitious alternative to theory-building based on 'economic men' in his two-volume work *Behavior and Location*. He began with a critique of existing location theory based on three groups of objections: those concerned with logical inconsistency – it is impossible for competing decision-makers to arrive at optimal location decisions simultaneously; those concerned with motives – maximizing versus satisficing; and those concerned with human ability to collect, assimilate and use all possible information. Thus (Pred, 1967):

> Bunge's theoretical geography is easily distinguished from geographical location theory because its optimal final goals are disassociated from the interpretation of real-world economic phenomena . . . and because these same goals can only yield a body of theory that for all intents and purposes is totally abehavioral and static rather than dynamic (p. 17).

Decisions on locations and on land use are made with imperfect knowledge by fallible individuals. As a result there is bound to be some disorder in the ensuing spatial patterns. (For another critique, see Barnes, 1988.)

As an alternative to the forms of theory-building which he attacked, Pred proposed the use of a behavioural matrix (Figure 5.2), whose axes are quantity and quality of information available and the ability to use that information: completely informed rational decision-makers are located in the bottom right-hand corner. Because of the nature and importance of information flows, position on the first axis depends in part on the decision-maker's spatial location; on the second, position would reflect aspiration levels, experience, and the norms of any groups to which the individual belonged. Different people in different positions in the matrix would vary in their decisions, therefore; indeed, two at the same position may act on different bases and in different ways.

Individuals do not stay at the same position in the matrix, and spatial patterns are not static. Thus in his second volume, Pred (1969) introduced a dynamic element by shifting individuals through the matrix; as they shift, and change their decisions, so the environment changes for others. As people learn, they both acquire more and better information, and become more skilled in its use; they shift towards the bottom right-hand corner of the matrix, some of them in advance of others, who benefit from the activities of the 'decision-leaders'. The unsuccessful are gradually eliminated, so that with time a concentration of 'good' decision-makers close to the optimum position evolves. But changes in the external environment produce parametric shocks, which result in decision-makers becoming less informed and less certain; as a consequence they are shifted back towards the upper left-hand corner and another learning cycle begins. As long as parametric shocks occur more frequently than the learning experience takes, an optimal location pattern will never emerge, except perhaps by chance.

Pred (1969) presented the behavioural matrix as a 'gross first approximation' (p. 91), arguing that any theory is better than none (p. 139), even if the model itself is literally untestable (p. 141: see also Pred and Kibel, 1968). Harvey (1969b) treated it to a scathing review, however, calling the two dimensions of the matrix vaguely defined, ambiguous, unoperational, and an oversimplification of the complex nature of behaviour. Indeed, Harvey (1969c) was generally sceptical about the potential of a behavioural location theory, a view shared by Olsson (1969), who pointed out the difficulties of studying processes and demonstrated that much behavioural geography involved only the inferring of processes from aggregated data on individual behaviour. Others argued that such inference could be very strong, however. Rushton (1969), for example, accepted that any one pattern of behaviour —

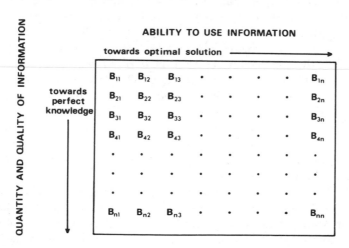

Fig 5.2 The behavioural matrix
Source: Pred (1967, p. 25)

what he termed *behaviour in space* – was largely a function of the spatial structure within which it occurred (the choice of shopping centres by a population, for example), but he claimed that general rules of *spatial behaviour* could be deduced from examining the types of preferences displayed within a particular pattern:

> To say that these preferences do not exist independently of the environment where the decision is made is to argue that environments could exist about which the person would be unable to reach a decision (p. 393).

Thus a distance-decay pattern reflects the details of the environment in which it is observed, but to produce it people must make decisions based on certain rules which they apply, and Rushton developed a procedure for isolating those rules. Its validity has been queried, however (Pirie, 1976), and, like Pred's behavioural matrix, it has not attracted many disciples. (Rushton's arguments suggest activity in a 'taken-for-granted world: see p. 179.)

Harvey (1969c) suggested two alternatives to behavioural location theory – further development of normative theory and the construction of a stochastic location theory. He felt that both of these offered more immediate pay-offs in terms of understanding spatial patterns than did behavioural efforts, because of the conceptual and measurement problems of the latter. The stochastic approach was also favoured by Curry (1967b), who argued that large-scale patterns are the outcomes of small-scale indeterminacy; individual choices may be random within certain constraints, but when very many of them are aggregated they may display considerable order (see above, p. 124). Similarly, Webber (1972) attempted to model locational decision-making processes in states of uncertainty using normative approaches: his conclusion was that 'uncertainty increases agglomeration economies' (p. 279), thereby leading to greater concentration of economic activities and people into cities than would be predicted by models based on 'economic men'. Game theory is a mathematical procedure developed to handle decision-making in uncertainty, but it has received little attention from human geographers (Gould, 1963); the most ambitious attempt to build on such theories, which has had very little impact, is Isard *et al.* (1969). To some, then, micro-analysis at the level of the individual is either impossible, unnecessary or misleading, and macro-analysis provides sufficient insight to the behaviour that produces aggregate patterns. Both are needed according to Watson (1978), however, with macro-analysis as the first step providing the overview that poses questions which can only be answered by behavioural study.

The behavioural approach has not brought about a revolution away from the spatial-science focus within human geography, therefore, and in effect has become an attachment to it. Whereas various normative approaches start with certain assumptions, usually simplifying ones, about human behaviour, and then deduce what spatial patterns follow from such axioms, the behaviourists have sought to modify the assumptions by an inductive procedure which seeks the rules of behaviour that can be used to predict (and therefore explain) spatial patterns (Gale and Golledge, 1982). In its entirety, this latter approach involves a sequence of interrelated investigations. An individual is faced with a decision, either one with a direct spatial input or one with spatial consequences. To make that decision, the individual sets criteria, collects information, and then evaluates the information against the criteria. As a result of the evaluation, a decision to act might be made, or instead the outcome is to change criteria, to collect more information, or to do both. (In this way, the problem-solving is very similar to the procedures of the scientific method outlined in Figure 3.1.) Many investigations have not gone through this full sequence, however, but have focused on certain aspects of it, such as the flow of information, from which characteristics of other elements in the sequence may be inferred.

Whereas very many of the studies in the spatial science school reviewed in earlier chapters could be conducted using either published data sources (such as censuses) or relatively small field-collection exercises, the behavioural approach has required much more effort on the part of human geographers in data collection from the individual decision-makers. This need to conduct social surveys of various kinds has furthered the growing links between geographers and sociologists, psychologists, and, to a lesser extent, political scientists, and has led to an expansion in the data-handling procedures necessary for the training of geographers. One of the problems in their use is that many of the topics studied in human geography involve very large numbers of individual decisions – as in migrations, journeys to work and to shop, voting decisions, and so on. Very large sample surveys may be necessary to produce valid generalizations about such behaviour, but resource limitations have meant concentration on both small selections and only limited segments of the full behavioural sequence. Thus, for example, Brown and Moore's (1970) schema for the study of intra-urban migration decisions has mainly been tested in part only (e.g. Clark, 1975, 1981). More success with use of the behavioural sequence has probably been achieved in those branches of human geography that deal with topics involving relatively few decision-makers. In the study of diffusion, for example, Brown (1975) has attempted to divert attention away from overall patterns of spatial spread and the reasons for adoption (or not) to the decision-making which brings certain innovations to places; most of these innovations involve the selling of products, and so he terms them 'consumer innovations' (see also Brown, 1981). Similarly, a number of industrial geographers have moved from investigations of aggregate patterns, which could be compared to those predicted by application of neo-classical economic analysis (Smith, 1971), to the study of decision-making behaviour within firms (e.g. Hamilton, 1974; Carr, 1983; Hayter and Watts, 1983).

Within behavioural geography, a major trend during the 1980s was the growing sophistication of its analytical procedures. In terms of output, most of this work involved analysing patterns of behaviour within the framework set by the spatial science approach and its general positivist orientation. The goal was to explain, through mathematical modelling and statistical analysis, variations in an aspect of behaviour (choice of travel mode for the journey-to-work, for example) in terms of variations in a number of independent variables (such as the characteristics of the decision-makers and the milieux in which their decisions were made). Data for such studies are usually categorical in form, involving classifications (which travel mode was used, for example, and the gender of the person concerned) rather than variables measured on interval or ratio scales. Much work was done by behavioural geographers exploring the relevant statistical procedures for the analysis of such data; Wrigley (1985) provided a major overview of the various methods, and Davies and Pickles (1985) explored the important issue of inferring secular trends from cross-sectional data. Similarly, methods of quantifying attitudes and other aspects of human characteristics and behaviour have been explored, involving both increasingly sophisticated survey instruments for investigating how people cognise and learn about their spatial environments (Golledge and Timmermans, 1990) and technical procedures for representing those cognitions quantitatively (see Aitken *et al.*, 1989).

Many of the choice models which underpin the work in behavioural geography, and which have become increasingly explicit in the more sophisticated work reported in the 1980s, are based on theories of utility maximization. This approach was heralded in early work by, for example, Cadwallader (1975), exemplified in fuller detail by Wrigley and Longley (1984), and became the basis for a burgeoning literature (as displayed in great detail in Golledge and Timmermans, 1988, and reviewed in Timmermans and Golledge, 1990). According to such theories, selections are made by decision-makers from within the choice sets presented to them (and which they perceive), according to the utility which they allocate to each of the alternatives evaluated: as Timmermans and Golledge (1990) express it, all 'are based on (variants of) a conceptual model that explicitly relates choice behaviour to the environment through consideration of perceptions, preference formation and decision-making' (utility being a measure of preference). Thus a full analysis of discrete choices involves knowing each of: the available choice set; the elements of the choice set considered by each individual; the criteria on which each member of the choice set was evaluated by individual decision-makers; and the relative importance they attached to each criterion. Bird (1989), following Desbarats (1983), illustrates this (Figure 5.3): the process starts with all possible opportunities, some of which are discarded to form an 'objective choice set'; some elements of that set are then discarded after evaluation, to produce an 'effective choice set'; and further evaluation leads to its reduction to a 'target choice set' within which the final selection is made. A potential house-buyer in a particular town, for example, 'discards' many of the possibles available through ignorance, and then whittles down those perceived as viable buys to a final list from which the selection is made.

Behavioural geography is now widely accepted within the positivist orientation. It seeks to account for spatial patterns within the environment by

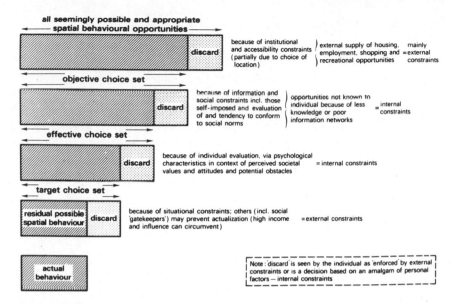

Fig 5.3 Bird's representation (after Desbarats) of choice sets in the spatial decision-making process
Source: Bird (1989, p. 145)

establishing generalizations about people-environment interrelationships, and then using these as a basis for change through environmental planning activities that 'modify the stimuli which affect the spatial behavior of ourselves and others' (Porteous, 1977, p. 12). According to Gold's (1980) text, this approach is built on four main features:

1   The environment in which individuals act is that which they perceive, which 'may well differ markedly from the true nature of the real world' (p. 4).
2   Individuals interact with their environments, responding to them and reshaping them.
3   The focus of study is the individual, not the group.
4   Behavioural geography is multidisciplinary.

Within this general framework, research methods vary substantially but the general orientation – inductive generalization leading to planning for environmental change – remains. Eventually, it is hoped, a 'powerful new theory' (Cox and Golledge, 1969) will emerge. As yet, it has not (Golledge, 1981a, p. 1338; see also p. 144), but Golledge argues that substantial advances in understanding spatial behaviour have been made by studying 'individual preferences, opinions, attitudes, cognitions, cognitive maps, perceptions, and so on' (p. 1339) – what he terms process variables.

Approaches to Behavioural Geography

Apart from the technical issues, the positivist foundation of most work in behavioural geography has been subject to considerable debate, as part of a wider consideration of the relevance of that philosophy of social science to human geography. Major contributions to this debate have been made by Golledge, a leading practitioner of behavioural geography. He argues that positivism is a constraining philosophy, and that (Couclelis and Golledge, 1983)

> behavioural geography has evolved by gradually shedding the tenets of the philosophy out of which it was born, as these have come to be seen as barriers to further progress and understanding (pp. 333–4).

He prefers' to use the term *analytical research* to describe his preferred approach, which is

> not so much a philosophy as a distinct mode of discourse, a space of possibilities for theoretical languages that meet the criteria of clarity, coherence, inter-subjective validity, and a concern never to lose sight of experience (p. 334).

Nevertheless, he retains one of the central tenets of the positivist programme, as illustrated by references to 'a search for generalizations' (Golledge and Couclelis, 1984, p. 181), 'significant generalizations . . . about particular sub-groups' (Golledge, 1980, p. 16) and the need to shift research away from 'the more narrow perspective of behaviour in space' towards 'a general under-standing of spatial behaviour' (Golledge and Rushton, 1984, p. 30; see also p. 152 above). A fuller discussion of the main aspects of positivism is provided by Hill (1982), who argues that 'those who adhere to many of its central tenets rarely describe themselves as positivists' (p. 43). He presents a ten-point self-assessment scale, on which many would probably find that they have 'positivist leanings'; how far you have to lean before you are one is not clear, however!

Golledge's preferred classification of the research approach that he espouses as *analytical behavioural geography* is based, according to Golledge and Stimson (1987, 9), on 'what is truly positive in positivist thought'. They reject what they call the 'classic positivist separation of value and fact' and argue for a positivist position which is able to 'interpret values and beliefs in a scientific manner'. This they term a transactional or interactionist position, which is characterised by: '(a) the importance of logical and mathematical thinking; (b) the need for public verifiability of results; (c) the search for generalisation; (d) the emphasis on analytic languages for researching and expressing knowledge structures; and (e) the importance of hypotheses testing and the importance of selecting the most appropriate bases for generalisation or theorising'. The goal is clearly the development of quantitatively verified theory (Macmillan, 1989b).

This continued emphasis of key elements of the positivist philosophy links to the second, much less important in volumetric terms, type of work within the behavioural approach. As Pipkin (1981) notes, much effort has been expended on the identification of behaviour patterns but little has been done on exploring the mental constructs that underpin behaviour. To this extent, understanding why people behave as they do has not been advanced very far; as Greenberg (1984) expresses it

> For the most part, the intention of behavioural – perceptual geographers has not been to explain the spatial organization of society, but to illuminate the spatial behavior of individuals (p. 193).

Recently, the field of Artificial Intelligence (AI) has been proposed as one which offers much to the study of cognitive processes (T. Smith, 1984), using computer-modelling procedures to represent the decision-making processes and thereby gaining insights (by analogy) to the nature of the human brain; as Couclelis (1986a) indicates, this involves the 'human computer' metaphor according to which

> cognitive functions such as problem-solving, pattern-recognition, decision-making, learning, and natural language understanding are investigated by means of computer programs that purport to replicate the corresponding mental processes (p. 2).

Clearly, the ability to replicate the processes by predicting their outcomes (as in Smith, Clark and Cotton, 1984) is not necessarily to be equated with understanding those processes (see p. 115 on the instrumentalist approach): as Couclelis (1986a) says in concluding a detailed discussion of the utility of AI to the study of human behaviour

> reliable predictions can be made about intentional systems even by theories which . . . are totally vacuous psychologically (p. 111).

Whether one wants to know *how* people behave, or *why*, is crucial: AI can reproduce the former, it is claimed, but can it help with the latter? Nystuen (1984) doubts the former claim, arguing that

> I see little potential in AI methods available today in addressing problems considered important in the spatial decision-making literature, such as the decision to migrate . . . These processes would require elaborate models of spatial cognition and tradeoff behavior whereas even the simplest model of a child's wayfinding is complex and contains major unresolved methodological problems (p. 358).

Nevertheless, if the claim could be sustained, Nystuen would welcome the output. He accepts that it would provide only a constructed explanation (see the discussion of Lukerman's arguments above, p. 76) but

> I am struck by the fact that careful empirical analysis by biologists describing the anatomy and behavior of bats did not lead to the discovery of how bats navigated in the dark. The explanation was beyond imagination until a purely

> human system (radar, followed by sonar) was invented and by analogy applied
> to the behavior and anatomy of the bat. Then all the things fell into place
> (p. 359).

In other words, if you can reproduce a process, then you may well gain some
appreciation of it. As Nystuen puts it

> If a constructed computer program can repeatedly resolve an issue under
> varying spatial conditions in a way that is considered useful to geographers, then
> one might say that we understand the issue. This is a sufficient claim: the
> problem has been solved by whatever logic or capacities the program has at
> hand. There is no need to claim that this is necessarily the way human spatial
> decision-making works (p. 359).

Such an instrumentalist argument is rejected by others however (e.g. Gregory,
1980), giving rise to the cases against positivist work outlined in other parts
of this book.

Moving On

In a review published in 1981, Thrift (1981, 359) suggested that:

> The halcyon days of behavioural geography are long gone. With them have
> passed the days when behavioural geographers made inflated claims for the
> explanatory power of their subject area. But the subject area still has its place
> in human geography.

He recognized the criticisms of behavioural work, both from those who
perceived it as presenting the individual decision-maker as little more than
an automaton responding to stimuli as if programmed and from those who
claimed that it ignored the importance of society as a whole greater than the
sum of its individual parts. (These two sets of criticisms represent the views
discussed in detail in Chapters 6 and 8 below.) This led him to accept that
behavioural geography might be presented as 'half-blind':

> But to say that behavioural geography is therefore half-blind is not to say that
> it can see nothing at all. Its explanations may be limited. That does not mean
> that they are therefore non-existent.

In other words, behavioural geography has provided a useful methodology
that can be validly employed within the wider set employed by human
geographers.

   If Thrift's conclusion were valid, this would lead one to anticipate a
slowing-down in the pace of work within behavioural geography. In many
ways, it could be argued that the opposite has occurred, that the volume of
work conducted and reported during the 1980s (and summarized in reviews
such as Golledge and Rushton, 1984; Golledge and Timmermans, 1990; and
Timmermans and Golledge, 1990) has remained substantial and, in the

context of the model of normal science outlined above (p. 13), achieved substantial progress. It could also be claimed, however, that behavioural geography has not only become a minority (albeit a strong minority) interest but has also become increasingly isolated within human geography, because of the theoretical and analytical sophistication achieved by its leading practitioners. While many human geographers have accepted the need to collect and analyse individual data through questionnaire and similar methods, in order to portray how people learn about, represent and behave in space, relatively few have kept pace with the methodological developments reviewed above. Thus what we appear to have is a topic which has both made a general impact upon geographical pratice and has been advanced by a small group of specialists somewhat apart from the mainstream.

An example of the vitality of that group of specialists is given by Golledge and Stimson's (1987) text on *Analytical Behavioural Geography*. They introduce the approach, and its origins in the 1960s, as a recognition that (p. 1):

> in order to exist in and to comprehend any given environment, people had to learn to organise critical subsets of information from the mass of experiences open to them. They sense, store, record, organise and use bits of information for the ultimate purpose of coping with the everyday task of living. In doing this, they create knowledge structures based on information selected from the mass of 'to whom it may concern' messages emanating from the world in which we live. Different elements from these various environments are given different

The Man-Environment Behavioural Interface

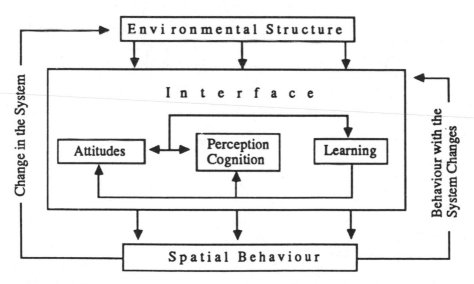

Fig 5.4 Golledge and Stimson's representation of the society-environment interface
Source: Golledge and Stimson (1987, p. 11)

meanings and have different values attached to them. It was the explicit recognition of the relationship between cognition, environment and behaviour that initially helped to develop behavioural research in geography.

They then illustrate how the work developed, and structure the subdiscipline's approach through a diagram which places the individual decision-makers at the interface between environment and behaviour, learning and acting within the environment and changing it as they act (Figure 5.4). The organization of their book, covering both the methods used by behavioural geographers and their substantive achievements in various topical areas, provides a clear view of a vital subdiscipline, as does the size of their bibliography, along with the large number of other pieces listed in the review papers on which parts of this chapter have drawn.

6

Humanistic Geography

Behavioural geography involves a reorientation of the work undertaken within the spatial science approach, but maintains its generally positivist framework. Alongside it, from the early 1970s on, though with roots extending much further back, a fundamental critique of the positivist approach emerged, including that of behavioural geography as practised by Golledge and others. It, too, promoted a focus on the individual as decision-maker, but denied the goal of explanation and prediction that was inherent to the behavioural approach. It was not a coherent body of opinion in terms of the alternatives that it proposed to positivism, but it was united in its critical stance of what was being promoted as the 'new geography'. (A recent, cogent presentation of this case is provided by Cosgrove, 1989a, 1989b.) The nature of the criticisms, the alternatives, and the developing practice are the subject of the present chapter. (For an alternative essay as part of the same task, see Pickles, 1986.)

Cultural and Historical Behavioural Geography

As indicated in earlier chapters, workers in cultural and historical geography were neither closely involved in nor attracted by the so-called quantitative and theoretical revolutions. There was some application of statistical procedures, as attempts to make work in these fields appear more 'modern' – several of these attempts were by non-historical (e.g. Pitts, 1965) and non-cultural geographers – but few changes of substance in the approaches adopted. But by the 1970s, historical and cultural geographers had taken the initiative, and were proposing alternative philosophies to that of positivism, philosophies which were humanistic in their orientation.

The beginnings of these changes can be traced to two papers, one of which had more impact than the other on the geographical discipline at large. In the first, John K. Wright (1947) introduced the term *geosophy*, defined as the study of geographical knowledge:

it covers the geographical ideas, both true and false, of all manners of people — not only geographers, but farmers and fishermen, business executives and poets, novelists and painters, Bedouins and Hottentots — and for this reason it necessarily has to do with subjective conceptions (p. 12).

Wright conceded that study of such subjective ideas was not open to the employment of the strict scientific principles of physical geography, but claimed that it provided indispensable background and perspective to geographical work:

geographical knowledge of one kind or another is universal among men, and is in no sense a monopoly of geographers . . . such knowledge is acquired in the first instance through observations of many kinds. . . . Its acquisition, in turn, is conditioned by the complex interplay of cultural and psychological factors . . . nearly every important activity in which man engages, from hoeing in a field or writing a book or conducting a business to spreading a gospel or waging a war, is to some extent affected by the geographical knowledge at his disposal (pp. 13–14).

These words could well have heralded an earlier start to behavioural geography than that chronicled here, but apparently, by the lack of reference to them in later published works, they had little impact until taken up by Wright's colleague at the American Geographical Society, David Lowenthal (1961), in a widely cited paper 'concerned with *all* geographic thought, scientific and other: how it is acquired, transmitted, altered and integrated into conceptual systems' (p. 259). In a wide-ranging survey, Lowenthal argues that the world of each individual's experience is intensely parochial and covers but a small fraction of the total available. There are consensus views about many aspects of the world, but often individuals will mistakenly assume that their view is the consensus. We all live in personal worlds, which are 'both more and less inclusive than the common realm' (p. 248). Our perceptions of these personal worlds are personal too; they are not fantasies, being firmly rooted in reality, but because 'we elect to see certain aspects of the world and to avoid others' (p. 251) behaviour based on such perceptions must have its unique elements. Different cultures have their own shared stereotypes, however, which are often reflected in language, and they attempt to create environments fitting into these stereotypes:

The surface of the earth is shaped for each person by refraction through cultural and personal lenses of custom and fancy. We are all artists and landscape architects, creating order and organizing space, time, and causality in accordance with our apperceptions and predilections (p. 260).

These ideas were put into practice in other papers concerned with the interpretation of landscapes as reflections of societal norms and tastes (e.g. Lowenthal, 1968; Lowenthal and Prince, 1965), thereby belatedly bringing Wright's ideas before a wider, and perhaps more readily appreciative, audience.

The second of the original papers was by a British geographer, although it was published in India (Kirk, 1951; it is reprinted in Boal and Livingstone, 1989): the main arguments were reiterated in a later article (Kirk, 1963). He, too, stressed that the environment is not simply a 'thing' but rather a whole with 'shape, cohesiveness and meaning added to it by the act of human perception' (Kirk, 1963, p. 365): once this meaning has been ascribed, it tends to be passed to later generations. Thus Kirk recognizes two, separate but not independent, environments; a phenomenal environment, which is the totality of the earth's surface, and a behavioural environment, which is the perceived and interpreted portion of the phenomenal environment:

> Facts which exist in the Phenomenal Environment but do not enter the Behavioural Environment of a society have no relevance to rational, spatial behaviour and consequently do not enter into problems of the Geographical Environment (p. 367).

Since much of geography is concerned with decision-making and its consequences, appreciation of the behavioural environment should be central to the study of geography. Indeed, according to Ley (1977a), one cannot proceed without such awareness of what is in the behavioural environment; even an apparently neutral statement such as 'Pittsburgh is a steel town' is, he argues, a value-laden view of a geographer-outsider, which may not accord with the perceptions of the resident-insiders. Thus:

> Too often there is the danger that our geography reflects our own concerns, and not the meanings of the people and places we write of. . . . The geographical fact is as thoroughly a social product as the landscape to which it is attached (p. 12).

Scientific disciplines, as indicated in Chapter 1, can be divided into their 'invisible colleges', groups of scholars working on the same topic who refer to each other's publications. Wright, Lowenthal and Kirk were not members of any major college during the early 1960s, and so had very little impact on the first phase of behavioural work identified earlier in this chapter. (None of the three, for example, is in Pred's (1967, 1969) bibliographies, nor is any one referred to by Wolpert: Golledge, Brown and Williamson (1972, p. 75) make only a passing reference to Lowenthal's work – 'Pursued by insightful researchers, the analysis of literary and other artistic data of past and present can have strong explanatory power. The subjective element in these attempts to assess the impact of spatial perception is acknowledged, but its presence in many other studies is more subtle and potentially damaging'. Note, however, Kirk's, 1978, p. 388, reference to his influence on non-geographers who adopted the concept of the behavioural environment. Spate, 1989, refers to Kirk's initial paper, and the discussion of it at an IBG Conference, as 'the Catalytic Crystal in the Saturated Solution', p. xix – for a detailed exegesis of Kirk's work, see Campbell, 1989.) The behavioural work of the mid-1960s was in the positivist mould; that of the three authors just discussed was not.

Several cultural and historical geographers took up the concepts of the behavioural or perceived environments. Among the former, one of the leaders was Brookfield, a British geographer with field experience, by the mid-1960s, of South Africa, Mauritius, New Guinea, and several Pacific Islands. In reviewing work by cultural geographers on alien societies, he noted (Brookfield, 1964):

> A difference of approach is apparent between those who have an overtly choro-
> graphic purpose, who scarcely ever seek explanations in matters such as human
> behaviour, attitudes and beliefs, social organization, and the characteristics and
> interrelationships of human groups, and those whose inquiries are not primarily
> chorographic, and who are more inclined to undertake a search for processes
> as a means of reaching explanation (p. 283).

Social organization, Brookfield argued, is the key to many explanations, so that:

> when an individual human geographer is sitting down in one small corner of
> a foreign land, and seeks to interpret the geography of that small corner, then
> it is difficult for him to do so without trying to comprehend the perception of
> environment among the inhabitants (p. 287).

But geographers had largely failed to delve into such details of social organization, because of the broad areal scale at which they had tended to work, their
concern with distributions rather than with processes, and their avoidance
of what he terms 'micro-geography'. Inquiry in human geography should
involve three stages:

1 general statements about areal patterns and interrelationships;
2 detailed local inquiries which follow up the questions about processes
   raised by these general statements; and
3 organization of the general and local material to produce explanatory
   generalizations.

Brookfield's argument was for more micro-geographical studies at the second
of these stages, providing the basis for the development of comparative
methods with which generalizations could be forged (Brookfield, 1962).

Brookfield (1969) later surveyed the literature which showed that 'decision-
makers operating on an environment base their decisions on the environment
as they perceive it, not as it is. The action resulting from decision, on the other
hand, is played out in a real environment' (p. 53). Referring to the 'modern'
behavioural work, as well as the studies of cultural geographers, he pointed
out the great problems involved in isolating the perceived environment –
something which is 'complex, monistic, distorted and discontinuous, unstable
and full of unwoven irrelevancies' (p. 74) – and in building it into an analytical methodology. Further data are needed, too, on such topics as work-
organization, time-allocation and budget-allocation, on the meaning of
consumption and of distance – all necessary tasks for the full understanding
of people-environment systems.

The concept of the perceived environment has a considerable pedigree in historical-geographical scholarship, though without the current terminology; a major example of its use is Glacken's (1956, 1967) survey of societal attitudes to environments (see also N. Smith, 1984, and Pepper, 1984). Historical geographers, it has been suggested (Prince, 1971a), must study a trilogy of worlds: the real world, as recorded in documents and in the landscape; the abstract world, as depicted by general models of spatial order in the past; and the perceived world: 'Past worlds, seen through the eyes of contemporaries, perceived according to their culturally acquired preferences and prejudices, shaped in the images of their assumed worlds' (p. 4). From these three, it may be possible to provide explanations of landscape changes, which cannot be obtained from the assumed processes provided by continua of data over time (see also Moodie and Lehr, 1976): as Prince (1961–2, p. 21) expressed it 'it (is) the province of the intellect to observe the facts, to reduce them to order and to discover relationships among them, but it (is) the imagination which (gives) them meaning through the exercise of judgement and insight'. Reconstruction of past environments is extremely difficult, however, for it involves seeing the written record through the cultural lens of the writer:

> A study of past behavioural environments provides a key to understanding past actions, explaining why changes were made in the landscape. We must understand man and his cultures before we can understand landscapes; we must understand what limits of physical and mental strain his body will bear; we must learn what choices his culture makes available to him and what sanctions his fellows impose upon him to deter him from transgressing and to encourage him to conform (Prince, 1971a, p. 44).

Perhaps the enormity of such a task is the reason why most success in such reconstructions has been with regard to the relatively recent past, for example, the perceptions which guided the settlement of the American West (e.g. Lewis, 1966), although Wright (1925) essayed a similar task for Europe at the time of the Crusades.

Not all perceived worlds refer to either past or present; some landscapes have been fashioned out of Utopian views of the future (Porter and Lukermann, 1975; Powell, 1971). In general, however, and whether of past, present or future, geosophy has not become a popular field of study, despite some intriguing essays (see Lowenthal and Bowden, 1975). But directly or indirectly, it has led to arguments for alternative approaches in human geography to those of the positivist, and it is those arguments which form the material for the rest of this chapter.

The Attack on Positivism and the Humanistic Approaches

From the early 1970s, work by some cultural and historical geographers has presented an attack on the positivism of spatial science. To replace the latter, a variety of humanistic approaches has been proposed, focusing on decision-makers and their perceived worlds and denying the existence of an objective world which can be studied by positivist methods. The intent is to reorient human geography towards a more humanistic stance, to resurrect its synthetic character, and to re-emphasize the importance of studying unique events rather than the spuriously general.

Anti-positivism, idealism, and historical geography

The various humanistic approaches have much in common, but they can be separated into different proposals in the present context. The first to be discussed here is associated with two workers who were together at the University of Toronto at the end of the 1960s; both are historical geographers.

The basic theme of a first paper (Harris, 1971) is that geography is a synthetic discipline, concerned with particular assemblages of phenomena and not with the science of spatial relations. Thus:

> When the history of North American geography in the 1950s and 1960s is written, a paradox with which it will have to deal is how, with little argued, logical justification, so many geographers came to see their subject as a science of spatial relations (p. 157).

With May and Sack (p. 112ff), Harris sees the spatial perspective leading to the dismemberment of geography, as specialists communicate more with their contemporaries in other disciplines than with geographers, and develop theories which are descriptions of how the world might operate under certain conditions, rather than of how it does actually work.

> The difficulty in conceiving of geographical theory comes down to this. The development of theory is necessarily an exercise in abstraction and simplification in which the complexities of particular situations are eliminated to the point which common characteristics become apparent. But if geography is thought to have a particular subject matter, it is certainly not individual phenomena or categories of phenomena which other fields do not study. Rather it is a whole complex of phenomena, many or all of which may be studied individually by other fields but which are not studied elsewhere in their complex interactions (p. 162).

The clear parallel, according to Harris, is with history, for:

> Few historians would attempt to develop a general theory of revolutions. In so doing they would lose grasp of the type of insight that characterizes good historical synthesis (p. 163).

The goal of both history and geography is synthesis, therefore. In developing syntheses, positivist methods may be applicable. Historians may be law-consumers, applying the generalizations of other social scientists to particular events, and geographers could operate likewise; alternatively, both historians and geographers could apply the idealist method, arguing that all activity is based on personal theories. Thus Harris (1978) writes elsewhere of a 'historical mind':

> Such a mind is contextual, not law-finding. Sometimes it is thought of as law-applying but, characteristically, the historical mind is dubious that there are overarching laws to explain the general patterns of human life (p. 126).

This mind, he argues, is open and eclectic, uses no formal research procedures, sees things in context, is sensitive to motives and values, excludes little, and is wary of sweeping generalizations. Its goal is understanding, not planning, and this should be the case with the 'geographical mind' too. (To understand an event is to appreciate why it took place, and is the humanistic goal: to explain an event is to predict it, as an instance of a general law or suite of such laws, and is the positivist goal.)

Developing his theme of the parallel between history and geography, Harris (1971, p. 167) suggests four major points of agreement concerning the nature of history:

1 Its primary concern is with the particular;
2 Explanation may take into account the thoughts of relevant individuals;
3 Explanation may make use of general laws; and
4 'Explanation in history relies heavily on the reflective judgement of individual historians'.

From these, he then argues:

> If geography aims to describe and explain not so much particular events or peoples, as particular parts of the surface of the earth, then these points of agreement about history also apply to geography (p. 167).

(The term 'particular parts' can be widely interpreted, it would seem, for Harris (1977) has himself sought to understand the nature of north-western European colonizing societies 'by a model': the implication is that colonists developed a common reaction to the 'new world'.) The landscape results from actions; behind those actions lie thoughts; study of thoughts allows understanding of landscape. Thus synthesis is crucial, since:

> the idea of synthesis itself becomes more important as it becomes obvious that our larger problems transcend narrow subject-matter fields . . . integration . . . in a larger understanding is still achieved, however aided by statistical methods and computers, by the judgement of wise men who have cultivated the habit of seeing things together (p. 170).

Geographers, presumably, are to be those wise individuals; not an original claim for, according to Buttimer (1978a), the basis of Paul Vidal de la Blache's work was that:

> The task which no other discipline with the possible exception of history claims is to examine how diverse phenomena and forces interweave and connect with the finite horizons of particular settings. Temporality and spatiality are

universal features of life so historical and geographical study belong together (p. 73).

Positivist work seeks the same end – interweaving parts of a whole – but its parts are instances of general laws, not unique events.

Many of Harris's arguments were extended by his Toronto colleague, Leonard Guelke, whose first paper (Guelke, 1971) was a strong criticism of the 'narrowly conceived scientific approach' (p. 38) to geography using the positivist method. Thus he argued against geography as a law-seeking activity by asking the proponents of the positivist approach to indicate how their laws would meet the basic standards of scientific acceptability, particularly with regard to prediction. Whereas they might be able to produce generalizations concerning the phenomena which they actually studied he felt it very unlikely that they could define laws applicable to all examples of the relevant phenomena. Statistical regularities are not laws and

> Until the new geographers have shown that the laws that might conceivably be discovered in geography will be more than generalizations, which describe common but non-essential connections between phenomena, their claims must be treated cautiously . . . there is little cause for optimism, especially as the statistical methods widely employed by geographers cannot be considered appropriate law-finding procedures (p. 42).

Regarding geography as a law-applying science, Guelke argues that laws of human behaviour are virtually impossible to conceive in anything but the most generalized form, because so much behaviour is culturally specific, and an a priori statement of the determining conditions for their operation is not feasible. Thus 'Human geographers cannot consider themselves to be law-applying scientists . . . because they have no laws to apply' (p. 45).

Turning to the use of theories and models in geography, Guelke points out that for them to serve a valid purpose in the pursuit of understanding, criteria must be erected which indicate how such devices are testable against reality (see also Newman, 1973, on the vague use of the term hypothesis). Such criteria have not been, and cannot be, stated, Guelke claims; to him, studies purporting to test central place theory seem to operate the rule that 'one counts one's hits but not one's misses' (p. 48; see also Guelke, 1978, p. 50). Too often, failure to reproduce reality is explained by claims that the test environment was not entirely suitable, and frequently *ad hoc* hypotheses are adduced to account for observed disparities. Models and theories may have heuristic value for human geographers, clarifying certain aspects, therefore, but they can have no explanatory power.

Guelke's (1971) conclusions are that:

> The new geography . . . has not yet produced any scientific laws and . . . appears unlikely to produce them in the future. . . . The theories and models . . . are not amenable to empirical testing. . . . The new geographers insisted on . . . logical and internally consistent theories and models. Yet, none of their theoretical constructs were ever complex enough to describe the real world

accurately. They had achieved internal consistency while losing their grip on reality (pp. 50–1).

His alternative to the so discredited procedure is the idealist approach mentioned by Harris, which is 'a method by which one can rethink the thoughts of those whose actions he seeks to explain' (Guelke, 1974, p 193). All actions, according to the idealist, are the result of rational thought, the parameters of which are constrained by a theory, which in turn is 'any system of ideas that man has invented, imposed, or elicited from the raw data of sensation that make connections between the phenomena of the external world' (p. 194). Many such theories are part of the society and culture inhabited by the actor under consideration, and include its religions, myths and traditions. Using them, 'the explanation of an action is complete when the agent's goal and theoretical understanding of his situation have been discovered. . . . One must discover what he believed, not why he believed it' (p. 197; but see Sayer, 1981). Thus human geographers do not need to develop theories, since the relevant theories, which led to the action being studied, already exist (or existed) in the minds of the actors. The task of the analyst is to isolate those theories (a task of considerable difficulty, according to Curry, 1982a, because people are not always able to identify the reason for an action). Some of them may be unique to particular individuals – such as that which led Columbus to sail westwards – but there are many consensus theories, shared in large part by large numbers of actors; they represent the order which people themselves have stamped on the world, and do not require further theories in order to be understood.

Guelke's argument was challenged by Chappell (1975), who pointed out that by focusing on the individual actor alone the idealist omitted any reference to the environmental constraints and influences on that person's actions (see also Gregory, 1978a). Guelke (1976) accepted the existence of such constraints and influences, but claimed that investigation of them lay outside the geographer's domain. Study of environmental causes would, he felt, lead into physiology and psychology and deviate attention from 'the most critical dimension of human behaviour, namely the thought behind it' (p. 169). Chappell (1976) responded that 'to go so far as to say that there is no possible respectable theory to explain man's rational theories and the actions which flow from them' (p. 170) is to be myopic: 'paradigms not only explain facts but they guide the research of whole disciplines' (p. 171). To him, Guelke's contention that the ultimate causes of actions lie outside the scope of human geography places geographers in an inferior position in the academic division of labour.

In a further essay, Guelke (1975) addressed his ideas on idealist approaches to historical geographers, as a counter to the arguments that they should adopt the approaches and techniques of positivism (see p. 89). He argued:

> It is obvious that quantitative techniques will often be useful. . . . Statistical methods put in harness with positivist philosophy are a dangerous combination. . . . Historical geographers need to rethink not their techniques but their

> philosophy. . . . This can best be achieved by moving from problem-solving
> contemporary applied geography towards the idealist approach widely adopted
> by historians. (p. 138).

Gregory (1976) agreed with the first part of this statement, but not with the
proposed solution. Like Chappell, he saw the need to investigate individual
action within its constraining structures (see below, p. 236 and Curry,
1982a).

Positivist approaches in human geography have been defended against the
idealist attack by Hay (1979a), who both responds to the criticisms and in
return raises points of contention in the proposed alternative. Thus he argues
that Guelke's case is ill-founded and rests on misconceptions of the nature of
positivism, such as that all theory must be both normative and based on conceptions of optimal decision-making, that to be scientific is to be nomological,
and that prediction is the same as prophesy (rather than simply testing, from
the known to the unknown). Further, he claims that Guelke presents an anti-
positivist argument by using a positivist test, and that he fails to realize the
value of *ad hoc* hypotheses in the improvement of theory (which is the basis
of Lakatos's concept of a research programme and its positive heuristic –
p. 17): Guelke should not, according to Hay, ask 'does this theory explain Y?'
but rather should ask 'does this theory contribute to an understanding of Y?'.

With regard to the idealist alternative, Hay raises the problem of studying
groups rather than individuals. To Guelke (1978):

> The assumption that thought lies behind human action is not related to the
> numbers involved. . . . If thousands of people drive motor cars to their places
> of work the idealist assumes that each of these journeys is a considered action
> involving thought. In such situations the investigator will not be able to look
> at each case individually, but he will seek to isolate the general factors involved
> in typical circumstances . . . [for which he] might well make use of statistical
> procedures . . . the value of statistical analysis will largely depend on its success-
> ful integration in the general interpretation or explanatory thesis being
> developed (p. 55),

which is a procedure akin to that employed by the behaviourist geographers
whose work has been reviewed in the previous chapter. Such a procedure does
not give ontological status to groups as collections of individuals in which, as
with 'traditional' regions, the whole is greater than the sum of the parts.
Secondly, Hay points out the objective facts must influence behavioural
outcomes, in addition to the thoughts of the actors: Columbus found America,
because it was there. Thirdly, he claims that the idealist position ignores the
possibility of either unconscious or subconscious behaviour. In sum, idealism
is reductionist, but the world is more than a large number of independent
decision-makers.

Idealism has also been criticized by Mabogunje (1977) who claims that
'Such a retreat from objective theory formulations as a means of seeking
explanation to certain events would exclude from our consideration the

exploration of the consequences of societal actions' (p. 368) and that instead of retreating to a focus on particular cases – 'seek[ing] special explanation for each situation in which a different value system can be shown to be operative' (p. 370) – geographers should attempt to build better theories encompassing these differences in value-systems. Others have asked how an idealist interpretation can be verified. (See also the same question regarding phenomenology, raised by Mercer and Powell (1972), who wonder whether two phenomenologists can ever have the same 'intuitions' of a phenomenon, or indeed know whether they have.) Guelke is prepared for this argument, presenting the analogy of the court-of-law, rather than the positivist's laboratory, for his Popperian procedure.

A well-verified idealist explanation will be one in which a 'pattern of behaviour can be shown to be consistent with certain underlying ideas. Where data are presented which are not in accordance with a proposed explanation a new hypothesis will be needed' (Guelke, 1978, p. 55), which is somewhat in contradiction to his earlier statements that theory should not be imposed from without by the observer. Even so, he says, 'one cannot guarantee mistake-free interpretations. The complex nature of human societies and lack of pertinent data makes it inevitable that many idealist interpretations will be of a tentative character' (p. 55), a position which is very similar to Moss's (1977) outline of deductive procedures in historical explanation.

The idealist philosophy, according to Guelke (1981), combines two positions: a metaphysical argument that 'mental activity has a life of its own which is not controlled by material things and processes'; and an epistemological argument

> that the world can only be known indirectly through ideas . . . all knowledge is ultimately based on an individual's subjective experience of the world, and comprises mental constructs and ideas. There is no 'real' world that can be known independently of mind (p. 133).

Positivist spatial science is thus criticized because it believes in the existence of a 'real' world, the nature of which it seeks to explain via general laws of behaviour. Behavioural geography is similarly criticized, not for its acceptable (to Guelke) premise that behaviour can be understood as a response to perceived images and subjective evaluations, but because of two assumptions within this field: 'that identifiable environmental images exist that can be measured accurately . . . [and] that there are strong relationships between revealed images and preferences and actual (real-world) behaviour' (Bunting and Guelke, p. 453). Such an approach, Bunting and Guelke believe, traps human geographers into a single-cause model, much like the earlier environmental determinism, and even if one accepted this model research in behavioural geography has failed to validate it. They argue for an idealist perspective, which focuses on overt behaviour and its interpretation: 'In searching for the truth a scholar conducts a critical dialogue with his evidence and in due course he puts the results before his colleagues for their appraisal'

(p. 458). In response, Downs (1979), Rushton (1979), and Saarinen (1979)
claim that Bunting and Guelke misrepresent much of behavioural geography
and argue that although the study of overt behaviour may give clues as to the
answers to 'why?', only the study of decision-making can provide an understanding that is of value in planning, as in the work on environmental hazards.
Golledge (1981a, p. 1328), also responding to Bunting and Guelke, claims
that to qualify as behavioural geography research may focus on the overt act,
but more importantly the set of explanatory variables must include 'one or
more process variables'.

   Curry (1982a) has criticized Guelke's idealist programme on a number of
grounds. Central to Guelke's argument is the claim that the methods of positivist science are irrelevant to the study of human behaviour; the latter results
from rational thought, and thus can only be explained by reconstructing that
thought. There is then a single answer to the question 'why did you do that?'
which forms the explanation. But, according to Curry,

> First, in our daily lives we do many things for which, at the time, we consciously
> entertain no reason; at the same time, we hardly consider these actions to be
> non-rational. Second, we often, both at the time and after the fact, give reasons
> that are not the 'real' reasons for our actions. And, third, we can often attribute
> reasons to behaviour in which they were patently not involved (p. 43).

Those reasons which are often not readily explored may be examples of individuals following rules, whether consciously or not, and such rules need not
be determinate – as in a game of chess, the rules identify what moves are
possible in a given situation but do not define which will be followed. Thus
we must study behaviour in its context

> Without appeal to rules human action would be random and, hence, incompre-
> hensible. The idealist geographer . . . must consider the human world as a
> whole as imbued with the same sort of normative significance as that found in
> the more limited area of rules or maxims of actions (p. 46).

In response, Guelke (1982) restated his position that geography is an ideo-
graphic discipline seeking to understand the 'complexity of human activity on
the land' (p. 52), drawing the boundaries such that

> The geographer is not concerned with explaining fluctuations in wheat prices
> or the level of interest rates, but he is concerned with the impact that these
> factors might have on, say, farming in western Canada (p. 53).

Thus, in seeking to understand the reasons for any action, he accepts that
stated reasons may not always help and that a 'historical reconstruction of
thought' is necessary to explicate the learned response that is 'part of an individual's cultural heritage' (p. 54); this does not require exploring the subconscious forces that may have influenced the composition of that heritage.
But Guelke accepts much of Curry's case, and argues that

for both of us human geography is concerned with understanding the meaning of human activity on the earth's surface in its unique cultural contexts
(p. 57).

Curry (1982b) disagrees, however, arguing that 'we remain very much farther
apart than he believes' (p. 59), because he is concerned to understand the
processes that produce the thoughts behind actions that are Guelke's sole
interest. Pickles (1986, p. 34) follows Curry in arguing that idealism, as
promoted by Guelke, is not concerned with understanding that is 'empathetic
in an emotional sense' but rather requires conformity 'to rules of inference and
evidence'.

Phenomenology and related approaches

Phenomenology has attracted more attention among human geographers than
has idealism. The first direct statement advocating a phenomenological
approach was by Relph (1970), who has also been associated with the Department of Geography at the University of Toronto. Despite a variety of specific
interpretations, he noted that the basic aim of phenomenology is to present
an alternative methodology to the hypothesis-testing and theory-building of
positivism, an alternative grounded in people's lived world of experience. Phenomenologists argue that there is no objective world independent of human
existence – 'all knowledge proceeds from the world of experience and cannot
be independent of that world' (p. 193). Thus, according to Entrikin (1976),
'phenomenologists describe, rather than explain, in that explanation is viewed
as [an observer's] construction and hence antithetical to the phenomenologist's
attempt to "get back" to the meaning of the data of consciousness' (p. 617).
(Seamon, 1984, p. 4, also defines phenomenology as a 'descriptive science'.)

   Phenomenology in human geography is concerned with what Kirk termed
the phenomenal environment (p. 163). The contents of that environment are
unique to every individual, for each of its elements is the result of an act of
intentionality – it is given meaning by the individual, without which it does
not exist but through which it influences behaviour. Phenomenology is the
study of how such meanings are defined. It involves the researcher seeking
to identify how the individual structures the environment in an entirely subjective way; the researcher is presuppositionless, using no personal ideas in
seeking to understand those of the subject. (Thus the subjectivity is that of
the focus of the study, not that of the researcher who, in the positivist method,
imposes a personal subjective view of the world: Ley, 1980.) The phenomenologist may be satisfied with such empathetic understanding. Some seek to go
further, however, to identify essences – elements in individual consciousness
which control the allocation of meanings (Johnston, 1983b: Pickles, 1988,
p. 252, distinguishes between 'transitional essences' and 'invariant and
universal structures (understood carefully)'). Phenomenology, then, studies
human appraisals. It works at the level of the individual, but may seek to
identify the common (imprinted not agreed) elements of those appraisals.

Relph's paper was followed by another from a geographer having associations with the <u>University of Toronto, Yi-Fu Tuan (1971), to whom geography is a mirror,</u> revealing the essence of human existence and human striving: to know the world is to know oneself, just as careful analysis of a house reveals much about both the designer and the occupant. Thus the study of landscapes is the study of the essences in the societies which mould them, in just the same way that the study of literature and art reveals much of human life. Such study, by geographers, has a clear base in the humanities, rather than the social or physical sciences. Tuan (1974, 1975b) has illustrated it in a number of essays, giving, for example, insights into such topics as the sense of place.

> Humanistic geography achieves an understanding of the human world by studying people's relations with nature, their geographical behaviour as well as their feelings and ideas in regard to space and place (Tuan, 1976, p. 266). . . . Scientific approaches to the study of man tend to minimize the role of human awareness and knowledge. Humanistic geography, by contrast, specifically tries to understand how geographical activities and phenomena reveal the quality of human awareness (p. 267).

Tuan exemplifies this with five themes: the nature of geographical knowledge and its role in human survival; the role of territory in human behaviour and the creation of place identities; the interrelationships between crowding and privacy, as mediated by culture; the role of knowledge as an influence on livelihood; and the influence of religion on human activity. Such concerns are best developed in historical and in regional geography; their value to human welfare is that they clarify the nature of the experience (see also Appleton, 1975). Indeed, Tuan (1978) claims that 'The model for the regional geographers of humanist leaning is . . . the Victorian novelist who strives to achieve a synthesis of the subjective and the objective' (p. 204). He quotes the first two pages of E. M. Forster's *A Passage to India* as a paradigm example.

Tuan's corpus of work has not involved philosophical explorations, and he rarely claims allegiance to any particular approach. Rather, he has been involved in a variety of explorations of the inter-relationships between people and environments. As he describes it himself (Tuan, 1984)

> my point of departure is a simple one, namely, that the quality of human experience in an environment (physical and human) is given by people's capacity — mediated through culture — to feel, think and act . . . I have explored the nature of human attachment to place, the component of fear in attitudes to nature and landscape, and the development of subjective world views and self-consciousness in progressively segmented spaces (p. ix).

Thus, for example, he shows that fear is both a representation of the environment and an influence on the creation of environments (Tuan, 1979), that the creation of patterns of spatial segregation reflects the retreat of individuals from wholes to segmented parts (Tuan, 1982), and that the creation of gardens reflects a desire to dominate the environment (Tuan, 1984). Such works are implicitly phenomenological in that they suggest the existence of general essences, or stimuli to behaviour, but the term is not in the index of any of the books.

Among others advocating the phenomenological approach, Mercer and Powell (1972) argue that application of positivism in geography 'left the subject with too many technicians and a dearth of scholars' (p. 28). Land-use patterns, they claimed, can never be understood 'by the elementary dictates of geometry and cash register' (p. 42); the world can only be comprehended through people's intentions and their attitudes towards it. In a lengthy discussion of the nature of phenomenology and its development in other disciplines, notably sociology, they point out 'a very real danger of the research worker assuming that concepts which are cognitively organized in his own mind "exist" and are equally clearly organized in the minds of his respondents' (p. 26), and argue instead for research methods which lead to empathy between observer and observed. Within geography this requires 'that we make every effort to view problems and situations not from our own perspective, but from the actor's frame of reference' (p. 48) – which is a scientific position of 'disciplined naivete'.

In similar vein, Anne Buttimer made a general case for study by geographers of the values which permeate all aspects of living and thinking (Buttimer, 1974). She feels that the order, precision and theory developed by positivist social sciences are dearly bought – 'we often lose in adequacy to deal with the values and meanings of the everyday world' (p. 3) – and that the behavioural geography of the sort discussed earlier in this chapter does not break away from the mechanistic, natural-science view of humans as preconditional responders to stimuli. Ley (1981) also points to the positivist elements in behavioural geography and the suggestion of operant conditioning: people react in predetermined ways to various stimuli, and so can be manipulated accordingly. On the other hand, according to Buttimer, 'An existentially aware geographer is . . . less interested in establishing intellectual control over man through preconceived analytical models than he is in encountering people and situations in an open, inter-subjective manner' (p. 24). The results of such activity are 'a meditation on life', with geographers providing more comprehensive mirrors on life experience than is possible for their colleagues from more specialized disciplines, and thereby clarifying the structural dynamics of life. Prediction would be impossible, apart for the 'most routinized aspects of experience' (p. 29), but the deeper understanding achieved would allow much more valid social action and planning than is currently possible.

In a later paper, Buttimer (1976) directs geographers' attention to the concept of the lifeworld, that amalgam of the worlds of facts and affairs with those of values which comprise personal experience – 'the pre-reflective, taken-for-granted dimensions of experience, the unquestioned meanings, and routinized determinants of behaviour' (p. 281). Positivism is rejected as a method for analysing the lifeworld because it separates the observer from that which is being studied, and who, as a result, fails to appreciate the human experience. Idealism is rejected, too, because it accepts that there is a real world outside the individual's consciousness. Phenomenology, on the other hand, is a path to understanding, on which informed planning can be built:

> It helps elucidate how . . . meanings in past experience can influence and shape the present . . . extremely important as preamble not only to scientific procedure, but also as a door to existential awareness. It could elicit a clearer grasp of value issues surrounding one's normal way of life, and an appreciation of the kinds of education and socialization which might be appropriate for persons whose lives may weave through several milieux (p. 289).

The result is an understanding of actions as those involved understand them, rather than in the terms of abstract, outsider-imposed models and theories. And having achieved that understanding, human geographers can transmit it to their subjects, thereby helping them to understand themselves and realize their potential. In this way, the applied geographer acts as a provocateur, stimulating human development but not forcing it (Buttimer, 1979).

Berry (1973b), too, has backed this phenomenological orientation, calling for

> a view of the world from the vantage of *process metageography*. By metageography is meant that part of geographic speculation dealing with the principles lying behind perceptions of reality, and transcending them, including such concepts as essence, cause and identity (p. 9).

But not all believe that phenomenology can entirely replace the positivist approach. Walmsley (1974), for example, accepts the merits of the case just presented because so many human decisions are based on 'experiential' rather than 'factual' concepts, but feels that the scale of geographical enquiry, and its long tradition of certain types of empirical work, will require maintaining the positivist orientation. That the perceived world is not necessarily the same as the real world must be realized, but 'logical consistency and empirical truth will remain central to geographical enquiry provided the importance of values is recognized' (p. 106).

Gregory (1978a) is critical of both positivism and phenomenology. Those favouring the former are criticized for making 'social science an activity performed *on* rather than *in* society, one which portrays society but which is at the same time estranged from it' (p. 51) and for supporting a procedure which, because it so often assumes *ceteris paribus* in testing its models, can never be sure why these fail, when they do, to replicate reality (p. 66). The necessity for humanistic approaches is recognized, but these will not be sufficient to provide a satisfactory foundation of themselves, because they ignore the 'constraints on social action which are so much part of the taken-for-granted life-world of the actors' (Gregory, 1978b, p. 166). Thus:

> A geography of the life-world must therefore determine the connections between social typifications of meaning and space-time rhythms of action and uncover the structures of intentionality which lie beneath them (Gregory, 1978a, p. 139).

But

> A major deficiency . . . is [the] restricted conception of social structure: in parti-
> cular, it ignores the material imperatives and consequences of social actions and
> the external constraints which are imposed on and flow from them (*ibid*).

Phenomenology and idealism, then, must be incorporated with investigations
of those imperatives and constraints; such incorporation produces a critical
science, whose nature is discussed in Chapter 8.

Whereas a key feature of the positivist/spatial-science approach has been
a great numerical superiority of practitioners over preachers, the phenomenological movement (like the idealist) was initially characterized by the
converse – much preaching but relatively little practice (Relph, 1981a, has
pointed to the absence of substantive applications of the phenomenological
approach in geography, though see Jackson and Smith, 1984, p. 44):

> There is an essential difference between the contemplative intentions of this
> transcendental philosophy and the practical concerns of a social science, so that
> it is scarcely surprising that . . . geographers' . . . efforts have been directed
> towards the destruction of positivism as a *philosophy* rather than the construc-
> tion of a phenomenologically sound *geography* (Gregory, 1978a, pp. 125–6).

Among the examples of the method's use, however, are Tuan's interpretative
essays, and Relph, who 'would much prefer to see substantive applications
rather than discussions of the possible uses of phenomenology' (1977, p. 178),
published his thesis on *Place and Placelessness* in which – implicitly, he
says – phenomenological methods are used 'to elucidate the diversity and
intensity of our experiences of place' (Relph, 1976, p. i): his essential themes
are the sense of place and identity in the human make-up and the destruction
of this through the growing placelessness of modern design (see also Porteous,
1988). Other work generally quoted as phenomenological includes pieces on
European settlement of the New World. Powell (1972), for example, has
written on images of Australia and in his major work on the settlement of
Victoria's western plains (Powell, 1970) has examined the conflict between
official and popular environmental appraisals, the dialogue between these,
and the learning process which resulted in the final settlement pattern (see
also Powell, 1977, who presents the study of eiconics, or image-making, in
the context of colonization processes). Billinge (1977), however, has queried
whether all such works are really phenomenological:

> the idea has spread that since certain branches of our discipline are less suscepti-
> ble to quantitative reduction (and, so the argument continues, by false exten-
> sion, to *scientific* analysis), we can justify our partially formulated hypotheses,
> exploit the atypicality of our data, cease worrying about the validity of our
> reconstruction and within some weakly articulated framework label the whole
> exercise phenomenological (p. 64).

The study of perceived environments represents an 'important and vigorous movement' (p. 65) but, Billinge argues, phenomenology is not just the study of such environments: it is an approach to the study of those subjective sources which in its method is presuppositionless, concerned with the human consciousness and not only its output; thus 'phenomenological we have by no means become' (p. 67). In fact, much of the work which is claimed as phenomenological is probably closer to the idealist position, in that it does not attempt to investigate essences.

Attempts by geographers to adopt a phenomenological approach have been trenchantly criticized by Pickles (1985), not because he is opposed to such attempts in principle but because he believes that those undertaken have been misconceived; he accepts that, if for no other reason than its attack on positivism, 'It cannot be denied that the founding and guiding intuitions of a phenomenological approach in geography as it exists at the moment are in the main sound and well intentioned' (p. 68) but argues that the output, as illustrated in the works of Buttimer and Relph, 'is ungrounded method, unfounded claims, and the actual imposition of unexamined propositions' (p. 71). His criticisms then lead him to contend

> we now need to move *from* what passes for phenomenology in the geographical
> literature, *towards* what is actually the case in phenomenology itself (p. 89).

Quoting substantially from the original works of Husserl and Heidegger, he argues that phenomenology is not concerned to explicate subjective meanings as an end in itself, but rather 'to be the science of science through explicating the science of beginnings' (p. 97). Its goal is to identify the essences that underpin individual meanings:

> The essential relation between an individual object and its essence − such that
> to each object there corresponds its essential structure, and to each essential
> structure there corresponds a series of possible individuals as its factual
> instances − necessarily leads to a corresponding relationship between sciences
> of fact and sciences of essence (p. 111).

Thus the subjectivity of the lived world is explored for the insights that it can provide on those essential structures, the underpinnings of knowledge itself.

According to this interpretation, phenomenology has much in common with certain forms of structuralism (see p. 220; Johnston, 1986f: Pickles, 1988, p. 252, implies this too) in its basic concern with neither empirical appearances nor actual decision-making but with the deep structures of consciousness. To that extent it does not fit easily into the humanistic concerns of most geographers who have espoused it. Instead, for Pickles, it involves seeking those essences that give rise to the necessity for geography, as the empirical science concerned with particular facets of behaviour. (Each empirical science should be grounded in such an essence.) Thus

> we seek an ontological, existential understanding of the universal structures
> characteristic of man's spatiality as the precondition for any understanding of
> places and spaces as such. That is, we seek to clarify the original experiences

on the basis of which geography can articulate and develop its regional ontology as a *human* science, concerned with *man's* [sic] spatiality, is to be possible at all (p. 155).

Spatiality is that essence, he claims, an essence best represented by the German noun *Raum* and verb *räumen*

> which means to clear away, to free from wilderness or to bring forth into an openness. *Räumen* is thus a clearing away or release of places, a making room for the settling and dwelling of man and things (p. 167).

In this context, space and place are closely related concepts. (See also Gould, 1981b.)

Closely associated with phenomenology is *existentialism*, and some geographers have experienced difficulty in separating the two (Entrikin, 1976). The basic difference is that phenomenology assumes the primacy of essence – the allocation of meanings results from the existence of consciousness – whereas to existentialists the basic dictum is 'being before essence – or man makes himself'. The process of defining oneself (creating an essence) involves creating an environment. Thus environments can be read as biographies – 'for every landscape or every existential geography there is someone who can be held accountable' (Samuels, 1981, p. 131). Generalization may be possible in the analysis of such landscapes. Appleton (1975), for example, suggests that landscapes reflect two primal needs – prospect (the need to search for the means of survival), and refuge (the need to hide from threatening others) – although individuals and groups may seek to satisfy these needs in different ways. And Lowenthal (1975; see also Lowenthal, 1985) has suggested that individuals seek to rewrite their biographies, and those of their ancestors, by their choices of what to preserve in the landscape.

All of this suggests that humanistic geography is concerned either with the study of individuals and their construction of, plus behaviour in, phenomenal environments (as in Rowles, 1978) or with the analysis of landscapes as repositories of human meaning. As such, it may be considered separate from the subject matter of much human geography, notably behavioural geography and its investigation of everyday activity within environments. But the phenomenological perspective has been adapted to the latter type of work also, in the writings of Schutz on what he terms the 'taken-for-granted' world (Ley, 1977b). Much everyday behaviour is unconsidered, in that it involves no original encounters. The behaviour is habitual, because all of the stimuli encountered are processed as examples of particular types. Those types are not externally defined for the individual, but are personally created. The phenomenology of the taken-for-granted world is the study of those individually-defined typifications – of the unconsidered 'world of social reality' rather than 'a fictional non-existing world constructed by the scientific observer' (Ley, 1980, p. 10, quoting Schutz): see also Curry's (1982a) discussion of 'the ordinary, everyday actions of individuals' which create for the geographer 'a complex world of complex places and actions' in which the role of the individual decision-maker 'can be determined only on an individual basis, case by case' (p. 38). It may be, of course, that interaction within communities leads to common typifications. Quantitative methods may be used to identify the common elements, but as descriptive tools only. (Quantification is not tied to positivism, except when it is used to suggest laws and other generalizations: Johnston, 1986a.)

Humanistic geography is based on a profound critique of positivist work, both that which makes major assumptions about the nature of decision-making and that which seeks inductive laws of human behaviour which can be scientifically verified (Ley and Samuels, 1978; Powell, 1980). Its argument is for an understanding of the individual as a 'living, acting, thinking' being. To some, it is just a criticism – Entrikin (1976, p. 616) argues that:

> humanist geography does not offer a viable alternative to, nor a presupposition-less basis for, scientific geography as it is claimed by some of its proponents. Rather the humanist approach is best understood as a form of criticism. As criticism the humanist approach helps to counter the overly objective and abstractive tendencies of some scientific geographers.

To others, however, the human condition can only be indicated by humanistic endeavour, for attitudes, impressions and subjective relations to places (the 'sense of place') cannot be revealed by positivist research. Thus, as Pickles (1986, p. 42) puts it 'The value of humanism has been its resilience in consistently raising questions which do not fit within other frameworks . . . humanism has been the voice of man against reason, against science'.

To some critics, humanistic geography is concerned with relatively trivial matters and not with the major concerns of an applied geography concerned with improving the world. To Buttimer (1979, p. 30) such an applied geography is managerial, manipulating individuals and their environments rather than seeking to advance the process of 'human becoming'. To Relph (1981b, pp. 139–41) it implies geographism:

> the view that people should behave rationally in geographical, two-dimensional space . . . that cities and industries and transportation routes should be arranged in the most efficient way

which when used as a basis for planning

> will diminish the distinctiveness and individuality of . . . communities and places. Geographism involves the imposition of generalizations onto specific landscapes; it breeds uniformity and placelessness.

To him, as to Buttimer, planning should emphasize subjectivity and individuality. Scientists, engineers and planners may have sought to improve well-being, but in so doing they have made people rootless and denied them individuality. Planning must be allied with environmental humility, by which

> places and communities would increasingly become the responsibility of those who live and work in them instead of being objects of professional disinterest (p. 201).

In this context, humanistic geography is not only a reaction against the dehumanizing treatment of people in spatial science and behavioural geography. It is also an argument against an applied geography which imposes that treatment on the landscape, and for a form of anarchism in which individuals are encouraged to realize what they are and how they can control themselves and their environments (see also Pickles, 1986, p. 47). Seamon (1987) has reviewed a substantial volume of phenomenological work, illustrating that it is 'a learning tool which can help us to discover more about ourselves, others, and the world in which we live' (p. 21), and which may then have practical value in environmental design.

The practice of humanistic geography

Much of the practice of humanistic geography has been concerned with exploring and explicating the subjectivity of human action and its base in meanings (both individual and shared), with relatively little concern for the claims of idealist, phenomenological, existentialist and other philosophies. To the extent that such work is explicitly influenced by philosophical and methodological writings, the stimulus is more often the *pragmatism* (and symbolic interactionism) developed by the Chicago School of sociologists in the 1920s and 1930s (and largely overlooked by human geographers who paid much more attention to the relatively small amount of spatial analysis undertaken by that school, as typified by the Burgess model of the internal structure of cities: Johnston, 1971). Pragmatism portrays life as a continuous process of experience, experiment and evaluation by which beliefs are continually being reconstructed; such reconstruction is a social process, whereby individuals learn and behave in the context of the beliefs of those with whom they interact (hence the term interactionism: see Jackson and Smith, 1984, Chapter 4: Smith, 1988, and Jackson, 1988, illustrate this in their own research).

Understanding social life within this broad framework involves participatory fieldwork (as detailed in Evans, 1988), the methodology of which (according to S. Smith, 1984) is 'a hallmark of much geographic humanism' (p. 353). This, she continues,

> requires a commitment to fieldwork, with the aim of securing data lodged in the meanings ascribed to the world by active social subjects. The strength of this strategy derives from the unique insight it offers into 'lay' or 'folk' perceptions and behaviors. True to the pragmatic maxim, the method allows the truth of a social reality to be established in terms of its consequences for those experiencing it (pp. 356–7).

How local societies work is thereby explicated, which was the goal of the ethnographic work of the Chicago School (Jackson, 1984, 1985); this has been achieved by Ley in his detailed portrayal of a Philadelphia community (Ley, 1974) and his general textbook on urban social geography (Ley, 1983).

The field, and interaction with people in it over long or short terms, is only one source of information about how people structure their lives, however. There are other *texts*, other repositories of meanings, so that Pocock (1983) can describe humanistic strategies ranging 'from library search, to the observational, to the experiential' (p. 356). One such text is the landscape, the creation of those who live/have lived in it. A particular perspective on this is provided by Lowenthal (1985), who uses the landscape not as a mirror of the past but as an insight to the present; as he expresses it

> . . . Traditions and revivals dominate architecture and the arts; schoolchildren delve into local history and grandparental recollections; historical romances and tales of olden days deluge all the media. The past thus conjured up is, to be sure, largely an artifact of the present. However faithfully we preserve, however authentically we restore, however deeply we immerse ourselves in bygone times, life back then was based on ways of being and believing incommensurable with our own. The past's difference is, indeed, one of its claims: no one would yearn for it if it merely replicated the present. But we cannot help but view and celebrate it through present-day lenses (p. xvi).

The present landscape is a conglomerate of relics from many different periods in most cases, and by preserving only parts of it we bias our representation of the past:

> Every act of recognition alters survivals from the past. Simply to appreciate or protect a relic, let alone to embellish or imitate it, affects its form or our impressions. Just as selective recall skews memory and subjectivity shapes historical insight, so manipulating antiquities refashions their appearance and meaning. Interaction with a heritage continually alters its nature and context, whether by choice or by chance (p. 263).

Thus when we use the landscape as a text, we are reading the outcome of a long sequence of selective retentions of earlier forms, so that we learn about what parts of their history people wanted to build into their own presents and futures. Thus

> We must concede the ancients their place . . . But their place is not simply back there, in a separate and foreign country; it is assimilated in ourselves, and resurrected into an ever-changing present (p. 412).

The past does not exist independently of those who seek to interpret it (as Taylor, 1987, makes clear in a very different context); the landscape may tell us more about the past people wanted to preserve than about the past as it was experienced. (It also tells us much about the people who describe it, as Porteous, 1986, illustrates in his discussion of body imagery as a metaphor for landscape description.)

An increasingly used text for the explication of meanings is literature – or 'creative literature' in White's (1985) term; Porteous (1985) refers to 'imaginative literature', within which geographers have been highly selective

> Plays are not considered, poetry is but occasionally used, the novel reigns
> supreme. The advantages of the novel lie in its length (meaty), its prose form
> (understandable), its involvement with the human condition (relevant), and its
> tendency to contain passages, purple or otherwise, which deal directly with
> landscapes and places in the form of description (geographical). (p. 117)

He argues that in using novels as texts, geographers have concentrated on
nineteenth century, rural contexts, with a particular focus on 'sense of place'.
To correct this, especially the latter, he proposes a two variable categorization
of situations according to whether the subject is an insider or an outsider and
whether the place being described is 'home' or 'away'. The 'home-insider'
provides material on sense of place, whereas the much less frequently reported
'away-outsider' refers to those experiencing alienation in what to them is a
placeless world. (White's, 1985, use of novels to describe the *situations* of
migrants – rather than the places that they live in – perhaps fits most readily
into this category.) 'Home-outsiders' are people who fail to develop insider
relationships with their milieux, whereas 'away-insiders' are travellers reporting their experiences (as in 'road, tramp, and down-and-out novels'; Porteous,
1985, p. 119).

Much humanistic geography has been written, therefore, in order to
describe and appreciate the variety of the human condition, as it is experienced. (Thus, for example, the essay by Eyles, 1989, in a volume designed
to 'introduce some of the most exciting challenges of the contemporary subject
to a wider audience' writes of place and landscape without reference to
philosophy.) It has been relatively unconcerned with philosophical issues,
such as the origins of meanings in human consciousness, and has focused
almost entirely on the empirical worlds of experience, even if these have
to be interpreted from secondary sources. (Note, however, Watson's, 1983,
claim that literature is not a secondary source but 'primary source material
for the whole world of images' – p. 397 – that illustrates the 'soul' of a place.)
Its relevance, according to Pocock (1983), is that

> it attempts to unravel the nature of being-in-the-world, as it explores the exist-
> ential significance of place as an integral part of human existence. In short, it
> is a geographical contribution to the most fundamental of questions, 'what is
> man?' (p. 357)

Meinig (1983) expresses this more vigorously

> By limiting ourselves to describing and measuring and analyzing certain aspects
> of the world as it seems geographers have denied themselves the possibility of
> probing very deeply into what it all means. Being unable to convey what it
> means we cannot help shape it toward what it might become (p. 325).

Explicating what it means involves practising geography as art, placing the
discipline firmly in the humanities as well as the sciences and the social
sciences.

One problem for such work, brought home to geographers by Olsson in a series of iconoclastic essays (Olsson, 1978, 1979, 1982: see also Pred, 1988), is that the medium of the text is enabling as well as constraining. His particular concern is with language as medium, and with the constraints that word definitions and usages put on their application, and hence the modes of thought that they support. Thus (Olsson, 1982)

> any social scientist is handicapped by the methodological praxis which requires him to be more stupid than he actually is. Thus, in the interests of discipline, verification and communication he relies mainly on the two senses of sight and hearing: what counts is what can be counted; what can be counted is what can be pointed to; what can be pointed to is what can be unequivocally named. Accumulation of knowledge about the nameable is consequently the point of the scientist's game (p. 227).

Thus ambiguity is translated into certainty; merely describing a phenomenon by words allocates it to a category, and can over-simplify the complexity of the world. Hence our ability to think is made possible by the richness of language yet at the same time constrained by the categorizations that it imposes; the former aids our understanding but the latter can hinder it (so that, as critical theorists have made clear – p. 227 – language, as the major medium of communication, can be employed ideologically to promote certain forms of understanding: Held, 1980).

Cultural Geography and Humanistic Geography in Practice

In earlier chapters it has been argued that the detailed debates about philosophy and methodology in geography have engaged only a minority of the discipline's practitioners, so far as the empiricist/positivist approaches are concerned, whereas a majority have conducted their own empirical enquiries informed by those debates but only marginally connected to them. To a considerable extent this has been the case with humanistic geography too. A small number of writers have been concerned with its philosophical underpinnings, and with the relative merits of idealism, existentialism, phenomenology, pragmatism and so forth. Others have accepted the general tenor of the argument, described by Boal and Livingstone (1989, pp. 7–8) in the following terms:

> We can give up the need to find direct empirical connections between terms and objects in the world; we can view knowledge not as presenting the world in some correct way, but as just helping us to get along in it, or to change it. Truth, to repeat, has nothing to do with accurately representing, or, as Rorty has it, mirroring reality; it is just, according to Rose, 'what we are well advised, given our present beliefs, to assert'. The purpose of geography, then, is not to tell us about how the world 'really' is: it tells us nothing about regions or landscapes or economic structures or human agency, because these are mere linguistic fictions; it is just the search for 'the right vocabulary, the right jargon, the best discourse in which to pursue the kinds of account which help us in the most basic sense, decide what to do'.

(The quote is from Rose, 1987.) Doing that, according to Pickles (1986, p. 29), involves 'archaeology', uncovering the layers of human behaviour to identify the experience that underpins it, which involves the explication of texts – the 'written records, cultural artefacts, urban landscapes or whatever' (Boal and Livingstone, 1989, p. 15) which are the repositories of human meanings, and whose interpretation is the goal of humanistic geography.

Some of the work undertaken within this humanistic framework, and without the explicit philosophical underpinnings, now goes under the rubric of *cultural geography*. As discussed earlier, cultural geography has a long and distinguished background, notably in the United States, based on the work of Sauer, and this continues there. Nevertheless, the suggestion of a break between an 'old' and a 'new' cultural geography is denied in the review in *Geography in America*, with Rowntree, Foote and Domosh (1989, p. 215) arguing that 'Although traditional cultural geography has preferred topics with historical depth, there is increasing interest and emphasis on the study of everyday life and landscapes'. But they recognize that the trends originating in Britain, and promoted by Cosgrove and Jackson (1987), do differ substantially from the more traditional concerns (as represented in the chapter on cultural ecology in the same volume: Butzer, 1989; see also Turner, 1989), and opine that 'Whether the British trajectory becomes an integral part of North American cultural geography remains to be seen': quoting Kofman (1988), they suggest that 'the "new" cultural geography is more talked about than done' (p. 209).

In their essay, Cosgrove and Jackson (1987) pointed not only to the continued vitality of cultural geography as the interpretation of past and present landscapes and other texts (for which they appropriated the term iconography, as in Cosgrove and Daniels, 1987: see also Powell, 1977, to whom they don't refer) but also to growing contacts with contemporary social geography. (Soon after, the Social Geography Study Group of the IBG was retitled the Social and Cultural Geography Study Group.) The field of contemporary cultural studies offered 'alternative ways of theorising culture without specific reference to the landscape concept' (p. 98), they claimed, with its emphasis on contemporary subcultures and their political struggles rather than 'the elitist and antiquarian predilections of traditional cultural studies'. This is illustrated in a special issue of *Society and Space* (Gregory and Ley, 1988), and in Jackson's (1989) text *Maps of Meaning*. Jackson begins his book with a definition of culture that marks the 'new' cultural geography (p. ix):

> This book employs a more expansive definition of culture than that commonly adopted in cultural geography. It looks at the cultures of socially marginal groups as well as the dominant, national culture of the elite. It is interested in popular culture as well as in vernacular or folk styles: in contemporary landscapes as well as relict features of the past.

The work of Sauer and the Berkeley School (p. 45 above) is criticized for being relatively narrow, culture is linked to the contested concept of ideology, and substantive chapters cover popular culture, gender and sexuality, racism, and language. An agenda for future work suggests an even wider coverage, into aspects of social relations that impinge upon the economic organization of society and thus link cultural geography more firmly with aspects of radical geography (as discussed below: p. 247). Work in this mould will presumably further the challenge to the content of traditional cultural geography as 'innocent' (Rowntree et al, 1989, p. 214).

Conclusions

There is a common thread which links the material discussed in this and the preceding chapter; both are concerned with positive rather than normative investigations, with attempts to uncover how humans behave in the world rather than with contrasts between actual patterns of behaviour in space and those predicted from normative theories. Both types are part of a more general trend towards an anthropocentric focus within the social sciences, which in turn reflects reorientations in the external environment. From the mid-1960s on there was a growing disillusion with science and technology, especially among students, and the popularity of the social sciences boomed. Within the latter, there was a shift in emphasis from study of the aggregate to the individual, an increase in the relative volume of research conducted at the micro-scale, and growing unease about the role of social scientists in planning mechanisms. Both behavioural (or behaviourist) geography and the various humanistic approaches reflect these trends.

Beyond the general concern with the individual as a decision-maker there is little else to connect the two types of work, however. Behavioural geography, as already pointed out, has maintained strong ties with the positivist/spatial-science tradition. Data are collected from individuals, but these almost all concern the conscious elements in action and their outcomes; they are usually aggregated in order to allow statistically substantive and significant generalizations to be made about spatial behaviour, almost certainly in the context of the normative models of the spatial science school. In the humanistic strand, on the other hand, the intent has been to understand and to recognize the dignity and humanity of the individual, but the output of substantive studies has not been great. This may indicate that the ethos of the positivist tradition has maintained a major constraint to the wholesale adoption of new philosophies and methodologies. Many investigations in human geography from 1970 onwards involved some behavioural concepts other than those of 'economic man', but relatively few human geographers have become humanistic geographers.

The two approaches are very much antithetical. One – behavioural geography – treats people as responders to stimuli. It seeks to identify how different individuals respond to particular stimuli (and also how the same individual responds to the same stimulus in different situations), to isolate the correlates of those varying responses and to build models that can predict the probable impact of certain stimuli. The end-product is input to processes aimed at either providing environments to which people respond in a preferred way or at changing behaviour by changing the stimuli. (Such environmental planning is considered social control by some.) The other approach – humanistic geography – treats the person as an individual constantly interacting with the environment and changing both self and milieu. It seeks to understand that interaction by studying it, as it is represented by the individual and not as an example of some scientifically-defined model of behaviour. And then by transmitting that understanding, it seeks to reveal people to themselves and to enable them to develop the interactions in ways that will be self-fulfilling. The two cannot be combined, since the concept of behavioural laws is not in sympathy with the humanist view that people are alone responsible for their circumstances and destinies, and are free – if they so choose – to exercise that responsibility as they will. Few adherents of either approach totally derogate the other. Humanists recognize that behavioural geography and spatial science may be valid approaches to certain aggregate phenomena – such as trade flows (Ley, 1981; see also Tuan, 1977) and the planning of transport systems, and behaviouralists recognize that their methods are irrelevant to the study of emotions and aspects of landscape (as suggested in the two main ways of studying space: Sack, 1980). But the two have little in common, and are competing for central positions as the philosophy of *human* geography.

For D. M. Smith (1988), humanistic work involves a 'new movement', and the chapters in the book that he edited with Eyles (p. 266)

> have provided persuasive accounts of ways of interpreting the geographical world which are capable of challenging if not displacing prevailing orthodoxy or at least of providing a convincing alternative. The positivist and empiricist paradigm fixated by mathematical process modelling with a promise of policy relevance . . . is already yielding to approaches more sensitive to actual human achievement.

For him, the struggle between paradigms apparently continues, with humanistic interpretative work now being rich in empirical example as well as strong in philosophical criticism.

7

Applied Geography and the Relevance Debate

The period since the late 1960s has contained traumatic years in the countries being studied here. The underlying problem has been economic uncertainty: after two decades of relatively high rates of economic growth and prosperity, the American and British economies began to experience serious difficulties. Further, it became increasingly clear that the prosperity of the previous decades had not been shared by all; this was highlighted in the United States by the growing tempo of the Civil Rights movement and in the United Kingdom by the unrest in Northern Ireland, which began as a civil rights movement, and a series of inner city riots, most of them linked to racial discrimination issues. Student protest erupted in several countries during 1968, much though not all of it related to the Vietnam War, and increasing concern was being expressed about despoliation of the physical environment. Other issues which gained increased attention included the relatively repressed state of women in western societies (this includes the geographical profession: Zelinsky, 1973a).

Much of the protest of the late 1960s was centred on particular issues and was relatively ephemeral. For many of those involved, the aim was to win reforms within society, in the classical liberal manner, while leaving its major structure untouched. For some, however, disillusion led to what Peet (1977) has termed a 'breaking-off' from liberalism and a move to more radical political stances. As he expressed it:

> The starting point was the liberal political social scientific paradigm, based on the belief that societal problems can be solved, or at least significantly ameliorated, within the context of a modified capitalism. A corollary of this belief is the advocacy of pragmatism — better to be involved in partial solutions than in futile efforts at revolution. Radicalization in the political arena involved, as its first step, rejecting the point of view that one more policy change, one more 'new face', would make any difference (p. 242).

Eventually, he says, the radicals exploded 'through the thick layers of ideology which in the most dangerous, mass-suicidal way, protect late capitalism'

(p. 243) and settled on forms of socialism (see also Blaut, 1979: Peet, 1985, has updated this history).

The substantive concerns of those termed 'radicals' from the late 1960s on are treated in detail in the next chapter. Here the concern is with the more general issues of applied geography and its role within the discipline. As noted in Chapter 1, the pressures for more applied work built up in the late 1970s and through the 1980s, initially as a reaction to the economic recession that afflicted the countries considered here during that period. In addition, the policies towards higher education, adopted from then on especially in the United Kingdom, placed an increased emphasis on applied work, both in terms of providing vocational and professional training for students and in the pressure to cover institutional costs through 'earnings' from research activity. Thus the debate over applied geography concerned pragmatic issues of disciplinary survival as well as concerns with regard to relevance.

Disenchantment and Disillusion in Academic Geography

A forthcoming revolution in human geography, against the innate conservatism of behavioural studies, was foreseen by Kasperson (1971):

> The shift in the objects of study in geography from supermarkets and highways to poverty and racism has already begun, and we can expect it to continue, for the goals of geography are changing. The new men see the objective of geography as the same as that for medicine − to postpone death and reduce suffering (p. 13).

This shift is illustrated by the writings of one senior geographer, Wilbur Zelinsky, who was president of the Association of American Geographers (AAG) in 1973. His views may not be entirely typical, and are certainly more firmly stated than those of his peers, but they reflect a growing disillusion within geographical circles with past achievements (see also Cooke and Robson, 1976) and a wondering about future directions.

Zelinsky's (1970) first statement began:

> This is a tract . . . The reader is asked to consider what I have come to regard as the most timely and momentous item on the agenda of the human geographer: the study of the implications of a continuing growth in human numbers in the advanced countries, acceleration in their production and consumption of commodities, the misapplication of old and new technologies, and of the feasible responses to the resultant difficulties (p. 499).

He developed three basic arguments:

1   that people are inducing for themselves a state of acute frustration and a crisis of survival;
2   that these conditions originate, and can only be solved, in the 'advanced' nations; and

3 that the current 'growth syndrome' has profound geographical
   implications.

Material accumulation can no longer be considered progress, he argues, for
it is not sustainable; effort is currently misallocated on a massive scale, and
there is a major geographical task involved in its sensible reallocation.

Zelinsky suggests five attitudes towards the problems of the growth
syndrome:

1 ignore them;
2 accept that major consequences will occur, eventually;
3 admit the existence of problems, but argue that they are easily solved
   by the free market, perhaps with state guidance;
4 claim that nothing can be done, but that in any case we will survive; and
5 realize the potential for immediate, unprecedented trouble.

Zelinsky's own attitude is clearly the last of these and he proposes three roles
for the geographer in facing the oncoming disasters. The first – which
involves a minimal political commitment and 'should not offend even the most
rock-ribbed conservative scholar' (p. 518) – is the geographer as diagnosti-
cian, applying 'the geographic stethoscope to a stressful demography'
(p. 519), mapping what he calls geodemographic load, environmental conta-
mination, crowding and stress. The second involves the geographer as
prophet, projecting and forecasting likely futures. Finally, there is the geographer as architect of utopia, educating with regard to problems and possible
solutions and providing support for the unknown leaders who have the
political will to guide society through the coming 'Great Transition'.

Ending his 'declaration of conscience' on a pessimistic note, Zelinsky argues
regarding geographers,

> how woefully deficient we are in terms of practitioners, in terms of both
> quantity and quality, how we are still lacking in relevant techniques, but most
> of all that we are totally at sea in terms of ideology, theory and proper institu-
> tional arrangements (p. 529).

His criticisms are not confined to geographers, however; in his presidential
address to the AAG (Zelinsky, 1975) he applied them to scientists en masse.
Science, to Zelinsky, is the twentieth-century religion, but he claims it has
failed to avert the oncoming crisis. (See also Harvey, 1973, 1989a, discussed
below on p. 196 and 255.) Its disciplinary specialisms and separatism 'fog perception of larger social realities' (p. 128), while 'fresher, keener insights, along
with much better prose' (p. 129) are produced by the brighter contemporary
journalists.

Zelinsky identifies five crucial axioms as foundations of science:

1 that the principle of causality is valid for studying all phenomena;
2 that all questions are soluble;
3 that there is a final state of perfect knowledge;

4   that findings have universal validity; and
5   that total scientific objectivity is possible.

The social sciences have failed to live up to these, he claims, for several reasons: their immaturity; their use as a refuge for mediocre personnel; the difficulty of their subject matter concerning interpersonal relationships; their problems of observation and experimentation; and the political and other problems involved in applying their proposed solutions. Furthermore, their major cause for failure is the irrelevance of the natural science model to the study of society:

> If we are in pursuit of nothing more than information or knowledge, then there is some value in copying the standard formula of a research paper in the so-called hard sciences. . . . But if we are in pursuit of something more difficult and precious than just knowledge, namely understanding, then this simple didactic pattern has very limited value (p. 141).

In other words, the natural science approach adopted by positivist spatial scientists helps to describe the world, but not to understand it.

Zelinsky's views were echoed in another presidential address to the same body, with Ginsburg (1973) writing that:

> Much so-called theory in geography . . . is so abstracted from reality that we hardly recognize reality when we see it. . . . The increasing demand for rigour to cast light on trivia has come to plague all of the social sciences . . . the most important questions tend not to be asked because they are the most difficult to answer (p. 2).

At about the same time, the Association established a Standing Committee on Society and Public Policy (Ginsburg, 1972), which White (1973) hoped would 'be alert to distinguishing the fatuous problems and the activities that are pedestrian fire-fighting or flabby reform' (p. 103). This statement was made at a session on geography and public policy at the Association's 1970 conference; a similar theme was chosen for the 1974 conference of the Institute of British Geographers (IBG). It should be noted, however, that not all geographers accepted White's aim – using the AAG to influence public policy – whilst not denying the value of geographic method in social engineering. According to Trewartha (1973):

> I must demur when he proposes that it should be a corporate responsibility of our professional society to become an instrument for social change. . . . From the beginning, the unique purpose of the Association of American Geographers has been to advance the cause of geography and geographers; it was never intended to be a social-action organization. . . . All kinds of research, pure as well as applied, should be equally approved and supported by the AAG (p. 79).

Two major arguments can be identified in the materials just reviewed: that geographical research should be relevant to the solution of major societal problems; and that the positivist-based spatial-science methodology may be inappropriate for such a task. As several have been quick to point out, neither of these concerns was particularly new, especially the first: House (1973), for example, has reviewed the tradition of involvement in public policy by British geographers, and Stoddart (1975b) has identified the late nineteenth-century views of Réclus and Kropotkin as 'the origins of a socially relevant geography' (p. 190) – the latter was later rediscovered by the 'radicals' (Peet, 1978). Nor was the more 'revolutionary' approach of those who had 'broken off' from liberalism particularly novel. Santos (1974), for example, has reminded English-speaking geographers of the marxist-inspired works of Jean Dresch on capital flows in Africa and of Jean Tricart on class conflict and human ecology, both prior to the Second World War; Keith Buchanan's presidential address on the need for studying 'the absolute geographical primacy of the state; especially in the non-Western world' (Buchanan, 1962) produced an acid response from Spate (1963).

Relevance, on What, and for Whom?

The claims that geographical work should be more relevant to major societal problems raised queries about the nature of that relevance, and it soon became apparent that there was no consensus on what should be done, and why. The ensuing debate is illustrated by a number of contributions to the British journal *Area* during the early 1970s.

The opening statement was by Chisholm (1971b), who identified differences between governments, with their interests in cost-effective research and their primacy in decision-making, and academics, some of whom are concerned to protect their academic freedom and their right to be the sole judges of what they study and publish. Traditionally, geographers had advised governments as information gatherers and 'masterful synthesizers' and had not been involved in the final stages of policy-making: they had been delvers and dovetailers, but not deciders. On the latter role, unfortunately:

> The magic of quantification is apt to seem rather less exciting when the specifications of the goods it can deliver are inspected at close quarters (p. 66). . . . The danger with empirical science is the absence of guidance at the normative level as to which of various options one should take (pp. 67–8).

The challenge to human geography, according to Chisholm, was to define such norms.

To Eyles (1971), the focus of relevant research should be 'some of the social and spatial inequities in society' (p. 242), and the challenge is to study the distribution of power in society, which is the mechanism that allocates scarce resources. Research would then identify the disadvantages of relative powerlessness – and would provide the basis for policy which redistributes resources.

Also in 1971, British readers were introduced to the ongoing debates in American geography with two reports on the 1971 AAG conference. This was not the first at which major social issues had been raised: the 1969 meeting should have been in Chicago, but it was transferred to Ann Arbor as a protest over events at the 1968 Democrat Party Convention in Chicago. At Ann Arbor, the radical journal *Antipode* was launched, and those attending were confronted by the problems of the inhabitants of Detroit's black ghetto. By the 1971 meeting, 'many geographers were deeply frustrated by a sense of failure' (Prince, 1971b, p. 152) to deal with major social issues, but while some members were taking notice of 'the sufferings of the outside world' (p. 152) other scholars remained 'locked in private debates, preoccupied with trivia, mending and qualifying accepted ideas' (p. 153).

In his report of the 1971 conference, Smith (1971) suggested that American geography was about to undergo another revolution, to counter a situation in which 'geography is overpreoccupied with the study of the production of goods and the exploitation of natural resources, while ignoring important conditions of human welfare and social justice' (p. 154). This forthcoming revolution would involve fundamental reevaluation of research, teaching activities, and basic social philosophies, and was represented at the conference by activities such as the foundation of SERGE (The Socially and Ecologically Responsible Geographer) by Zelinsky and others and by a motion at the Annual General Meeting condemning United States involvement in Vietnam. Smith was unsure, however, whether this revolution, with its emphasis on social as against economic concerns, would spread to Britain:

> The conditions which have helped to spawn radical geography in the United States include the existence of large oppressed racial minorities, inequalities between rich and poor with respect to social justice, a power structure and value system largely unresponsive to the needs of the underprivileged, and an unpopular war which is sapping national economic and moral strength. These conditions do not exist in Britain or exist in a less severe form, and the stimulus for social activism in geography is thus considerably less than in America (pp. 156–7).

(A decade later, Smith might have changed his mind.) Dickenson and Clarke (1972) responded that British geographers had long been concerned with 'relevant' issues, with particular respect to the Third World.

Another commentary on the 1971 conference of the AAG at Boston came from Berry (1972c), who felt that he had observed just a new fad involving 'new entrants to the field seeking their "turf" '. He could identify no real commitment:

> The majority of the new revolutionaries, it seems, are essentially 'white liberals', quick to lament the supposed ills of society and to wear their bleeding hearts like emblems or old school ties – and quicker to avoid the hard work that diagnosis and action demand. A smaller group of hard-line marxists keeps bubbling the potage of liberal laments. *In neither group is there any profound*

> *commitment to producing constructive change by democratic means. . . . If*
> *either of these will be the 'new geography' of the 1970s, count me out*
> (pp. 77–8).

To him, the academic geographer should provide a base of knowledge on
which policy can be built, and this involves a close involvement with the
education of future generations of policy-makers. But to Blowers (1972), 'The
issue is not how we can cooperate with policy-makers, but whether and in
what sense we should do so. It is a question of values' (p. 291). To him, the
activities proposed by Berry would be strongly supportive of the status quo,
and unlikely to produce fundamental social reform. Smith (1973a) responded
to Berry that 'bleeding hearts sometimes help to draw attention to important
issues, and marxists can make valuable contributions in the search for alternatives to existing institutions and policies' (p. 1), and he pointed out that the
current 'fad' was no more pronounced than that of the quantifiers a decade
earlier. The results of that earlier 'revolution' offered little for the solution of
social problems, however, and Smith doubted the value of the large projects
established by the AAG as part of its geography and public policy drive.
Instead the research focus should highlight particular problems, while
teaching should have emphases on 'a man in harmony with nature rather than
master of it, on social health rather than economic health, on equity rather
than efficiency, and on the quality of life rather than the quantity of goods'
(p. 3). Chisholm (1973) advocated caution in the corridors of power, because
geographers had done insufficient substantive research to back up a 'hard sell';
Eyles (1973, p. 155) argued that any entry to those corridors 'assumes that
the structure underlying policy alternatives is basically sound'; and Blowers
(1974) wrote that in the corridors one can only influence, not decide, and that
for the latter task geographers must develop their political convictions and act
accordingly.

   This debate on if, and how, geographers should contribute to the solution
of societal problems was a major item at the 1974 annual conference of the
IBG. In his presidential address, Coppock (1974) presented the challenges,
opportunities and implications of geographical involvement in public policy,
an involvement which he felt the current generation of students welcomed.
Policy-makers, he felt, were largely ignorant of the potential geographical
contribution, while at the same time geographers seemed unaware that 'there
is virtually no aspect of contemporary geography which is not affected to some
degree by public policy' (p. 5). Coppock sought to change this, to have geographers identify the contributions that they could make, to encourage research
relevant to those contributions, and to enter a dialogue with those who advise
on and implement public policy.

   Other conference contributors were neither as optimistic nor as committed as Coppock. Hare (1974), himself an adviser to the Canadian government, reacted to cries that geographers were not consulted enough with the
reply 'Thank goodness'. His argument was that geography, as a discipline, is

irrelevant to the separate domain of public-policy-making, although geographers, as individuals, because of the breadth of their training, could offer much that was valuable: his conclusion was 'Geography no, geographers yes' (p. 26). His was a different response to mounting social concerns from that of Steel (1974) who told the British Geographical Association:

> As geographers we often get hot under the collar over the number of theoretical economists who are called on to advise the governments of developing countries. We comment on how much better World Bank surveys of countries would be if they were prepared, at least in part, by geographers. . . . We wonder why university departments of geography are not engaged on a consultancy basis more often than they are, and we marvel that the Overseas Development Administration in London has only a handful of geographers on its staff where, we feel, an army would be more appropriate (p. 200).

In a later paper, Hare (1977) argued that a major reason for a lack of geographical contributions to public policy in recent years may be the poverty of their training: in recent years we have 'swept geography departments into the social-science divisions of faculties of arts and sciences where, from playing second fiddle to geologists or literary critics, we learned to play second fiddle to economists and sociologists' (p. 263). Geographers, he argued, would have to rebuild their discipline based on the centrality of society-environment interactions, with a new brand of physical geography that leans heavily on biological ideas and sources. Thus:

> We must reassert the old, essential truth that geography is the study of the earth as the habitat of man, and not some small sub-set of that gigantic theme (p. 266)

and regional syntheses should be stressed, because

> Realizing that regional perspectives are necessary in politics is to get one's manhood back (p. 269).

(See also Steel, 1982; Hart, 1982.)

Hare's views on the current irrelevance of geography to public policy were supported by Hall (1974) who argued that

> geography, most clearly of all the social sciences, has neither an explicit nor an implicit normative base . . . spatial efficiency . . . is rather a description of what men seek to do in actuality . . . not . . . any objective to be achieved or objective function to be maximized. (p. 49).

Policy-makers must seek their norms elsewhere; geographers, meanwhile, must develop a new political geography which will aid in their understanding of the crucial role of political decisions in structuring spatial systems (Johnston, 1978b).

Two other papers given at the 1974 IBG conference argued against Coppock's programme. Leach (1974), for example, claimed that governments, as paymasters, already constrained what geographers could do research on, and as a result geographers were being used; their only alternative was political action. Harvey's (1974c) contribution was entitled 'What kind of geography for what kind of public policy?'. Individuals wishing to become involved in policy-making were, he argued, stimulated by motives such as personal ambition, disciplinary imperialism, social necessity and moral obligation: at the level of the whole discipline, on the other hand, geography had been coopted, through the universities, by the growing corporate state, and geographers had been given some illusion of power within a decision-making process designed to maintain the status quo. Indeed, to Harvey the corporate state is 'proto-fascist' (p. 23), a transitional step on the path to the barbarism of Orwell's 1984. The function of academics, he claimed, was to counter such trends, to expunge the racism, ethnocentrism and condescending paternalism from within their own discipline and to build a humanistic subject and thereby assist all human beings 'to control and enhance the conditions of our own existence' (p. 24).

Harvey (1973) had argued previously that the current mode of analysis in geography offered little for the solution of pressing societal concerns:

> There is an ecological problem, an urban problem, an international trade problem, and yet we seem incapable of saying anything of depth or profundity about any of them. When we do say anything, it appears trite and rather ludicrous. . . . It is the emerging objective social conditions and our patent inability to cope with them which essentially explains the necessity for a revolution in geographic thought (p. 129).

He recognized three types of theory:

1   status quo, which represents reality accurately but only in terms of static patterns, and therefore cannot make predictions which will lead to fundamental social change;
2   counter-revolutionary, which also represents reality, but obfuscates the real issues because it ignores (deliberately or accidentally) the important causative factors and so can be used to promote changes that will not bring about significant alterations to the operation of those factors. It is 'a perfect device for non-decision making, for it diverts attention from fundamental issues to superficial or non-existent issues' (p. 151); and
3   revolutionary, which is grounded in the reality it seeks to represent, and is formulated so as to encompass the contradictions and conflicts which produce social change.

Harvey clearly wished to write revolutionary theory, thereby overthrowing the current paradigm; his blueprint for geography

> does not entail yet another empirical investigation. . . . In fact, mapping even more evidence of man's patent inhumanity to man is counter-revolutionary in the sense that it allows the bleeding-heart liberal in us to pretend we are contributing to a solution when in fact we are not. This kind of empiricism is irrelevant. There is already enough information. . . . Our task does not lie here. Nor does it lie in what can only be termed 'moral masturbation' of the sort which accompanies the masochistic assemblage of some huge dossier of the daily

injustices. . . . This, too, is counter-revolutionary for it merely serves to expiate guilt without our ever being forced to face the fundamental issues, let alone do anything about them. Nor is it a solution to indulge in that emotional tourism which attracts us to live and work with the poor 'for a while'. . . . These . . . paths . . . merely serve to divert us from the essential task at hand.

This immediate task is nothing more nor less than the self-conscious and aware construction of a new paradigm for social geographic thought through a deep and profound critique of our existing analytical constructs. This is what we are best equipped to do. We are academics, after all, working with the tools of the academic trade . . . our task is to mobilize our power of thought, which we can apply to the task of bringing about a humanizing social change (pp. 144–5).

To Harvey, then, relevant geography involves the revision of geographic theory; such new theory will be built on a marxist base, and its dissemination will achieve social reform through the education process. (This gradualist view, promoting reform through education, is only implicit in Harvey's work; Johnston, 1974, p. 189; 1986g.) To Blaut (1979), the benefit of marxist theory was that it can handle two crucial issues that positivist theory cannot: increasing injustice and heightened economic and social instability.

Harvey (1984) presented a forceful elaboration of his views a decade later in a paper subtitled 'an historical materialist manifesto'. Geography, he contended, not only records, analyses and stores information about society but also 'promotes conscious awareness of how such conditions are subject to continuous transformation through human action' (p. 1). But the nature of the knowledge that it collects and propagates reflects the social context of place and time, hence the role of geography in the 'Bourgeois era' as an 'active vehicle for the transmission of doctrines of racial, cultural, sexual, or national superiority' (p. 3). The positivist movement then sought to establish a universal science of spatial relations, which was countered by both humanistic and Marxist critiques. Together the latter suggested the development of a revitalized geography, but they lacked

a clear context, a theoretical frame of reference, a language which can simultaneously capture global processes restructuring social, economic and political life in the contemporary era and the specifics of what is happening to individuals, groups, classes, and communities at particular places at certain times (p. 6).

Historical materialism provides that framework, he argues (though see Eliot Hurst's, 1985, argument that, if Harvey continues to accept his 1972b contention that disciplinary boundaries are counter-revolutionary, then it is hard to understand how he can later promote a disciplinary-based manifesto).

Geographers cannot be neutral, Harvey argues, so their work must be of value to some special interest group within society. He is clear which that group should be, not 'generals, politicians, and corporate chiefs' (p. 7) but the disenfranchised. His people's geography, 'threaded into the fabric of daily life with deep taproots into the well-springs of popular consciousness'

> must also open channels of communication, undermine parochialist world
> views, and confront or subvert the power of the dominant classes or the state.
> It must penetrate the barriers to common understanding by identifying the
> material base to common interests (p. 7).

Such a geography will not only reveal to the disenfranchized how societies
are structured and restructured so that

> centers exploit peripheries, the first world subjugates the third, and capitalist
> powers compete for domination of protected space (markets, labor power, raw
> materials). People in one place exploit and struggle against those in another
> place (p. 9).

It will also help them to

> Define a political project that sees the transition from capitalism to socialism
> in historico-geographical terms . . . we must define, also, a radical guiding
> vision: one that explores the realms of freedom beyond material necessity, that
> opens the way to the creation of new forms of society in which common people
> have the power to create their own geography and history in the image of liberty
> and mutual respect of opposed interests. The only other course . . . is to sustain
> a present geography founded on class oppression, state domination, unnecessary
> material deprivation, war, and human denial (p. 10).

The Liberal Contribution

In the present context, liberalism is defined as the idea 'shared by many
modern American liberals who, characteristically, combine a belief in democratic capitalism with a strong commitment to executive and legislative action
in order to alleviate social ills' (Bullock, 1977, p. 347). Liberals, then, are concerned that all members of society do not fall below certain minimum levels
of well-being (variously defined), and are prepared for state action within the
capitalist structure in order that this can be achieved. Within geography,
much of the work conducted in this ethos has focused on description rather
than on theory-construction: the few exceptions include Chisholm's (1971a)
investigation of the potential of welfare economics as a basis for normative
theory which does not involve profit-maximization goals (see also Wilson,
1976b).

There is a long tradition of liberal contributions by 'applied geographers',
both in their research and associated activities and in their teaching (see
House, 1973, and Hall, 1981b, for reviews). In Britain, applied geography –
as information gathering and synthesizing – has a long and substantial
record. Stamp's Land Utilization Survey of Britain in the 1930s, his involvement in the preparation for post-war land-use planning, and the use of
geographical material in that preparation, provide a major example (Stamp,
1946). Other aspects of land-use planning were of interest to geographers
in the 1930s and 1940s, and were discussed several times at the Royal

Geographical Society (Freeman, 1980b); there was similar geographical involvement in the United States (Kollmorgen, 1979). After the Second World War – during which geographers made many contributions as information synthesizers and gatherers, the latter including the development of air-photo interpretation – land-use planning was established on a large scale, and trained geographers provided a large proportion of its personnel. Many academic geographers remained active in applied work. Technical developments in cartography and data handling have seen them involved in redistricting for Congressional elections (Morrill, 1981), a wide range of mapping activities (Rhind and Adams, 1980), and developing regional bases for the presentation of Census statistics (Coombes *et al.*, 1982), for example. Policies have been evaluated (e.g. Keeble, 1976), and much of the entropy-maximizing systems modelling (p. 125) was developed to provide procedures for the joint activities of land-use and transport planning (Wilson, 1974; see Batty, 1989).

Most of this work is set in an empiricist and (usually implicit) positivist framework. With regard to the former, geographers are perceived as having valuable skills in the collection and ordering of data, as in land use surveys. For the latter, the use of such data frequently assumed the existence of certain relationships and the desirability of maintaining them; the planning of agricultural land use, for example, assumed a clear causal relationship between the physical environment and agricultural productivity and that of industrial location assumed the need for efficiency via the minimization of total travel costs. (Interestingly, as some critics have pointed out, the greatest use of such optimizing models has been made not in the 'capitalist west' but in the 'socialist east'.) As positivist work developed, in the allocation of land uses and traffic flows, for example, so the potential for geographic inputs to spatial planning was promoted (and many people initially trained as geographers became professional planners). Most of this was pragmatic application of technical skills, though there were some attempts to evaluate policy impacts (e.g. Hall *et al.*, 1973) and to develop a theory of decision-making in this context (Hall, 1981a, 1982).

The empiricist role of geographers is one that continues to be advanced in the 1980s, both as a continued reaction to economic and linked crises and the need for valid data (a need not always recognized by some governments, which seek, for example, to reduce the amount of public data collection) and as a response to pressures from the state on universities and other institutions to contribute more to the attack on society's problems. In Britain, for example, the government introduced a three-year programme in 1983 designed to provide 'new blood' for university research efforts; 792 lectureships were available, in open competition between universities, with a further 146 in the fields of information technology. Geography departments received 11.5 of these posts (1.1 per cent of the total; the staff of geography departments comprised 2 per cent of all university posts in 1982–3). D. M. Smith (1985) argues that not only did geography lose out relatively in that contest (the 'winners' were engineering and technology and the physical and biological sciences) but also that within geography the posts allocated selectively focused on certain aspects of the discipline: five were for research in remote sensing/digital mapping, for example, and three more for various aspects of mathematical modelling (two in physical geography); only one reflected 'place-specific' issues, a post in historical-cultural geography. Smith interprets this as follows:

> The predominance of remote sensing (and associated digital mapping) reflects a view of geography as a technologically sophisticated means of gathering and displaying information, in the tradition of the geographer as map-maker linked to the contemporary preoccupation with information technology . . . [that] appears to conflate the needs of the discipline with a conception of the needs of society in which the emphasis is much more economic than social. It is hard to see more than one or two of the posts contributing much to the solution of *social* problems. The predominant impression is of an a-social view of the world, in which social relations, class structure and political power seem strangely absent (p. 241–2).

Clayton (1985a) responded that this was unlikely to be the only example of much greater state interference with the direction of academic research (see also his analysis of how geographers should react to that: Clayton, 1985b). Indeed, in 1986 the University Grants Committee produced a rating of the research record of every University department – on criteria that were not clear but within which externally-earned research income was clearly important – and began a selective allocation of funds to universities that reflected those ratings (see Smith, 1986).

Alongside those who argued for a greater commitment to applied geography in the empiricist/positivist mould, and therefore for an implicit acceptance of a particular ideology (Johnston, 1981a), there were those who challenged this view as the best way to respond to pressing societal problems. For them, the need was for a reappraisal of how geographers could assist in understanding the genesis of those problems rather than in the suggestion of solutions which rarely tackled the root causes. The major contributions of the two groups are the subject of the next sections.

Mapping welfare

During the 1960s, a lot of research was reported, under the general title of factorial ecologies (p. 82), on the application of multivariate statistical procedures to large data matrices representing spatial variations in population characteristics. These works, according to Smith (1973b, p. 43), were over-reliant on certain types of census data and therefore provided little information on social conditions. There had been some earlier attempts to structure analyses of such data towards particular ends, as in the work of rural sociologists on farmers' levels of living (Hagood, 1943), a concept introduced to the geographical literature by Lewis (1968), and Thompson *et al.*'s (1962) investigation of variations in levels of economic health among different parts of New

York State. Only in the 1970s, however, was the factorial ecology set of procedures adapted to the task of mapping social welfare on any significant scale.

Two workers led in this adaptation. For Knox (1975), a fundamental objective for geography is to map social and spatial variations in the quality of life, both as an input to planning procedures and as a means of monitoring policies aimed at improving welfare. The concept of level-of-living was divided into three sets of variables for this reporting task – physical needs (nutrition, shelter and health); cultural needs (education, leisure and recreation and security); and higher needs (to be purchased with surplus income) – and statistical procedures were used to provide accurate portrayals of the spatial variations in meeting these needs. With the resultant maps, geographers must then decide whether they are playing a sufficient role in awakening human awareness of the extent of the disparities or are 'under an obligation to help society improve the situation' (p. 53).

Smith's (1973b) very similar work was set in the context of the American social indicators movement and the growing belief there that GNP and national income 'are not necessarily direct measures of the quality of life in its broadest sense' (p. 1). His aim was to initiate the collection and dissemination of territorial social indicators, to point out the extent of discrimination by place of residence which occurs in the United States. Again, multivariate statistical procedures were employed to provide the needed maps, at inter-state, inter-city and intra-urban scales. (See also Cox, 1979, who extended the treatment to the international scale.) In a later book, Smith (1979) sought to present 'the basis for a better understanding of the origins of equality as a geographical condition and of the difficulties in the way of plans to promote greater equality in human life chances' (p. 11).

To use Chisholm's terms, these two works represented the geographer as delver and dovetailer, as a provider of information on which more equitable social planning could be based. Several other studies of individual elements in that planning performed similar roles, and also suggested spatial policies which could lead to social improvements. Harries (1974), for example, studied spatial variations in crime rates and the administration of justice, and argued that predictive models of criminal patterns, in the positivist mould, could aid in the organization of police activities; Shannon and Dever (1974) and Phillips and Joseph (1984) investigated variations in the provision of health-care facilities and argued for spatial planning which would improve the services offered to the sick (which is different from a geography of prophylaxis: Fuller, 1971); and Morrill and Wohlenberg (1971) studied the geography of poverty in the United States, proposing both social policies – higher minimum wages, guaranteed incomes, guaranteed jobs, and stronger anti-discrimination laws – and spatial policies – such as an extensive programme of economic decentralization to a network of regional growth centres – which would alleviate this major social problem.

An alternative, and highly personal, programme of mapping variations in human welfare was advanced by Bunge, who had prepared a 'geobiography' of his home area, part of the black ghetto of Detroit (Bunge, 1971). His is a deeply humanitarian concern for the future of mankind, which he interprets as a need to ensure a healthy existence for children; he wants a 'dictatorship of the children' (Bunge, 1973b, p. 329) with regions – 'may the world be full of happy regions' (p. 331) – designed for them. This requires a reduction in the worship of machines, which are inimical to children's health (Bunge, 1973c), and a mapping of the sorts of variables never collected by external agencies and therefore requiring the development of geographical expeditions within the world's large cities; these maps would include roach regions, parkless spaces, toyless regions, and rat-bitten-children regions (Bunge, 1973d), and some have been prepared for Detroit and for Toronto (Bunge and Bordessa, 1975).

Attempts at understanding

The mapping investigations just discussed are very largely descriptive, and any prescriptions offered are based on limited theoretical foundations. Other investigations included attempts to develop the necessary theoretical under-standing. Cox (1973), for example, looked at the urban crisis in the United States – the racial tensions and riots, municipal bankruptcies, and the role of the government in the urban economy – presenting his analysis in terms of conflict over access to sources of power. This was intended as part of an educational exercise, for:

> It would be utopian to think that we can propose solutions on the basis of our analysis. The locational problems and locational consequences of policies weave too intricate a web for that to be possible. All we can hope to do is inform. To be aware of the problems and of their complexity may induce some sensitivity in a citizenry which has shown as yet precious little tolerance for the other point of view (p. xii).

Nevertheless, his final chapter is entitled 'Policy implications' and discusses two imperatives towards greater equity in the provision of public services – the moral imperative and the efficiency imperative (the latter applies to the total level of welfare in society as well). The policies presented involve spatial reorganization to achieve the desired equity, including metropolitan integra-tion, community control, population redistribution, and transport improve-ments. A similar focus on spatial reorganization is provided in Massam's (1975) review of geographical contributions to social administration: his evaluation of service provision is in terms of the spatial variables of distance and accessibility, with major chapters on the size and shape of administrative districts and on the efficient allocation of facilities within such districts (see also Hodgart, 1978).

   Cox's work heralded an increased geographical interest in a much neglected field, the role of the state in capitalist society (see also Cox, Reynolds and Rokkan, 1974; Dear and Clark, 1978; Johnston, 1982a; Cox, 1979). Traditionally, political geography had been concerned with the state at the macro-scale only, dealing with political regions and boundaries and with the operations of the international political system (e.g. Muir, 1975). The similarly underdeveloped field of electoral geography had highlighted spatial variations in voting, but there had been little work on both the geographical inputs to voting and the geographical consequences of the translation of votes into political power (Taylor, 1978, 1985a; Taylor and Johnston, 1979). The state is involved in many aspects of economic and social geography, however, as both Buchanan (1962) and Coppock (1974) have stressed, but few geographers have investigated this involvement in any detail, or the electoral base on which it is founded (Brunn, 1974; Johnston, 1978b).

An attempt to present an understanding of spatial variations in well-being was presented by Coates, Johnston and Knox (1977). After defining the components of well-being and mapping their variations at three scales – international, intra-national, and intra-urban – they introduced three sets of causes of such variations: the division of labour; accessibility to goods and facilities; and the political manipulation of territories. (See also Cox, 1979.) Finally, they evaluated spatial policies aimed at the reduction of spatial inequalities, such as various forms of positive discrimination by areas. Their conclusions were that, of their three sets of causes, the division of labour is the primary determinant of levels of social well-being. Creation of this division is a social and not a spatial process, though it has clear spatial consequences, so that:

> The root causes of spatial inequalities cannot be tackled by spatial policies alone, therefore. Inequalities are products of social and economic structures, of which capitalism in its many guises is the predominant example. Certainly inequalities can be alleviated by spatial policies . . . but alleviation is not cure: whilst capitalism reigns, however, remedial social action may be the best that is possible . . . the solution of inequalities must be sought in the restructuring of societies (pp. 256–7).

(See also Johnston, 1986h.) Hägerstrand (1977) was drawn to similar, if not more pessimistic, conclusions:

> When the world is stable and/or unhampered liberalism prevails, then there is probably not much to do for geographers except surviving in academic departments trying to keep up competence and train schoolteachers in how wisely arranged the world is (p. 329).

(Hägerstrand's definition of liberalism in this case is undoubtedly that of economic liberalism, which favours price competition in the 'market place' and frowns on 'state interference': Brittan, 1977, p. 188.)

A more ambitious attempt at explaining spatial variations in well-being is Smith's (1977) book, in which he argues that:

> the well-being of society as a spatially variable condition should be *the* focal point of geographical enquiry . . . if human beings are the object of our curiosity in human geography, then the quality of their lives is of paramount interest (pp. 362–3)

and he acts on this by essaying

> a restructuring of human geography around the theme of *welfare* . . . to provide
> both positive knowledge and guidance in the normative realm of evaluation and
> policy formulation (p. ix).

The book proceeds from theory through measurement to application. The theoretical section is an amalgam of normative welfare economics with marxian
perspectives on the creation of value, plus the political conflict for power.

> The analysis will inevitably reveal certain fundamental weaknesses of the con-
> temporary capitalist-competitive-materialistic society, but the temptation to
> offer a more radical critique of existing structures has been resisted, in favour
> of an approach that builds on the discipline's established intellectual tradition
> (p. xi).

Two types of solution to perceived spatial inequalities are identified: liberal
intervention, and radical, structural reform – the former is emphasized
because 'most social change is incremental rather than revolutionary' (p. xii).
Thus one concluding chapter – entitled 'Spatial Reorganization and Social
Reform' – emphasizes reorganization of administrative areas, although geographers are later urged to be 'open-minded enough to see that there may be
greater merit to some of the development strategies practised with evident if
not painless success in the USSR, China, Cuba and so on' (p. 358). Further,
counter-revolutionary possibilities are foreseen – 'overpreoccupation with
spatial reorganization may serve the interests of the existing rich and powerful
by helping to obscure the more fundamental issues' (p. 359) – and some
socialist arguments are forthcoming – 'That spaces and natural resources
should be privately owned, with their use subject to the chances of individual
avarice, altruism or whim, is increasingly an anachronism' (p. 360). The conclusion is that:

> As geographers we have a special role – a truly creative and revolutionary
> one – that of helping to reveal the *spatial* malfunctionings and injustices, and
> contributing to the design of a spatial form of society in which people can be
> really free to fulfil themselves. This, surely, would be progress in geography
> (p. 373).

That design, he argued in a later book on the same theme (Smith, 1979),
would involve public control of multinational corporations, and greater
public participation in that control, with a decentralization of power, but he
was not optimistic that this would lead to the equality relevant in socialist
arguments because 'Striving to become unequal seems almost to be an imperative of human existence' (p. 363).

Environmentalism

The late 1960s was a period of rapidly increasing concern about environmental problems; as Mikesell (1974) described it for the United States:

> Towards the end of the 1960s the American public was overwhelmed with decla-
> rations of an impending environmental crisis. . . . Since that time, crisis
> rhetoric and a yearning for simple answers to complicated questions has given
> way to a more sophisticated and deliberate search for environmental under-
> standing. Ecology has been institutionalized (p. 1).

Two of the leaders of the public debate disagreed as to the cause of the
problems (O'Riordan, 1976, pp. 65–80): Ehrlich argued for the primacy of
population growth, and popularized the concept of zero population growth;
Commoner claimed that technological advances and the consequent rapid
depletion of resources plus deposition of pollutants created the major
problems.

Both of these arguments have clear geographical components, as Zelinsky
and others realized, and geographers have a considerable record of activity
in resource conservation. In the United States, for example, George Perkins
Marsh had written on the topic in 1864 (Lowenthal, 1965) and in the 1930s
the climatologist Warren Thornthwaite had been closely involved in the soil
conservation movement established as a consequence of the Dust Bowl phenomenon. Their interest in landscape modification was advanced by Sauer and
his followers, and reflected in the symposium *Man's Role in Changing the
Face of the Earth*: there was similar interest elsewhere, as exemplified by
Cumberland's (1947) pioneering classic on soil erosion in New Zealand.
Nevertheless, Mikesell wrote that 'developments in geography have been such
that the several phases of national preoccupation with environmental
problems have not produced a general awareness of our interests and skills'
(p. 2).

As part of the AAG's increased commitment to public affairs, its Commission on College Geography established a Panel on Environmental Education
and sponsored a Task Force on Environmental Quality. The latter reported
(Lowenthal *et al.*, 1973) that geographers would make excellent leaders for
the educational tasks in hand because of:

1   the breadth of their training and their ability to handle and synthesize
    material from a range of sources;
2   their acceptance of the complexity of causation;
3   the range of information which they are trained to tap;
4   their interest in distributions; and
5   their long tradition of study in this area.

All of these had fostered the development of expertise in work on environmental perception, on vegetation succession, and on relationships between land
use and soil erosion, which could be used as the bases for environmental
impact statements, the elaboration of environmental choices, and international research collaboration.

Geographical efforts in the area of society-environment interrelationships
were of two types. The first, traditionally geographical, was concerned
with description and analysis. Review volumes such as *Perspectives on*

Environment (Manners and Mikesell, 1974) were prepared, and a particular interest in problems of the physical environment of urban areas was generated (Detwyler and Marcus, 1972; Berry and Horton, 1974; Berry *et al.*, 1974; a later, British, addition was Douglas, 1983). The second type of effort focused more precisely on issues of environmental management (O'Riordan, 1971a, 1971b), with particular emphasis on its economic aspects and on societal response to environmental hazards (Hewitt, 1963): as Kates (1972, p. 519) pointed out, economics provided the theories and prescriptions of the 1960s (and later; see Rees, 1985). A topic of especial interest was the study of leisure, of the growing demand for recreational facilities, and the impact of recreational activities on the environment (Patmore, 1970, 1984; see the critique of much of that work in Owens, 1985).

Despite such activity, Mikesell concluded in 1974 that up to then the geographical contribution to environmentalism had not been great. Regarding the prognostications of *The Limits of Growth* (Meadows *et al.*, 1972), for example, he commented that 'the debate on this most relevant of all issues has attracted remarkably little attention from geographers' (Mikesell, 1974, p. 19) – though see Eyre (1978) – and he concluded more generally that: 'one must add hastily that many of the environmental problems exposed in recent years and also many of the social and philosophical issues debated during the environmental crusade have not been given adequate attention by geographers' (p. 20). Such a conclusion is supported by perusal of the contents of recent geographical journals, and of O'Riordan's (1976) lengthy bibliography.

A powerfully-argued case not only for more work on the society-environment interface but also for its centrality to the whole of geographical activity has been presented by Stoddart (1987). He begins by contending that instead of celebrating the achievements of a century of professional geography, many of his colleagues are 'despondent, morose, disillusioned, almost literally devoid of hope, not only about Geography as it is today but as it might be in the future' (p. 328). He believes that this is because so many of them 'have either abandoned or failed ever to recognize what I take to be our subject's central intent and indeed self-evident role in the community of knowledge' (p. 329). For him, geography has become diffuse and lacking a central focus, which should be (p. 331):

> Earth's diversity, its resources, man's survival on the planet.

This involves a unified discipline, human and physical, in which:

> The task is to identify geographical problems, issues of man and environment within regions – problems not of geomorphology or history or economics or sociology, but geographical problems: and to use our skills to work to alleviate them, perhaps to solve them.

This, he claims, involves geographers claiming 'the high ground back' (p. 334), focusing on 'the big questions, about man, land, resources, human potential', and abandoning much that is currently done:

> Quite frankly I have little patience with so-called geographers who ignore these challenges. I cannot take seriously those who promote as topics worthy of research subjects like geographical influences in the Canadian cinema, or the distribution of fast-food outlets in Tel Aviv. Nor have I a great deal more time for what I can only call the chauvinist self-indulgence of our contemporary obsession with the minutiae of our own affluent and urbanized society . . . We cannot afford the luxury of putting so much energy into peripheral things. Fiddle if you will, but at least be aware that Rome is burning all the while.

Bird (1989, 212) points out that although Stoddart calls for a geography that is 'real, united and committed', 'we are not told exactly what it is, though for Stoddart such a geography obviously exists'.

Others have made similar, though less strident, calls (e.g. Douglas, 1986; Goudie, 1986; see also Cosgrove and Daniels, 1989); in response, the relevance of much that Stoddart would disregard in contemporary social science has been promoted as necessary to appreciation of society-environment relations (Blaikie, 1985; Blaikie and Brookfield, 1987; Johnston, 1989).

Stoddart's argument, in a paper which was first given as the ninth Carl O Sauer Memorial Lecture at the University of California, Berkeley, was clearly set in the cultural ecology mould. A similar case was made in the same year by Kates (1987), who regretted the dominance of spatial science within geography and argued that when environmental issues became important on the public and political agenda in the early 1970s (p. 526):

> No discipline was better situated than was geography to provide intellectual and scientific leadership. The natural science for the environmental revolution should have been the science of the human environment. Instead, intellectual leadership was split among biology, economics, and engineering, each of which transferred onto the human environmental realm their own theories of nature, of economy, or of technology, but none of these offered a truly integrated view . . . The theory of the human environment, then, was the theory of plant or animal ecosystems, or of pervasive externalities, or of technological and managerial fixes.

For geographers, then, the lack of an ability to respond to the demand for environmental scientists (producing 'geographers who can sit astride the natural and social science boundary to provide analysis, integration and leadership') was an opportunity lost, a 'road not taken'. But the Malthusian dilemma is still present, posing great questions for society which geographers can bring their special disciplinary advantages to in the search for answers (p. 532):

> We possess more than passing knowledge of both the natural and social sciences . . . We have some useful tools for organizing data and information . . . We possess a strong tradition of empirical field research . . . And perhaps most important we have and we teach a respect for other peoples' theories. Our answer, then, as to why geography . . . is that we are needed and that we are useful. When they go forth, our students understand the nature of the great questions, have more than a passing knowledge of natural and social science,

have been in the field, have collected and organized new data, and have placed these data into a theoretical perspective.

But to be sure that they will be called upon to perform in this way, geographers must put their house in order and some departments should rebuild centres of expertise in the human environment tradition.

Geographers have turned their attention to other 'great questions' within contemporary society, such as nuclear weapons and nuclear power. Regarding the use of nuclear technology in warfare, geographers have criticized attitudes to civil defence policies and likely deaths from nuclear blast and fallout (Openshaw, Steadman and Green, 1983) and have set that concern within a developing geographical contribution to peace studies (Pepper and Jenkins, 1985). With reference to the peaceful uses of nuclear energy, they have analysed, inter alia, issues relating to the siting of nuclear power stations (Openshaw, 1956) and the transport of nuclear waste. Others argue for geographical contributions to other aspects of peace studies (Pepper and Jenkins, 1983), such as international relations (van der Wusten and O'Loughlin, 1986), none more forcibly than Gilbert White (1985), who sees the human family as 'tortured and driven by its newfound capacity to throw the whole set of processes out of kilter by more violent action' (p. 14). The two editions of A World in Crisis? (Johnston and Taylor, 1986, 1989) have focused on many of these issues, ranging from the macro-scale in the study of geopolitics to the investigation of individual human rights.

The breadth of study in modern environmentalism is indicated by O'Riordan's volume. Much of the work is set in the liberal humanitarian tradition already illustrated in this section. O'Riordan draws four conclusions: environmentalism challenges many aspects of Western capitalism; it points out paradoxes rather than clear solutions; it involves a conviction that better modes of existence are possible; and it is a politicizing and reformist movement, based on a realization of the need for action in the face of impending scarcity and a lack of faith in the western democracies (pp. 300–1). A new social, environmental order is required. O'Riordan identifies three possibles – centralized, authoritarian, and anarchist; his choice is the liberal one, for the middle-of-the-road:

> we must individually and collectively seize the opportunities of the present situation to end the era of exploitation and enter a new age of humanitarian concern and cooperative endeavour with a driving desire to re-establish the old values of comfortable frugality and cheerful sharing (p. 310).

This new era, which will involve a new political order based on a combination of local self-determination and supranationalism, can be achieved through education – environmental education will form a preparation for citizenship.

To some writers, the revival of interest in environmental issues – mainly through the study of resources and their management – provides a contemporary linking of human and physical geography. Relatively little of the research and textbook writing indicates any integration of the two, however

(Johnston, 1983a; 1989b), because the focus is almost invariably on the processes studied in one of the sub-disciplines only. Thus physical geographers
study human action as a catalyst for environmental processes, as a result of
trends such as demographic growth, technological sophistication, urbanization, and demands for resources, but they take those trends for granted and
do not ask what processes generate them. Similarly, human geographers take
the resources of the physical environment as given and do not inquire of their
genesis. Thus while bridges have been built across the human-physical
geography interface, there has been no integration of the study of physical
and societal processes; for human geographers their links with other social
scientists are very much stronger than those with environmental scientists (as
illustrated, for example, by the lack of references to the physical geography
literature in O'Riordan, 1976).

Geographers and Policy

Most of the studies referred to here have been concerned with the identification of problems within societies − including their inter-relationships with
the physical environment − and suggesting solutions to them. Underlying
their varied approaches has been the basic thesis that geographers should be
much more involved in the creation and monitoring of policies. But what sort
of policies, and what sort of involvement?

Berry (1973a) has suggested that planning policies can be categorized into
four types. The first, *ameliorative problem-solving*, involves identifying
problems and proposing immediate solutions − as with the removal of a
traffic bottleneck. Such solutions are likely to stimulate further problems in
the future, since it is only the proximate cause that is tackled (the features
of the bottleneck) rather than the real cause (the growth of traffic). The
second type − *allocative trend-modifying: planning toward the future* −
involves identification of trends, evaluating what is likely to be the best outcome of the several implied by those trends, and then allocating resources to
steer the system being planned towards that end. The third − *exploitative
opportunity-seeking: planning with the future* − identifies trends and then
seeks to gain the maximum benefit from them, irrespective of the possible
long-term consequences; compared to the previous category, this one has a
dominantly short-term focus. Finally, *normative goal-oriented planning for
the future* begins with a statement of goals, of a vision of the future, and then
prepares a strategy which will ensure that they are achieved.

Relatively little policy-making is of the fourth type; most involves elements
of the other three, with general statements about goals but no clear strategy
with regard to a foreseeable future. To some critics, as detailed below, this
means that geographers who become involved in policy-making and evaluation are uncritically accepting the dominant forces in society, and leads to

arguments that their claimed scientific objectivity and neutrality is an (often unrealized) cloak for ideological political judgements about the nature of society. Whatever their individual motives, such geographers are acting on behalf of interest groups (private and public) whose sustenance depends on maintaining an unjust and unequal structure to society.

Such arguments are recognized by Clark (1982), who accepts that

> the academic community is not independent: there are no objective standards between competing explanations and thus policy advice (p. 43)

but who nevertheless agrees 'with the principle of policy analysis and the involvement of academics in policy-making' (p. 48). That involvement cannot be presented as neutral and objective, however, since all social science 'explanations' are incomplete and therefore compete with others to provide plausible accounts and prescriptions. Thus, Clark suggests four propositions that should guide academic contributions to policy analysis (pp. 55–9):

1 Academics must acknowledge their own values and beliefs in presenting policy alternatives and impact assessments.
2 Policy analysts must be advocates for particular causes rather than supposedly independent and objective adjudicators of knowledge.
3 Policy science should be critical of the status quo.
4 Sponsoring institutions must encourage advocate briefs and make those briefs accessible to the public.

In accepting these, academics who become involved in policy analysis should be considered 'part of the political process' (p. 57) whose role would be to ensure that

> Choices would be brought squarely into the open and be dependent upon the political, as opposed to expert, process (p. 59).

The present situation idolizes experts, and promotes a myth of social science as objective, neutral knowledge. Clark's case is that social scientists cannot be neutral experts, because their 'values, interests and normative views of the world' mean that their presentations, although scholarly and rigorous, are necessarily partial. (Sayer, 1981, has made a similar case in a slightly different context, arguing that any rigorous social scientific inquiry must be based on rationally defended value judgements; objectivity does not require neutrality.)

In another essay on the role of geographers – in this case urban geographers only – in applied work, Pacione (1990a) has argued that practitioners have paid insufficient attention to conceptual issues underlying what they do. He derives nine 'principles or guidelines' to remedy those failings: (1) the notion of value-free research is an illusion; (2) towns, as examples of places, are meaningful entities on which to work; (3) a spatial perspective is of substantial value; (4) the main emphasis of applied urban geography is on problem-solving; (5) a realist position provides the context for such work (see below

p. 222); (6 and 7) analysis must integrate various spatial scales; (8) a wide methodological tool-kit of quantitative and qualitative procedures must be employed; and (9) geography must integrate the findings of many disciplines. Johnston (1990b) responded by asking six questions of Pacione: what is a problem?; are problems always soluble?; what is science?; what is a geographic perspective?; who solves?; and what sort of society?. He concludes that some of the principles/guidelines are trivial and/or irrelevant, some are unsupported, and some are wrong, so that Pacione's contribution to a rationale for an applied urban geography is slight. For him, unless Pacione 'is prepared to tackle the fundamental issues of what problems are and how they can be tackled, he is unlikely to help those of us who want *both* an end to the problems that we currently perceive *and* a society which would no longer produce such problems'. Few problems are soluble, he argues, pointing instead to the need for resolution between opposing points of view, none of which have any claim to absolute truth. (This point is made in another way in a debate over how different geographers perceive the geography of Israel: Waterman, 1985; Falah, 1989: Khot and Waterman, 1990.)

Undertaking research characterized as 'relevant' – being pertinent to tackling societal problems – raises major issues for the individuals concerned, therefore. Thus, according to Mitchell and Draper (1982)

> when functioning as an advocate or consultant, the geographer must consciously decide how to resolve a conflict which may arise regarding the promotion of one perspective versus critical assessment and balanced judgement about all viewpoints (p. 2).

There are issues of *ethics*, as well. Mitchell and Draper argue that

> when functioning as a pure researcher, the geographer must balance a concern for obtaining necessary information against a concern for respecting the dignity and integrity of those people or things being studied (p. 3)

and this applies to 'relevant' research as well. Geographers have largely ignored these ethical issues, they claim, and their professional bodies, unlike those of other disciplines, have promulgated no codes of conduct. They show that conflict is frequently likely between striving to 'discover truth' and respecting the rights of those being studied, and they advocate individual, institutional and external controls.

These critiques of the arguments for greater involvement by geographers in policy analysis are entirely sympathetic. They make a case for *sensitive* geographical involvement; others question the grounds for such involvement and instead focus on the development of revolutionary theory (see p. 196). These contributions are discussed in the next chapter.

Changing Contexts and Applied Geography

As noted above, the demands for greater involvement in what is generally termed applied geography have grown in recent decades, largely, it seems, as a response to changes in the societal contexts within which Anglo-American human geographers work. This is not a surprising trend, according to Taylor's (1985c) analysis of the history of geography. In periods of economic recession, he argues, cutbacks in public funding of higher education and research can be expected, and to counter the loss of support geographers are forced to seek financial backing elsewhere (including arms of the state which contract for research); that backing is only likely to come if individuals within the discipline, and even collectivities representing the discipline, are able to convince potential sponsors of the value (i.e. potential 'profitability') of investing in geography and geographers. From this observation, and following Grano (1981), he identifies two external influences on disciplinary developments: 'Within academia geographers had to be given an intellectual foundation to satisfy intellectual peers, and outside in the wider world geography had to be justified as a useful activity on which to spend public money' (p. 100). These produce 'pure' and 'applied' geography respectively. Both are necessary to a discipline's future, but in different times and places the relative emphasis placed on each will vary. Thus:

> Outside pressures will be particularly acute in periods of economic recession when all public expenditure has to prove its worth. All disciplines will tend to emphasize their problem-solving capacity and we can expect applied geography to be in the ascendancy . . . In contrast in a period of expanding economies and social optimism outside pressures will diminish and academia can be expected to be under less external pressure. Geographers will thus be able to contemplate their discipline and feel much less guilty about this activity. We can expect bursts of 'pure' geography to occur in these periods . . .

Based on this argument, Taylor identifies cycles of pure and applied geography corresponding to cycles in economic prosperity.

The late 1970s and early 1980s should clearly be part of a period of applied geographical ascendancy, according to Taylor's analysis, and this expectation is borne out by experience of those years. Pressure to justify the discipline in terms of utility to economic goals was strong, and the search for research contracts of all types became much more determined (so that learned journals, such as *Area*, began to report quarterly on the new grants and contracts won by geographers and institutions such as the IBG, seeking to promote the discipline and emphasizing its utilitarian aspects). As the 1980s progressed, so the recession became less severe, but the pressure for applied geography was not released. In large part this was because the attitude within the state apparatus, particularly but not exclusively in the United Kingdom, did not favour a return to the type of funding of higher education which would sustain a further period of pure geography. Instead, academic departments were continually required to canvass for research funds from outside sponsors.

Changing the focus

The desirability of a continued period within which applied geography is in the ascendancy has been the focus of further debate of the type discussed above. Some clearly accepted the ethos, and argued strongly for a revised approach within geography. But their main concern was either with geography using its perceived particular skills in what Harvey (1973; see p. 196) terms the application of status quo theory (as in Pacione, 1990) or with exploring how geographers could make a committed contribution towards the achievement of change (Clark, 1982).

Bennett (1989) has based a case for a reorientation of what geographers do on a belief that there has been a major shift in the 'culture of the times', away from 'welfarism' – a consensus ideology aimed at 'improving the qualty of life and provision of needs through collective and governmental intervention' (p. 273) – towards what he terms 'post-welfarism'. This latter emphasizes individual rather than collective decision-making, and the role of markets rather than states (p. 286):

> the emergent 'culture of the times' has been happier to see the market as both the creator and the provider of new wants. Rather than markets being seen as an inhumane and exploitative system, socialism and even corporatist social democracy have come to be associated with the odious and paternalistic treatment of individuals.

This leads him to criticize geographers who work with 'social theory', and who accept the welfarist ethos, as being necessarily of the 'political left', and he challenges their 'core concept of relative deprivation and its consequential focus on relative inequality and hence "social" and "spatial" justice' (p. 285). Rather than a society in which 'every difference in outcome is translated into an entitlement to state intervention', which inevitably leads to a situation of 'total state intervention in everything', Bennett (p. 286) argues:

> Where the Thatcher era has heralded consumer choice and economic change, social theory and socialist politics has sought to defend the mode of production and to trap people in labour-intensive work practices and unattractive jobs vulnerable to technological change; the spirit of market freedom of individuals has heralded a consumer and service economy which has offered the release from the least attractive toils and labours, and has seemed to offer the potential to satisfy many of people's most avaricious dreams.

He sees this new, market-oriented society as posing an important challenge to geographers regarding the nature of their applied role.

For Bennett, geographical research whose main relevance is seen as aiding government intervention, without questioning the validity of that intervention, is no longer viable, and he also rejects the critical stance discussed in the next chapter which is based on a critique of capitalism. To him, the intellectual challenge for geographers involves dismissing notions of a welfare state founded on a social theory which emphasizes rights and relative needs, because policies based on such theory 'cannot be proved to work . . . Even social democracy offers no easy solutions' (p. 287). But markets do fail, and so:

> The two key questions for a post-welfarist society are: first how can support be improved by practical policies that can be demonstrated to work and are reasonably cost-effective; and second at what point does governmental action end . . . Hence what is needed is a better definition of what is 'socially' possible through collective action and what is not. Social theory and social democracy has, perhaps, promised too much and hence led to disillusionment in its own promises (pp. 287–8).

Answering those questions is central to the role he casts for geographers:

> The grand objective of the discipline should be to contribute to the debate around these issues. But it must be a contribution to practice.

This calls for a discipline in which practical concern with means is more important than theoretical debate about ends. In a post-welfarist society

> The welfare state, and its associated public decision-making, no longer has the privileged status that it can be justified by mere statements of belief in public or governmental goods: public goods and the policy that provides them have to be demonstrated to be *effective* in meeting social needs; policies have to work and be more effective than alternatives. (pp. 288–9)

Bennett provides no detail regarding what such a post-welfarist geography would look like, though he refers approvingly to Openshaw's (1989) arguments (see p. 130 above). He offers two brief suggestions, however. The first is a criticism of Marxist and related work (p. 289):

> The key aspect . . . is a better understanding of the structure of economic incentives and rights, rather than class . . . We need to identify a new language not of class but of 'rights' or 'nature'. By which I mean 'choice' conceptions of rights which promote autonomy, freedom, self-determination and human development, and not 'interest' conceptions of rights which make people passive beneficiaries of the services of others.

The other is a recommendation that:

> For the academic discipline of geography this means adaptation of its frameworks of teaching and research. I would argue that one aspect of this requires more intensive training in analytical methods including model-based approaches, information systems and elementary analytical skills.

Thus geographers are called upon to participate in a reevaluation of the welfare state, focusing attention on the limits to both individual choice and collective action, and to develop the analytical skills which will advance policy appraisal and so contribute 'useful knowledge to the research process, to policy debate and to practice' (p. 290). The extent to which the call will be followed, in the creation of a new form of applied geography, waits to be seen: in his commentary at the end of the book in which Bennett's chapter appears, Macmillan (1989b, p. 306) comments that 'the idea that the welfarist tradition is in terminal decline seems highly debatable'.

8

'Radical' Approaches

From the late 1960s on, there has been a growth within human geography of a group of related approaches for which a single, descriptive adjective is difficult to identify. Initially, the approach adopted was termed 'radical' (see Peet, 1977, 1978, 1985b), but in the 1980s this became less popular as the term was also applied to the political movements associated with the 'new right', 'Thatcherism' and 'Reaganomics'. Other terms, such as structuralist and realist, were proposed and adopted by some, whereas to yet others the radicalism was clearly associated with the adoption of a marxist (or marxian; on the difference see, Harvey, 1973) approach. But although Walker (1989a, p. 135) has argued that 'While not every realist is a marxist as regards theory of society . . . every marxist must be a realist', the latter term has not been generally accepted, and the so-called 'radical' approaches lack a consensus definition and coherence.

More recently, the approaches have been categorized in two new ways. In his evaluation of their contribution to American geography, Walker (1989b) writes of 'Geography from the left', which involves 'bringing the analytic framework and progressive social agenda of marxism and allied schools of thought into most of the traditional subject areas of the discipline' (p. 619). As he expresses it, the goal of achieving a 'more explicitly spatialized theory of capitalist societies' involved some scholars developing Marxist theory more fully, some looking at methods and 'welcoming the clarifications that realism, critical theory, and structuration theory might add to the understanding of social processes and how to grasp them' (p. 620), while others still sought to develop 'middle level' theories of such topics as local labour markets. And he argues that:

> Left geographers can be proud of their achievements in a discipline that is not always noted for its explanatory depth or overriding concern with human oppression and liberation. The left can claim a good deal of credit for broadening the intellectual respectability of the geographic enterprise

following this with a review which clearly indicates the breadth of work undertaken by 'the left'.

Rather than use 'the left' as the collective term within which to group a wide range of work, and no longer favouring the adjective 'radical', Peet and Thrift (1989, p. 3) have selected 'political economy':

> to encompass a whole range of perspectives which sometimes differ from one another and yet share common concerns and similar viewpoints. The term does not imply geography as a type of economics. Rather economy is understood in its broad sense as social economy, or way of life, founded in production . . . Clearly, this definition is influenced by Marxism . . . But the political-economy approach in geography is not, and never was, confined to Marxism . . . So, while political economy refers to a broad spectrum of ideas, these notions have focus and order: political-economic geographers practise their discipline as part of a general, critical theory emphasizing the social production of existence.

This group of approaches began as 'radical geography' in the 1960s, as a (lukewarm) reaction to the crises of capitalism made clear in both the response to the Vietnam War and the US Civil Rights movement; in the 1970s, led by David Harvey, it explored marxism in depth; and in the 1980s it became 'more sober and less combative' (p. 7) as marxism was subjected to criticism, the recession of the 1980s led to more disciplined inquiry, greater knowledge of the problems of socialist economies made the prospects of revolutionary change less likely, geography became more narrowly professional, and some of the 'radical, anti-establishment Young Turks' joined the establishment. Nevertheless, they conclude (p. 7) that:

> The political-economy approach . . . has survived counterattack, critique, and economic and professional hard times, and has matured into a leading and, for many, *the* [their emphasis] leading school of contemporary geographic thought.

It is with the activities of that school that the present chapter is concerned.

Radical Beginnings

Peet (1977) has pointed out that the early 'radical' work by geographers in the late 1960s was liberal in its attitudes (p. 142):

> Radicals investigated only the surface aspects of these questions — that is, how social problems were manifested in space. For this, either we found the conventional methodology adequate enough or we proposed only that 'existing methods of research must be modified to some extent if they are to serve the analytic and reconstructive policies of . . . radical applications' (Wisner, 1970, p. 1) . . . we were fitting into an established market . . . we were amenable to established ways of thinking . . . we were useful in providing background ideas for the formulation of 'pragmatic' public policy directions, and so could not, and were not, engaging in radical analysis and practice (p. 245).

This was illustrated by his own paper on poverty in the United States (Peet, 1971) — in which, like Morrill and Wohlenberg (see p. 201), he argued for a series of growth centres in the poverty areas – and also by the tenor of the articles in early issues of the radicals' journal, *Antipode*. Morrill (1969), for example, argued

> against the 'New Left' premise that a revolution is the only route to progress . . . the dreams of revolution are naive . . . the New Left vastly exaggerates potential support . . . a 'revolutionary program' is hopelessly dated and simplistic . . . the 'New Left' underestimates the capacity of our society for change. . . . All revolutions seem to have been betrayed by incompetents who preferred exercising power to executing reform (pp. 7–8)

and later (Morrill, 1970b) that

> A simple marxist-type change in the ownership of business from private to a government (or union) bureaucracy would in all probability decrease production, and would not necessarily bring any improvement in basic conditions. The key is to retain the institution of private property while instituting social control over its exchange and circumscribing its power over people (p. 8).

The case for a marxist approach was first presented formally by Folke (1972) in a critique of Harvey's (1972) paper on ghetto formation and counterrevolutionary theory. To Folke, geography and the other social sciences are 'highly sophisticated, technique-orientated, but largely descriptive disciplines with little relevance for the solution of acute and seemingly chronic societal problems . . . theory has reflected the values and interests of the ruling class' (p. 13). Liberal arguments such as Morrill's are dismissed as unlikely to succeed. Morrill had argued in his two papers in *Antipode* for change to be brought about by persuasion, producing a capitalist-socialist convergence. But this is the social democrat method practised in Sweden

> where it has been shown over and over again that the idea of equal influence for employers and employees is an illusion. After half a century of social-democratic rule injustices and inequalities still prevail. . .*. No small group of experts can accomplish anything . . . when it runs counter to the interests of the dominant social forces. These are not interested in equality or justice, but in profit (Folke, 1972, p. 15).

Radical change requires mass mobilization, and so, to Folke, Harvey's call for a new paradigm within geography was insufficient. What is needed is a new paradigm for a unified social science, containing geography, which deals with problems in all their complexity and provides not only theory but the basis for action: 'Revolutionary theory without revolutionary practice is not only useless, it is inconceivable . . . practice is the ultimate criterion of truth' (p. 7). (See also Eliot Hurst, 1980, 1985.)

The major contribution to the case for a marxist-inspired, materialist theory-development within geography was made by David Harvey, initially in his book of essays *Social Justice and the City* (Harvey, 1973). The book is presented as autobiographical, illustrating the evolution of Harvey's views towards an acceptance of Marx's analysis:

as a guide to enquiry . . . I do not turn to it out of some *a priori* sense of its inherent superiority (although I find myself naturally in tune with its general presupposition of and commitment to change), but because I can find no other way of accomplishing what I set out do or of understanding what has to be understood (p. 17).

The first part of the book is entitled 'Liberal Formulations' and comprises essays which analyse problems of inequality within societies in terms of the mechanisms which allocate income; the role of accessibility and location in those mechanisms is stressed. This leads him to an attempt to define territorial social justice, which separates the processes allocating incomes from those which produce them. Only in the second part of the book – 'Socialist Formulations' – is it

> finally recognized that the definition of income (which is what distributive justice is concerned with) is itself defined by production. . . . The collapse of the distinction between production and distribution, between efficiency and social justice, is a part of that general collapse of all dualisms of this sort accomplished through accepting Marx's approach and technique of analysis (p. 15).

The transition in Harvey's approach is marked by the paper on the ghetto (Harvey, 1972). He begins with a critique of Kuhn's model of scientific development (p. 11), asking how anomalies to the current paradigm arise and how they are translated into crises. The problem with Kuhn's analysis, he claims, is that it assumes that science is independent of its enveloping material conditions, when in fact it is very much geared to its containing and constraining society. Recognition of this point is important for geographers because:

> the driving force behind paradigm formulation in the social sciences is the desire to manipulate and control human activity in the interest of man. Immediately the question arises as to who is going to control whom, in whose interest is the controlling going to be exercised, and if control is going to be exercised in the interest of all, who is going to take it upon himself to define that public interest? (Harvey, 1973, p. 125).

To Harvey (1973), Marxist theory provides

> the key to understanding capitalist production from the position of those *not* in control of the means of production . . . an enormous threat to the power structure of the capitalist world (p. 127).

It not only provides an understanding of the origins of the present system, with its many-faceted inequalities, but also propounds alternative practices which would avoid such inequalities:

> we become active participants in the social process. The intellectual task is to identify real choices as they are immanent in an existing situation and to devise ways of validating or invalidating these choices through action (p. 149).

In such a context, geography can no longer be simply academic, isolated in its 'ivory towers'. Its practitioners must become politically aware and active, involved in the creation of a just society which involves replacement, not reform, of the present one. The remainder of Harvey's (1973) book does not make this commitment clear, however; it contains one essay on land use and land-value theory, investigating the difficult concept of rent, and another on the nature of urbanism, presenting a marxist interpretation of the process of urbanization. His later (1984: see p. 197) historical materialist manifesto is a very clear statement of that goal, however (though see Eliot Hurst's, 1985, critique), and his (1982) *The Limits to Capital* is presented as an attempt to extend Marx's theory.

Peet, too, moved from a liberal to a marxist position, replacing his earlier paper on poverty (Peet, 1971) by a marxist interpretation (Peet, 1975a) based on the assumption that inequality is inherent in the capitalist mode of production. This led him to a 'metatheory dealing with the great forces which shape millions of lives' (p. 567) within which

> Environmental, or geographic, theory deals with the mechanisms which perpetuate inequality from the point of view of the individual. It deals with the complex of forces, both stimuli and frictions, which immediately shape the course of a person's life (pp. 567–8).

Such environmental resources act as constraints because they define the milieux within which individuals are socialized and presented their opportunities for participation within the capitalist system. (See also Soja, 1981.) Mere redistribution of income through liberal mechanisms, based on taxation policies, will not solve the problems of poverty, therefore; according to Peet, the requirement is for geographers to seek alternative environmental designs, with removal of central bureaucracies and their replacement by anarchistic models of community control. (Harvey – 1973, p. 93 – disagrees with the latter, pointing out that unless resources are equalized among communities and territories, community control will only result in 'the poor controlling their own poverty while the rich grow more affluent from the fruits of their riches'.)

Structuralism

As a mode of analysis, marxism is a variant of the philosophy of structuralism (of which there are many different forms: cf. Johnston, 1983b). In general, structuralism identifies three levels of analysis: (1) the level of appearances, or the *superstructure*; (2) the level of processes, or the *infrastructure*; and (3) the level of imperatives, or the *deep structure*. Of these three, only the first can be directly apprehended; the superstructure of society comprises its social, cultural, political, and spatial organization. But this superstructure cannot be used to account for its own existence. The processes creating it are in the infrastructure. This cannot be observed: its nature can only be theorized and compared with its outputs in the superstructure.

In most forms of structuralism, there is no deterministic relationship between the infrastructure and the superstructure. A particular process can result in a considerable number of outcomes, depending on a variety of factors. To illustrate this, the French social anthropologist Claude Lévi-Strauss developed the analogy of the cam-shaft driving a machine for cutting the outlines of jig-saw puzzles (Figure 8.1). The machine is constrained to produce only certain movements, but the order in which they come is random and means that it can produce a large number of unique puzzles. Study of one of these puzzles alone could not reveal the nature of the machine; only study of the machine could do that. Structuralism is the study of the machines but, unlike the analogy, these are not available for investigation. The structuralist researcher must develop a theory of the machine, and see whether the contents of the superstructure are consistent with that theory. (Note that the contents of the superstructure cannot be predicted because, to continue the analogy, the particular operation of the machine cannot be foreseen.)

In some forms of structuralism, such as Lévi-Strauss's social anthropology (Leach, 1974), it is further argued that the nature of the processes operating in the infrastructure is a consequence of the imperatives of the deep structure. Study of the patterns in the superstructure should reveal the nature of the deep structure, therefore (in somewhat similar fashion to the identification of essences in phenomenology: p. 173). Thus, according to Lévi-Strauss, all incest taboos are variants of a basic taboo which is imprinted in everybody's conscience. That taboo comes out in a slightly different form in each society and culture, but careful comparison of all taboos should reveal their common elements, and thus that aspect of human neural structure.

This search for deep structures does not characterize work in human geography, although it could be claimed that certain spatial concepts – the

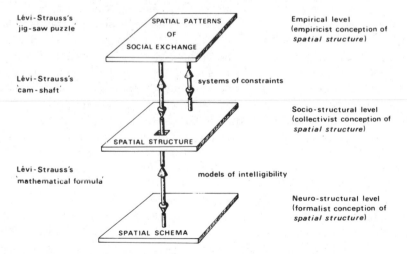

Fig 8.1   A geographical interpretation of Lévi-Strauss's cam-shaft analogy for structuralism
Source: Gregory (1978a, p. 100)

sense of place; territoriality; orientation – investigated by some humanistic geographers are realizations of deep structures. (In his important essay on territoriality, for example, Sack, 1983, decides to 'skirt the issue of whether human territoriality is a biological drive or instinct': see also Johnston, 1986c.) Only the work of the Swiss structuralist, Piaget, has received much attention. He claims the existence of a deep structure which allows the individual to assimilate and accommodate to new material. Golledge (1981a) argues that this approach informs some of the work in behavioural geography, but there is little evidence that it has had a major impact.

Marxism and realism

Marxist structuralism for the most part ignores issues relating to deep structures and focuses on the infrastructure and superstructure. Marxism has a materialist base, and so argues that the infrastructure comprises a set of economic processes. The contents of the superstructure at any one place and time reflect the operations of the infrastructure, within a milieu representing previous operations. They are not determined, however, because the super-structure is created, maintained and changed by human actors. These can interpret the economic processes in a variety of ways, for there is no one way in which a process must be realized – as illustrated in the different forms of government in the world and the different party and electoral systems of Western Europe and North America (Taylor and Johnston, 1979; Johnston, 1984a, 1986d). The interpretation must be consistent with the processes, which enable, but also constrain, human decision-making. The results of those interpretations will probably constrain the environment of the future. They will also inform the processes, but will not deflect them.

Marxist analysis seeks to identify the processes operating in the infrastructure and to relate them to the patterns in the superstructure. In human geography, this means deriving general theories of historical materialism that will account for particular patterns. The patterns themselves cannot be used to identify the processes – although they may offer clues as to their contents. The processes can only be identified theoretically, and compared with the superstructure to see if the outputs are consistent with the postulated economic driving forces. Within human geography, for example, Harvey (1975a) has suggested why socio-economic segregation takes place in urban residential areas, as a means of reproducing the class system and defusing inter-class conflict. The basic process is one of distancing (Johnston, 1980b). This can account for the existence of segregation, but not the particular pattern that it takes: suburbanization of the rich is a sufficient but not a necessary response to this process (Walker, 1981a). And for political geography, Taylor (1982, 1985b) has provided a materialist framework for the operation of the world-economy, within which states act. Again, this provides a theory of what the state is, and what it does, but not of how it reacts to a particular, time-place specific, stimulus (Johnston, 1982a).

The philosophy of *realism* (sometimes known as transcendental realism to distinguish it from direct realism), within which much marxist work can be located, is based on the separation out of three domains (Bhaskar, 1978): the domain of the empirical is concerned solely with experiences, with the world as it is perceived; the domain of the actual is concerned with events as well as experiences, accepting that an event (a particular item of human behaviour, for example) may be interpreted in different ways by individuals (by the actor, perhaps, and by another person experiencing it); and the domain of the real is concerned with structures that are not directly apprehendable, but which contain the mechanisms that lead to the events and their empirical perception. To realists, all science deals with these three domains, but the natural and the social sciences differ in the type of mechanism with which they deal.

The goal of realism, like that of positivism, is to explain events, discovering causes by 'finding out what *produces* change, what *makes* things happen, what *allows* or *forces* change' (Sayer, 1985, p. 163). But it differs from positivism because it contends that

> what causes something to happen has nothing to do with the matter of the number of times it has happened or been observed to happen and hence with whether it causes a regularity (p. 162).

Indeed, in the social sciences 'regularities' (i.e. laws and law-like generalizations) are very unlikely to occur. As Sayer (1984) makes clear in his detailed examination of realism, for such regularities to appear two conditions are necessary: the mechanisms must be invariant; and the relationships between the mechanisms and the conditions in which they occur must be constant. If both hold, then the science involved is studying closed systems: regular sequences of events should occur (either naturally or in laboratory conditions). If one or both is absent, however, the object of study is an open system, and regularities will then not occur. The social sciences study open systems:

> we can interpret the same material conditions and statements in different ways and hence learn new ways of responding, so that effectively we become different kinds of people. Human actions characteristically modify the configuration of systems, thereby violating the . . . [first] conditions . . . while our capacity for learning and self-change violates the . . . [second] condition (p. 113).

Thus the tendencies which comprise the mechanisms of human societies are interpreted in different ways, with the outcomes of those interpretations creating new sets of conditions for future interpretations. The mechanisms are abstract concepts, that are actualized in contingently related conditions: for example,

> the law of value, which concerns mechanisms which are possessed necessarily by capital by virtue of its structure (as consisting of competing and independently directed capitals, each producing for profit and being reliant on the production of surplus value, etc.), produces effects which are mediated by such

things as the particular kinds of technology available, the relative power of capital and labour and state in[ter]vention. No theory of society could be expected to know the nature and form of these contingencies 'in advance' purely on the basis of theoretical claims (pp. 128–30).

Thus whereas the mechanisms can be theorized, their particular realizations cannot, since they depend on human agency, on individuals interpreting the mechanisms in the context of their interpretations of the empirical world (see Johnston, 1989a).

The study of causation in a realist context involves what Sayer and Morgan (1985) term *intensive* research programmes. In these, the questions asked are of the form 'What did the agents actually do?', which involves examining causal processes in a particular case or group of cases. The answers will not be generalizable, in contrast to those produced in *extensive* research programmes, common in empiricist/positivist human geography, which are 'mainly concerned with discovering some of the common properties and general patterns in a population as a whole' (p. 150). Because the latter are almost certainly not investigating closed systems, however, generalizations are impossible; thus they are descriptive and synoptic only, whereas intensive research programmes are explanatory and

> Because intensive studies allow the identification of causal agents in the particular contexts relevant to them, it provides a better basis than extensive studies for recommending policies which have a 'causal grip' on the agents of change (p. 154).

Thus, as Massey and Meegan (1985) make clear, extensive research seeks to identify common outcomes through large scale studies that cancel out idiosyncratic behaviour in aggregate data, whereas intensive research views idiosyncracy as the complex interactions of necessary relations with contingent conditions; the goal of intensive research is to tease out those necessary relations. Nevertheless, Chouinard, Fincher and Webber (1984) argue that there are similarities between positivist and realist research strategies:

> Because social scientists (by definition) cannot guarantee an invariant relation between specific causal mechanisms, processes and empirical events, the 'laws' posited by theory must be treated as *tendencies* and not as empirical regularities . . . even non-realist human geographers have adopted these interpretations of testing and scientific laws in practice (p. 374).

Those non-realists assume, however, that with sufficient research behaviour will be predictable once all the possible interactions are accounted for; realist social scientists do not accept that argument.

It is the time-place specificity of the contents of the superstructure which provides one of the major elements in the realist critique of positivism. Positivism, in geography as elsewhere, seeks to identify laws of general applicability; realists deny that this is possible (Sayer, 1979, 1984). It is not quantification which is the basis of the criticism, but its use in the search for positivist goals (although see Sayer's, 1984, criticism, and the response by Johnston, 1986a); quantification as a descriptive tool is perfectly acceptable (Walker, 1981b; Taylor, 1981).

Positivist work in human geography is criticized by realists, including marxists, because it seeks 'laws' of the superstructure which are unrelated to the processes in the infrastructure, and which in any case cannot exist because of the change that is inherent in the infrastructure. Behavioural and humanistic work is subject to similar criticism, for apparently giving individual actors complete freedom and therefore removing them from the context in which they operate. With regard to the first, for example, Cox (1981, p. 275) argues that 'behavioral geography . . . unwittingly accepts the assumption of the separation of individual and society'; with regard to the latter, N. Smith (1979, p. 467) claims that 'The phenomenological approach . . . fails to take seriously the society external to the individual', and Wagner (1976, p. 84) argues that 'Existentialism and its close relatives in the Phenomenological camp seem to abdicate concern with the processes of history and the wider panoramas of geography, and so perhaps lack direct relevance': Warf (1986, p. 279) similarly writes that 'Phenomenology's exuberant voluntarism overstates the efficacy of intentional actions and assumes a fixed set of social relations asserting that consciousness is produced in an historical vacuum'.

In both positivist and humanistic geography, therefore, the individual is not treated as an actor constrained by society:

> In 'classical' location theory, agents were individual, autonomous, rational economic automatons. In behavioural theory, the main agents of interest were 'decision-makers' whose prime position is exaggerated by a disregard for economic conditions, thereby producing voluntaristic accounts where 'locational preferences rule' (Sayer, 1982, pp. 80–1).

The realist alternative emphasizes that behaviour is constrained by economic processes, but it does not deny human agency. The infrastructure provides 'determinants of activity of which actors are unaware' (p. 81), but within these the individual makes decisions, which in themselves may add to the constraints for future decisions: the infrastructure is thus both constraining and enabling, it restricts yet stimulates choice.

The acceptance of 'knowing actors' operating within structural constraints means that realism, like other forms of structuralism depicted by the analogy in Figure 8.1, does not argue that the contents of the superstructure are determined by the processes of the infrastructure. Rather it argues that the former can only be understood by the development and 'testing' (Sayer, 1982, pp. 85–7) of theories relating to the latter. Marxism, for example, is a theory of the processes. It is not an empirical discipline – its lack of an apparent focus on the details of the superstructure led Jones (1980, p. 257) to criticize its 'withdrawal from the patterns of distribution which are usually deemed the starting-point of geographical enquiry' – but it provides the framework within which empirical details can be studied and without which their understanding is impossible. However, a marxist geography does accept that the environment itself is an influence on the content of the superstructure. Cultural regions are formed (note that Gregory, 1978a, ends his book with a call for a renewed regional geography focusing on spatial variations in the realization of economic processes). According to Peet (1979, p. 167), in a statement that Duncan and Ley (1982, p. 37) call irresponsible:

> neither environment nor space is passive as social relations pass over and through them. . . . As class relations move over space, they pick up qualities from the regions of a social formation. . . . Class relations become infused with the direct and indirect contents of regions and environments. . . . They are transformed, thereby, into socio-spatial-environmental relations. Spatial relations are at base class relations; class relations contain the effects of space and environment.

Class conflict governs capitalist economic processes. Variations in the interpretation of this conflict from place to place create subtle variations in the superstructure, however. These may become self-sustaining, separate cultures within the overall capitalist framework, with the variations stimulating further spatial differences in actors' interpretations of the ongoing class conflict. (Culture never becomes a determinant, however – Duncan 1980 – only a secondary constrainer and enabler, secondary that is to the demands of economic processes.) The spatial/environmental dimension is thus important to the marxist analysis of empirical variations (see Quaini, 1982, and also N. Smith, 1984, on the marxist analysis of capitalist concepts of nature).

Marxism, then, is a form of realism, which seeks to relate the contents of an empirical world to a set of infrastructural determinants – economic processes. It is much more than this, however; it is also the basis for a political programme aimed at changing those economic processes. According to Peet and Lyons (1981, p. 205)

> If we want to understand what is happening to us, the people of the capitalist world, . . . we need a powerful, logical, sequential, political form of analysis to give an accurate, deep portrayal of the causes of events.

Marxism, including marxist geography, does this, and also provides 'a powerful theoretical and political base for resistance'. The marxist goal is to change the economic processes, and thereby to remove the dominance of the capitalist imperatives on individual action. This goal is based on Marx's humanism. He argued that people are alienated by the capitalist system; in particular that the proletariat is exploited and has its human dignity removed. To restore this dignity, to give the individual full control over self and destiny, capitalism must be overthrown and replaced by communism. The argument is that (Relph, 1981b, p. 122):

> truly human relationships can be achieved only when everyone can take responsibility for the conditions of their own lives and when there is freedom from the ideologies and actions of a bourgeois professional class.

Capitalism can only be overthrown by revolution, which should be achieved by the proletariat realizing their exploitation and determining to end it. Achievement of that realization requires emancipation, whereby individuals are made increasingly aware of their exploited position (Johnston, 1988). Such achievement is the goal of critical theory (Gregory, 1978a) which combines a marxist realism to the development of communicative skills (hermeneutics) so as to enable individuals to understand the real processes operating in society – to appreciate the infrastructure. Human agency is encouraged, by increasing awareness. (There is little reference to the deep structure that is assumed to exist in some forms of structuralism – as well as in phenomenology – p. 221. Marxists believe that all human behaviour patterns are socially created, hence their difficulty in dealing with the concept of territoriality when it is presented on a basic human drive.)

This political goal of marxist work leads to a major element of its critique of positivism – as indicated by Harvey's identification of three types of theory (p. 196). Positivist empiricism describes the present situation in the superstructure as a series of laws. Use of these laws in planning therefore seeks to maintain the present situation. Since that situation is one of exploitation, then positivist planning serves to further exploitation, to retain the present unjust capitalist structure rather than moving it on towards the desired social and economic change. Such work, in any case, rarely understands what is happening in the superstructure, it only describes it. Application of such incomplete understanding is termed instrumentalism (Gregory, 1978a; 1980). Positivist planning seeks to impose its laws on society, rather than recognizing its findings as descriptions of instances of a dialectically changing process that never exactly reproduces itself (Marchand, 1978).

To human geographers, therefore, marxist and related realist work suggests:

1 that explanation of patterns of spatial organization and of society-environment relations within the superstructure can only be understood as realizations of economic processes operating in the infrastructure;

2 that those economic processes cannot be apprehended directly, but only appreciated through the development of theories that are consistent with the outputs in the superstructure;

3 that those economic processes are continually changing, and with them the outputs – and as a result universal laws of the superstructure cannot be derived;

4 that class conflict (bourgeoisie v proletariat) is central to the economic processes;

5 that how the processes are realized in the superstructure reflects the actions of individuals operating within the constraints set by the processes and their preceding realizations – individuals are constrained yet enabled, not determined;

6 that any attempt to retain the present superstructure, by planning

procedures based on positivist examination of the present, can only help
the present unjust system to survive;

7   that understanding the processes and their realizations requires much
closer cooperation among, if not integration of, the social sciences than
heretofore; and

8   that the goal of academic work must be emancipation, leading to social
change.

Adoption of this programme involves altering the model of modern western
society. There are two main models, according to Eyles (1974, p. 39):

> one based on consensus, the other on conflict. The first would stress that social
> life is based on cooperation and reciprocation with norms being the basic
> element. Such societies would also be characterized by cohesiveness, integration
> and persistence and life within them would depend on the recognition of legiti-
> mate authority, mutual commitments and solidarity. The conflict model sees
> sectional interests as being the basis of social life which is, therefore, divisive,
> involving inducement and coercion as well as generating the structural conflicts
> . . . [that are] the central element in a social system.

Conflict – between classes in a capitalist society – and power – unequally
distributed in favour of the bourgeoisie – are the key elements in the latter
model, of which marxism is a particular form. Understanding that conflict
and how power is distributed and used is basic to understanding how resources
are allocated in a society. Its spatial organization is the result of the competition and conflict whose ethic (Eyles, 1964, p. 64)

> implies winners and losers and the winners in economic competition will be
> those with the powers of ownership and control in the productive process. In
> this way, growth under such a system will most probably lead to greater
> inequalities. It would seem obvious, therefore, that poverty and the distribution
> of real income in a spatial system cannot be understood without reference to
> power and inequality.

The Uses of Realist Approaches

The research tradition generated by the introduction of the realist approach
has several components. (Realist is used as a collective term to embrace a
variety of approaches.) The first is the critiques of positivist spatial science
and behavioural geography, and of humanistic geography, exemplified by
Rieser (1973) and Massey (1975). The second is to provide general theoretical
frameworks, within which empirical work can be set (as in Taylor, 1982,
1985b; Harvey, 1982; and major collections of essays on urbanization and
industralization – Dear and Scott, 1981; Scott and Storper, 1985). Thirdly,
there is work that seeks to establish how individuals act within the structural
imperatives (Johnston, 1983c, illustrates this): Eyles (1981, p. 1386), for

example, has argued that although 'no geography or social science can be complete without Marxism', this is insufficient. It must focus on the world of lived experience, the microworld of 'family, network, community, neighbourhood' if it is to be complete, and this requires integrating structuralist marxism with humanistic philosophies. According to a growing number of writers, this involves appreciation of the importance of places (frequently termed 'locales' or 'localities') as the context within which people live and act, and has led to calls for a 'new regional geography' (Gilbert, 1988; Pudup, 1988).

Initially, the purpose of much writing in the emerging realist framework was to demonstrate the shortcomings of positivist-inspired research, especially that categorized here as behavioural geography. In urban geography, for example, Gray (1975) presented a critique of studies of the operations of housing markets which focused on mapping people's residential moves and inferring these as the outcomes of choice and as expressions of preferences. He argued that such research: (i) assumes that people are free to choose in what homes, and where, they live, when most are actually constrained to particular types of dwellings in certain parts of urban areas only; (ii) assumes that residential patterns are the consequence of a large number of residents' decisions rather than those of a few developers and institutional managers; and (iii) implies that the study of consumers provides the key to understanding the structure of urban areas. But people are not free to choose:

> Instead, many groups are constricted and constrained from choice and pushed into particular housing situations because of their position in the housing market, and by the individuals and institutions . . . controlling the operation of particular housing systems (p. 230).

Research in line with Gray's critique focused on the controllers of access to housing, individuals who became known as 'urban managers'. According to a seminal paper by Pahl (1969), urban residential patterns are the consequence of two basic sets of constraints: the spatial constraints on access to resources and facilities, which are usually expressed in terms of time/cost distance; and the social constraints — the bureaucratic rules and procedures operated by gatekeepers — that also govern access and reflect the distribution of power in society. Study of the latter thus focused on the key managerial groups, such as building societies and their lending policies (Boddy, 1976; Dingemans, 1980), the managers of local government housing stock (Gray, 1976; Taylor, 1979), the local authority agents who influence the redevelopment of private housing (Duncan, 1974, 1975), and the real estate agents who structure access to housing submarkets (Palm, 1979). Pahl (1975) later revised his ideas, however, pointing out that planners, for example, are merely 'the bailiffs and estate managers of capitalism, with very little power' (p. 7; see, however, Pahl, 1979) so that focusing on them and other gatekeepers tends to

> view the situation through the eyes of disadvantaged local populations and to attribute more control and responsibility to the local official than, say, local

> employers or the national government . . . such 'a criticism of local managers of the Caretaking Establishment' and 'of the vested interest and archaic methods of the middle dogs' may lead to an uncritical accommodation to the national elite and society's master institutions (pp. 267–8).

The managers are important actors in the production of empirical worlds, therefore, but are not independent agents: in the analogy of Figure 8.1 they can be equated with the camshaft. Without care, treatment of managers outside the constraints within which they must operate could become as reductionist as some behavioural geography (see also Williams 1978, 1982; Leonard, 1982).

Whereas the managerial approach focuses on the agents who interpret and activate the real mechanisms, producing patterns of residential segregation, the work of Harvey has paid much more attention to the mechanisms themselves (though with reference to particular outcomes: Harvey, 1974e). Residential separation is one of the means of reproducing class differences in a capitalist society. It is brought about by the actions of those managing finance capital interpreting the basic mechanisms of the capitalist mode of production, and it produces a series of spatially separated housing sub-markets within which individual households may express their preferences, producing micro-scale migration patterns.

> But there is a scale of action at which the individual loses control of the social conditions of existence . . . [sensing] their own helplessness in the face of forces that do not appear amenable, under given institutions, even to collective political mechanisms of control (Harvey, 1975a, p. 368).

Such forces in the American context include those promoting suburbanization, a major means, according to Harvey (1975b, 1978), of stimulating consumption (of housing, automobiles, consumer durables etc.) at a time of dangerous latent overproduction (see also Walker, 1981a; for the particular outcomes, see Johnston, 1984b). Thus for urban geographers who accept the realist argument, the basic task is to bring together discussions of the mechanisms that drive capitalist (and other) societies, the interpretations of those mechanisms by key agents (the managers and gatekeepers), and the empirical outcomes and experiences. Thus they focus on how and why society operates, not on seeking to generalize the empirical outcomes (as in Bassett and Short, 1980; Badcock, 1984; Johnston, 1980b).

The study of urban residential patterns is just one element of the study of urbanization, which Scott (1985) relates directly to the nature of capitalism:

> the mechanisms of production, the interlinkages of firms, and the formation of local labor markets . . . combine to create a process in which the profit-seeking (cost-reducing) proclivities of producers lead directly to the dense spatial massing of units of capital and, as a corollary, of labor (p. 481).

Thus cities are both labour markets and places for the reproduction of labour, involving what Castells (1977) and others term 'collective consumption' of commodities produced by the state rather than purchased in the market place (see also Pinch, 1985); today, as Scott makes clear, some of them are also 'global cities' which are the control centres of the international corporate economy (see also Johnston, 1987). Scott (1986, 1988) has carried this work forward, presenting an outline theory for both the initiation of capitalist urbanization and the recent urban trends within the 'advanced industrial' countries.

Urbanization, according to these arguments, is just one element of the continuing process of uneven geographical development under capitalism (see Harvey, 1985a; N. Smith, 1984). In general, however, study of patterns of development has traditionally been the concern of economic rather than urban geographers. For some years, a major focus was on the study of patterns and processes (i.e. changing patterns: Hay and Johnston, 1983) of modernization, which involved using a series of variables chosen to represent various aspects of social and economic change (according to capitalist, technological definitions) which were statistically manipulated to produce maps of what were termed modernization surfaces (e.g. Gould, 1978b; Riddell, 1970; Soja, 1968). Such work presented Drysdale and Watts (1977) with the analogy that

> At times, geographers have resembled spectators who, seated on a hill overlooking a battlefield, are fascinated by the direction in which clouds of smoke are blowing (p. 41).

Brookfield (1975) was also very critical, arguing that such value-laden depictions, useful though they were as descriptive exercises, were redolent of

> a superb craftsman ignorant of the material with which he is working. The folly of such an approach was never better demonstrated than on the prolonged failure of . . . [Gould's] group to make its real contribution in an area where the direct participation of geographers is increasingly wanting (p. 116).

That participation would involve geographers becoming involved in policy prescription, but Brookfield found attempts in that direction even more worrying. Berry (1972a), for example, had produced a paper likening the spread of development to the diffusion of innovations and diseases within central place hierarchies; Brookfield described this as 'a highly mathematical paper on hierarchical diffusion employing his well-known, but doubtfully relevant data on the diffusion of TV in the United States' (p. 110). Similarly, Blaikie (1978) has criticized such diffusion studies as a 'spatial cul-de-sac' (see also Blaut, 1987) and Slater (1973, 1975) used them to launch a critique of the positivist approach, what he termed the 'Anglo-Saxon mainstream' abstracted empiricism.

Against the empiricism of the students of modernization surfaces and diffusion patterns, scholars of realist (including Marxist) persuasions have sought to develop theories of uneven development, emphasizing (Slater, 1975) that

> A crucial factor in the development of any spatial structure is the way in which surplus is circulated, concentrated and utilized in space (p. 174).

The major contribution to this has been a book by Harvey (1982) – *The Limits to Capital* – which is a substantial reworking of Marx's economics to incorporate the spatial factor which was largely ignored in the original formulations. The key element of the operations of a capitalist system on which Harvey focuses is that of 'those seemingly irreconcilable contradictions that lead capitalism into the cataclysms of crises' (p. xvi). Having examined the economic causes of such crises (in both the falling rate of profit and inflation, for example) he turns to examinations, in abstract, of geographical mobility of capital and labour to show

> how the contradictions of capitalism are, in principle at least, susceptible to a 'spatial fix' – geographical expansion and uneven geographical development hold out the possibility for a contradiction-prone capitalism to right itself (p. xvii).

Such 'spatial fixes' are not permanent crisis-avoidance mechanisms, however – 'Indeed spatial configurations are as likely to contribute to the problem as resolve it' (p. 429) – so that although capital is becoming increasingly mobile (hypermobile according to some: Ross, 1982) in attempts to avoid it, eventually global crises will emerge (see also the essays in Johnston and Taylor, 1986, 1989).

The spatial structuring of development is a topic of immense interest to realist geographers, at all spatial scales, and it has attracted a range of alternative theoretical formulations (for a critique, see Corbridge, 1986; Barnes, 1985, 1989a, 1989b uses an alternative, neo-Ricardian approach which he contrasts to Marxist and neoclassical approaches). Harvey's (1982) theoretical analysis implies that uneven spatial development is a necessary precondition for the processes of capitalist accumulation; others suggest that it is an inevitable consequence. Browett (1984) has contested both of these positions, however, claiming that:

> Whilst it is recognized that existing regional imbalances may well be taken advantage of and be exacerbated by capital in the process of restructuring, it is nonetheless maintained that they are not *necessary* to nor *systematic* consequences of, the *logic* of the capitalist mode of production (p. 156).

He argues that the real exploitative relationship is not between developed and underdeveloped places (to him a reification of space) but between labour and capital, and that focusing on space diverts attention from the real issue. N. Smith (1986) terms this 'reverse fetishism', as distorting as the spatial fetishism that Browett attacks, and presents the counter case (developed more fully in N. Smith, 1984)

> that uneven geographical development at different (and differing) spatial scales is a necessity of the logic of capital accumulation (p. 97).

Corbridge's (1986) detailed critique of much of what he terms 'radical development geography' is based on a perception that too much of it follows 'the path of dogma and determinism (wherein capitalism and its law of motion are assumed to remain essentially unchanged in time and space)' (p. 245) rather than a 'path of critical engagement (wherein the emphasis is on capitalism's temporal and spatial variation and its conditions of existence)'. He is unsure which path will eventually be followed. Harvey's (1982, 1985b) work is criticised for following the former path, for example. Initially, the problems of over-accumulation are tackled by a 'temporal fix' – the credit system – and when this fails capitalism turns to a 'spatial fix' – imperialism. But imperialism will eventually fail too, and bring global war in its wake.

> This sort of determinism is not at all what I have in mind when I talk of time, space and conditions of existence . . . If we are really to grasp the fundamentally different impact that the capitalist world system has had on (say) Brazil and Taiwan, then we must have done with models of capitalist development which oppose a fixed core and a fixed periphery (neo-Marxism) or which theorise the Third World in terms of the needs . . . of the imperialist powers alone (structural Marxism). More positively, our accounts of differential development must recognise that the dynamics of a changing capitalist world economy are always mediated by conditions of existence (population growth rates, gender relations, state policies and so on) which vary in space and time and which are not directly at the beck and call of a grand 'world system'. (pp. 246–7).

This view is somewhat akin to that presented below in the arguments about locales and structuration (p. 236). Watts (1988, p. 163) characterizes Corbridge's arguments as 'rash accusations of determinism' and contends that much radical development geography is concerned with the issues that Corbridge raises. The latter (1988, p. 239) accepts that there is 'a continuing dialogue *within* Marxist development studies' (and he cites Watts's own work in this regard: see Watts, 1989). Nevertheless, he maintains his contention that 'the theoretical heart of Marxism is seriously deficient and must always be rendered problematic' (p. 254), and for this reason he anticipates greater benefits from studies within the French Regulationist School, and their conception of different regimes of accumulation (such as flexible accumulation: see p. 251).

In a later essay, Corbridge (1989) reviewed the development of what he termed 'a more tolerant post-Marxism' (p. 225) which is less deterministically economistic than the classical variety and its offshoots, is sympathetic to the case regarding temporal and spatial variations in the process of capitalist accumulation, and thereby links development studies to the trends categorized as the 'new regional geography' (p. 245). Such a post-Marxism draws on Marxist analysis for its foundations, but is at the same time critical of its basic organizing concepts. The links to Marxism are especially strong in its materialist base, its emphasis on inequalities in the distribution of assets and power, its acceptance of contradictions within the accumulation process, and its agreement with the tenet that people make their own history but not in conditions of their own choosing. Post-Marxism differs from Marxism, however, in its refusal to accept that any non-Marxist concepts are incommensurate with it — Corbridge instead argues for a '*careful* wedding of concepts from Marxism and non-Marxism' (p. 246). It opposes the view that economic concerns are necessarily of primary importance, is sceptical of the labour theory of value on which classical marxism is founded, draws insights for its putative general theory of power and civil society from other approaches, such as feminism, and is not necessarily committed to revolution as the sole acceptable political practice. Works in this mould have already been written within development geography, he argues, though much remains to be done: an agenda covering seven tasks is set out.

The role of the state in various aspects of the production of geographies of uneven development has stimulated increased interest in the field of political geography. The nature of the state as an institution within society has been the topic of considerable theoretical and empirical interest, with attempts to appreciate its necessity to the dynamic of capitalist accumulation, its relative autonomy as an institution within the superstructure of capitalist social formations, and its particular features as an institution with a clear territorial identity (see, for example, Clark and Dear, 1984, for a full discussion of these issues; Taylor and Johnston, 1985, look at the British state in a similar context). The crucial role of the state is recognized by Harvey (1982), for example, who links the processes of uneven development to global geopolitics, and by Taylor (1985b, 1989), who has presented a reorganization of much of the basic subject matter of political geography around an appreciation of the functions of the state in promoting and legitimating capitalism. This allows spatial variations in state operations to be appreciated (as in Taylor, 1986), but that appreciation is never deterministic; in line with the realist approach the actions of the state (i.e. those with power within it) are those of knowing agents interpreting their roles in particular ways (as both Clark, 1985, and Johnston, 1984b, illustrate with regard to the courts in the USA; see also Johnston and Taylor, 1986).

Study of uneven development also involves work on the relationships between society and nature. As noted above (p. 204), liberal concerns over environmental issues increased substantially during the late 1960s and early 1970s. Harvey (1974d) introduced a marxist perspective to this issue, however, arguing that contemporary statements on resource-population ratios are ideo-logically based, an argument sustained through an examination of the works of Malthus, Marx, and Ricardo. Resources are not defined outside the context of societal appraisals of nature, and those appraisals reflect the current mode of production. Thus, predictions such as those of the *Limits of Growth* study (p. 206) represent a status quo theoretical perspective (p.196), whereas other perspectives may lead to different conclusions:

> let us consider a simple sentence: 'Overpopulation arises because of the scarcity of resources available for meeting the subsistence needs of the mass of the popu-lation'. If we substitute our definitions [of subsistence, resources and scarcity] into this sentence we get: 'There are too many people in the world because the particular ends we have in view (together with the form of social organization

we have) and the materials available in nature, that we have the will and the way to use, are not sufficient to provide us with those things to which we are accustomed (p. 272).

With the first version of the sentence, the policy option seems clear – a reduction of the population. But the second allows Harvey to identify three possibilities: (i) changing the desired end and the social organization; (ii) changing technical and cultural appraisals of nature; and (iii) changing views about the capitalist system and its scarcity basis. The Ehrlich-Commoner arguments (p. 206) accept the first version of the sentence and, according to Harvey, have been grasped by the elite of the capitalist world to provide the underpinning for a popular ideology (the need for birth control). Similarly, Buchanan (1973) has argued that the arguments for birth control in the Third World are part of the 'white north's' imperialist policy of ensuring its continued access to the resources of the international periphery (even to the extent of stimulating environmental destruction and famine: Bradley 1986; Blaikie, 1986), and Johnston, Taylor and O'Loughlin (1987) have explored the geography of what Buchanan (1973), along with other peace scientists, terms structural poverty:

> The poverty which is regarded as symptomatic of reckless population growth is rather a *structural poverty* caused by the irresponsible squandering of world resources by a small handful of nations (p. 9).

Under capitalism, the environment (or nature) is treated as a commodity, to be bought, exploited, and sold, in the same way that labour is. As N. Smith (1984) points out, in the ideology of capitalism nature is presented as some-thing external to society, as the 'antithesis of human productivity . . . the realm of use-values rather than exchange values' (p. 32). But analysis shows that in fact nature is produced by capitalism. Thus

> In its uncontrolled drive for universality, capitalism creates new barriers to its own future, it creates a society of needed resources, impoverishes the quality of those resources not yet devoured, breeds new diseases, develops a nuclear technology that threatens the future of all humanity, pollutes the entire environ-ment that we must consume in order to reproduce, and in the daily work process it threatens the very existence of those who produce the vital social wealth (p. 59).

Just as spatial organization and reorganization is a product of the continuing processes of capitalist accumulation, so is nature (Fitzsimmons, 1989). As Pepper (1984) expresses it, nature as an abstract concept is of no value to society; it is of interest only as a sphere of human activity. This allows him to separate the 'historicity of nature' (how the concept of nature in a particular time and place is related to the human activities there) from the 'naturalness of history' (the relationship between natural conditions and human activity – a relationship crudely expressed in theories of environmental determinism, p. 40). Part of the creation of a society involves its historicity of nature

> Labour is the means whereby man converts nature into forms useful to him. In the main nature does not offer ready-made subsistence to man, neither does man take direct possession of nature's resources. He has to transform them. This process of transformation is a *social* one — it is done with other people who are organized in a particular way . . . Thus through shaping nature, men shape their own society and their relations with their fellows (p. 162).

From this, it is clear that just as the creation of social relations (the means of exploiting surplus value from labour by capital) is part of the making of a society, so too is the creation of society-nature inter-relations; and just as those social relations contain within them the seeds of crisis for capital accumulation (the class conflict) so too do the society—nature inter-relations (environmental problems). Johnston (1989b) has carried this argument forward in an account of society-nature relationships under various modes of production and of the role of the state in their regulation: the essays in Blaikie and Brookfield (1987) illustrate that general theme.

Locales, Structuration, and a 'New Regional Geography'

In the 1980s, marxist and other realist work on topics such as those reviewed above has led to the growing integration of geographical understanding of the nature of capitalist society with that of other social scientists, notably sociologists. This has come about very largely through the realization that though it is a global phenomenon, capitalism works at a variety of spatial scales which are interdependent. This linkage has been made clear by Taylor's (1981b, 1982) writing on scales, of which he identifies three. The first is the global world-economy, what he terms the *scale of reality*; capitalism operates with little respect for the constraints of international boundaries, and the mechanisms that drive it (the domain of the real) are global in their reach. The scale of reality is beyond the apprehension of those subject to global capitalism, however, whose daily lives form their *scales of experience*: they do not encounter capitalist forces directly, but only as they are played out in the spatially restricted areas that form their life worlds. Between these two scales is the state — the *scale of ideology* — which is the major ideological force linking people's experiences of capitalism to its reality. These three scales provide the trilogy of the subtitle to Taylor's (1985b, 1989) *Political Geography* — world-economy, nation-state and community (see also Short's, 1984, trilogy — capital, state and community) — which captures his basic thesis that capitalism is organized globally, justified nationally, yet experienced locally.

Structuration and locale

The scale of experience is central to much recent writing on the spatial structuring and restructuring of capital, in a variety of contexts. Giddens (1984), for example, expresses it through his concept of a *locale*.

> Locales refer to the use of space to provide the *settings* of interaction, the settings of interaction in turn being essential to specifying its *contextuality* . . . Locales provide for a good deal of the 'fixity' underlying institutions . . . It is usually possible to designate locales in terms of their physical properties, either as features of the material world or, more commonly, as combinations of those features and artefacts. But it is an error to suppose that locales can be described in those terms alone . . . A 'house' is grasped as such only if the observer recognizes that it is a 'dwelling' with a range of other properties specified by the modes of its utilization in human activity (p. 118).

Locales can vary in size, according to Giddens, from rooms to the territories of states; they provide the settings within which interactions are organized, and are thus the contexts of economic, social, and political life.

Recognition of the contextuality of life, of its structuring and restructuring in locales, has led to the development of both geographically-informed social theory and cases for a restructuring of the discipline of geography. With regard to social theory, Thrift (1983) has developed an important distinction, derived from Hägerstrand, between what he terms compositional and contextual theory. *Compositional* theories classify individuals on certain criteria and allocate beliefs and behaviour patterns to them accordingly (as with both marxist and Weberian conceptions of class). *Contextual* theories, on the other hand, focus on the role of locales as the settings within which people learn how to act as human agents; their interpretations of their compositional categories are learned in particular places. Thus *structuration* – a theoretical approach developed by Giddens (1984) to account for the ways in which people learn about and transform social structures – is a place-bound (and time-bound) process; one's context (including one's language: see p. 184) is a major influence on one's individual development. (For an exegesis and application by geographers, see Moos and Dear, 1986; Dear and Moos, 1986.)

Structuration, as an example of a contextual approach, makes clear the falseness of any distinction between social relations and spatial structures; as Gregory and Urry (1985) express it

> spatial structure is now seen not merely as an arena in which social life unfolds, but rather as a medium through which social relations are produced and reproduced (p. 3).

Together they produce the process of *spatiality* (or socio-spatial dialectic), used by Soja (1980, 1985) to characterize the conjoint social production of space (*à la* Harvey, 1982) and the spatial construction of society. To Giddens and others, there is much in common between his conception of structuration and Hägerstrand's of time geography (though see Gregson, 1986), and Pred has used the two in a number of essays to illustrate their relevance to understanding the unfolding of both his own career (Pred, 1979, 1984a) and the development of particular places (Pred, 1984b, 1984c). Thus

> The meanings of interpretations I have imposed upon the past, the there and then in Berkeley and Sweden, are a result of the knowledge, attitudes and values I hold now, the ever fading here and now in Berkeley. Yet, the knowledge, attitudes and values I hold here and now are rooted in my past path, my past participation in projects and the institutional and societal context which generated those projectes (Pred, 1984a, p. 101)

and

> Biographies are formed through the becoming of places, and places become through the formation of biographies (Pred, 1984b, p. 258).

Relatively few authors have adopted structuration as a research methodology. Gregson (1987b), for example, argues that she has identified 'some quite major, and unresolved, problems in front of us before Giddens's theory of structuration can be demonstrated to be of real import for empirical enquiry' (p. 89). She discusses Moos and Dear's (1986) usage in which they present two levels of analysis: first (level 1) there is analysis of the individuals involved in the production of a particular event; and second (level 2) there is a higher-order analysis of the structural properties within which those agents are operating. These are tied together, they argue, by Giddens's concept of the 'duality of structure', the interdependent relationships among structure and agency. This they term 'abstraction' but Gregson doubts whether they have provided a way of moving 'between what are often universal theoretical categories and the specifics of the events which occur in particular times and places' (p. 81): thus, she says, they have provided only 'abstraction without specification'. Further, she argues that (p. 83):

> it would be unreasonable to expect structuration theory to generate either empirical research questions or appropriate categories for empirical analysis as it stands, and . . . to transfer structurationist concepts directly into empirical analysis is misconceived.

This is because structuration is about second-order questions, which are questions *about* social science that cannot be answered by an appeal to methods of obtaining facts, rather than about first-order questions *in* the social sciences.

Gregson's argument that 'structurationist concepts and categories will not, and should not, be expected to specify particular empirical research projects' (p. 84) appears to have been adopted by others, who instead take it as an organizing framework within which empirical work can be set. They accept that locales comprise social systems which provide the contexts within which individuals become 'knowledgeable actors': Sarre *et al.* (1989, p. 43) define 'knowledgeability' as:

> individuals' ability to infer from the complex and contradictory situations and processses of society both the prevailing rules and the most advantageous strategies and tactics.

Their ability to apply their knowledge then reflects their 'capability' to act in the ways that they wish. Their locale is thus both enabling and constraining, therefore: it is enabling in that it provides them with resources – knowledge – on which they can base action, and it is constraining in that it limits how they can act (both in the knowledge provided and the milieux in which it can be used). As they act, so they reproduce the rules, and thus ensure that the social system remains to constrain and enable further actions (their's and others'). But as they act, and make their choices, so they may change the rules somewhat, creating a new set of enabling and constraining conditions for future action. In this way, 'The course of history is therefore neither determined nor open, but a process in which rules and resources are both reproduced and to some degree changed' (p. 45).

How can such a theoretical framework be made empirically operational? Sarre *et al.* (1989, p. 46) claim that:

> Giddens offers few prescriptions about methods, though he stresses that the task is essentially hermeneutic, indeed it is doubly hermeneutic: the social scientist must interpret a social reality which crucially involves the actor's own interpretations. The way-in to study is an immersion in a particular area of society which allows the observer to 'get to know' 'how to be able' to act in it. However, this must not result in assimilation – the observer must be more aware than the actors of the nature of the rules and resources involved and of the way particular situations relate to wider structures.

Thus researchers interested in actions in a particular locale must both appreciate its social system and gain an understanding of how its residents interpret that system: they must both set the scale of experience in its wider context and study how the actors do the same. This, they argue, involves adopting a realist approach as developed by Sayer (1984; see also Sarre, 1987). However, 'the practicalities of what it means to do realist research are still emerging' (Sarre, 1987, p. 10), so:

> Our response was to utilise familiar methods of data gathering and analysis but to seek to interpret the data we collected in the light of emerging realist and structurationist views (Sarre *et al.*, 1989, p. 53).

Lovering (1987) has essayed a similar task, arguing that realism allows a non-eclectic synthesis to be achieved which avoids the empiricism, eclecticism and reductionism of other approaches (as demonstrated in his diagram: Figure 8.2). Nevertheless, this type of argument has led some to equate realist research with empiricism (e.g. Bennett and Thornes, 1988), and has led to substantial arguments among those who accept the basic realist-structurationist case. Those arguments are clearly illustrated by one major research programme.

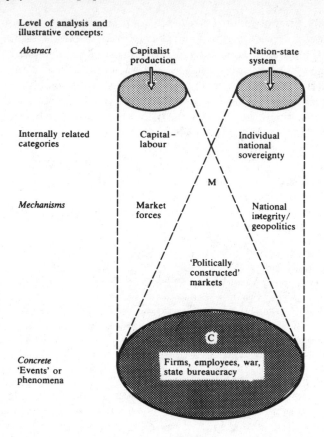

Level of analysis and
illustrative concepts:

Fig 8.2   Lovering's realist conception of the defence industry. The abstract categories are the domain of the real (p. 223); the mechanisms form the domain of the actual; and the events form the domain of the empirical: thus the mechanisms related to two abstract categories (capitalist production and the nation-state system) intersect to produce the events in which the military–industrial complex operates
Source: Lovering (1987, p. 298)

'Localities'

The localities research programme in the United Kingdom had its origin in Massey's (1984a) work on the changing geography of economic activity there. A central argument was that understanding the changing locational patterns of industries required an appreciation of the links between economic and social change. The social structures of local areas vary, she contended, in terms of how the labour process is organized, and from comparing two case study regions she concluded that (p. 194):

> although both . . . are now being drawn into a similar place in an emerging wider division of labour, their roles in previous spatial divisions of labour have

> been very different; they have different histories. They bring with them different class structures and social characteristics, and, as a result, the changes which they undergo . . . are also different.

(Without the terminology, this argument parallels that of Giddens's structuration theory discussed above.) Thus we get a changing industrial geography linked to a changing social geography as new 'layers of investment' are superimposed on those of earlier eras.

The outcome of these processes is areal differentiation, a regional mosaic of unique areas reflecting the interpretations of the actors involved in creating the United Kingdom's changing industrial geography. (A measure of the seminal importance of *Spatial Divisions of Labour* is the series of ten commentaries produced by Australian-based authors, published in Volume 12, Number 5 (May 1989) of *Environment and Planning A*.) Massey later generalized this in her essay 'Geography matters' (Massey, 1984b) in terms of each of its three traditional concerns – space, environment and place. Regarding space, for example, she argues that (p. 5)

> aspects of 'the spatial' are important in the construction, functioning, reproduction and change of societies as a whole and of elements of society. *Distance* and separation are regularly used by companies to establish degrees of monopoly control.

Regarding the environment, she argues that conceptions of the 'natural' are socially produced, and so might vary between areas as a reflection of separate social systems there, whereas with regard to place she contends that general processes can have particular outcomes in unique areas, in exactly the same way that Giddens does. Thus the study of geography involves unravelling the unique and the general:

> the fact of uneven development and of interdependent systems of dominance and subordination between regions on the one hand, and the specificity of place on the other (p. 9).

is thus a central concern for the discipline.

Massey illustrated her general contention through a number of case studies in *Spatial Divisions of Labour* (1984a), and provided others in an essay on women in the labour force (McDowell and Massey, 1984: see also Rose, 1988). She was also instrumental in the development of a major research programme, financed by the British Economic and Social Research Council, into the Changing Urban and Regional System (CURS). This initiative was introduced by the coordinator (Cooke, 1986) and summarized by him in a volume which reported on the seven case studies financed through the programme (Cooke, 1989a). The substantive focus of that work, as with Massey's earlier book, was the spatially varying processes of economic restructuring taking place in Britain during the 1980s. Thus (p. ix):

> The overall objectives of the programme were to explore the impact of economic restructuring at national and local levels, and to assess the role of central and

local government policies in enabling or constraining localities, through their various social and political organizations, to deal with processes of restructuring.

(The terminology is direct from Giddens.) But in addition

an important dimension of the research involved seeking to establish the conceptual status of the idea of 'locality' by taking account of a wide range of social scientific theory and research.

The concept of 'locality' was chosen after both the traditional term – community – and Giddens's own – locale – were rejected. As Cooke expressed it (p. 10)

There is a gap in the social science literature when it comes to a concept dealing with the sphere of social activity that is focused upon place, that is not only reactive or inward-looking with regard to place, and that is not limited in its scope by a primary stress on stability and continuity.

Locale was rejected because its spatial scope is vague, it suggests a passive rather than an active context for action, and lacks any specific social meaning. A locality, on the other hand, is (p. 12):

the space within which the larger part of most citizens' daily working and consuming lives is lived

and in which their citizenship rights are defined.

At the end of the summary volume, Cooke argued that the research reported from the seven case studies sustains his earlier contention regarding the crucial role of localities in the restructuring process and the creation and recreation of uneven development. The case studies illustrate, he contends (p. 296):

the argument that the relationship between the different scales is not simply a one-way street with localities the mere recipients of fortune or fate from above. Rather localities are actively involved in their own transformation, though not necessarily as masters of their own destiny. Localities are not simply places or even communities: they are the sum of social energy and agency resulting from the clustering of diverse individuals, groups and social interests in space. They are not passive or residual but, in varying ways and degrees, centres of collective consciousness. They are bases for intervention in the internal workings of not only individual and collective daily lives but also events on a broader canvas affecting local interests.

This conclusion, and the path towards it, has been the subject of considerable debate, much of it unfavourable on conceptual grounds because, as Cox and Mair (1989) express it, what is necessarily local and what is contingently so has not been defined.

One of the initial critiques came from Neil Smith (1987), who argued that the CURS programme as formulated was likely to be submerged in a morass of statistical information and contained within it the potential for producing no more than those earlier empiricist studies of particular places 'which deliberately examined individual places for their own sake, and [did] not attempt to draw out theoretical or historical conclusions' (p. 62). He was also concerned about the vagueness of the spatial scale in defining localities. Nevertheless, he welcomed the attempt to blend theoretical analysis with local understanding. The empiricism charge was refuted by Cooke (1987), who argued that the objective of the CURS initiative was 'theorised interrogation' (p. 75) of available data. His general position was supported by Urry, who initially (1986, p. 239) argued the general point that 'there are some significant locality-specific processes' and followed this with a list of ten different ways in which social scientists have addressed those processes (Urry, 1987; see also Urry, 1985).

Other critiques included Cochrane's (1987), who wondered whether CURS was 'just a cover for structural Marxism with a human face, or . . . the cover for a return to empiricism with a theoretically sophisticated face' (p. 355). His conclusion was that the programme contained within it the danger that as a guide to political action it might suggest that local struggle could suffice (what he terms 'micro-structuralism') rather than the realization that parts cannot readily be isolated from wholes. Gregson (1987a) was perhaps even less sanguine, arguing that the theoretical purpose of undertaking the seven case studies was far from clear, thus making the likelihood of falling into the empiricist trap high. Thus, she says, without a properly-articulated theoretical core 'CURS simply replicates the mistakes of previous local studies; with such a core it could be so much more' (p. 370). Beauregard's (1988) criticism is that the programme lacks any clear directions for practice, for using the radical theory to achieve social change, whilst Jonas (1988) sustains the 'drift into empiricism' argument.

One of the fullest critiques is provided by Duncan (1989), who accepts that the concept refers to something important – spatial variability and specificity – but concludes that 'the locality concept is misleading and unsupported' (p. 247: elsewhere he concludes – Duncan and Savage, 1989 – that it is 'confused, unsatisfactory, and largely redundant . . . a mystification', pp. 202–204). He accepts that 'space makes a difference' in three ways. First, social processes are constituted in places, which may differ because of previous 'layers of investment' (to use Massey's term). Second, actions take place locally and so can vary spatially. And, finally, spatially-varying actions can create spatially-varying contexts. But for him, the concept of locality implies 'social autonomy and spatial determinism' (p. 247), both of which he rejects. And he is unconvinced that local differences are that important (relative to more general processes). Thus (p. 248)

> Locality is . . . only important if and when locality effects are part of the causal group explaining any event. And locality may well not be important

which implies a verdict of 'not proven'. Cooke's (1989, p. 272) response (to the Duncan and Savage paper in particular) was trenchant:

> Local social processes are clearly an abiding feature of contemporary social life. Duncan and Savage's injunction to ignore them and settle on the structural level, supra-local, supra-national or whatever, in order to describe spatial variation in terms which deny agency to the social groups comprising localities, is both dated and redundant.

And he concludes that:

> 'Locality' can be seen to be a fascinating, complex concept of considerable value to geographical theory and empirical research.

The debate over 'localities' as the term has been used in the CURS programme is just one part of a wider attempt to identify the role of place in the creation of social scientific understanding. Thus, for example, Agnew and Duncan (1989, p. 1) open their introduction to *The Power of Place* with the statement that the book is 'an attempt to make the case for the intellectual importance of geographical place in the practice of social science and history . . . [through] bringing together what can be called the geographical and sociological "imiginations" '. Agnew (1989) then analyses why place has been devalued in 'orthodox social science' in recent decades, and in particular focuses on the confusion of place with community. The orthodox treatment, he argued, identified a decline in community with 'modernisation' and its replacement by a 'placeless' society, a transition seen as 'natural, lawful, and universal' (p. 16), with nationalism growing as a 'place-transcending ideology'. Similarly, the alternative view presented by Marxism devalued place with its emphasis on 'freeing people from places' (p. 22). (A similar elegant argument is provided in the companion chapter by Entrikin, 1989.) The goal of the book is to right those tendencies, and, through both theoretical argument and empirical illustration, to 'argue against the prevalent tendency in history and social science to overvalue the sociological imigination at the expense of the geographical' (p. 7: see also Agnew, 1990, on the similarities and differences between his structuration-based focus on locales and Hartshorne's arguments – p. 42 – for geography as the study of areal differentiation/variation).

Agnew's (1987b) detailed monograph on political behaviour presents his arguments at greater length, in a critique of political sociology. He answers his question 'Why adopt the place perspective?' in the following way.

1   First, adoption of the place perspective allows abstract categories such as class to be analysed in the context of everyday life. As a mobilizing force, class may be present or absent in a particular place, and where it is present it may be weak or strong as a focus of social organization. Class, like other catogories such as religious affiliation, means different things in different places, and understanding behaviour requires an appreciation of its nature in the milieux under consideration.

2   Secondly, by adopting place as the context within which structuration occurs one avoids the search for laws of behaviour that are universal in

both space and time, which is central to the positivist approach. The place perspective allows one to recognize the uniqueness of places without abandoning a commitment to causation:

Thus, the structuration of social relations in everyday life contains many similar elements from place to place (e.g. class, central-local government relations etc.), but produces many different outcomes in different places. (p. 42).

3   Thirdly, by focusing on place one can resolve the structure-agency problem, because this 'recognizes human action as both motivated and intended but, at the same time, as both mediated by social structure and generative of it'. Agnew realises that this is difficult, and can easily lead into either voluntarism or determinism (what Johnston, 1985d, calls, respectively, the 'singularity trap' and the 'generality trap').

4   Fourthly, the recognition of differences between places means that the division of history into stages can be avoided, because societies evolve differently, and at different rates, in separate localities whilst under the same general operative processes. (Here, Agnew previews the later arguments of Soja, 1989, and others regarding postmodernism: see, p. 249 below).

5   Finally, recognition of local differences that reflect cultural variations allows a counter to the arguments founded in economic determinism. Cultural phenomena are not simply reflections of economic determinants, but rather reflect the modus operandi established by people as they develop practices within which the economic imperatives can be pursued. The 'practical nature of everyday life' (p. 43) provides the context within which people act, and is the environment that they recreate as a consequence of their actions.

Agnew illustrates the benefits of this approach with a number of case studies, notably one on the geography of support for Scottish nationalism, which he claims that contemporary political sociology has failed to deal with satisfactorily. He argues that his approach brings together the 'geographical and sociological imiginations' in a microsociological procedure in which the macrosociological outcome (the pattern of voting for the Scottish National Party, for example) is the sum of the microsociological processes in the area considered. Such a perspective is based on the tenet (p. 233):

that political order is produced and reproduced through microsociological routines (locale and sense of place). Whatever the specific nature of power relationships, they cannot be separated from the realm of action and everyday practices. The macro-order (location) is represented in routines and practices of people in places.

Thus Agnew is arguing not only for a rejuvenation of the study of place (or locality) within geography but also for the firmer integration of that work with the other social sciences.

A 'new regional geography'

The debate over locality research is one element in a wider literature relating to the importance of studying the specific characteristics of places. The works using an implicit contextual approach are already numerous, and include Agnew's (1984, 1987b) argument that voting behaviour is strongly influenced by the local context of the electorate (see also Johnston, 1986e) and a detailed analysis of variations between local states in their provision of public housing, which is also informed by the realist perspective (Dickens *et al.*, 1985). Some have translated this general concern into a plea for a revived, and restructured, regional geography. Massey (1984b), for example, ended her plea for that cause with the argument that it is

> necessary to reassert the existence, the explicability, and the significance, of the particular. What we [must do] . . . is take up again the challenge of the old regional geography, reject the answers it gave while recognizing the importance of the problem it set (p. 10).

This echoes an earlier call, by Gregory (1978a):

> Ever since regional geography was declared to be dead . . . geographers, to their credit, have kept trying to revive it in one form or another . . . This is a vital task . . . We need to know about the constitution of *regional* social formations, of *regional* articulations and *regional* structures . . . [producing] a doubly human geography: human in the sense that it recognizes that its concepts are specifically human constructions, rooted in specific social formations, and capable of − demanding of − continual examination and criticism; and human in the sense that it restores human beings to their own worlds and enables them to take part in the collective transformation of their own human geographies (pp. 171–2).

This call was not immediately taken up, though Fleming (1973), Steel (1982), Hart (1982) and others called for a revival of traditional regional geography − which to Hart meant 'producing good regional geography − evocative descriptions that facilitate an understanding and an appreciation of places, areas and regions' (p. 2). More recently, however, people have followed Gregory's lead (see also Gregory, 1985b), and argued − as do Lee (1984, 1985) and Johnston (1984c, 1985a) − for a reconstituted regional geography which recognizes (Lee, 1985) that:

1   Social processes operate in historically and geographically specific circumstances, although they are also wholes − their understanding requires a sensitivity to geographical variations (regional mosaics);
2   Society is not a fixed phenomenon but something that is constantly being recreated by human actions. Since those actions occur in historically and geographically specific contexts, then societal recreation is similarly historically and geographically variable;

3 Those local transformations occur in the context of wider social relationships; and

4 The regions that emerge are not fixed divisions of territory but are changing social constructions.

A major goal of geography should be to uncover the nature of those regions.

The emphasis on change in these arguments indicates the lack of any clearly distinct niche for historical geography within the overall programme for the discipline. The claim that a major route to understanding the present lies in the study of the past is not new, but the development of an approach based on structuration/contextual theory makes clear the importance of an historical perspective. Indeed, historical geographers have been major contributors to the debate over the issues discussed here (see Baker and Gregory, 1984), drawing on such sources as the writings of the French *Annales* school of history (Baker, 1984; Pred, 1984d, draws heavily on the work of Braudel, for example). Their interpretations of the long-term evolution of a society (e.g. Dunford and Perrons, 1983) and its regional components (Langton, 1984), of basic transformations in a region, whether industrial (e.g. Gregory, 1982a) or agricultural (Pred, 1985, 1986), and of the constitution of particular places (as in Harvey's, 1985c, detailed analysis of nineteenth century Paris as an example of how consciousness is created in a particular context) all draw upon the basic realist conceptions, and illustrate how changes take place as the result of general tendencies being played out in particular milieux by particular human agents. (Not all historical geographers agree, however: see Meinig, 1978, especially p. 1215.) Similarly, cultural geography is no longer clearly distinguished from other aspects of the discipline. For long, this has been a peculiarly North American subdiscipline, focusing mainly on human artefacts in the landscape and, as Duncan (1980) has argued, paying relatively little attention to the concept of culture itself. If culture is interpreted as the entire heritage – material and nonmaterial – of a community, then the 'contents' of a region can be equated with its culture, providing the foundations for a revived cultural geography (Cosgrove, 1985; Thrift, 1985; Jackson, 1989) – while not precluding the continued study of landscapes as reflections of cultures and contributors to their recreation (Cosgrove, 1984).

The differences between the 'new' and the 'traditional' approaches to regional geography are made clear in an essay by Pudup (1988), who characterizes the latter as empiricist in its orientation: 'Theoretically neutral observations are the basis for areal description' (p. 374). That is now being replaced by a reconstructed regional geography, the foundations of which 'rest in a clarified status of regions as objects of study – put simply, why geographers bother to study regions in the first place' (p. 379). The answers to that 'why?' question, she argues, are given by works such as Pred's (1984c) on southern Sweden and Gregory's (1982) on West Yorkshire: regions are territorial entities, produced, reproduced and transformed through human agency. Here we have an argument similar to those of Taylor (see p. 236) on the scale of experience and Giddens (p. 237) on structuration; regions are the places in which people learn a culture, and contribute to its continuation (what Thrift, 1983, calls 'settings for interaction': p. 40). The nature of those processes is appreciated through a theorized approach, with the appreciation being provided through a narrative which draws on a defined vocabulary which then permits 'theory to speak through subsequent empirical accounts' (p. 383: see also Sayer, 1989a, 1989b). What those empirical accounts should focus on still remains to be debated – if indeed any agreement can be reached on the salient features of a region which should be the focus of enquiry. (See Johnston, 1990a, for some suggestions on that: in the context of the argument for a 'new' regional geography, he argues that 'we do not need regional geography, but we do need regions in geography' – p. 139. Warf, 1988, p. 57, argues that with the replacement of traditional regional geography by positivism 'a geography of "regions without theories" quickly became a geography of "theories without regions".)

Pudup's characterization of the 'new' regional geography is extended by Gilbert (1988), who identifies three separate concerns with regional specificity in recent writings.

1   The concern with regions as local responses to capitalist processes, which she identifies as probably the most prominent among English-speaking writers. As Harvey and others have argued in their work on uneven development (see p. 231), there are local variations in reactions to, and hence restructuring of, capitalist social relations, and their understanding, within a political economy (probably marxian) theory, is the goal of the new approach.

2   The concern with the region as a focus of identification (or 'sense of place'), which is especially strong among French writers concerned with the analysis of culture. To them, appropriation of a place (region) is part of the creation and recreation of cultural identity.

3   The concern with the region as a medium for social interaction, playing 'a basic role in the production and reproduction of social relations' (p. 212). The work on 'localities' (p. 240) fits into this concern, though Gilbert is able to show that it has been developed by French- as well as English-speaking geographers.

All three represent a break from 'traditional' regional geography, she claims, because of: the recognition that the persistence of regional diversity in the face of the homogenizing tendencies within capitalism (see also Peet, 1989) provides regional geography with a practical significance, in the mobilization of resistance to those tendencies; the 'new' work is dependent on structural theory (as illustrated in Agnew's, 1987a, book on the United States within the capitalist world-economy); the recognition of regional processes relies on dialectical rather than naturalistic theories; and the importance of human agency in the creation, recreation and transformation of regions is recognised. Together, these suggest a mode of study committed to understanding and achieving social change, which provides the challenge of making 'geography a science useful for society' (p. 223).

Postmodernism

Linked to this 'new' regional geography by some, but separate from it for others, is postmodernism, an approach which has become increasingly popular within both the social sciences and the humanities in recent years. The rise of postmodernism, according to Soja (1989), is part of the attack on the predominance of historicism in modern thought, with its emphasis on biography (individual and collective) and the consequent neglect of spatiality: Soja (p. 15) defines historicism as:

> an overdeveloped historical contextualization of social life and social theory that actively submerges and peripheralizes the geographical or spatial imagination . . . [which produces] an implicit subordination of space to time that obscures geographical interpretations of the changeability of the social world.

Because of this, geography did not attain a rightful position in the development of theory in the social sciences earlier in the present century: a 'superficially similar historical rhythm' (p. 33) was assumed to occur, rather than a realization that social processes were constituted differently in separate places, so that the historical flow was not the same everywhere (hence the apparent 'chaos' in the organization of postmodern novels, which lack a continuous narrative, and the lack of a clear, functional structure to postmodern architecture: Knox, 1987). Soja draws on most of the work reviewed above, and seeks to set it in the wider context of postmodernist social thought. To others, postmodernism is part of the response to modernism, a world-view (see p. 16) which concentrated (1989a, p. 68, as Gregory) asserts, on 'the power of reason and the progress of rationality': it was a homogenizing force, reflected in the literary and the functional architectural styles of the 'enlightenment'. Post-modernism rejects such 'totalizing' approaches, and instead stresses the discontinuities and disjunctures that are characteristic of modern life – increasingly so, according to Lash and Urry (1987), who contrast the homogeneity of the era of 'organized capitalism' (what others call 'Fordism') with the heterogeneity of economic, social and political life in contemporary 'disorganized capitalism' (what others call 'flexible accumulation': see Harvey and Scott, 1989, and the special issue of *Environment and Planning D: Society and Space*, Volume 6(3), 1988, edited by Scott and Cooke, 1988, but also Hudson, 1989). For some geographers, the appeal of this approach, with its emphasis on 'heterogeneity, particularity and uniqueness' (Gregory, 1989a, p. 70) is that it provides a theoretical context for the study of regional diversity. And, as Gregory puts it (pp. 91–92), this involves recognition that

> there is more *disorder* in the world than appears at first sight is not discovered until that disorder is looked for . . . we need, in part, to go *back* to the question

of areal differentiation: but armed with a new theoretical sensitivity towards the world in which we live and to the ways in which we represent it.

Dear (1988), too, is drawn to postmodernism because it represents an attack on the generalizing approaches of modernism and their search for 'universal truths'. With postmodernism, one theoretical viewpoint cannot be promoted over another because their relative merit is 'undecidable' (p. 266). As a consequence, there can be no grounds for promoting consensus within geography, but instead anarchy should reign: language lies at the heart of all knowledge, so that our use of language to order our experience reflects our cultures and not any true 'nature of things'. Thus geography (and every other discipline) cannot aspire to a 'grand theory', but instead can only interpret the 'contemporaneity in social process over time and space' (p. 272), within which Dear accords priority to economic, social and political geography over other subdisciplines. If geography is reconstructed in this mould, then it can 'claim its place alongside history as one of two key disciplines concerned with the time-space reconstruction of human knowledge'.

The argument for a postmodernist approach is thus, like most of the 'radical' case, very much against spatial science and its (sometimes only implicit) basis in positivism. Gregory (1989b) traces this 'modernist' approach to the particular aspects of anthropology, sociology and then economics which influenced the developing practice of geography in the nineteenth and twentieth centuries. He focused on two elements of the dominant 'modernist' paradigm:

1   the strong base in *naturalism* (likely to have 'special significance in a discipline like ours, where human geography is yoked to physical geography': p. 352), and the reliance on the aims and procedures of the natural sciences as relevant to the study of humans and their societies; and

2   a *totalization* conception of science, which involves the search for a 'systematic order whose internal logic imposes a fundamental coherence on the chaos of our immediate impressions', hence the dominance of spatial science.

In recent years, however, that totalizing, naturalistic approach has come under attack because of its perceived irrelevance to an understanding of the changing world. Thus in political economy, marxism, 'shackled to the baggage-trains of a traditional naturalism' (p. 356), cannot cope with the growth of 'disorganised capitalism' (Lash and Urry, 1987); in social theory, the totalizing discourses cannot comprehend the time-space variation made clear in Giddens's theory of structuration; and in the 'cultural sciences' (such as the study of literature) the attack on meta-narratives (see below) similarly discredits the belief in the validity of general theories. For Gregory, the 'crisis of modernity' that these elements of the attack represent is answered by a postmodernism which:

provides a particularly vibrant statement of the polyphony that characterizes (and ought to characterize) contemporary social theory (p. 379).

If general theories (or meta-narratives) cannot account for the variety which geographers observe, then an approach which can is needed. Postmodernism offers a framework for that, within which Gregory situates both structuration theory and Habermas's work on critical social theory, but – as perhaps with many 'academic bandwagons' – it 'needs to be saved from both its antagonists and its advocates. Its claims need to be approached openly, scrupulously, and vigilantly' (p. 379).

One of the fullest explorations of the many interpretations of post-modernism and their meaning for geographers, especially in the context of the assumed shift from Fordism to flexible accumulation, has been provided by Harvey (1989a). His assessment is as follows (p. 113–5):

> in its concern for difference, for the difficulties of communication, for the complexity and nuances of interests, cultures, places, and the like, it exercises a positive influence. The meta-languages, meta-theories, and meta-narratives of modernism . . . did tend to gloss over important differences, and failed to pay attention to important disjunctions and details . . . [it] sees itself as a wilful and rather chaotic movement to overcome all the supposed ills of modernism

but Harvey is less convinced by that claim than some. He accepts the case regarding 'historicism' (as developed by Soja), but is not prepared (as indicated below: p. 255) to reject certain meta-narratives, notably marxism. Thus to him, postmodernism reflects (p. 116):

> a particular kind of crisis within . . . [modernism], one that emphasizes the fragmentary, the ephemeral, and the chaotic side . . . (that side which Marx so admirably dissects as integral to the capitalist mode of production) while expressing a deep scepticism as to any particular prescriptions as to how the eternal and immutable should be conceived of, represented, or expressed.

To him, most postmodernists go too far, and border on the nihilistic. He remains a firm believer in the power of the marxist meta-theory and meta-narrative, while accepting that it is integral to the empirical operation of the capitalist dynamic that one gets the sort of spatial variation which the post-modernists and other 'new regional geographers' promote (see his agenda on p. 355). Like Graham (1988), he cannot accept that postmodernism offers 'fragments where there was wholeness' (p. 60). Marxism should be deepened as a meta-theory, she claims, because Graham, 1988, (p. 65):

> post-modernism resists the subordination of all experience and social life to class struggle and the laws of accumulation, as Marxism can and should.

The result would be a theory that accounted for the general trends, with which was integrated an appreciation of the differences among places that lead to the regional geography which we observe.

Feminism

In marxist theory, the conflict between classes is fundamental to the operation of capitalist society but, as recent developments in cultural geography indicate, analysis of that conflict alone is insufficient to appreciate the empirical variations between places in the operation of capitalist processes. Thus to Jackson (1989, p. x), culture:

> is a domain, no less than the political and the economic, in which social relations of dominance and subordination are negotiated and resisted, where meanings are not just imposed, but contested.

Within that domain, a topic of increased interest in recent years, and one which has contributed substantially both to the broadening of cultural geography and to the appreciation of variations in the operation of capitalist economic systems, is the conflict between the sexes.

Feminist geography, according to McDowell (1986a, p. 151), 'emphasizes questions of gender inequality and the oppression of women in virtually all spheres of life'. A part of its goal is to identify such inequality and discrimination within the geographical profession (Zelinsky, 1973a; Zelinksy, Monk and Hanson, 1982; Jackson, Smith and Johnston 1988: Johnson, 1989), but its larger task is (McDowell, 1980, p. 137):

> to demonstrate that women do matter in geography, and to argue that the failure to take gender differences into account impoverishes both geographical scholarship and teaching . . . [in addition] it is not enough just to add women in as an additional category. Feminist geography, as opposed to a geography or geographies of women, entails a new look at our discipline. It poses several awkward questions about how we currently divide the subject matter into convenient academic parcels and also challenges current practice in teaching and research.

Thus the goal is not to add a separate feminist thread to geographical practice, with the potential for its ghettoization, but rather to ensure that a feminist perspective informs all work in human geography.

According to Johnson (1989), feminist geography involves recognizing women's common experience of, and resistance to, oppression by men, and a commitment to end that oppression 'so that women can define and control themselves' (p. 85). This involves, among other things, evaluating geographical practice, to demonstrate that it is 'sexist, patriarchal, and phallocentric' and as such contributes to the oppression of women. Through such demonstration, emancipation should be achieved, in the same way that critical theory as applied to inter-class exploitation paves the way for emancipation. In this way, feminist geography differs from a geography of women, because, like radical geography generally, the explanations that it produces are to be used as guides to political practice (Bowlby, Lewis, McDowell and Foord, 1989).

Walby (1986) has identified five approaches to the study of gender inequality:

1   The demonstration that it is either theoretically insignificant or non-existent;
2   Indicating that it is derivative of capitalist relations;
3   Showing that it is the result of an autonomous system of patriarchy which is the primary form of social inequality;
4   Demonstrating that it results from patriarchal relations that are so intertwined with capitalist social relations that they make a single system of capitalist patriarchy; and
5   Showing that it results from the interaction of autonomous systems of patriarchy and capitalism.

Bowlby *et al.* (1989) claim that the second and the fourth of these have been most commonly adopted, thus focusing on the ways that gender inequality is structured by capitalism. However, Foord and Gregson (1986) adopted the fifth approach, arguing that patriarchy is separate from capitalist social relations, though the two are clearly empirically linked. They argue that just as capitalism can be seen as a particular example of a necessary condition – mode of production – which has unique individual instances in terms of its operation at different times and places, so patriarchy can be seen as a particular example of a necessary general condition – gender relations – which has unique instances also.

Regarding the general condition, Foord and Gregson argue that the necessary inter-relationship between humans and the environment requires a social organization to ensure human survival, and that '*all* social relations must involve gender, and . . . gender relations will be embedded in all forms of social relations' (p. 199). Thus gender relations are a necessary element of any social relations, and as such are independent of the mode of production: capitalist social relations and gender relations may be linked empirically, but they are not part of the same structure. Patriarchy is a particular form of gender relations, in which men dominate the process of species reproduction, and empirical work is concerned with the nature of that domination 'in particular periods and places' (p. 206): 'Just as other relations vary and combine differently over time and space, so too must the practices which comprise these relations' – hence the importance of studying gender relations in the context of locality research.

Foord and Gregson's argument leads to the conclusion that marxist and feminist theories cannot be integrated, because gender and social relations are separate spheres. McDowell (1986b), however, promotes a capitalist class analysis and argues against the notion of a universal feminine experience. Biological reproduction is part of the process of capitalist reproduction, and (p. 313):

> Patriarchal social relations are further strengthened by the political and ideological functions of the state that has a vested interest in supporting the domination of individual women in the exploited class by individual men in that class.

Within capitalism, she argues, the contradiction arising from the need to create surplus wealth is the source of women's oppression, not any necessary gender relations (p. 317):

> The social construction of male sexuality and the dominance of family forms based on sexuality and kinship networks in class societies are historical resolutions of the contradiction, rather than necessary elements of gender relations.

Gier and Walton (1987), on the other hand, take issue with Foord and Gregson on the issue of whether gender relations are necessary to all social relations, claiming that (p. 56–7):

> Evidence from anthropology and history as well as other disciplines indicates that gender has not always been used to identify male and female sexual difference and its attendant physical and psychological archetypes . . . [so that] the very identification of the concept is the product of human consciousness and human society.

Gender differences are created within societies, along with all other differences, according to this view, and are not necessarily there (see also Knopp and Lauria, 1987). Gregson and Foord (1987, 373–4) responded by defending their view that mode of production and gender relations are 'distinct and separate objects of analysis which interlock as particular forms (capitalism and patriarchal gender relations) but not as conceptual categories', but were not prepared to admit that this was the preface to the creation of a universal theory of women's oppression.

This debate has illustrated that feminist geography involves much more than the empirical demonstration that women are repressed in contemporary societies and that there are important gender differences in a wide range of activities, times, and places. Particular studies (Women and Geography Study Group, 1984; Little, Peake and Richardson, 1988) have provided the raw material for examination of those differences, but, as Mackenzie (1989) and Bowlby *et al*'s (1989) agenda demonstrate, feminist geography is contributing to the theoretical debates within geography (Foord and Gregson's work is explicitly realist in conception) and illustrating the great variety of ways in which social relations are constituted and reconstituted over time and space.

Radicals in Debate

The 'radical camp' is not a united body of scholars, and although marxism has remained the focus of some workers' activities it has recently come under attack from others, who would generally be categorized as within the 'camp' themselves. Thus in 1986 Saunders and Williams equated the recent literature on urban studies with an unchallenged 'taken for granted orthodoxy . . . [which] thrives on an unspoken and largely unexamined political and theoretical consensus' (p. 393). This, they claim, has opposition to positivism as its lynchpin, and within it arguments occupy 'a very narrow spectrum embracing left Weberianism and the different varieties of marxism, but excluding almost everything else'. This leads to their conclusion that urban studies currently:

> makes little pretence of being 'value-free' or 'ethically neutral' and . . . is sheltered from the possibility of empirical disconfirmation. This in turn means that approaches (such as the philosophy of the so-called 'New Right') which cannot be subsumed under the orthodoxy can be dismissed almost a priori. Such work is rarely read, still less seriously considered on its own terms. Rather a pejorative label is attached to it (for example, 'Thatcherism', 'Reaganism', or 'authoritarian populism') which enables us to pigeonhole it within our existing conceptual apparatus . . . without ever having to engage with its intellectual content. In this way alternative ideas are dismissed but never discussed, explained away but never critically evaluated (pp. 393–4).

Elements of both marxism and realism are then criticized, with the latter, for example, being characterized as a 'justification for subordinating history to theory' (p. 394) and the source of 'causes which can only be identified theoretically and which are guaranteed immunity from falsification even where there is no manifest evidence for their existence' (p. 395): works which are explicitly anti-positivist are therefore castigated for not being subjected to positivist and critical rationalist procedures!

According to their critique theories of structures have primacy in these approaches, and as such are outdated: the major changes in British society over the last century are ignored, it is claimed – 'we still employ an essentially outdated class theory in our analyses' (p. 397) – and the many changes are dismissed as:

> having done little or nothing to change the essential features of capitalism. As social change takes place under our noses, so we risk a situation where our methods and theories ensure that we pay it little heed. The orthodoxy is safeguarded and reproduced as the society changes

Even the challenge of feminism, and of the renewed interest in ethnicity issues, has largely been disregarded, according to Saunders and Williams, so that the conceptual tools of the 'radical camp' are not reexamined, and urban studies is castigated as 'safe rather than innovative, conservative rather than critical'.

One of the subjects of Saunders and Willams' criticisms, and one of the strongest adherents to the Marxist position, is Harvey, who characterized the goal of 'my academic concerns these last two decades . . . [as] to unravel the role of urbanisation in social change, in particular under conditions of capitalist social relations and accumulation' (1989b, p. 3). In a 1987 paper, written in response to Sauders and Williams, he noted 'a marked strategic withdrawal from Marxian theory within the field of urban analysis and a broadening reluctance to make explicit use of Marx's conceptual apparatus in articulating arguments' (Harvey, 1987, p. 367). In reply, he launched what some saw as an unwarranted attack against those whom he identified as abandoning the 'tough rigour of dialectical theorizing and historical materialist analysis', because:

> The case for retiring Marx's *Capital* to the shelves of some antiquarian bookstore . . . is not yet there. Indeed, in many respects the time has never been more appropriate for the application of Marx's conceptual apparatus to understanding processes of capitalist development and transformation. Further more, I believe the claim of Marxian analysis to provide the surest guide to the construction of radical theory and radicalizing practices still stands.

His critics have caved in too readily to right-wing pressures, he argues.

Harvey begins by agreeing with Saunders and Williams that realism and the conceptualization of agency and structure:

> are nothing more than weak disguises, soft versions of a traditional left orthodoxy ranging from left Weberianism to 'different varieties of Marxism' (p. 368).

But he disagrees with their perceived way forward. He identifies 'three myths' which have been pervasive in the critique of marxist scholarship. One is that of economism, as reflected in the critique by Duncan and Ley (1982: see below, p. 263). The second is that

> The abstractions of Marxian theory cannot explain the specificities of history and the particularities of geography' (p. 370).

to which he clearly takes great exception. Harvey believes that 'it is in principle possible to apply thoretical laws to understand individual instances, unique events' (p. 371), particularly since Marx's most interesting law-like statements were about capitalist processes, not events. He illustrates this by quoting the chapter in *Capital* on 'The Working Day', arguing that such a detailed empirical description of how humans respond to their conditions on a daily basis allows

> categories like money, profit, daily wage, labour time, the working day, and ultimately value and surplus value [to] arise through an examination of historical materials (p. 372).

thereby illustrating how theory is both derived from and developed through the unravelling of particular situations.

Harvey believes that this myth is being advanced from 'within the ranks of the left itself' (p. 373), quoting Massey and Sayer and their 'very deep and serious concerns for the particularities of places, events and processes'. Sayer's realist approach involves combining 'wide-ranging contingency with an understanding of general processes', but

> The problem with this superficially attractive method is that there is nothing within it, apart from the judgement of individual researchers, as to what constitutes a special instance to which special processes inhere or as to what

contingencies (out of a potentially infinite number) ought to be taken seriously. There is nothing, in short, to guard against the collapse of scientific understandings into a mass of contingencies exhibiting relations and processes special to each unique event (p. 373).

This, he fears, is a path to 'simple empiricism' (p. 374), which he believes Saunders and Williams (1986) also promoted (he characterized their agenda as 'nothing short of an abrogation of scientific responsibility and a caving in of political will'). Against that, he insisted on 'the viability of the Marxist project' (p. 375), with its focus on 'universalising statements and abstractions' (p. 375) and its ability to guide political practice.

Harvey's stance was also adopted by Smith (1987) in the ensuing debate, who defends Marxism as providing both a broad analytical framework and a 'quintessentially political discourse', and who finds that the 'realist project . . . has become the theoretical justification for the belief that there can be no general theory *at all* concerning questions of geographical space, and that any attempt to devise such a theory is fundamentally misconceived' (p. 379). But others were less supportive, Ball (1987, p. 393), for example, taking issue with Harvey's:

> total dismissal of anyone who does not repeatedly declare their Marxist label, who does not believe that everything Marx said is unambiguous and correct, and who fails directly to apply the most abstract propositions of Marxist theory to the empirical situations they are investigating.

Sayer (1987) similarly resents the attack, and its impugning of motives, and replies to both Saunders and Williams and Harvey, 'even if it means breaking off from what I had hoped and still hope is a broad but common project, the search for a social science with an emancipatory potential'. (p. 395).

In his response, Sayer agrees very much with Harvey that empirical research enables a clarification of theoretical understanding, being 'partly responsible for making me revise my abstract ideas about the nature of capital, competition, class and the division of labour' (p. 397). He also defends realism against the charges of both reductionism and theoreticism (Saunders and Williams) and empiricism (Harvey). Regarding the latter, he argues that, because of the impossibility of theoretically-neutral observation, claims that realism (or any other approach) is atheoretical and empiricist cannot be sustained; instead, he argues that 'capital-labour relations, class, gender, as well as many other phenomena of interest, are historically constituted in particular localities (though not only in them) and that the manner of this constitution must be explained' (p. 399). Thus the abstract categories of Marx's general theorizing about capitalist processes are employed to appreciate the nature of particular realisations (which, he argues elsewhere, 1989b, calls for a combination of humanism and historical materialism; see also Storper, 1987). Similarly, Cooke (1987c) argues for the study of the interactions of universal and local processes, and for the use of the understanding so achieved to forge local political practice: 'I find it distinctly odd that thinking globally and thinking or acting locally should be thought somewhat "parochial" ' (p. 412). And Thrift (1987) believes that Marxian political economy has been so successful in Britain that 'it now forms a vital subtext to most theorising' (p. 401): further, he argues that 'the realist project is the reconstitution of dialectical materialism so that it preserves the best of the Enlightenment tradition but incorporates the verities of twentieth century developments in social theory' (p. 405). To him, social theory such as marxism is a hand torch that helps to illuminate particular instance, but not the 'searchlight flooding every nook and cranny of society with light' (p. 405), which is the interpretation of Harvey's case. For Thrift, this involves the study of agency, in places, as well as of structure.

Saunders and Williams (1987) begin their response with the following categorization of Harvey (pp. 427–8):

> Harvey eschews fraternization with the enemy, and he adopts a quasi-religious, almost messianic tone in delivering his epistle. He tells us . . . of his unswerving *belief* that Marxism provides the *surest guide* to radical salvation . . . Harvey's statement provides a good example of precisely that tendency in contemporary urban studies which we suggested could stifle fresh initiatives and hamper intellectual debate. If you believe, as Harvey apparently does, that the eternal verities have largely been established by Marx's *Capital*, then you have effectively closed off the possibility of open debate, and even more the possibility of learning from, others who disagree.

(Gould, 1988, similarly criticizes Marxist writers in general and Harvey in particular for what he terms their 'claim to exclusiveness'.) Saunders and Williams then criticize him for sustaining a 'totalizing' form of theory, which embraces the whole of society and thus has a privileged starting point (or set of initial assumptions) which are not open to empirical refutation/confirmation: 'It is difficult to see how you can get to the whole by studying the parts and building up from there . . . Totalising discourses are thus always unalterably committed to a priori assumptions – Marx's theories of exploitation, class struggle, and historical evolution came, not from studying people in Manchester, but from ideas about society 'as a whole', and these ideas were then mapped onto existing empirical observations' (pp. 428–9). Thus Harvey's marxism is not susceptible to effective falsification; nor, they assert, despite Sayer's arguments, is realism. These, they argue, are 'closed' approaches, and although they share the same goal as Harvey and Sayer, they believe (p. 430):

> you will not develop an emanicipatory social science before social science itself is opened up.

Hence the debate, which the editor argues is necessary because: capitalist society is changing; the nature of politics is altering; and 'social theory has to take account of these cumulative changes' (Dear, 1987, p. 363).

Liberals and radicals in debate

The material discussed in this chapter illustrates a world view very different from that employed by many human geographers during the 1970s and 1980s. It has formed the basis for a debate which, in its published components at least, is much more heated than that generated by the 'quantitative revolution'. It has also been developed in more depth and detail, using forums, such as the journal *Area*, which were not available twenty years earlier, when publication outlets for 'views and opinions' were few. Whereas the behaviourists caused little real concern within the discipline, and their views were soon coopted within the corpus of acceptable approaches, the so-called radicals of the 1970s and 1980s have had much more impact, because they attack not only the basis of most geographical work but also, in their clear inter-disciplinarity, the bureaucratic structure of the discipline and the existence of geography itself (Johnston, 1978c); some, such as Eliot Hurst (1980, 1985), argue explicitly for the abolition of geography as a separate discipline. (Most of the debate has involved the empiricalists/positivists on the one hand and the radicals on the other. Relatively little has involved responses to the humanistic approach – but see Billinge, 1983, and Flowerdew, 1989.)

A clear example of the liberal-radical polarization is given by a debate on the geography of crime. This was initiated by Peet (1975b), who argued that in attempting to make their work relevant geographers avoided asking 'relevant to whom?'; the political consequences of their work were ignored. The studies of crime reviewed (e.g. Harries, 1974) referred only to the surface manifestations of a social problem and could not provide solutions to that problem, but only ways of ameliorating it. 'So it is that "useful" geography comes to be of use only in preserving the existing order of things by diverting attention away from the deepest causes of social problems and towards the details of effect' (p. 277). Furthermore, geographers study only the crimes for which statistics are collected, thereby accepting the definition of crime by the elite; the maps which they produce, which are useful to police patrols, can therefore be employed to help maintain the status quo of power relations within society. The implicit position of the geographers involved is one of protecting the 'monopoly-capitalist' state.

Harries (1975) responded by attacking the simplistic nature of Peet's arguments, and claimed that geographers would have no influence at all if they argued merely that crime is a consequence of monopoly capitalism. He contended that it is best to work within the system, to make the administration of justice more humane and equitable, to protect the potential victims of crime, and to provide employment opportunities for graduate geographers. Approaches based on the control of crime are likely to be more influential than polemics relating its cause to the mode of production: as Lee (1975) also pointed out, Peet 'failed to provide us with any clues as to how he or other radical geographers would study crime' (p. 285).

Peet (1976a) responded to Lee's challenge, presenting a radical theory which would 'contribute directly, through persuasion, to the movement for social revolution' (p. 97). The theory argues that capitalism harnesses human competitive emotions and produces inequalities of material and power rewards. Aggression is an acceptable part of being competitive, and is often released on the lower classes, who are encouraged to consume but provided with insufficient purchasing power. As the contradictions of this paradox increase, so does the pressure to turn to crime. Thus crime occurs where the lower classes live, and at the spatial interface between them and the middle class. Harries (1976) replied that being a radical was a luxury few academics could afford; working at a publicly-financed university demanded a pragmatic rather than a revolutionary approach. To him, Peet's theory is overly economic and deterministic; it fails to account for cultural elements, such as the disproportionate criminal involvement of blacks, the sub-culture of violence in the southern United States and other areas, and the fact that all economic systems produce minorities disadvantaged in terms of what they want and what they can get by socially legitimate means. He could offer no alternative theory, however: 'I do not carry in my head a theory of crime causation, and I am quite incapable of synthesizing and attaching value judgements to existing theoretical formulations within a couple of pages of typescript' (p. 102). He encouraged Peet to come off the fence, and to get involved in the production of change within the present system. Wolf (1976), on the other hand, claimed that by concentrating on the traditional concerns of marxism Peet was not radical enough.

Two geographers who were involved in a considerable, often virulent, debate in the 1970s are Brian Berry and David Harvey. Berry (1972b) initiated the exchanges with his comments on Harvey's (1972) paper on revolutionary theory and the ghetto. Berry wondered whether Harvey's rational arguments on the need for a revolution would be accepted: 'because of "commitment", the opposition will quietly drift into corners, the world will welcome the new Messiah, and social change will somehow, magically, transpire' (p. 32). The power to achieve change, he contended, needs more than logical argument to produce it in the twentieth century – 'nothing less than cudgels has been effective' (p. 32) – and Harvey's belief in logical rationalism will be to no avail. He also argued that, in any case, Harvey is wrong about the ghetto, for liberal policies are succeeding and the inequalities between blacks and whites are being reduced (Berry, 1974a). Harvey (1974a) responded that scarcity must continue in a capitalist economy, which will leave some people – probably those in the inner city – relatively disadvantaged.

In reviewing *Social Justice and the City* (Harvey, 1973), Berry (1974b) criticized Harvey's dependence on economic explanations. Basing his case on the arguments of Daniel Bell (1973) on post-industrial society, Berry (1974b) claimed that the economic function is now subordinate to the political: 'the autonomy of the economic order (and the power of the men who run it) is coming to an end, and new and varied, but different, control systems are emerging. In sum, the control of society is no longer primarily economic but political' (p. 144). (His comments clearly pre-date the economic recession of the mid and late 1970s and the political response of the 'New Right' in both the USA and the UK, which was to reduce political control substantially and 'free' the market processes.) Harvey's (1974b) response was that marxism could not be considered as passée while the selling of labour power and the collusion between the economically and the politically powerful continue, and that the state has to be considered within a marxist framework too (Harvey, 1976). Berry (1974b) retorted:

> I believe that change can be produced *within* 'the system'. Harvey believes that it will come from sources *external* to that system, and then only if enough noise is produced at the wailing wall. . . . The choice, after all, is not that hard: between pragmatic pursuit of what is attainable and revolutionary romanticism, between realism and the heady perfumes of flower power (p. 148).

Harvey's (1975c) review of Berry's (1973a) *The Human Consequences of Urbanization* − a study of urbanization processes at various times and places and of the planning responses to these − concluded that the book is 'all fanfare and no substance' (p. 99), revealing that Anglo-American urban theory is 'substantively bankrupt' and that 'it is scholarship of the Brian Berry sort which typically produces such messes' (p. 99).

> It is doubtful if it makes any sense even to consider urbanization as something isolated from processes of capital formation, foreign and domestic trade, international money flows, and the like, for in a fundamental sense urbanization is economic growth and capital accumulation − and the latter processes are clearly global in their compass (p. 102).

To Harvey, Berry has nothing to say of any substance, but as Berry 'is influential and important . . . his influence is potentially devastating' (p. 103). Berry's only response was a general comment on the Union of Socialist Geographers (Halvorson and Stave, 1978):

> there's no more amusing thing than goading a series of malcontents and kooks and freaks and dropouts and so on, which is after all what that group mainly consists of. There are very few scholars in the group (p. 233).

Apart from these very polarized exchanges, several other statements indicate that whereas some 'liberals' have been prepared to consider the radical case seriously, others have tended to avoid the issues, more or less. Chisholm, for example, has (1975) claimed that:

> while I am fully sympathetic to the view that the 'scientific' paradigm is not adequate to all our needs, and must be supplemented by other approaches, I am not persuaded that it should be replaced. . . . Harvey wants us to embrace the marxist method of 'dialectic'. This 'method' passes my understanding; so far as it has a value, it seems to be as a metaphysical belief system and not − as its protagonists proclaim − a mode of rational argument (p. 175)

(see also Chisholm, 1976; Sayer, 1981). More frequently, reviewers accept that the radical view is valuable but not, to them, tenable in its entirety. Thus Morrill (1974) writes of Harvey's *Social Justice and the City* that 'I am pulled most of the way by this revolutionary analysis but I cannot make the final leap that our task is no longer to find truth, but to create and accept a particular truth' (p. 477). King (1976), too, seeks a middle course,

> An economic and urban geography that will be concerned explicitly with social change and policy. . . . Such a middle course will not find favour with the ideologues, who will see it either as another obfuscation favouring only 'status quo' and 'counter-revolutionary' theory, or as a distraction from the immediate task of building elegant quantitative-theoretic structures, but some paths are being cut through the thicket of competing epistemologies, rambling lines of empirical analysis, and gnarled branches of applied studies that now cover the middle ground (pp. 294–5).

He accepts that much quantitative-cum-theoretical geography has sought mathematical elegance as an end in itself, at the sacrifice of realism; he believes that social science must feed into social policy and generate social change; he accepts the 'intellectual power' of marxist analysis but believes that the prescriptions based on it are acceptable only if the ideological framework is: his conclusion suggests the need for more quantification, aimed at being operationally useful rather than mathematically elegant (see also Bennett, 1985a, 1985b). He later notes that '*space* . . . should be seen as an element in the political process, an object of competition and conflict between interest groups and different classes' (King and Clark, 1978, p. 12). And finally, Smith (1977) concluded that:

> Marx may have been able to dissect the operation of a capitalist economy with particular clarity, and see the essential unity of economy, polity and society that we so often miss today. But Marx does not hold the key to every modern problem in complex, pluralistic society (p. 368).

The debates continue, very largely it seems because many geographers are unable/unwilling to accept both the marxist analysis of society and the marxist programme for action. In part, this reflects a partial reading of marxism – in particular a concentration on strict structural interpretations which do not apparently allow for the activities of knowing individuals and which do not accept the concept of structuration (see p. 236). Thus Ley (1980, p. 12) identifies in marxism 'some hidden transcendental phenomenon . . . directing the course of human society'. This commits an epistemological error, denying or at least suppressing the subjective; a theoretical error that devalues the power of human action to redirect the course of events; and a moral error, which makes humans into puppets and threatens basic freedoms of speech, assembly and worship. Muir (1978) attacks interpretations of marxism, and similarly implies that it threatens individual freedom of the academic 'to pick and choose from among the . . . literature' (p. 325). Respondents point to the lack of such 'intellectual orthodoxy' and 'sterilized geography' (Manion and Whitelegg, 1979; Duncan, 1979), but Muir (1979, p. 127) remains convinced of the threat implicit in 'the commands from such little men as Marx, Lenin, Trotsky, Stalin and Mao concerning the primacy of activism, the obligations of party membership and the necessity to subordinate individual judgement to the will of the party'. Radical geography is contributing to understanding, he says, but to call it marxist is to give it a certain programmatic base. To Walmsley and Sorensen (1980) marxism is just irrelevant, and deflects attention from 'reformism and relevance'.

Duncan and Ley (1982) have published an extensive critique of structural marxism in geography. This contains four major themes. First, marxist analysis is a form of holism, in which the whole – variously termed capital, the economic structure, economic processes, etc. – is given a life of its own: an abstraction is assumed to exist. Such an act (a reification: see also Gould, 1988) offends their belief in individuals as conscious, free agents (see Duncan, 1980, on holism in cultural geography, and Agnew and Duncan, 1981) – although they do not proclaim an idealist alternative and they accept that 'individual action cannot be fully explained without reference to the contexts under which individuals act' (p. 32). Secondly, individuals are represented as agents of the whole – the means of implementing its goals – not free decision-makers in their own right. Thirdly, the materialist infrastructure of marxism is a form of economism, in that it presents economic processes as the ultimate cause of all behaviour. This excludes, to them, many other influences and leads to the final theme, 'the attempt to cast explanation continually and everywhere in terms of economic imperatives, leading . . . to a crisis in empirical exposition' (p. 47). Here, they make what is essentially a positivist critique:

> the form of the explanations is both tautological and empirically untestable. The result is a mystification in explanation of how real processes operate (p. 55).

They conclude that structural marxism in human geography presents a passive view of the individual, and offers explanations in terms of abstract wholes which are obfuscatory and not verifiable. Later work by Duncan (1985) shows that he is attracted to the structuration approach, which allows for the operation of human agency within structural constraints – as indeed do most interpretations of marxism.

Structural marxism is criticized by others who disagree with its treatment of the individual, and who wish to build more convincing models of the inter-relationships between infrastructure and superstructure in the process of societal change. Gregory (1981) presents four such models (Figure 8.3):

1 Reification, in which the individual's actions are entirely determined by the whole – as in a structural marxism that denies human agency.
2 Voluntarism, in which society has no separate identity but is constructed from the actions of free individuals.
3 Dialectical reproduction, in which the whole creates the individuals, whose actions influence the whole – which in turn creates the next generation of individuals.

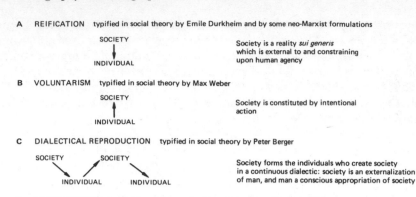

A   REIFICATION   typified in social theory by Emile Durkheim and by some neo-Marxist formulations

SOCIETY

INDIVIDUAL

Society is a reality *sui generis* which is external to and constraining upon human agency

B   VOLUNTARISM   typified in social theory by Max Weber

SOCIETY

INDIVIDUAL

Society is constituted by intentional action

C   DIALECTICAL REPRODUCTION   typified in social theory by Peter Berger

SOCIETY   SOCIETY

INDIVIDUAL   INDIVIDUAL

Society forms the individuals who create society in a continuous dialectic: society is an externalization of man, and man a conscious appropriation of society

D   STRUCTURATION   typified in social theory by Jürgen Habermas and Anthony Giddens

SOCIETY ——————— SOCIETY

INDIVIDUAL ——————— INDIVIDUAL

Social systems are both the medium and the outcome of the practices that constitute them: the two are recursively separated and recombined.

Fig 8.3 Four models of the relationships between society and the individual. *Source*: Gregory (1981, p. 11)

4   Structuration, which starts with individuals (not with the whole) and portrays individuals and society in a continuous dialectic from then on.

The last of these is preferred by Gregory, because it offers a full integration of humanist and materialist (or structuralist) perspectives – in a way that critiques such as those of Duncan and Ley do not. (See also Thrift, 1983.) Such an integration, he claims, will recognize the materialist base to society – the infrastructure – while accepting the important role of human agency. Humanistic geography should not compete with a scientific approach, but should acknowledge:

> the recurrent and recursive relations between the individual and society as being fundamentally implicated in the production and reproduction of both social life and social structure (p. 15).

These different approaches are based on a variety of conceptions of the nature of the human agent (or 'models of man' as they are frequently termed). For critiques of those conceptions, see Barnes (1988), Claval (1983), Harrison and Livingston (1982) and van der Laan and Piersma (1982).

Alongside these debates on the relevance of marxist ideas, other geographers have been defending quantitative spatial science against critiques such as Gregory's (1978, 1980). Bennett (1981d, p. 24), for example, argues that

> much of the critique of quantitative geography as 'positivism' has been misplaced and has accepted uncritically the representation of science as positivism given by Harvey in 1969. This has had a pernicious and destructive effect on the subject in three main ways: first, it has suggested that scientific and empirical enquiry is largely socially worthless; second, it has often rejected the links between physical and human geography; and third, it has often rejected the existence of geography as a discipline at all.

(Elsewhere, he has characterized the critique as 'at best a mis-representative irrelevance, and at worst a fatuous distraction': Bennett and Wrigley, 1981, p. 10.) The argument is that quantification need not be allied with positivism. Bennett identifies three messages from Harvey's *Explanation in Geography*: geography is primarily inductive, is an objective science, and seeks universal laws. But 'each is only a partial representation of the literature and ideas it seeks to describe' (Bennett, 1981d, p. 13). He argues that radical and quantitative approaches must be integrated:

> by empirical analyses, from the integration of environmental, social, political, and economic aspects with space, historical stimuli, and specific modes of thought and their spatial-political manifestations, . . . by the re-establishment of the geographical subject matter (p. 24).

He wishes to maintain a separate discipline of geography (human plus physical), in which quantitative geography – 'never . . . truly positive' (Bennett and Wrigley, 1981, p. 10) – occupies a central place, answering 'the fundamental questions of social norms, social distribution, policy impacts and humanistic concerns which the critics rightly emphasize' (p. 10). To many 'radicals', this would appear to be a *status quo* approach (p. 196).

In 1985, Thrall (1985) reported on a conference on 'Scientific geography', where the consensus was that 'Research in the unified areas of theory and modelling, data measurement and simulation, estimation and verification is central to the discipline of geography' (p. 254); such a perspective, he contended, should be used to promote the image of geography among the sciences and the 'acceptance of scientific approaches within geography'. His equation of science with mathematics, statistics and computer literacy was challenged by Driver and Philo (1986), who argued that 'science is more than a matter of technique' (p. 161) and that a clearly technocratic approach 'effectively marginalizes all other modes of interpretation and explanation' (p. 162). Thrall's (1986) response identified three major geographical traditions: humanistic; scientific; and pure theoretical. Scientific geography, he claims, is a 'philosophy of research . . . clearly distinct from the earlier quantitative geography movement' (p. 162); he advocates research that involves hypothesis-testing leading to theory-creation and verification, rather than the empiricism of regional geographies or the sterile output of pure theoretical research.

This presentation of geography as an applied, quantitative discipline, but one which does not accept the canons of positivism, continues to be criticized. An extreme example is D. Smith (1984) who concludes an autobiographical essay with the statement that

> To be quite honest, I no longer care very much about geography, with its smug self-satisfaction and nauseating narrow-minded chauvinism. Who else but geographers would dignify their puerile pursuit of statistics, models and paradigms as a 'revolution' as though it mattered to anyone but themselves? . . . And who else would want to read such trivia? How can we take it all so seriously,

when it contributes so little to the improvement of the human condition? Most geography is inconsequential claptrap, and never more so than during the 'quantitative revolution' (p. 132).

Mercer (1984) presents a somewhat similar summary, though noting that

> the last few years have witnessed a small – though perhaps temporary – retreat from the more lunatic excesses of flat earth quantitative geography towards a growing recognition that reality is not in fact beautifully ordered but that it is characterized much more by *contradictions, tension and disharmony*. The daunting . . . task for the critical geographer – whether 'Marxist' or humanist – [includes] . . . the fight against the hegemony of naive, blinkered, technocratic thinking (p. 194).

His goal is to unmask what he terms 'technocratic geography' and to divert attention away from topics such as 'where are the regions of health care need based on access to hospitals?' to more fundamental questions like 'What leads to ill health?'. The basic theme that he and similar critics stress is that selection of a particular research style, with the connotations of how its output may be used, involves an (albeit possibly unconscious) ideological choice: different conceptions of science are based on different views of both the utility of science and the social order within which that utility is to be employed.

Other writers have sought to integrate elements of the positivist, humanistic and structuralist approaches to human geography (e.g. Christensen, 1982; for a fuller review, see Johnston, 1986f). Some attempts have been short-lived, such as an essay on the links between catastrophe theory (p. 127) and the discontinuities central to marxist economic theory (Day and Tivers, 1979, 54–8; Alexander, 1979, 228–30). Hay (1979a, p. 22) has argued for an empirical, analytical geography that is:

> at the same time a *nomological* geography which seeks, for example, to understand the workings of urban rent theory as positivistically observed, a *hermeneutic* geography which seeks to identify the meaning of the urban rent system for those who are participants (active or passive) within it, and a *critical* geography which points to the extent to which present urban rent systems are themselves transformations of the capitalist system, but which admits that some of its features may indeed be 'invariant regularities'.

Livingstone and Harrison (1981, p. 370) somewhat similarly present the case for:

> a humanistic geography which is, at the same time, critical, in questioning rather than bracketing our presuppositions, hermeneutic, in interpreting the meanings behind action, and empirical, in examining the subjectively interpreted objective world.

They, it should be noted, include no nomological – or generalizing – component.

To some, particularly the critics of positivism, such an attempted integration is not possible because the approaches are incompatible: Gregory (1978a, p. 169) terms it 'inchoate eclecticism' (see also Gregory, 1982b; Eyles and Lee,

1982, Hudson, 1983. Positivist and structuralist approaches sit unhappily together in Rhind and Hudson, 1981.) The biggest problem is with positivism – not quantification (Walker, 1981b; though see Sayer, 1984, and the response in Johnston, 1986a) – because of its nomological orientation and its belief that human geographers can discover 'invariant regularities'. At present, the major links are between the structuralist and the humanistic approaches (as suggested in Eyles, 1981), which treat the knowing actor operating within structural constraints. Most of the humanistic approaches, as they have been presented to human geographers, focus entirely on the human as a free decision-maker, with no reference to either structural constraints or to how an individual's decision-making capabilities develop in a societal context. But, as several authors have indicated (e.g. S. Duncan, 1981), human geography as an empirical discipline must marry the ability to develop realist theories of the infrastructure with methods of studying human action within the superstructure (Johnston, 1983c). Such marrying represents a positive critique, rather than the almost entirely negative debate reviewed earlier in this section.

Increasingly the debate is not directly between different philosophies of geography, but rather over the utility of different approaches. As a consequence of the demands on education and research from governments of the 'new right' in the context of the major economic recession of the 1970s and 1980s in Britain and North America, there is considerable pressure within the geographical profession to advance the study and practice of applied geography. (Taylor, 1985c, sets such pressures in historical context.) To some, such as Bennett (1985b), Openshaw (1989), and others, this involves putting the technical competence of geographers to use in applied situations, without any necessary reference to philosophical issues; applied geographers are thus technicians (as in Gatrell, 1985), who implicitly accept the context within which their skills are used. To others, however, the philosophical issues remain important. Golledge *et al.* (1982) counter Hart's (1982) argument in his case for regional geography that

> We cannot allow ourselves to be intimidated by those who flaunt the banner of science (p. 5)

with

> We equally cannot allow ourselves to be intimidated by those who flaunt the banner of anti-science, those who would reject all that is scientific about the discipline, and those who would urge a return to the descriptive morass from which we have recently emerged (p. 558).

Implicit in most arguments for applied geography is that it should be based in empiricist/positivist philosophies, however; the counter-arguments that humanistic science can be applied to improve self- and mutual awareness and that realistic science can be applied to advance social transformation are rarely presented (Johnston, 1986a).

A further reason for the decline in the volume of debate over philosophical issues is that a consequence of what has taken place since *c*.1970 is that some believe that an eclectic pluralism is possible (see the discussion in Johnston, 1986f), some conduct empiricist work (often in the behavioural geography mould) unconcerned with any philosophical ramifications of that practice (see Flowerdew, 1986), and others have generally accepted the realist case and seek to situate their activities within that context. Gould (1985a), for example, has written that

> There is no question in my mind that the appearance of Marxist concern in geography, and its concomitant shaping of the lens through which the world is seen, has greatly enriched our methodological approach. There is an insistence that the things at the surface are not always what they seem, and that it is crucial to dig down underneath the superficial appearances to get at the 'deep structures'. I think this is quite right (p. 296).

but he then criticizes marxists for their claims to truth, their condescending attitudes to 'non-believers', their over-concentration on economic forces, and the 'messianic claims that seem to lead so readily and so often to the sacrifice of human beings today for some promise tomorrow' (p. 300).

Conclusions

This chapter has brought the debate on the nature of human geography up to date at the time of writing, and has indicated the depth and breadth of the discussions which have occupied much of the 1970s and 1980s. The clearest conclusion which can be drawn from Chapter 7 is that there is an increasing proportion of geographers who wish to be involved in the re-shaping of societies, either through ameliorative correction of current problems and trends or by designing desirable spatial organizations (Berry, 1973a): to some, this is necessary if human geography is to retain its institutional position. Their motives range along the continuum from 'pure altruism' to 'devoted self-seeking'. Their methods vary from those who accept the present mode of production and see humanitarian goals as achievable within its constraints, through those who subscribe to the phenomenological view (Buttimer, 1974) that:

> the social scientist's role is neither to choose or decide for people, nor even to formulate the alternatives for choice but rather, through the models of his discipline, to enlarge their horizons of consciousness to the point where both the articulation of alternatives and the choice of direction could be theirs (p. 29),

and ending with those who believe that a revolution is necessary to remove the causes of society's myriad problems and replace them by an equitable social structure.

Perhaps paradoxically, the 'revolutionaries' in the above classification are not 'activists' in the sense of being deeply involved in contemporary issues. It is the liberals who argue most strongly for geographical contributions to the solution of societal problems, particularly those which involve public sector intervention (e.g. Bennett, 1983), and who press for academic engagement in policy-making; many of the radicals, on the other hand, argue that their longer-term goals are best served through educational programmes (e.g. Huckle, 1985), although some are involved in policy-making activities for institutions (such as local governments) that are seeking to promote alternative (socialist) strategies, especially in the support for employment initiatives (e.g. Duncan and Goodwin, 1985). The two groups are members of the same discipline, and practice in the same academic environments, yet their goals and methods seem totally incommensurable. Alongside them are many others, who continue to research and teach in an empiricist context, with some recognition of the range of the philosophical arguments but little detailed consideration of their implications for the practice of geography. (Flowerdew, 1986, argues that, on the basis of papers submitted to him as Editor of *Area* over a three-year period, the vast majority of geographical work is empiricist with 'unexamined value positions, no explicit theory and no clear criteria for establishing the truth of statements' – p. 263.) For them, perhaps the majority of human geographers, the task is to assemble material, thereby to sensitize their readers to the world as they perceive it.

Currently, therefore, Anglo-American geography is characterized by a plurality of approaches (Gould and Olsson, 1982). These can be classified into three philosophies, each with a separate epistemology, or theory of knowledge. First there is the positivist philosophy, with its belief in the objectivity of scientific description (empiricism) and analysis of the world, its goal of formulating laws about that world, and its assumption that explanation (causal laws) can be derived by studying the outcomes of the laws; the laws of spatial organization and behaviour can be revealed by analysing spatial patterns. At least some of those who promote the empiricist foundation to this philosophy deny this necessarily leads to the full positivist commitment. They do agree, however, over the use of scientific procedures for the evaluation of hypothesis, such as the critical rationalism usually associated with Popper (Hay, 1985a, Marshall, 1985, Bird, 1989). Secondly, there are the humanistic philosophies based on a belief that people live in subjective worlds of their own creation, within which they act as free agents. Their actions cannot be explained (predicted) as examples of general laws of behaviour, but only understood – or appreciated – through methodologies that pierce their subjectivity. Finally there are the various structuralist and realist philosophies which argue that explanations for observed patterns cannot be discovered simply in the analysis of the patterns themselves, but only by the development of theories of the underlying – although inapprehendable – processes that generate the conditions within which human agents can create those patterns. Foremost within this group is marxism (particularly humanistic marxism) which argues that the processes are themselves changing – and can be altered by concerted political action – so that no laws of spatial organization are possible. For human geographers, this plurality is a focus of debate, and even a source of confusion. For some, it presents a polarization that can only be solved when one (paradigm?) is proved triumphant. (Others argue that this cannot be done logically, since there are no common criteria for comparing the approaches.) For many, the plurality offers potential for developing a newer, more robust human geography (eg Wilson, 1989), though the nature of that development is as yet far from clear. (The summaries of the statements made by six geographers – Hall et al., 1987 – to a review by the British Economic and Social Research Council on *Horizons and Opportunities in Social Science* clearly illustrate the pluralism: British geography was warmly commended: ESRC, 1987.) For a considerable number, however, it seems as if the debates are of little relevance to them. They continue to undertake empirical work, accepting the general structuration/realist thesis but believing that this is of little use in shedding light on the worlds of experiences and events.

9

Evaluation

The previous six chapters have outlined the major debates that have taken place within Anglo-American human geography since 1945 with regard to the discipline's contents – what it studies, how, and why. The chapter titles themselves indicate that several very different approaches to the discipline have been advocated. (For more detail on the approaches themselves, and on the substantial applications, see Johnston, 1986f.) The purpose of this final chapter is not to assess progress within those approaches (Lowe and Short, 1990), let alone to establish whether they have contributed towards the attainment of 'higher levels of intellectual, social and physical well-being for [our] fellow men' (Wise, 1977, p. 10). Rather, the evaluation here returns to the issues raised in Chapter 1, where several different models of the development of scientific disciplines were presented. No formal testing of those models is presented, for no methodology has been outlined that would allow such a task. Instead the general relevance of the ideas of Kuhn, Lakatos, Popper, Mulkay and Foucault is assessed against the material outlined above.

Human Geographers and Models of Disciplinary Progress

Along with members of almost every other academic discipline, human geographers have been attracted to the ideas and language of Kuhn's paradigm model. As Harvey and Holly (1981, p. 11) express it:

> the use of the word paradigm has become fashionable in geography as well as having become a pivotal concept for courses in geographic thought on both sides of the Atlantic. Thomas Kuhn has become as familiar to students of geography as Hartshorne or Humboldt.

In general, the use of Kuhnian ideas has been undertaken with relatively little research into the major debates that they have stimulated throughout Anglo-American academia. Most human geographers rely on the first, 1962, edition of *The Structure of Scientific Revolutions*; they seem to be unaware either that 'The loose use of "paradigm" in his book has made [it] amenable to a wide variety of incompatible interpretations' (Suppe, 1977a, p. 137) or that 'Kuhn's views have undergone a sharply declining influence on contemporary philosophy of science' (Suppe, 1977a, p. 647). Kuhn (1977) himself has substantially revised his ideas. (See also the exegesis of his work in Barnes, 1982.) Agnew and Duncan (1981, p. 42), for example, have argued that

> Recent reviews and programmatic statements concerning trends in Anglo-American human geography leave the impression that little attention has been given by geographers to the philosophical compatibility of borrowed ideas . . ., that the political implications of different ideas have largely been ignored . . ., and that controversy on source disciplines or literatures has not excited much interest.

Their examples do not include the import of Kuhnian ideas into geography, but their conclusions certainly hold in this case too. (For a critical discussion of that importing of Kuhnian ideas by geographers, see Mair, 1986.)

Kuhnian concepts were first used in the geographical literature by Haggett and Chorley (1967), in a normative sense as part of an argument for a revolution in geographical method. They identified an inability of the then dominant paradigm as they defined it (discussed in Chapter 2 of the present book) to handle both the explosion of relevant data for geographical research and the increasing fragmentation and compartmentalization of the sciences. They proposed a new 'model-based' paradigm

> able to rise above this flood-tide of information and push out confidently and rapidly into new data-territories. It must possess the scientific habit of seeking for relevant pattern and order in information, and the related ability to rapidly discard irrelevant information (Haggett and Chorley, 1967, p. 38).

The launch of the new paradigm had occurred more than a decade previously (see Chapter 3 above); Haggett and Chorley's goal was to diffuse the new ideas, and to win British converts to a new orientation of work in geography. (In the same book, Stoddart, 1967b, accepted the paradigm model and used it in promoting an 'organic paradigm' as a 'general conceptual model' – p. 512. When that essay was reprinted in 1986, he added a footnote 'that I would now take a less enthusiastic view of Kuhn's analysis' – p. 231.)

It was the concept of scientific revolutions that attracted Haggett and Chorley. A very similar concept was argued by Burton (1963), whose paper appeared almost contemporaneously with Kuhn's book, and contained no reference to it. Burton introduced the term 'quantitative and theoretical revolution', and argued that

> *An intellectual revolution* is over when accepted ideas have been overthrown or have been modified to include new ideas. *An intellectual revolution* is over when the revolutionary ideas themselves become part of the conventional wisdom. When Ackerman, Hartshorne and Spate are in substantial agreement

about something, then we are talking about the conventional w
my belief that the quantitative revolution is over and has been
Further evidence may be found in the rate at which schools o
North America are adding courses in quantitative methods to the
for graduate degrees (Burton, 1963, p. 153).

Similarly, Davies (1972b) used Kuhnian terminology in the title of his book, *The Conceptual Revolution in Geography*. The revolution that he identified involves a change from the contemplation of the unique to the adoption of 'the more rational scientific methodology' (p. 9): none of the contributions to his book refer to Kuhn, but the whole is clearly set in a context strongly influenced by Kuhnian ideas. And a little later, Harvey (1973) used the term, like Haggett and Chorley, in a normative sense in his search for a new world view.

The authors cited so far have used the paradigm concept at either the macro-scale of a world view or the meso-scale of a disciplinary matrix (see above, p. 16, and Mair, 1986). Others have used it as a general descriptive tool (e.g. Buttimer, 1978b, 1981; Holt-Jensen, 1981, 1988 – see also Asheim, 1990; it has the largest number of entries in the index to James and Martin, 1981); and as a framework for summarizing sub-disciplinary changes (Herbert and Johnston, 1978). And yet others have used Kuhn's micro-scale concept of a paradigm as an exemplar. Taylor (1976), for example, identified seven separate revolutions during the period under review here and Webber (1977) proposed an entropy-based paradigm (see p. 126). Harvey and Holly (1981) have made explicit use of the exemplar concept. They identify five paradigms within geography during the last century, associating each with an individual scholar

> we can tentatively assign paradigmatic status to . . . Ratzel with the paradigm of determinism, Vidal with that of possibilism, Sauer with the landscape paradigm, Hartshorne with the chronological paradigm and Schaefer with the spatial organization paradigm (Harvey and Holly, 1981, p. 31).

In effect, they are identifying 'schools of thought' associated with particular scholars, some of which existed concurrently rather than consecutively. In the 1960s, they claim, a single paradigm dominated (whether its leader was Schaefer is open to question, despite the views of Bunge, 1979, and others), but the 1970s was characterized by a 'diversity of viewpoints' (p. 37), within which spatial organization remains important. Zelinsky (1978, p. 8) calls the 1970s

> a decade of confused calm, or rather of pluralistic stalemate, as geographers explore a multiplicity of philosophical avenues and research strategies . . . without that single firm conviction as to destination that guided most of us in the past.

The discipline has become technically more capable, substantively more catholic, philosophically more mature, internationally more merged, socially more relevant, and academically more linked to other disciplines, he claims.

And this will probably lead to a continued plurality of approaches:

> I happen to believe that, more than anything else, this philosophical coming of age, this rising above the superficiality and tunnel vision that blemished so much geographical work earlier in this century, justifies (p. 10)

the title 'Human geography: coming of age'.

Although some are uncertain about the relevance of Kuhn's concepts to the 1970s and 1980s, in comparison with the 1950s and 1960s, others are less equivocal. In his introduction to a series of essays on *The Nature of Change in Geographical Ideas*, Berry (1978a) claims that

> The changes in geographical ideas that we have discussed are distinctly Kuhnian . . . What, then, is progress in geography? The perspective provided by the essays in this book is distinctly Kuhnian (pp. vii, ix).

There is little evidence of this in the essays by other contributors, however, and Berry's own contribution suggests that pluralism and inter-paradigm conflict have been much more common than have periods of normal science. Writing of geographical theories of social change, he notes (Berry, 1978b, pp. 19, 22):

> a diversity arising from the mosaic quality of modern geography . . . they have . . . moved from one paradigm to another, and in the last decade they have been extremely dynamic. . . . With multiple ideas and multiple origins, modern geography could rightly be characterized as a 'mosaic within a mosaic' (Mikesell, 1969).

Human geographers and a critique of Kuhnian applications

Kuhnian concepts and terminology are widely used in recent human geography literature, therefore, although it should be noted that some recent treatments of disciplinary history entirely ignore this literature (Freeman, 1980a, 1980b). Many of the presentations are superficial, however (see Graves, 1981), and are both cavalier and uncritical in basing their descriptions on Kuhnian foundations. (Mair, 1986, includes previous editions of this book in that category.)

But not all geographers are so convinced of the value of a Kuhnian interpretation, with two authors going so far as to claim that this has 'distorted even perverted the development of geography' (Haines-Young and Petch, 1978, p. 1). The concepts of revolutions and of normal science have both been criticized as poor descriptions of geography in recent decades (eg Holt-Jensen, 1988). Individual geographers may have experienced personal revolutions and rapid shifts from one paradigm (at the meso- if not the macro-scale) to another (Harvey, 1973, indicates this for himself: see the essays in Billinge, Gregory and Martin, 1984; the editors – p. 11 – quote Cox, Gould, Olsson, Scott and D. M. Smith as additional examples). But to claim that such experiences can be amalgamated into disciplinary revolutions, of which a number have been identified, strikes some observers as both inapt and inconsistent with the evidence:

> Perhaps so many revolutions in so short a time indicate in themselves either a continuously rolling programme, or something basically wrong with the overturning metaphor (Bird, 1977, p. 105).

The reason for this, Bird (1978, p. 134) suggests, is that mono-paradigm dominance of a discipline is inconsistent with 'the fact that society itself is organized around more than than one major principle'.

More pointed criticism is made by Stoddart, who initially saw some value in the paradigm model (Stoddart, 1967b). He argues (Stoddart, 1977, p. 1) that

> the concept sheds no light on the processes of scientific change, and readily becomes caricature. I suggest that as more is understood of the complexities of change in geography over the last hundred years, and especially of the subtle interrelationships of geographers themselves, the less appropriate the concept of the paradigm becomes.

His case is based on an analysis which shows both the absence of consensus (normal science) and the slow pace of change (which is more readily represented in Lakatos's schema). The concept of a paradigm, he claims, has become part of the 'boosterism' image with which geographers conduct debates. Thus (Stoddart, 1981a):

> the paradigm terminology has been used to illuminate either the establishment of views of which a commentator approved, or to advocate the rejection of those he did not (p. 72) . . . the concept of revolution bolsters the heroic self-image of those who see themselves as innovators and who use the term paradigm in a polemical manner . . . those who propound the Kuhnian interpretation have done so in ways which tend to make it self-fulfilling (p. 78).

and (Stoddart, 1977, p. 2):

> There is scope for sociological enquiry into the extent to which the concept has been used in recent years as a slogan in interactions between different age-groups, schools of thought, and centres of learning

The use of Kuhnian terminology has also been criticized by Billinge, Gregory and Martin (1984), who claim that the initial usage by Chorley and Haggett was 'In some measure . . . only gestural' because although they clearly distinguished between normal science and extraordinary research

> the 'anomalies' within the traditional paradigm which were central to Kuhn's thesis were never identified in any detail (p. 6).

They were arguing for a revolution in the nature of geography, but it was not a revolution generated by the failure of the previous paradigm, using failure in a Kuhnian context. With Stoddart (1981a), Mair (1986) and others, Billinge *et al.* point out that the term paradigm was being used more for propaganda – thereby gaining prestige by locating their would-be revolution alongside those in physics described by Kuhn (Taylor, 1976) – than for historiography. With regard to the latter, they accept rejection of the Kuhnian model (as presented in earlier editions of this book), but argue that since Kuhn himself did not expect the model to fit the social sciences, such a conclusion is hardly surprising. Mair (1986) takes the criticism further, contending that, with the single exception of Billinge, Gregory and Martin

> geographers have entirely misinterpreted Kuhn's contributions. They have been wrong on Kuhn in the simple sense that the skeletal Kuhnian model is misrepresented as Kuhn's major contribution. More fundamentally, however, they have been wrong on Kuhn in misconceiving his entire project (p. 359).

For him, the main values of Kuhn's work are: the concept of the exemplar as an analogy to be used in the creative process; the notion of incommensurability in the comparison on competing paradigms; and the clear need to study the sociology of scientific communities.

Despite such criticisms, little has been done to suggest an alternative sociology, either based in another model of the history of science or developed specifically to represent the situation in human geography. Wheeler (1982) finds Lakatos's work attractive, arguing that several separate programme cores can be identified in contemporary human geography (he cites areal differentiation, spatial science, cognitive-behavioural approaches and marxist structuralism), in each of which the operation of positive heuristics (see p. 17) can be identified. These research programmes are in continuing competition, whose nature will change over time (Wheeler, 1982, p. 4):

> Given the deficiencies in Kuhn's scheme and the rather ill-defined nature of geography, it seems unlikely that the future of the discipline will be characterized by sequences of revolutionary change interspersed with efficient problem solving. Moreover expectations of revolutionary progress appear to be unjustified. Instead it seems that a variety of approaches, which will undoubtedly wax and wane in popularity, will continue to be employed.

Geography and its Environment

A thesis developed by some geographers is that the major influence on the content of the discipline is its environment, particularly its economic, social and political milieux (the contents of which may influence other disciplines more directly, which then transmit changes to human geography). Stoddart (1981b, p. 1), for example, introduces a book of essays which demonstrates

> that both the ideas and the structure of the subject have developed in response to complex social, economic, ideological and intellectual stimuli.

Evidence for this is presented, as a second theme of the essays, in the reciprocal relationship between geographers and their milieux:

thoughout its recent history geographers have been not only concerned with narrowly academic issues, but have also been deeply involved with matters of social concern.

Many geographers writing on a contextual approach stress that the content of the discipline (indeed of any discipline) must be linked to its milieu, so that disciplinary changes (revolutionary or not) should be associated with significant events in the milieu. Thus Berdoulay (1981, p. 10) writes about the role of the *Zeitgeist* (or spirit of the age) as an influence on what geographers do. Grano (1981) takes this much further, showing (Figure 9.1) that geographers are a subcommunity within the community of scientists, which is itself a subset of wider society, that society has a culture, including a scientific culture within which the content of geography is defined. Action is predicated on the structure of society and its knowledge base: research praxis is part of that programme of action, and includes geographical research. The community of geographers is an 'institutionalizing social group' (p. 26), a context within which individual geographers are socialized and which defines the internal goals of their discipline in the context of the external structures within which they operate. When geography was established, one of the major goals was to create a disciplinary identity, to 'establish an object of study that could be regarded as geography's own and that differed from that of other disciplines' (p. 30); this, he claims, was a 'passive education role' (p. 32) disseminating knowledge of society-environment inter-relationships, but it was replaced in the 1970s when

> geography began to contribute actively to a transformed and replanned world. Applied geography was created and geography became a *profession* outside the small world of the university (p. 32).

(See also Goodson, 1981.)

It was, then, geographers who made geography. As Grano (1981) expresses it

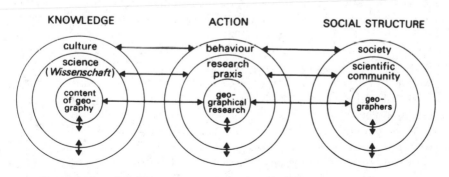

Fig 9.1   The context of geography (from Grano, 1981, p. 19)

It was the external goals of society that brought the establishment of geography as an academic discipline. This took place without any noticeable contribution from any other scientists (p. 30).

(See, however, Stoddart, 1986.) The initial period of institutionalization, as both Capel (1981) and Taylor (1985c) show, involved geography largely as a pedagogic subject, meeting the needs for the training of teachers whose activities would promote the interests of the expanding 'nation-states'. Thus Capel (1981) writes of the creation of geography as a discipline resulting from

the presence of geography in primary and secondary education at the time when the European countries begin the rapid process of diffusion of elementary education; the necessity to train geography teachers for primary and middle schools was the essential factor which led to the institutionalization of geography in the university and the appearance of the scientific community of geographers (p. 36).

(See also Freeman 1961, 1980a and, for a more critical account, Rieser, 1973.) As the context changed, however, so did geography for

The established community employs strategies tending to reproduce and amplify itself. Never will it opt for self-liquidation; the community will defend its survival, even if other communities of scientists investigate similar problems with like methods, or if the logical incoherence of the conceptions that they defend is revealed . . . Everything will be sacrificed for the reproduction and growth of the community, including the coherence of the very conception of the discipline: different conceptions can defend themselves in distinct moments or even simultaneously, without putting into doubt the continuity of the science practised (p. 66).

Thus the promotion of both national interests and those of commerce (as reflected by the nineteenth-century geographical societies) provided the context for the creation of geography. Later, changing social structures and needs created new demands to which geographers responded.

An example of the reconstruction of the discipline in the context of changed circumstances is provided by Scott's (1982) attempt to answer the question 'why do geographers, regional scientists, urban economists and others study the spatial patterning of social events?' (p. 141). His answer concentrates on the ways in which late capitalism is organized, largely, he claims, not through market relations but rather by bureaucratic intervention, by an all-embracing state. Because 'the geography of late capitalist society is shot through with problems and predicaments' (p. 145: Scott there uses geography in the vernacular sense – Johnston, 1986b – rather than the professional) this calls for state action in 'more subtle forms of social, cultural, and psychological management' (p. 146) on which science thrives. However, in participating in those managerial tasks, scientists contribute to the creation of countervailing forces, with which scientists may also become involved:

the endemic crisis of economic production and growth in late capitalist society creates the need for specific problematics and policy discourses out of which technical control may be accomplished. But technical control creates an advanced set of social conditions in which a countervailing set of human predicaments makes its appearance – alienation, the destruction of affective human relations, the repoliticization of human and regional planning, and so on (p. 152).

Hence the radical and humanistic responses to spatial science.

Geographers, then, make and remake geography in context. There is no necessity for geography, no 'specific necessities in scientific knowledge' (Grano, 1981, p. 65). Rather, according to Taylor (1985c),

Geography is a social institution. Like all such institutions its value to society varies over time and place. The creation of any social institution is a result of a group of people who identify a particular need and are able to find the resources to meet that need. As needs change the institution has to adopt to survive (p. 93).

It may fail; the particular forms of scientific discourse created may not command sponsorship and resources. Scott (1982) argues strongly that success requires identification of clear social needs:

only discourses that are posited upon existing problems of social life and practice, and upon existing political interests, stand any likelihood of commanding a significant consensus of scholars and scientists (p. 151).

There is nothing deterministic in these arguments, for they depend on geographers identifying what is and is not sustainable in a particular context and successfully promoting themselves as able to meet the perceived needs. How they do this will reflect what Berdoulay (1981) calls their individual 'circles of affinity', their social networks outside their disciplinary base. To appreciate those one must appreciate biographies, as Buttimer (1981) has argued and as two volumes of autobiographical recollections suggest (Buttimer, 1983; Billinge, Gregory and Martin, 1984). Buttimer (1983) defends such an approach because

In each person's life echoes the drama of his or her times and milieu; in all, to varying degrees, the propensity to submit or rebel. Through our own biographies we reach toward understanding, being and becoming (p. 3).

Autobiography, she argues, provides what she terms 'choreographic awareness', the 'moral, esthetic, and emotional commitments which are related to lived experience and which underpin a scholar's eventual choice of epistemological presentation and style of practice' (p. 12), and can retail that which may not be available in the written record, the influence of 'pioneers of geographic thought whose inspiration flowed through their teaching and field experiences, through their counselling and listening' (Buttimer, 1981, p. 88). This is the theme taken up explicitly by Pred (1979, 1984a), using the language of time geography (p. 146). What is perhaps particular to a scientist's autobiography, however, is that the encounters which influence career development and change need not be interpersonal. As Bird (1975, 1985) makes clear, using Popper's concept of World Three (the world of recorded knowledge), we can be strongly influenced by our reading of the ideas (both ancient and contemporary) of those who have written down their thoughts, so that our milieux are not as bounded as those who rely much more on inter-personal transmission of information (see Johnston, 1984e) – though, of course, we are reliant on what materials are, or can be, made available to us locally. (Biography is an alternative source, but few biographies are avail-able of geographers who have contributed significantly to the contemporary period: Paterson, 1985; Johnston, 1986g.)

The case for understanding the changing nature of geography contextually closely parallels the case made by realists for appreciating all human activity; the operation of human agency must be analysed within the constraining and enabling conditions provided by its environment. Thus Johnston (1983d) has enlisted structuration theory as a framework for analysing the changes in human geography that are the concern of this book, arguing that

> the content of a discipline at any one time and place reflects the response of the individuals involved to external circumstances and influences, within the context of their intellectual socialization (p. 4).

This is the position taken by Mikesell (1981), though without the language of structuration, in a description of the history of geography in the United States. That history has been characterized, he claims, by a sequence of 'tem-porary enthusiasms or episodes' (p. 9). The content of those episodes is a response to the stimuli of the contemporary American environment – hence the popularity of urban studies in recent decades, the decline in foreign-area studies after the Viet-Nam withdrawal, and the impact of national concern about the physical environment in the 1970s. Furthermore, he also suggests the role of environmental influences on the culture of individual geographers:

> The first generation of American geographers grew up in a country that was still strongly influenced by the *mores* of small towns. Most of the students now attracted to geography are products not only of an urban but increasingly of a suburban environment . . . the geographical profession has changed and is changing as a consequence of the suburban, middle-class origin of most of its current members (pp. 11–12).

Porter (1978) has advanced similar arguments, identifying two types of American geography: a Midwest version that 'was a characteristically opti-mistic, action-oriented, "can-do" kind' (p. 17); and a Californian geography, based on Sauer, 'historical, uncompromisingly academic, speculative, suspic-ious of government, keenly interested in cultures other than the dominant Anglo culture of the United States' (p. 18).

This environmental influence thesis can be taken too far, of course, and should not be allowed to become environmental determinism: Mikesell notes that urban geography flowered in the 1950s and 1960s not only in Chicago but also in Iowa. But it does suggest that human geography and human geographers must be studied in the context of their milieux, and that, as Capel (1981) so clearly points out, the disciplinary community (or major elements within it) will seek to maintain its identity by bending to the perceived shifts in their milieux (as clearly demonstrated for anthropologists by Patterson, 1986). Further, as Mikesell (1981, p. 13) argues – following Harvey (1973) and others – this reaction to environmental shifts is undertaken by individual scholars, who are seeking not only to defend and promote their chosen discipline but also to defend and promote their own status and careers within it:

> innovation will continue to be regarded as a virtue. Much of the development that has already taken place in American geography is a consequence of the attempt of individual scholars to stake a claim for themselves, to be or at least to seem to be different from their rivals. The fact that most academics see virtue in innovation means that there is reward for innovation.

What Mikesell does not discuss is the scale of the innovation; does it have to involve developments within the positive heuristic of a research programme, to use Lakatos's terms, or does it require the launch of a new research programme? Can one bring potentially greater rewards, and disasters, than the other?

The relevance of the environmental influence thesis has been illustrated several times in this book. It has been especially relevant in the late 1970s and early 1980s as a consequence of the economic recession, the cut-backs in higher education, the attacks on social science research and then the response to the policy prescriptions of the 'New Right' designed to achieve recovery from the recession by sustaining what has become widely known as 'flexible accumulation' (Hudson, 1988) through a 'Free economy and a strong state' (Gamble, 1988: Johnston and Pattie, 1990). Many have reacted to this by promoting human geography as an 'applied discipline', offering relevant skills for the attack on contemporary problems. (This is illustrated in Chapter 7.) Writing in the December 1981 issue of the *Newsletter* of the Association of American Geographers (AAG), under the title 'A survival package for geography and other endangered disciplines', Kish and Ward (1981, p. 8) state that:

> On 19 June, 1981, the Board of Regents of the University of Michigan decided, by unanimous vote, to terminate the Department of Geography at the end of the 1981–82 academic year.

From their experience of this decision, Kish and Ward offer comments on how other departments of geography may counter similar attacks. They emphasize the teaching role, seeking to attract students in a competitive market and presenting 'our wares in a stimulating and excellent way'. This should involve examining the virtues of applied geography. As students become more conscious of careers, there may be a corresponding need to increase a skill-oriented curriculum. This could demonstrate the relevancy of geography and enhance its appeal to students (p. 14).

Kish and Ward — 'To appease some traditionalists' — claim that they do not advocate reorganizing the entire corpus of geography, 'but only attempt to broaden the appeal of geography to the student population'. (See also Ford, 1982; Powell, 1981.)

In research as well as teaching the trend towards geography as an applied discipline is being heavily emphasized. Thus in announcing a new editorial policy for *The Professional Geographer*, the April 1982 issue of the AAG *Newsletter* reports that (p. 1)

> Brunn hopes to emphasize work in applied geography and to include information on corporation activities, state and local government projects, Federal government activities, activities by United Nations and other international agencies, and research projects.

The need for more applied work is widely accepted among American human geographers as a necessary means for the reproduction and even growth of their discipline. It takes a variety of forms (some argue, for example, for a greater concentration on cartography and geographical information systems: see p. 109), as Mikesell (1981, p. 14) indicates:

> geographers fortunate enough to have secure teaching positions will worry about what they should do. The best response to this concern could be a decision to do what they have been doing, but with a keener appreciation of context and a greater willingness to be influenced by environment.

In Britain, the external pressures became just as great during the 1980s, and there has been substantial expression of the need for applied geography, as a contribution from the discipline to the solution of current economic and social problems (see Chapter 7). Thus, for example, Bennett (1982, p. 69), writing of the 1982 conference of the Institute of British Geographers, found it

> possible to discern a strong and growing set of foci which, if they do not yet demark a new core, at least show an emerging commonality of interest. For this writer these foci were a widespread assertion of 'relevant' research, the reassertion of quantitative and analytical methods, and the rejection of recent anti-empirical movements.

Bennett welcomed these, noting that

> hot [i.e. relevant] issues are not ones which British geographers are particularly noted for tackling *en masse* — and, as a result, the discipline has suffered a lack of public exposure, and a marked inability to influence public and private decisions.

and

At a time when higher education as a whole is under considerable challenge, and when geography as a discipline may suffer particularly severe pressure in some institutions it is heartening to see the emergence of concern with the hot issues expressed at this meeting (p. 71).

Beaumont (1989, p. 172) echoed this a few years later, when he argued that

the issues raised for the next twenty years are a practical and developmental, rather than a research, orientation. The future is unknown, but it could be exciting, if geographers are prepared to become involved (probably with new partners) in doing geography.

Against this, there are those who see the changes in society as presenting a challenge: Harvey (1989a, p. 16), for example, in looking for alliances that will 'mitigate if not challenge the hegemonic dynamic of capitalist accumulation to dominate the historical geography of social life'.

A generational model?

The importance of context as an influence on the nature of human geography as a discipline has suggested that the paradigm model might be rephrased as a generational model (Johnston, 1978c, 1979b). This argues that changes in the external environment provide a necessary, but not sufficient, stimulus to changes within the discipline that can be interpreted as attempts to develop a new research programme, if not to launch a revolution and create a new normal science. Associated with the external changes must be a set of conditions within the discipline itself which is sympathetic to the new demands of the milieux. In most cases, these conditions are best met by younger members of the discipline. Stegmuller (1977, p. 148) agues that:

it is mostly young people who bring new paradigms into the world. And it is young people who are most inclined to champion new causes with religious fervour, to thump the propaganda drums.

In order to obtain influence, however, especially in times of resource shortage within higher education, such younger workers need the patronage of some established members of the discipline (see Chapter 1). According to Lemaine *et al.* (1976, p. 5):

Mendel's work, and that of his successors, was a response to scientific problems. But the scientific implications of their results were not pursued until there existed a strong group of scientists who, owing to their academic background and their position in the research community, were willing to abandon established conceptions.

Such reactions to environmental shifts may involve attempts to create a new paradigm or new research programme, or they may only require new branches of an existing paradigm/programme. Whichever it is, even when establishment support has been obtained, success is more likely to occur − or a bridgehead is more likely to be built − when certain criteria are met. These include (van den Daele and Weingart, 1976): an autonomous system of evaluation and reputation; an autonomous communication system; acknowledgement of the new ability to solve puzzles within the confines of the disciplinary matrix; a formal organization providing training programmes which allow reproduction and expansion of the new group's membership; an informal structure with leaders; and resources for research. In periods of academic expansion, these criteria rarely create problems; as Capel, Mikesell, Taylor and others indicate, innovation is encouraged if it brings status, charisma and resources to the discipline. In periods of stagnation and retrenchment, the conditions are less favourable, and major shifts can only be achieved by revolutions among the existing members of the discipline. The generational model suggests that the latter is rare. With regard to the research record, Law (1976, p. 228) has counselled that:

> it may well be the case that scientists do lay special emphasis on the accounts in scientific papers, but my hunch is that there is immense (and non-trivial) variation between scientists on this count. For some, science is something you do in the laboratory, something you talk about, and something you get excited about. For others, science is what they write and what they read in the journals. I would even hypothesize (in conformity with the invisible college notion) that those who are generally felt to be of higher status locate science less in their journals than in their own and other people's heads.

Many academics publish rarely, if ever, in their discipline's research journals, and for some as changes occur in their discipline so they get 'left-behind'. The 'normal science' that they continue to teach is probably based on the worldview, disciplinary matrix and exemplars into which they were socialized. But their colleagues, socialized later and influenced by subsequent environmental conditions, operate in different ways. The academic career cycle, in combination with a changing milieu, can produce a multi-paradigm teaching, if not research, discipline.

The key elements in the generational model (modified after Johnston, 1978c) are:

1   The external environment is a major influence on the contents of a discipline, especially one in the social sciences which is closely linked with that environment.
2   At times, the nature of this environment may shift. This provokes a reaction among a minority of members of the discipline who seek to stimulate change in disciplinary practice by its established members and to generate interest in that change among the youngest generation of research workers. The latter is usually much more successful than the former.
3   Together, this grouping presents a new 'school of thought'. In some cases, opposing new schools may be stimulated.
4   The new school is coopted into the disciplinary career structure.
5   The publications of the new school come to dominate the disciplinary

research output, as the productivity of the earlier generation declines.

6   Students face two or more separate generational schools in a department's teaching syllabus.

7   Over time, members of the new school attain seniority within the discipline.

Several consequences may follow from operation of this model. One is that if a discipline fails to react to a changing milieu, it will stagnate. Thus innovators are to be encouraged. Another is that some potential innovators may find that they are unable to influence their discipline, because the environment is not right and the establishment need not react to their suggestions. Duncan (1974b, p. 109) has illustrated these 'processes of resistance to new scientific ideas within science itself', using the example of Hägerstrand's (1968) work on spatial diffusion. Hägerstrand's ideas were originally published in 1953, but Duncan's study of citations shows that widespread recognition was much delayed, compared to the average for all publications in geography (Stoddart, 1967a). The reasons for this, Duncan claims, were neither language nor Hägerstrand's relative isolation in Sweden, but the apparent irrelevance of his work to those steeped in another paradigm. Only when spatial science had been established was Hägerstrand's seminal contribution recognized:

> Hägerstrand's own attempts to disseminate his work met rejection from adherents to orthodoxy, but enthusiasm from the new geography group. The eventual relay of information to this community owed more to dogged personal effort than to the formal communication system of normal science, and general recognition was not achieved until professional allegiances were extremely reorganized (p. 130).

Even when a new idea has been recognized, however, those working on it may be divided into two or more virtually independent groups (Gatrell, 1982).

Human Geography: Paradigms, or Research Programmes, or . . .?

The previous sections have discussed the application of various models of scientific progress to human geography. Clearly a number of possible interpretations of the last four decades is possible. This final discussion suggests the general relevance of Kuhn's concept of a paradigm (at all three scales of definition), without necessarily accepting either substantial periods of mono-paradigm dominance and normal science for the discipline as a whole or major revolutionary events that involved large numbers of geographers switching from one paradigm to another. (In some ways, paradigms as disciplinary matrices can be equated with research programmes in Lakatos's terminology; the Kuhnian term is preferred here.) In seeking to understand the relative popularity of various paradigms at different times, however, it is necessary to employ the contextual approach largely ignored by the modellers of scientific progress.

The 1950s and 1960s

At the beginning of the period studied here, regionalism – with its empiricist and implicit exceptionalist philosophy – dominated the discipline. There were several versions of it: in the United States, areal differentiation was stressed by geographers emanating from the Midwest, notably Chicago and Madison, whereas those from Berkeley focused on the evolving cultural landscape, and there was also a distinct school based in Clark University (Bushong, 1981; Prunty, 1979). The regional theme dominated in Britain, too, though with a greater emphasis on physical geography and less evidence of distinct 'schools' (Freeman, 1979; Johnston and Gregory, 1984). Then, in the first post-war decade systematic studies became dominant. Their stated (though often unrealized) aims were to increase the content of regional descriptions, advancing the understanding of particular places by gaining knowledge of the general processes that interacted to produce unique characteristics.

Regionalism was a disciplinary matrix with several different exemplars, therefore; the one belief shared by members of the community was that regional synthesis is the *raison d'être* of geography. But during the 1950s and 1960s there came what Entrikin (1981, p. 1) terms 'transition between reigning orthodoxies . . . in which the spatial theme superseded the regional theme'. This was marked by the growth of systematic studies, the distancing of many geographers from the core belief in regional synthesis, and an increasing emphasis on finding laws of spatial organization, involving distance as a basic influence on human behaviour. As Guelke (1977a, 1977b, 1978) and Entrikin (1981) have indicated, the distancing was not rapid – in part no doubt because of the political need to sustain the unity and identity of the discipline – and some of those promoting the new paradigm argued that all that quantitative analysis and spatial science offered was better and more rigorous procedures for identifying and understanding regions (as in Berry, 1964b). There was, then, a methodological shift (Chisholm, 1975), which implies new exemplars but not a new disciplinary matrix, let alone a new world view.

Increasingly, the methodological shift alone was portrayed as insufficient, and a philosophical shift slowly emerged (elsewhere termed a 'quiet revolution': Johnston, 1978c, 1979b, 1981b). The link to regional synthesis was unattractive (Gould, 1979) and increased contact with other social scientists introduced geographers to the excitements of systematic specialisms practised according to the positivist model of science and perceiving a clear societal need for their products: the links with the regional core were severed and a new disciplinary matrix of spatial science established. (Batty, 1989, argues that by the time its models were well developed and applicable the demand for them had gone: 'It is an irony of history that such good models finally exist which could well have produced excellent advice in their day had they been available. But that day has passed' – p. 156.) The term region took on a very different meaning (Johnston, 1984d). The shared values of the new disciplinary matrix clearly varied from those of regionalism, and to the extent that the adherents of spatial science, most of them from the new generation of geographers who were part of the educational boom of those decades, came to dominate the discipline (see Mikesell, 1984, on whether they did) so a revolution can be said to have occurred. Whether it was a revolution in the traditional Kuhnian terms is doubtful, however, since – as noted above (p. 272) – the shift hardly fits into the 'response to anomalies' component of Kuhn's model. This suggests that it was not only a shift in disciplinary matrix but also a shift in world view, in the conception of the nature of science. Whether that is so is also doubtful, however, for, as Hartshorne makes clear (p. 56), traditional regional geography (at least as he conceived it) did not deny the possible relevance of generalizations about processes for the under- standing of places. Bird (1989), does identify a 'one and only' revolution, however, and dates it to June 1966 with the publication of Bunge's (1966) note criticising the uniqueness of location argument as a defence against positivism in science.

The new disciplinary matrix of spatial science was firmly established in Anglo-American human geography by the end of the 1960s, and has been sus- tained since. Over nearly thirty years it has seen many shifts in exemplars, a lot of them linked to methodological – especially technical – developments in data analysis. (Compare, for example, Haggett, 1965 with Haggett, Cliff and Frey, 1977, for shifts in the general orientation; Cliff and Ord, 1973 with Cliff and Ord, 1981, for a single methodological issue; and Hägerstrand, 1968, with Cliff et al., 1987, for a particular substantive topic. Clarke and Wilson, 1985, provide a useful review of later developments.) Such paradigm shifts at the level of exemplar have been closer to Kuhn's original presentation, in that new ways of doing research have been accepted as superior to those previously used, thereby assimilating anomalies. They have brought greater substantive success, too: Haggett (1978), writing on 'The spatial economy', claims that it:

> is more carefully defined than before, we know a little more about its organi- zation, the ways it responds to shocks, and the way some regional sections are tied to others. There now exist theoretical bridges, albeit incomplete and shaky, which span from pure, spaceless economics through to a more spatially disaggre- gated reality (p. 161).

As well as the shifting among exemplars with regard to methods there were also changes within the spatial science disciplinary matrix which had a wider import. The first of these was the reorientation away from normative modelling and the testing of spatial organization against a priori models towards behavioural studies; as Cox (1981) indicates, the disciplinary matrix was not queried but there were major shifts in emphasis and style. The second was the advocacy for 'welfare geography' (p. 200), described by Eyles and Smith (1978) as a response to social conditions and a desire to make contemporary human geography more relevant to them.

What we can identify in the 1950s and 1960s, therefore, is the establishment of a new disciplinary matrix for human geographers, with its twin concentrations on the spatial organization of society and human spatial behaviour. During those decades, and much more so since, exemplars have waxed and waned. They have introduced new methodological procedures and new focuses of substantive interest, in part as reactions to anomalies thrown up within the discipline (the failure of certain normative models, for example, and the shortcomings of certain quantitative procedures) and in part as responses to trends in society. Indeed, there are many branches and sub-branches of the disciplinary matrix, reflecting the substantive interests of geographers (urban social, agricultural etc.) and the technical arsenal that they deploy. (The review of American geography published at the end of 1980s is almost entirely structured within those systematic specialisms: Gaile and Willmott, 1989.)

The 1970s and 1980s

Although the spatial science disciplinary matrix expanded rapidly in the 1960s, and continued to do so in the early 1970s, it never dominated human geography at that time, as has been shown in the discussions of historical geography. It was, however, relatively unchallenged, for a variety of reasons (Taylor, 1976). During the subsequent decade challenges developed, both as a response to the output of that disciplinary matrix and as a reaction to events and issues elsewhere in society. Two major challenges emerged, contesting not just the exemplars, nor even the disciplinary matrix, but the world-view implicit in the disciplinary matrix of spatial science.

The first of these challenges – termed the humanistic here – was a response both to the nature of spatial science and to the ideology of society that it reflected. Spatial science is technocratic in its orientation and application; it tends to reduce people to terms in equations, to ignore their individuality and freedom of action (Ley, 1981), and to ignore the immense variety of places in favour of a universalistic view of how people think and act. Its view of science is rejected by humanistic geographers who, from their reading of the other social sciences and philosophy, have argued for a different conception of science, one that focuses on subjectivity. Such a science is clearly incommensurable with positivistic spatial science, and the choice of which to practice is an ideological one (Johnston, 1986a).

Humanistic geography was introduced as an alternative science of geography, therefore, and not as a reorientation of the existing way, though some proponents claimed roots in earlier geographical practices such as those of the French geographer Vidal de la Blache (Buttimer, 1978a). It has its own disciplinary matrix, and its own variety of exemplars – in terms of both their philosophy and their subject matter. Its introduction has not brought about a revolution, for there has been no major switch in the contents of the discipline as a whole. Rather, it has offered an alternative conception of human geography and competes with the others on that basis.

The second challenge – summarized here as realist – was a response to the contents of the spatial science disciplinary matrix also, but was influenced much more by the external environment than was the humanistic. As detailed above (p. 217), those who launched what was initially known as radical geography were concerned with the failure of positivist science, including spatial science, to tackle and solve pressing societal problems. They, too, advocated applied geography, but defined relevance in a very different way (Harvey, 1974; Johnston, 1981a). As with humanistic geography, this involved promoting a scientific revolution at the level of the world view; the realist science that they advanced was incommensurable with both positivist and humanistic science.

Once established, realist-Marxist science also became a disciplinary matrix with a variety of exemplars. The core of its programme is the desire to uncover the mechanisms that drive society and which provide explanations for how people act and how the empirical world is organized. The means for achieving such understanding, and what use can be made of the knowledge that it provides, is the subject of much debate – between marxists and nonmarxists, for example, as well as among the various types of marxist – and exemplars have waxed and waned rapidly in recent years. The debates within the realist conception of science are about how to achieve agreed scientific goals; the debates with positivist and humanistic geographers are about the nature of science. The former produce internal revolutions; the latter seek to promote major disciplinary revolutions.

The decades reviewed here have been turbulent ones for human geography, a turbulence which Ley (1981) finds exciting but also confusing, in part because of the rapidity with which human geographers have explored new ideas. Ley feels that such exploration is often superficial, with ideas discarded almost as soon as they are adopted – 'In true North American fashion, obsolescence is setting in more and more speedily' (p. 209); others argue that such ideas are often taken out of their original context, and that geographers who import them may be unaware of the controversies surrounding them (Agnew and Duncan, 1981; Duncan, 1980). Some seek to reconcile the various world-views (Harrison and Livingstone, 1982; Hay, 1979a; Johnston, 1980, 1982c; Livingstone and Harrison, 1981); others argue that it is impossible (Eyles and Lee, 1982). Others still contend that the various world-views are informed by the others (eg Thrift, 1987, p. 401 and his claim that Marxist political economy now 'forms a vital subtext to most theorising'), and geographers should be active in using their synthesizing powers to integrate the various perspectives (Brookfield, 1989, p. 314).

Evaluating these turbulent years, when the turbulence is still continuing and shows little sign of abating, is not easy. There is no doubt that Kuhn's model, as sometimes presented to geographers of periods of normal scientific progress punctuated by major revolutions, is not relevant to what has happened within human geography since 1945. But, as Mair (1986) argues, the concept of the paradigm as a scientific community with shared values has considerable relevance to appreciating what has occurred and is occurring. At the lowest definitional level of a paradigm, the exemplar, there is clear evidence too that human geographers socialized within a disciplinary matrix have shifted the orientation of their work as 'better' ways have been suggested to them; minor revolutions have occurred, and frequently. Such shifts have gone in a variety of directions, presenting an apparent anarchy − not chaos, which is the vernacular use of that term, but 'free and voluntary cooperation of individuals and groups' (Labedz, 1977, p. 22). But the core values hold.

At the largest scale definition of a paradigm, the world view, there is also considerable evidence of its relevance to an appreciation of contemporary human geography. Currently, three very different conceptions of the nature of science (conceptions that are entirely incommensurable) are competing for geographical attention. They differ in their scientific and their societal goals, and demand choice. Clear evidence can be provided of geographers making such a choice, switching from one conception of science to another because, as Harvey (1973) expressed it with regard to Marxism, 'I can find no other way of accomplishing what I set out to do or of understanding what has to be understood' (p. 17).

In some ways, the intermediate definition of paradigm − the disciplinary matrix − appears redundant. But not entirely so. The shift from regionalism to spatial science was basically a shift of disciplinary matrix. The world view remained constant − that of positivist science with its foundation in empiricism − although it was hidden until relatively late in the shift. But within that world view, the shared goals altered very considerably, and this can readily be interpreted as a shift in disciplinary matrix. Within the other two world views, perhaps insufficient time has elapsed for such shifts to be clearly detected; the growth of structuration theory within the realist conception is very suggestive of one, however.

Kuhn's model as usually presented does not fit the experience of human geography since 1945. But the major elements of the model are of value in appreciating much of what has happened within the discipline over that period. In summary, the following five points present the salient elements of the period.

1   In the early years (up until the late 1960s) there was mono-paradigm dominance at the level of the world view, with the clear acceptance of empiricism and the increasingly explicit acceptance of positivism.
2   Within that period, there was a steady switch from one disciplinary matrix (regionalism) to another (spatial science) but the former was never entirely ousted by the latter.

3 Within the spatial science disciplinary matrix, which remains buoyant through to the present, a substantial number of exemplars have provided the framework for the conduct of research, reflecting both technical developments and the systematic subdivision of the discipline.

4 Since the late 1960s, two further world views have been promoted by human geographers, representing two very different views of science, both from each other and from spatial science. Both are now well established within the discipline, with substantial numbers of adherents, but neither has been able to achieve disciplinary hegemony.

5 Within both of these world views, different disciplinary matrices have been advocated. No one has dominated humanistic geography; realism (incorporating maxism) has increasingly come to dominate the 'radical structural' world view.

At the present time, then, human geography is characterized by a multi-paradigm situation at the world view level, by competition between disciplinary matrices within at least two of those world views, and by a wealth of exemplars on which research is based in all three. It is because of the last element, and because many human geographers have not been deeply schooled into any one disciplinary matrix, let alone the use of any one exemplar, that the discipline appears replete with fickle allegiances, as individuals explore (often via World Three rather than through interpersonal links) various ways of practising geography. Thus (Johnston, 1981b)

> Much geographical work is exploratory, and is conducted by individuals who operate independently. Indeed, many, although influenced by what they read, are in no sense socialized into a particular matrix or set of exemplars which might be associated with a 'research school' and its leader. The charisma of certain individuals and their published works may occasionally produce the prophet and disciple situation. Much more usual, however, is a situation of fickle allegiances (pp. 313–4).

Such fickleness suggests anarchy, in the sense used by Feyerabend (1975; Johnston, 1976b, 1978c). Some human geographers shift frequently among exemplars, sometimes between disciplinary matrices, and just occasionally between world views.

How can the nature of human geography summarized in the five points above, and the fickle allegiances just described, be accounted for? Clearly, Foucault's notion of an *episteme*, a dominant mode of discourse in society as a whole (see p. 22), is too general, since neither the frequency of the shifts described here nor the multi-paradigm situation of three competing, incommensurable, world views can be accommodated by that concept. No doubt changes within geography are linked to changes both in society as a whole and in other disciplines (as Claval, 1981, argues), but they lack mono-paradigm dominance also. What we have is individual geographers occasionally seeking to promote a particular paradigm (world view, disciplinary matrix, or exemplar) in opposition to prevailing practice. They are very unlikely to do that in isolation; either contacts with others or reading (or both) will suggest the argument to them, and they then seek support within the discipline, and resources/sponsorship in society.

Why are some people better able to promote paradigm change than others? Little work has been done on the sociology of geography as a discipline, especially with regard to power over the acceptance/rejection of proposed paradigm shifts and the ability to convince others of the (at least temporary) 'rightness' of any approach. (Though see Duncan, 1974b, on the belated recognition of Hägerstrand's pioneering work.) Some work has been done on the influential figures in the discipline's early development (e.g. in Blouet, 1981, and in the biobibliography series edited by Freeman, 1977ff) and the nature of the profession in Britain has been explored (Johnston and Brack, 1983), but the dynamics of the discipline in recent years have not been the subject of detailed analysis. Citation analysis has been used to identify frequently referenced works which could be categorized as exemplars (e.g. Whitehand, 1985; Wrigley and Matthews, 1986) and to discover research communities, groups of scholars who refer to each other's writings on a particular topic (Gatrell, 1984a, 1984b); journals have been rated and their interdependence charted (e.g. Whitehand, 1984; Gatrell and Smith, 1984) and departments in the United States and the United Kingdom have been ranked in terms of publications produced, publications cited, and peer evaluation, for example (see Morrill, 1980; Jones, Lindsey and Coggeshall, 1982; Turner and Meyer, 1985 on the U.S.; on the UK, see Bentham, 1987; Smith, 1988b); and exploratory studies of particular subdisciplines have sought the main stimuli to how individuals practice (e.g. Phillips and Unwin, 1985). All of these describe the structure of the discipline and its various subsystems, but tell us little of its processes; like spatial science they provide valuable descriptive data, but not necessarily much understanding.

For that understanding, it is necessary not only to appreciate the contexts in which people were working, but also to realize that those contexts are not determinate. A change in the level of economic prosperity in a country will not necessarily bring forth a certain reaction from geographers; individual geographers will respond (or not) to their interpretations of that change, and their responses may stimulate others to follow them in the initiation of a paradigm shift. This is the most likely reason for shifts at the level of the world view and, probably, the disciplinary matrix, as exemplified by the introduction of a radical/structuralist world view and by the shift within the empiricist world view from regionalism to spatial science. But such shifts can produce reactions, which was the case with the advancement of humanistic geography as a counter to spatial science, though clearly those promoting that cause were influenced both by currents of thinking outwith geography and by their explorations of World Three. At the level of the exemplar, shifts are most likely to occur as a response to events within the discipline, as Kuhn suggests; this occurred within the spatial science disciplinary matrix with the movement from normative to behavioural analyses, but the latter move towards welfare geography was strongly influenced by external factors.

There is, then, no simple model that can be applied to the changes within human geography that provides an explanation of why the discipline has altered in the ways described here. Kuhn's work provides a valuable vocabulary and organizing framework within which to analyse the alterations, but what has occurred reflects the perceptions and actions of individual human geographers. Like all other aspects of society, geography is a discipline created by and for geographers, and is continually recreated by them, in places, at a variety of scales. The last point is crucial, for – as the realist approach to human geography stresses – people are socialized in particular contexts and they then create part of the milieux within which others are socialized. Those places are not isolated, and changes in one can influence changes in others. But, as illustrated here, within the Anglo-American realm there have been substantial differences from one place to another in how geography is practiced, reflecting both the nature of those places and the people in them; at the international scale, the differences are even greater (Johnston and Claval, 1984).

And the Future?

Within the social sciences, and probably in the natural sciences too, the contents of a discipline vary over time and space; the nature of such change can be appreciated and accounted for, but not predicted, and certainly future change cannot be predicted with any certainty. In the early 1970s, a selection of leading geographers were asked to present their views of the discipline's future (Chorley, 1973). Little of what they wrote is clearly reflected in what exactly happened, and the contents of a somewhat similar book produced twelve years later (Johnston, 1985c) are very different. Debates about the nature of the discipline, on how it should be practiced and taught (Gould, 1977, 1978, 1981, 1975a, 1985b, has been a major contributor), continue and will continue, reflecting not only internal division within the discipline but also trends in the societies to which human geographers belong. What will be the contents and contexts of those future debates cannot be predicted; one could suggest with some certainty, however, that human geography will not be characterized by mono-paradigm dominance in the next decade.

In the introduction to his autobiographical essay, D. Smith (1984) wrote that

> my own professional activities seem to have been a continual struggle to come to terms with (or keep up with) the rapidly shifting focus of human geography. The struggle arises in large measure from the difficulty of breaking free from one's own intellectual heritage. . . . If my own struggles represent anything more than one half-life experience, it may well be the theme of the geographer or social scientist as creature of his or her times. . . . If anything is to be learned

from the instant replay of such recent events . . . it is that 'scientific' advance is not conducted in a social vacuum but as an integral part of human history, within which the element of chance arising from individual personality and creativity plays an important part. So let us proceed with the recollection of one of the random variables (p. 118).

We all, it seems, are random variables. (Robson, 1984, uses a similar turn of phrase when he writes that 'it is clear how small a part in my own development seems to have been played by clearly guided aims and how much has been contributed by the collage of rather random influences and serendipitous events to which I both responded and contributed' – p. 104.) Hence our individual projects and life-paths can be appreciated and set in context, but no more. We are very uncertain where we, as individuals, are going, let alone where geography as a set of linked yet anarchistic communities is going. We are making the future of geography as we practice it, just as I have been remaking its past by writing this book.

Bibliography

ABLER, R. F. 1971: Distance, intercommunications, and geography. *Proceedings, Association of American Geographers* 3, 1–5.

ABLER, R. F., ADAMS, J. S. and GOULD, P. R. 1971: *Spatial organization: the geographer's view of the world*. Englewood Cliffs, NJ: Prentice-Hall.

ACKERMAN, E. A. 1945: Geographic training, wartime research, and immediate professional objectives. *Annals of the Association of American Geographers* 35, 121–43.

—— 1958: *Geography as a fundamental research discipline*. Chicago: University of Chicago, Department of Geography Research Paper 53.

—— 1963: Where is a research frontier? *Annals of the Association of American Geographers* 53, 429–40.

ADAMS, J. S. 1969: Directional bias in intra-urban migration. Economic Geography 45, 302–23.

AGNEW, J. A. 1984: Place and political behaviour: the geography of Scottish nationalism. *Political Geography Quarterly* 3, 191–202.

—— 1987a: *The United States in the world-economy: a regional geography*. Cambridge: Cambridge University Press.

—— 1987b: *Place and Politics: The Geographical Mediation of State and Society*. Boston: Allen and Unwin.

—— 1989: The devaluation of place in social science. In J. A. Agnew and J. S. Duncan (eds.) *The Power of Place*. Boston: Unwin Hyman, 9–29.

—— 1990: Sameness and difference: Hartshorne's *The Nature of Geography* and geography as areal variation. In J. N. Entrikin and S. D. Brunn (eds.) *Reflections on Richard Hartshorne's The Nature of Geography*. Washington: Association of American Geographers, 121–40.

AGNEW, J. A. and DUNCAN, J. S. 1981: The transfer of ideas into Anglo-American human geography. *Progress in Human Geography* 5, 42–57.

—— and DUNCAN, J. S. 1989: Introduction. In J. A. Agnew and J. S. Duncan (eds.) *The Power of Place*. Boston: Unwin Hyman, 1–8.

AITKEN, S. C., CUTTER, S. L., FOOTE, K. E. and SELL, J. S. 1989: Environmental perception and behavioral geography. In G. L. Gaile and C. J. Willmott (eds.) *Geography in America*. Merrill, Columbus, 218–38.

ALEXANDER, D. 1979: Catastrophic misconception? *Area* 11, 228–30.

ALEXANDER, J. W. and ZAHORCHAK, G. A. 1943: Population-density maps of the United States: techniques and patterns. *Geographical Review* 33, 457–66.

AMEDEO, D. and GOLLEDGE, R. G. 1975: *An introduction to scientific reasoning in geography*. New York: John Wiley.

ANDERSON, J. 1973: Ideology in geography: an introduction. *Antipode* 5(3), 1–6.

APPLETON, J. 1975: *The experience of landscape*. London: John Wiley.

ARCHER, J. C. and TAYLOR. P. J. 1981: *Section and party*. Chichester: John Wiley.

ASHEIM, B. T. 1990: Review of Holt-Jensen. *Progress in Human Geography* 14.

BADCOCK, B. A. 1970: Central-place evolution and network development in south Auckland, 1840–1968: a systems analytic approach. *New Zealand Geographer* 26, 109–35.

—— 1984: *Unfairly structured cities*. Oxford: Basil Blackwell.

BAHRENBERG, G., FISCHER, M. M. and NIJKAMP, P. (eds.) 1984: *Recent developments in spatial data analysis: methodology, measurement, models*. Aldershot: Gower Press.

BAKER, A. R. H. 1972: Rethinking historical geography. In A. R. H. Baker (ed.), *Progress in historical geography*. Newton Abbott: David & Charles, 11–28.

—— 1979: Historical geography: a new beginning? *Progress in Human Geography* 3, 560–70.

—— 1981: An historico-geographical perspective on time and space and on period and place. *Progress in Human Geography* 5, 439–43.

—— 1984: Reflections on the relations of historical geography and the *Annales* school of history. In A. R. H. Baker and D. Gregory (eds.) *Explorations in historical geography*. Cambridge: Cambridge University Press, 1–27.

—— and GREGORY, D. 1984: Some terrae incognitae in historical geography: an exploratory discussion. In A. R. H. Baker and D. Gregory .(eds.) *Explorations in historical geography*. Cambridge: Cambridge University Press, 180–94.

BALL, M. 1987: Harvey's Marxism. *Environment and Planning D: Society and Space* 5, 393–4.

BALLABON, M. B. 1957: Putting the 'economic' into economic geography. *Economic Geography* 33, 217–23.

BARNES, B. 1974: *Scientific knowledge and sociological theory*. London: Routledge & Kegan Paul.

—— 1982: *T. S. Kuhn and social science*. London: Macmillan.

BARNES, T. J. 1985: Theories of international trade and theories of value. *Environment and Planning A* 17, 729–46.

—— 1988: Rationality and relativism in economic geography: an interpretive review of the *homo economicus* assumption. *Progress in Human Geography* 12, 473–96.

—— 1989a: Place, space and theories of economic value: contextualism and essentialism in economic geography. *Transactions, Institute of British Geographers* NS14, 299–316.

—— 1989b: Structure and agency in economic geography and theories of economic value. In A. Kobayashi and S. Mackenzie (eds.) *Remaking human geography*. Boston: Unwin Hyman, 134–48.

BARROWS, H. H. 1923: Geography as human ecology. *Annals of the Association of American Geographers* 13, 1–14.

BASSETT, K. and SHORT, J. R. 1980: *Housing and residential structure: alternative approaches*. London: Routledge & Kegan Paul.

BATTY, M. 1976: *Urban modelling: algorithms, calibrations, predictions*. London: Cambridge University Press.

—— 1978: Urban models in the planning process. In D. T. Herbert and R. J. Johnston (eds.), *Geography and the urban environment*, vol. 1 London: John Wiley, 63–134.

—— 1989: Urban modelling and planning; reflections, retrodictions and prescriptions. In B. Macmillan (ed.) *Remodelling Geography*. Oxford: Basil Blackwell, 147–69.

BEAUMONT, J. R. 1987: Quantitative methods in the real world: a consultant's view of practice. *Environment and Planning A* **19**, 1441–8.
—— and GATRELL, A. C. 1982: *An introduction to Q-analysis*. CATMOG 34, Geo Books, Norwich.
BEAUREGARD, R. A. 1988: In the absence of practice: the locality research debate. *Antipode* **20**, 52–59.
BELL, D. 1973: *The coming of post-industrial society*. New York: Basic Books.
BENNETT, R. J. 1974: Process identification for time-series modelling in urban and regional planning. *Regional Studies* **8**, 157–74.
—— 1975: Dynamic systems modelling of the Northwest region: 1. Spatio-temporal representation and identification. 2. Estimation of the spatio-temporal policy model. 3. Adaptive parameter policy model. 4. Adaptive spatio-temporal forecasts. *Environment and Planning A* **7**, 525–38, 539–66, 617–36, 887–98.
—— 1978a: Forecasting in urban and regional planning closed loops: the examples of road and air traffic forecasts. *Environment and Planning A* **10**, 145–62.
—— 1978b: *Spatial time series: analysis, forecasting and control*, London: Pion.
—— 1979: Space-time models and urban geographical research in D. T. Herbert and R. J. Johnston (eds.), *Geography and the urban environment: progress in research and application*, vol. 2. London: John Wiley, 27–58.
—— 1981a: Quantitative geography and public policy. In N. Wrigley and R. J. Bennett (eds.), *Quantitative geography*. London: Routledge & Kegan Paul, 387–96.
—— 1981b: A hierarchical control solution to allocation of the British Rate Support Grant. *Geographical Analysis* **13**, 300–14.
—— (ed.) 1981c: *European progress in spatial analysis*. London: Pion.
—— 1981d: Quantitative and theoretical geography in Western Europe. In R. J. Bennett (ed.), *European progress in spatial analysis*. London: Pion, 1–32.
—— 1982: Geography, relevance and the role of the Institute. *Area* **14**, 69–71.
—— 1983: Individual and territorial equity. *Geographical Analysis* **15**, 50–87.
—— 1985a: A reappraisal of the role of spatial science and statistical inference in geography in Britain. *L'Espace Geographique* **14**, 23–8.
—— 1985b: Quantification and relevance. In R. J. Johnston (ed.) *The future of geography*. London: Methuen, 211–24.
—— 1989a: Whither models and geography in a post-welfarist world? In B. Macmillan (ed.) *Remodelling Geography*. Oxford: Basil Blackwell, 273–90.
—— 1989b: Demography and budgetary influence on the geography of the poll tax: alarm or false alarm? *Transactions, Institute of British Geographers* **NS14**, 400–17.
BENNETT, R. J. and CHORLEY, R. J. 1978: *Environmental systems: philosophy, analysis and control*. London: Methuen.
BENNETT, R. J. and HAINING, R. P. 1985: Spatial structure and spatial interaction: modelling approaches to the statistical analysis of geographical data. *Journal of the Royal Statistical Society A* **148**, 1–36.
—— HAINING, R. P. and WILSON, A. G. 1985: Spatial structure, spatial interaction and their integration: a review of alternative models. *Environment and Planning A* **17**, 625–46.
BENNETT, R. J. and THORNES, J. B. 1988: Geography in the United Kingdom, 1984–1988. *The Geographical Journal* **154**, 23–48.
BENNETT, R. J. and WRIGLEY, N. 1981: Introduction. In N. Wrigley and R. J. Bennett (eds.), *Quantitative geography*. London: Routledge & Kegan Paul, 3–11.
BENTHAM, G. 1988: An evaluation of the UGC's rating of the research of British university geography departments. *Area* **19**, 147–54.
BERDOULAY, V. 1981: The contextual approach. In D. R. Stoddart (ed.), *Geography, ideology and social concern*. Oxford: Blackwell, 8–16.
BERRY, B. J. L. 1958: A critique of contemporary planning for business centers. *Land Economics* **25**, 306–12.

—— 1959a: Ribbon developments in the urban business pattern. *Annals of the Association of American Geographers* **49**, 145–55.

—— 1959b: Further comments concerning 'geographic' and 'economic' economic geography. *The Professional Geographer* **11**(1), 11–12.

—— 1964a: Cities as systems within systems of cities. *Papers, Regional Science Association* **13**, 147–63.

—— 1964b: Approaches to regional analysis: a synthesis. *Annals of the Association of American Geographers* **54**, 2–11.

—— 1965: Research frontiers in urban geography. In P. M. Hauser and L. F. Schnore (eds.), *The study of urbanization*. New York: John Wiley, 403–30.

—— 1966: *Essays on commodity flows and the spatial structure of the Indian economy.* Chicago: University of Chicago, Department of Geography, Research Paper 111.

—— 1967: *The geography of market centers and retail distribution*. Englewood Cliffs, NJ: Prentice-Hall.

—— 1968: A synthesis of formal and functional regions using a general field theory of spatial behavior. In B. J. L. Berry and D. F. Marble (eds.), *Spatial analysis*. Englewood Cliffs, NJ: Prentice-Hall, 419–28.

—— (ed.) 1971: *Comparative factorial ecology. Economic Geography* **47**, 209–367

—— 1972a: Hierarchical diffusion: the basis of development filtering and spread in a system of growth centers. In N. M. Hansen (ed.), *Growth centers in regional economic development*. New York: The Free Press, 108–38.

—— 1972b: 'Revolutionary and counter-revolutionary theory in geography' – a ghetto commentary, *Antipode* **4**(2), 31–3.

—— 1972c: More on relevance and policy analysis, *Area* **4**, 77–80.

—— 1973a: *The human consequences of urbanization*. London: Macmillan.

—— 1973b: A paradigm for modern geography. In R. J. Chorley (ed.), *Directions in Geography*. London: Methuen, 3–22.

—— 1974a: Review of H. M. Rose (ed.), *Perspectives in geography 2. Geography of the ghetto, perceptions, problems and alternatives. Annals of the Association of American Geographers* **64**, 342–5.

—— 1974b: Review of David Harvey, *Social Justice and the City. Antipode* **6**(2), 142–5, 448.

—— 1978a: Introduction: a Kuhnian perspective. In B. J. L. Berry (ed.), *The nature of change in geographical ideas*. de Kalb: Northern Illinois University Press, vii-x.

—— 1978b: Geographical theories of social change. In B. J. L. Berry (ed.), *The nature of change in geographical ideas*. de Kalb: Northern Illinois University Press, 17–36.

BERRY, B. J. L. and BAKER, A. M. 1968: Geographic sampling. In B. J. L. Berry and D. F. Marble (eds.), *Spatial analysis*. Englewood Cliffs, NJ: Prentice-Hall, 91–100.

BERRY, B. J. L. and GARRISON, W. L. 1958a: The functional bases of the central place hierarchy. *Economic Geography* **34**, 145–54.

—— and GARRISON, W. L. 1958b: Recent developments in central place theory. *Papers and Proceedings, Regional Science Association* **4**, 107–20.

BERRY, B. J. L. and HORTON, F. E. (eds.) 1974: *Urban environmental management: planning for pollution control*. Englewood Cliffs, NJ: Prentice-Hall.

BERRY, B. J. L. *et al.* 1974: *Land use, urban form and environmental quality.* Chicago: Department of Geography, Research Paper 155, University of Chicago.

BHASKAR, R. 1978: *A realist theory of science*. Brighton: Harvester Press.

BILLINGE, M. 1977: In search of negativism: phenomenology and historical geography. *Journal of Historical Geography* **3**, 55–68.

—— 1983: The mandarin dialect: an essay on style in contemporary geographical writing. *Transactions, Institute of British Geographers* NS8, 400–20.

BILLINGE, M., GREGORY, D. and MARTIN, R. L. (eds.) 1984: *Recollections of a revolution: geography as spatial science*. London: Macmillan.

—— 1984: Reconstructions. In M. Billinge, D. Gregory and R. Martin (eds.) *Recollections of a revolution: geography as spatial science*. London: Macmillan, 1–26.

BIRD, J. H. 1975: Methodological implications for geography from the philosophy of K. R. Popper. *Scottish Geographical Magazine* 91, 153–63.

—— 1977: Methodology and philosophy. *Progress in Human Geography* 1, 104–10.

—— 1978: Methodology and philosophy. *Progress in Human Geography* 2, 133 40.

—— 1985: Geography in three worlds: how Popper's system can help elucidate dichotomies and changes in the discipline. *The Professional Geographer* 37, 403–9.

—— 1989: *The changing worlds of geography: a critical guide to concepts and methods*. Oxford: Clarendon Press.

BIRKIN, M. and CLARKE, M. 1988: SYNTHESIS: a synthetic spatial information system: methods and examples. *Environment and Planning A* 20, 645–71.

—— 1989: The generation of individual and household incomes at the small area level using synthesis. *Regional Studies* 23, 535–48.

BIRKIN, M. and WILSON, A. G. 1986: Industrial location models 1. a review and integrating framework *and* 2. Weber, Palander, Hotelling and extensions within a new framework. *Environment and Planning A* 18, 175–206 and 293–306.

BLAIKIE, P. M. 1978: The theory of the spatial diffusion of innovations: a spacious cul-de-sac. *Progress in Human Geography* 2, 268–95.

—— 1985: *The political economy of soil erosion*. London: Longman.

—— 1986: Natural resource use in developing countries. In R. J. Johnston and P. J. Taylor (eds.) *A world in crisis? geographical perspectives*. Oxford: Basil Blackwell, 107–26.

BLAIKIE, P. M. and BROOKFIELD, H. C. (eds.) 1987: *Land degradation and society*. London: Methuen.

BLAUG, M. 1975: Kuhn versus Lakatos, or paradigms versus research programmes in the history of economics. *History of Political Economy* 7, 399–419.

BLAUT, J. M. 1979: The dissenting tradition. *Annals of the Association of American Geographers* 69, 157–64.

—— 1987: Diffusionism: a uniformitarian critique. *Annals of the Association of American Geographers* 77, 30–47.

BLOUET, B. W. (ed.) 1981: *The origins of academic geography in the United States*. Hamden Conn: Archon Books.

BLOWERS, A. T. 1972: Bleeding hearts and open values. *Area* 4, 290–2.

—— 1974: Relevance, research and the political process *Area* 6, 32–6.

BLUMENSTOCK, D. I. 1953: The reliability factor in the drawing of isarithms. *Annals of the Association of American Geographers* 43, 289–304.

BOAL, F. W. and LIVINGSTONE, D. N. 1989: The behavioural environment: worlds of meaning in a world of facts. In F. W. Boal and D. N. Livingstone (eds.) *The Behavioural Environment*. London: Routledge, 3–17.

BODDY, M. J. 1976: The structure of mortgage finance: building societies and the British social formation. *Transactions, Institute of British Geographers* NS1, 58–71.

BOOTS, B. N. and GETIS, A. 1978: *Models of spatial processes*. Cambridge: Cambridge University Press.

BOWLBY, S. R., FOORD, J. and MCDOWELL, L. 1986: The place of gender in locality studies. *Area* 18, 327–31.

—— LEWIS, J., McDOWELL, L. and FOORD, J. 1989: The geography of gender. In Peet, R. and Thrift, N. J. (eds.) *New models in geography (Volume Two)*. London: Unwin Hyman, 157–75.

BOYLE, M. J. and ROBINSON, M. E. 1979: Cognitive mapping and understanding. In D. T. Herbert and R. J. Johnston (eds.) *Geography and the urban environment*, volume 2. Chichester: John Wiley, 59–82.

BRACKEN, I., HIGGS, G., MARTIN, D. and WEBSTER, C. 1990: *A classification of geographical information systems literature and applications*. CATMOG 52. Norwich: Environmental Publications.

BRADLEY, P. N. 1986: Food production and distribution – and hunger. In R. J. Johnston and P. J. Taylor (eds.) *A world in crisis? geographical perspectives*. Oxford: Basil Blackwell, 89–106.

BREITBART, M. M. 1981: Peter Kropotkin, the anarchist geographer. In D. R. Stoddart (ed.), *Geography, ideology and social concern*. Oxford: Blackwell, 134–53.

BRITTAN, S. 1977: Economic liberalism. In A. Bullock and O. Stallybrass (eds.), *The Fontana dictionary of modern thought*. London: Fontana Books, 188–9.

BROOKFIELD, H. C. 1962: Local study and comparative method: an example from Central New Guinea. *Annals of the Association of American Geographers* 52, 242–54.

—— 1964: Questions on the human frontiers of geography. *Economic Geography* 40, 283–303.

—— 1969: On the environment as perceived. In C. Board *et al.* (eds.), *Progress in Geography* 1, London: Edward Arnold, 51–80.

—— 1973: On one geography and a Third World. *Transactions, Institute of British Geographers* 58, 1–20.

—— 1975: *Interdependent development*. London: Methuen.

—— 1989: The behavioural environment: how, what for, and whose? in F. W. Boal and D. N. Livingstone (eds.) *The Behavioural Environment*. London: Routledge, 311–28.

BROWETT, J. 1984: On the necessity and inevitability of uneven spatial development under capitalism. *International Journal of Urban and Regional Research* 8, 155–76.

BROWN, L. A. 1968: *Diffusion processes and location: a conceptual framework and bibliography*. Browett Regional Science Research Institute, Bibliography Series 3, Philadelphia.

—— 1975: The market and infrastructure context of adoption: a spatial perspective on the diffusion of innovation. *Economic Geography* 51, 185–216.

—— 1981: *Innovation diffusion: a new perspective*. London: Methuen.

BROWN, L. A. and MOORE, E. G. 1970: The intra-urban migration process: a perspective. *Geografiska Annaler* 52B, 1–13.

BROWN, R. H. 1943: *Mirror for Americans: likeness of the eastern seaboard 1810*. New York: American Geographical Society.

BROWN, S. E. 1978: Guy-Harold Smith, 1895–1976. *Annals of the Association of American Geographers* 68, 115–18.

BROWNING, C. 1982: *Conversations with geographers: career pathways and research styles*. University of North Carolina at Chapel Hill, Department of Geography, Occasional Paper 16.

BRUNN, S. D. 1974: *Geography and politics in America*. New York: Harper & Row.

BRUSH, J. E. 1953: The hierarchy of central places in southwestern Wisconsin. *Geographical Review* 43, 380–402.

BUCHANAN, K. 1962: West wind, east wind. *Geography* 47, 333–46.

—— 1973: The white north and the population explosion. *Antipode* 5(3), 7–15.

BULLOCK, A. 1977: Liberalism. In A. Bullock and O. Stallybrass (eds.), *The Fontana dictionary of modern thought*. London: Fontana Books, 347.

BUNGE, W. 1962: second edition, 1966. *Theoretical geography*. Lund Studies in Geography, Series C 1, Lund: C. W. K. Gleerup.

—— 1966: Locations are not unique. *Annals of the Association of american Geographers* 56, 375–6.

—— 1968: Fred K. Schaefer and the science of geography. *Harvard Papers in Theoretical Geography*, Special Papers Series, Paper A, Laboratory for Computer Graphics and Spatial Analysis, Harvard University, Cambridge, Mass.

—— 1971: *Fitzgerald: geography of a revolution*. Cambridge, Mass: Schlenkman.
—— 1973a: Spatial prediction. *Annals of the Association of American Geographers* **63**, 566–8.
—— 1973b: Ethics and logic in geography. In R. J. Chorley (ed.), *Directions in geography*. London: Methuen, 317–31.
—— 1973c: The geography of human survival. *Annals of the Association of American Geographers* **63**, 275–95.
—— 1973d: The geography. *The Professional Geographer* **25**, 331–7.
—— 1979: Fred K. Schaefer and the science of geography. *Annals of the Association of American Geographers* **69**, 128–33.
BUNGE, W. and BORDESSA, R. 1975: *The Canadian alternative: survival, expeditions and urban change*. Geographical Monographs, Atkinson College, York University. Downsview, Ontario.
BUNTING, T. E. and GUELKE, L. 1979: Behavioral and perception geography: a critical appraisal. *Annals of the Association of American Geographers* **69**, 448–62, 471–4.
BURNETT, K. P. (ed.) 1981: *Studies in choice, constraints, and human spatial behavior*. *Economic Geography* **57**, 291–383.
BURTON, I. 1963: The quantitative revolution and theoretical geography. *The Canadian Geographer* **7**, 151–62.
BURTON, I., KATES, R. W. and WHITE, G. F. 1978: *The environment as hazard*. New York: Oxford University Press.
BUSHONG, A. D. 1981: Geographers and their mentors: a genealogical view of American academic geography. In B. W. Blouet (ed.), *The origins of academic geography in the United States*. Hamden, Conn: Archon Books, 193–220.
BUTLIN, R. A. 1982: *The transformation of rural England c. 1580–1800*. Oxford: Oxford University Press.
BUTTIMER, A. 1971: *Society and milieu in the French geographical tradition*. Chicago: Rand McNally.
—— 1974: *Values in geography*. Commission on College Geography, Resource Paper 24, Association of American Geographers, Washington.
—— 1976: Grasping the dynamism of lifeworld. *Annals of the Association of American Geographers* **66**, 277–92.
—— 1978a: Charism and context: the challenge of La Géographie Humaine. In D. Ley and M. S. Samuels (eds.), *Humanistic geography: prospects and problems*. Chicago: Maaroufa Press, 58–76.
—— 1978b: On people, paradigms and progress in geography. Institutionen for Kulturgeografi och Economisk Geografi vid Lunds Universitet, *Rapporter och Notiser* **47**.
—— 1979: Erewhon or nowhere land. In S. Gale and G. Olsson (eds.), *Philosophy in geography*. Dordrecht: D. Reidel, 9–38.
—— 1981: On people, paradigms and 'progress' in geography In D. R. Stoddart (ed.), *Geography, ideology and social concern*. Oxford: Blackwell, 70–80.
—— 1983: *The practice of geography*. London: Longman.
BUTTIMER, A. and HÄGERSTRAND, T. 1980: *Invitation to dialogue: a progress report*. DIA Paper 1, University of Lund, Lund.
BUTZER, K. W. 1989: Cultural ecology. In G. L. Gaile and C. J. Willmot (eds.) *Geography in America*. Columbus: Merrill, 192–208.
—— 1990: Hartshorne, Hettner, and *The Nature of Geography*. In J. N. Entrikin and S. D. Brunn (eds.) *Reflections on Richard Hartshorne's The Nature of Geography*. Washington: Association of American Geographers, 35–52.
CADWALLADER, M. 1975: A behavioral model of consumer spatial decision making. *Economic Geography* **51**, 339–49.

—— 1986: Structural equation models in human geography. *Progress in Human Geography* 10, 24–47.

CAMERON, I. 1980: *To the farthest ends of the earth*. London: Macdonald.

CAMPBELL, J. A. 1989: The concept of 'the behavioural environment', and its origins, reconsidered. In F. W. Boal and D. N. Livingstone (eds.) *The behavioural environment*. London: Routledge, 33–76.

CAMPBELL, J. A. and LIVINGSTONE, D. N. 1983: Neo-Lamarckism and the development of geography in the United States and Great Britain. *Transactions, Institute of British Geographers* NS8, 267–94.

CAPEL, H. 1981: Institutionalization of geography and strategies of change. In D. R. Stoddart (ed.), *Geography, ideology and social concern*. Oxford: Blackwell, 37–69.

CAREY, H. C. 1858: *Principles of social science*. Philadelphia: J. Lippincott.

CARLSTEIN, T. 1980: *Time, resources, society and ecology*. Department of Geography, University of Lund, Lund.

CARLSTEIN, T., PARKES, D. N. and THRIFT, N. J. (eds.): *Timing space and spacing time* (three volumes). London: Edward Arnold.

CARR, M. 1983: A contribution to the review and critique of behavioral industrial location theory. *Progress in Human Geography* 7, 386–402.

CARROLL, G. R. 1982: National city-size distributions: what do we know after 67 years of research? *Progress in Human Geography* 6, 1–43.

CARROTHERS, G. A. P. 1956: An historical review of the gravity and potential concepts of human interaction. *Journal, American Institute of Planners* 22, 94–102.

CASTELLS, M. 1977: *The urban question*. London: Edward Arnold.

CHAPMAN, G. P. 1977: *Human and environmental systems: a geographer's appraisal*. London: Academic Press.

CHAPPELL, J. E., Jr 1975: The ecological dimension: Russian and American views. *Annals of the Association of American Geographers* 65, 144–62.

—— 1976: Comment in reply. *Annals of the Association of American Geographers* 66, 169–73.

CHAPPELL, J. M. A. and WEBBER, M. J. 1970: Electrical analogues of spatial diffusion processes. *Regional Studies* 4, 25–39.

CHISHOLM, M. 1962: *Rural settlement and land use*. London: Hutchinson.

—— 1966: *Geography and economics*. London: G. Bell & Sons.

—— 1967: General systems theory and geography. *Transactions, Institute of British Geographers* 42, 45–52.

—— 1971a: In search of a basis for location theory: micro-economics or welfare economics? In C. Board *et al.* (eds.), *Progress in Geography* 3, London: Edward Arnold, 111–34.

—— 1971b: Geography and the question of 'relevance'. *Area* 3, 65–8.

—— 1973: The corridors of geography. *Area* 5, 43.

—— 1975: *Human geography: evolution or revolution?* Harmondsworth: Penguin Books.

—— 1976: Regional policies in an era of slow population growth and higher unemployment. *Regional Studies* 10, 201–13.

CHISHOLM, M., FREY, A. E. and HAGGETT, P. (eds.), 1971: *Regional forecasting*. London: Butterworth.

CHISHOLM, M. and MANNERS, G. (eds.) 1973: *Spatial policy problems of the British economy*. London: Cambridge University Press.

CHISHOLM, M. and O'SULLIVAN, P. 1973: *Freight flows and spatial aspects of the British economy*. Cambridge: Cambridge University Press.

CHORLEY, R. J. 1962: Geomorphology and general systems theory. *Professional Paper* 500-B, United States Geological Survey, Washington.

—— 1964: Geography and analogue theory. *Annals of the Association of American Geographers* 54, 127–37.

—— 1973a: Geography as human ecology. In R. J. Chorley (ed.), *Directions in geography*. London: Methuen, 155–70.

—— (ed.) 1973b: *Directions in geography*. London: Methuen.

CHORLEY, R. J. and BENNETT, R. J. 1981: Optimization: control models. In N. Wrigley and R. J. Bennett (eds.), *Quantitative geography*. London: Routledge & Kegan Paul, 219–24.

CHORLEY, R. J. and HAGGETT, P. 1965a: Trend-surface mapping in geographical research. *Transactions and Papers, Institute of British Geographers* 37, 47–67.

—— (eds.) 1965b: *Frontiers in geographical teaching*. London: Methuen.

—— (eds.) 1967: *Models in geography*. London: Methuen.

CHORLEY, R. J. and KENNEDY, B. A. 1971: *Physical geography: a systems approach*. London: Prentice-Hall International.

CHOUINARD, V., FINCHER, R. and WEBBER, M. 1984: Empirical research in scientific human geography. *Progress in Human Geography* 8, 347–80.

CHRISMAN, N. R., COWEN, D. J., FISHER, P. F., GOODCHILD, M. F. and MARK, D. M. 1989: Geographic information systems. In G. L. Gaile and C. J. Willmott (eds.) *Geography in America*. Columbus: Merrill, 776–96.

CHRISTALLER, W. 1966: *Central places in southern Germany* (translated by C. W. Baskin). Englewood Cliffs, NJ: Prentice-Hall.

CHRISTENSEN, K. 1982: Geography as a human science. In P. Gould and G. Olsson (eds.), *A search for common ground*. London; Pion, 37–57.

CLARK, A. H. 1954: Historical geography. In P. E. James and C. F. Jones (eds.), *American geography: inventory and prospects* (Syracuse: Syracuse University Press), 70–105.

—— 1977: The whole is greater than the sum of the parts: a humanistic element in human geography. In D. R. Deskins *et al.* (eds.), *Geographic humanism, analysis and social action: a half century of geography at Michigan*. Michigan Geographical Publication No. 17, Ann Arbor, 3–26.

CLARK, D., DAVIES, W. K. D. and JOHNSTON, R. J. 1974: The application of factor analysis in human geography. *The Statistician* 23, 259–81.

CLARK, G. L. and DEAR, M. J. 1984: *State apparatus*. Boston: George Allen & Unwin.

CLARK, G. L. 1985: *Judges and the cities*. Chicago: University of Chicago Press.

—— 1982: Instrumental reason and policy analysis. In D. T. Herbert and R. J. Johnston (eds.) *Geography and the urban environment, volume 5*. Chichester: John Wiley, 41–62.

CLARK, K. G. T. 1950: Certain underpinnings of our arguments in human geography. *Transactions, Institute of British Geograpers* 16, 15–22.

CLARK, W. A. V. 1975: Locational stress and residential mobility in a New Zealand context. *New Zealand Geographer* 31, 67–79.

—— 1981: Residential mobility and behavioral geography: parallelism or interdependence? In K. R. Cox and R. G. Golledge (eds.), *Behavioral problems in geography revisited*. London: Methuen, 182–205.

CLARKE, M. and HOLM, E. 1988: Microsimulation methods in spatial analysis and planning. *Geografiska Annaler* 69B, 145–64.

—— 1987: Towards an applicable human geography: some developments and observations. *Environment and Planning A* 19, 1525–41.

CLARKE, M. and WILSON, A. G. 1985a: A model-based approach to planning in the National Health Service. *Environment and Planning B: Planning and Design* 12, 287–302.

—— 1985b: The dynamics of urban spatial structure: the progress of a research programme. *Transactions, Institute of British Geographers* NS10, 427–51.

—— 1989: Mathematical models in human geography: 20 years on. In R. Peet and

N.J. Thrift (eds.) *New Models in Geography (Volume Two)*. London: Unwin Hyman, 30–42.

CLARKSON, J. D. 1970: Ecology and spatial analysis. *Annals of the Association of American Geographers* **60**, 700–16.

CLAVAL, P. 1981: Epistemology and the history of geographical thought. In D. R. Stoddart (ed.), *Geography, ideology and social concern*. Oxford: Blackwell, 227–39.

—— 1983: *Models of man in geography*. Syracuse: Department of Geography, Syracuse University, Discussion Paper 79.

CLAYTON, K. M. 1985a: New blood by (government) order. *Area* **17**, 321–2.

—— 1985b: The state of geography. *Transactions, Institute of British Geographers* **NS10**, 5–16.

CLIFF, A. D. *et al.* 1975: *Elements of spatial structure: a quantitative approach*. London: Cambridge University Press.

—— *et al.* 1981: *Spatial diffusion*, Cambridge: Cambridge University Press.

CLIFF, A. D. and HAGGETT, P. 1989: Spatial aspects of epidemic control. *Progress in Human Geography* **13**, 315–47.

—— and ORD, K. J. 1987: *Spatial aspects of influenza epidemics*. London: Pion.

CLIFF, A. D. and ORD, J. K. 1973: *Spatial autocorrelation*. London: Pion.

—— 1981: *Spatial process* London: Pion.

COATES, B. E., JOHNSTON, R. J. and KNOX, P. L. 1977: *Geography and inequality*. Oxford: Oxford University Press.

COCHRANE, A. 1987: What a difference the place makes: the new structuralism of locality. *Antipode* **19**, 354–63.

COFFEY, W. J. 1981: *Geography: towards a general spatial systems approach*. London: Methuen.

COLE, J. P. 1969: Mathematics and geography. *Geography* **54**, 152–63.

COLE, J. P. and KING C. A. M. 1968: *Quantitative geography*. London: John Wiley.

CONZEN, M. P. 1981: The American urban system in the nineteenth century. In D. T. Herbert and R. J. Johnston (eds.), *Geography and the urban environment*, vol. 4. Chichester: John Wiley, 295–348.

COOKE, P.N. 1986: The changing urban and regional system in the United Kingdom. *Regional Studies* **20**, 243–52.

—— 1987a: Clinical inference and geographic theory *Antipode* **19**, 69–78.

—— 1987b: Individuals, localities and postmodernism. *Environment and Planning D: Society and Space* **5**, 408–12.

—— (ed.) 1989a: *Localities: The changing face of urban britain*. London: Unwin Hyman.

—— 1989b: Locality theory and the poverty of 'spatial variation' (A response to Duncan and Savage). *Antipode* **21**, 261–73.

COOKE, R. U. 1985a: Applied geomorphology. In A. Kent (ed.) *Perspectives on a changing geography*. Sheffield: The Geographical Association, 36–47.

—— 1985b: *Geomorphological hazards in Los Angeles*. London: George Allen & Unwin.

COOKE, R. U. and ROBSON, B. T. 1976: Geography in the United Kingdom, 1972–1976. *Geographical Journal* **142**, 3–22.

COOMBES, M.G. *et al.* 1982: Functional regions for the population census of Great Britain. In D. T. Herbert and R. J. Johnston (eds.), *Geography and the urban environment*, vol. 5. Chichester: John Wiley, 63–111.

COOPER, W. 1952: *The struggles of Albert Woods*. London: Jonathan Cape.

COPPOCK, J. T. 1974: Geography and public policy: challenges, opportunities and implications. *Transactions, Institute of British Geographers* **63**, 1–16.

CORBRIDGE, S. 1986: *Capitalist world development*. London: Macmillan.

—— 1988: Deconstructing determinism. *Antipode* **20**, 239–69.

—— 1989: Marxism, post-Marxism, and the geography of development. In R. Peet and N. J. Thrift (eds.) *New models in geography (Volume One)*. London: Unwin Hyman, 224–54.

COSGROVE, D. E. 1983: Towards a radical cultural geography: problems of theory. *Antipode* **15**, 1–11.

—— 1984: *Social formation and symbolic landscape*. London: Croom Helm.

—— 1989a: Geography is everywhere: culture and symbolism in human landscapes. In D. Gregory and R. Walford (eds.) *Horizons in Human Geography*. London: Macmillan, 1181–135.

—— 1989b: Models, description and imagination in geography. In B. Macmillan (ed.) *Remodelling geography*. Oxford: Blackwell, 23–44.

—— and DANIELS, S. J. (eds.) 1988: *The iconography of landscape*. Cambridge: Cambridge University Press.

—— 1989: Fieldwork as theatre: a week's performance in Venice and its region. *Journal of Geography in Higher Education* **13**, 169–82

—— and JACKSON, P. 1987: New directions in cultural geography. *Area* **19**, 95–101.

COUCLELIS, H. 1986a: Artificial intelligence in geography: conjectures on the shape of things to come. *The Professional Geographer* **38**, 1–10.

—— 1986b: A theoretical framework for alternative models of spatial decision and behavior. *Annals of the Association of American Geographers* **76**, 95–113.

COUCLELIS, H. and GOLLEDGE, R. G. 1983: Analytic research, positivism, and behavioral geography. *Annals of the Association of American Geographers.* **73**, 331–9.

COURT, A. 1972: All statistical populations are estimated from samples. *The Professional Geographer* **24**, 160–1.

COWEN, D. J. 1983a: Automated geography and the DIDS. *The Professional Geographer* **35**, 339–40.

COX, K. R. 1969: The voting decision in a spatial context. In C. Board *et al.* (eds.), *Progress in Geography* **1**. London: Edward Arnold, 81–118.

—— 1973: *Conflict, power and politics in the city: a geographic view*. New York: McGraw Hill.

—— 1976: American geography: social science emergent. *Social Science Quarterly* **57**, 182–207.

—— 1979: *Location and public problems*. Oxford: Basil Blackwell.

—— 1981: Bourgeois thought and the behavioral geography debate. In K. R. Cox and R. G. Golledge (eds.), *Behavioral problems in geography revisited*. London: Methuen, 256–79.

—— 1989: The politics of turf and the question of class. In J. Wolch and M. Dear (eds.) *The Power of Geography*. Boston: Unwin Hyman, 61–90.

COX, K. R. and GOLLEDGE, R. G. 1969: Editorial introduction: behavioral models in geography. In K. R. Cox, and R. G. Golledge (eds.), *Behavioral problems in geography: a symposium*. Northwestern University Studies in Geography 17, Evanston, 1–13.

—— (eds.) 1969: *Behavioral Problems in Geography: A Symposium*. Evanston: Northwestern University Studies in Geography, 17.

—— 1981: Preface. In K. R. Cox and R. G. Golledge (eds.), *Behavioral problems in geography revisited*. London: Methuen, xiii–xxix.

—— 1981: *Behavioural Problems in Geography Revisited*. London: Methuen.

COX, K. R. and McCARTHY, J. J. 1982: Neighbourhood activism as a politics of turf: a critical analysis. In K. R. Cox and R. J. Johnston, (eds.), *Conflict, politics and the urban scene*. London: Longman, 196–219.

—— and MAIR, A. 1989: Levels of abstraction in locality studies. *Antipode* **21**, 121–32.

COX, K. R., REYNOLDS, D. R. and ROKKAN, S. (eds.) 1974: *Locational approaches to power and conflict*. New York: Halsted Press.

COX, N. J. 1989: Modelling, data analysis and Pygmalion's problem. In B. Macmillan (ed.) *Remodelling Geography*. Oxford: Basil Blackwell, 204–10.

COX, N. J. and JONES, K. 1981: Exploratory data analysis. In N. Wrigley and R. J. Bennett (eds.) *Quantitative geography*. London: Routledge & Kegan Paul, 135–43.

CRANE, D. 1972: *Invisible colleges*. Chicago: University of Chicago Press.

CROWE, P. R. 1936: The rainfall regime of the Western Plains. *Geographical Review* 26, 463–84.

—— 1938: On progress in geography. *Scottish Geographical Magazine* 54, 1–19.

—— 1970: Review of *Progress in Geography* 1. *Geography* 55, 346–7.

CUMBERLAND, K. B. 1947: *Soil erosion in New Zealand*. Wellington: Whitcombe & Tombs.

CURRAN, P. J. 1984: Geographic information systems. *Area* 16, 153–8.

CURRY, L. 1967: Quantitative geography. *The Canadian Geographer* 11, 265–74.

—— 1972: A spatial analysis of gravity flows. *Regional Studies* 6, 131–47.

CURRY, M. 1982a: The idealist dispute in Anglo-American geography. *The Canadian Geographer* 26, 37–50.

—— 1982b: The idealist dispute in Anglo-American geography: a reply. *The Canadian Geographer* 26, 57–9.

DACEY, M.F. 1962: Analysis of central-place and point patterns by a nearest-neighbor method. In K. Norborg (ed.), *Proceedings of the IGU Symposium in Urban Geography, Lund 1960*. Lund: C. W. K. Gleerup, 55–76.

—— 1968: A review on measures of contiguity for two and k-color maps. In B. J. L. Berry and D. F. Marble (eds.), *Spatial analysis*. Englewood Cliffs, NJ: Prentice-Hall, 479–95.

—— 1973: Some questions about spatial distributions. In R. J. Chorley (ed.), *Directions in geography*. London: Methuen, 127–52.

DANIELS, P.W. 1982: *Service industries: growth and location*. Cambridge: Cambridge University Press.

—— 1985: *Service industries: a geographical appraisal*. London: Methuen.

DARBY, H. C. 1953: On the relations of geography and history. *Transactions and Papers, Institute of British Geographers* 19, 1–11.

—— 1962: The problem of geographical description. *Transactions and Papers, Institute of British Geographers* 30, 1–14.

—— (ed.) 1973: *A new historical geography of England*. London: Cambridge University Press.

—— 1977: *Domesday England*. London: Cambridge University Press.

—— 1983a: Historical geography in Britain, 1920–1980: continuity and change. *Transactions, Institute of British Geographers* NS8, 421–8.

—— 1983b: Academic geography in Britain, 1918–1946. *Transactions, Institute of British Geographers* NS8, 14–26.

DAVIES, R. B. and PICKLES, A. R. 1985: Longitudinal versus cross-sectional methods for behavioural research: a first-round knockout. *Environment and Planning A* 17, 1315–930.

DAVIES, W. K. D. 1972a: Geography and the methods of modern science, In W. K. D. Davies (ed.), *The conceptual revolution in geography*. London: University of London Press, 131–9.

—— 1972b: Introduction: the conceptual revolution in geography. In W. K. D. Davies (ed.) *The conceptual revolution in geography*. London: University of London Press, 9–18.

DAVIS, W. M. 1906: An inductive study of the content of geography. *Bulletin of the American Geographical Society* 38, 67–84.

DAY, M. and TIVERS, J. 1979: Catastrophe theory and geography: a Marxist critique. *Area* 11, 54–8.

DAYSH, G. H. J. (ed.) 1949: *Studies in regional planning*. London: Philip & Son.

DEAR, M. J. 1987: Society, politics and social theory. *Environment and Planning D: Society and Space* 5, 363–6.

—— 1988: The postmodern challenge: reconstructing human geography. *Transactions, Institute of British Geographers* NS13, 262–74.

DEAR, M. J. and CLARK, G. L. 1978: The state and geographic process: a critical review. *Environment and Planning A* 10, 173–84.

—— and MOOS, A. I. 1986: Structuration theory in urban analysis: 2. empirical application. *Environment and Planning A* 18, 351–74.

—— and SCOTT, A. J. (eds.) 1981: *Urbanization and urban planning in capitalist society*. London: Methuen.

DENNIS, R. J. 1984: *English industrial cities in the nineteenth century: a social geography*. Cambridge: Cambridge University Press.

DESBARATS, J. 1983: Spatial choice and constraints on behavior. *Annals of the Association of American Geographers* 73, 340–57.

DETWYLER, T. R. and MARCUS, M. G. (eds.) 1972: *Urbanization and environment*. Belmont, California: Duxbury Press.

DICKEN, P. 1986: *Global Shift*. London: Harper and Row.

DICKENS, P., DUNCAN, S.S., GOODWIN, M. and GRAY, F. 1985: *Housing, states and localities*. London: Methuen.

DICKENSON, J. P. and CLARKE, C. G. 1972: Relevance and the 'newest geography'. *Area* 3, 25–7.

DICKINSON, R. E. 1973: The distribution and functions of smaller urban settlements of East Anglia. *Geography* 18, 19–31.

—— 1947: *City, region and regionalism*. London: Routledge & Kegan Paul.

DINGEMANS, D. 1979: Redlining and mortgage lending in Sacramento. *Annals of the Association of American Geographers* 69, 225–39.

DOBSON, J. E. 1983a: Automated geography. *The Professional Geographer* 35, 135–43.

—— 1983b: Reply to comments on 'Automated geography'. *The Professional Geographer* 35, 349–53.

DOUGLAS, I. 1983: *The urban environment*. London: Edward Arnold.

—— 1986: The unity of geography is obvious. *Transactions, Institute of British Geographers* NS11, 459–63.

DOWNS, R. M. 1970: Geographic space perception: past approaches and future prospects. In C. Board *et al.* (eds.), *Progress in Geography* 2. London: Edward Arnold, 65–108.

—— 1979: Critical appraisal or determined philosophical skepticism? *Annals of the Association of American Geographers* 69, 468–71.

DOWNS, R. M. and MEYER, J. T. 1978: Geography and the mind. *Human geography: coming of age. American Behavioral Scientist* 22, 59–78.

DOWNS, R. M. and STEA, D. (eds.) 1973: *Image and environment*. London: Edward Arnold.

—— 1977: *Maps in mind*. New York: Harper & Row.

DRIVER, F. and PHILO, C. 1986: Implications of 'scientific' geography. *Area* 18, 161–2.

DRYSDALE, A. and WATTS, M. 1977: Modernization and social protest movements. *Antipode* 9(1), 40–55.

DUNCAN, J. S. 1980: The superorganic in American cultural geography. *Annals of the Association of American Geographers* 70, 181–98.

—— 1985: Individual action and political power: a structuration perspective. In R. J. Johnston (ed.) *The future of geography*. London: Methuen, 174–89.

DUNCAN, J. S. and LEY, D. 1982: Structural marxism and human geography: a critical assessment. *Annals of the Association of American Geographers* 72, 30–59.

DUNCAN, O. D. 1959: Human ecology and population studies. In P. M. Hauser and O. D. Duncan (eds.), *The study of population.* Chicago: University of Chicago Press, 678–716.

DUNCAN, O. D., CUZZORT, R. P. and DUNCAN, B. 1961: *Statistical geography.* New York: The Free Press.

DUNCAN, O. D. and SCHNORE, L. F. 1959: Cultural, behavioral and ecological perspectives in the study of social organization. *American Journal of Sociology* 65, 132–46.

DUNCAN, S. S. 1974a: Cosmetic planning or social engineering? Improvement grants and improvement areas in Huddersfield. *Area* 6, 259–70.

—— 1974b: The isolation of scientific discovery: indifference and resistance to a new idea. *Science Studies* 4, 109–34.

—— 1975: Research directions in social geography: housing opportunities and constraints. *Transactions, Institute of British Geographers* NS1 10–19.

—— 1979: Radical geography and marxism. *Area* 11, 124–6.

—— 1981: Housing policy, the methodology of levels, and urban research: the case of Castells. *International Journal of Urban and Regional Research* 5, 231–54.

DUNCAN, S. S. 1989: What is a locality? In R. Peet and N.J. Thrift (eds.) *New models in geography (Volume Two).* London: Unwin Hyman, 221–54.

DUNCAN, S. S. and GOODWIN, M. 1985: The local state and local economic policy. *Capital and Class* 27, 14–36.

DUNCAN, S. S. and SAVAGE, M. 1989: Space, scale and locality. *Antipode* 21, 179–206.

DUNFORD, M. F. and PERRONS, D. 1983: *The arena of capital.* London: Macmillan.

EILON, S. 1975: Seven faces of research. *Operational Research Quarterly* 26, 359–67.

ELIOT HURST, M. E. 1972: Establishment geography: or how to be irrelevant in three easy lessons. *Antipode* 5(2), 40–59.

—— 1980: Geography, social science and society: towards a de-definition. *Australian Geographical Studies* 18, 3–21.

—— 1985: Geography has neither existence nor future. In R. J. Johnston (ed.) *The future of geography.* London: Methuen, 59–91.

ENTRIKIN, J. N. 1976: Contemporary humanism in geography. *Annals of the Association of American Geographers* 66, 615–32.

—— 1980: Robert Park's human ecology and human geography. *Annals of the Association of American Geographers* 70, 43–58.

—— 1981: Philosophical issues in the scientific study of regions. In D. T. Herbert and R. J. Johnston (eds.), *Geography and the urban environment,* volume 4. Chichester: John Wiley, 1–27.

—— 1989: Place, region, and modernity. In J. A. Agnew and J.S. Duncan (eds.) *The Power of Place.* Boston: Unwin Hyman, 30–43.

—— 1990: Introduction: *The Nature of Geography* in perspective. In J. N. Entrikin and S. D. Brunn (eds.) *Reflections on Richard Hartshorne's The Nature of Geography.* Washington: Association of American Geographers, 1–16.

ESRC 1988: *Horizons and opportunities in social science.* London: ESRC.

EVANS, M. 1988: Participant observation: the researcher as research tool. In J. Eyles and D.M. Smith (eds.) *Qualitative methods in human geography.* Cambridge: Polity Press, 197–218.

EYLES, J. 1971: Pouring new sentiments into old theories: how else can we look at behavioural patterns? *Area* 3, 242–50.

—— 1973: Geography and relevance. *Area* 5, 158–60.

—— 1974: Social theory and social geography. In C. Board *et al.* (eds.), *Progress in Geography* 6. London: Edward Arnold, 27–88.

—— 1981: Why geography cannot be Marxist: towards an understanding of lived experience. *Environment and Planning A* 13, 1371–88.

—— 1989: The geography of everyday life. In D. Gregory and R. Walford (eds.) *Horizons in human geography*. London: Macmillan, 102–17.

EYLES, J. and LEE, R. 1982: Human geography in explanation. *Transactions, Institute of British Geographers* NS7, 117–12.

EYLES, J. and SMITH, D. M. 1982: Social geography. *Human geography: Coming of Age. American Behavioral Scientist* 22, 41–58.

EYRE, S. R. 1978: *The real wealth of nations*. London: Edward Arnold.

—— and JONES, G. R. J. (eds.) 1966: *Geography as human ecology*. London: Edward Arnold.

FALAH, G. 1989: Israelization of Palestine human geography. *Progress in Human Geography* 13.

FEYERABEND, P. 1975: *Against method*. London: New Left Books.

FINGLETON, B. 1984: *Models of category counts*. Cambridge: Cambridge University Press.

FISHER, P. F. 1989a: Geographical information system software for teaching. *Journal of Geography in Higher Education* 13, 69–80.

—— 1989b: Expert system applications in geography. *Area* 21, 279–87.

FITZSIMMONS, M. 1989: The matter of nature. *Antipode* 21, 106–21.

FLEMING, D. K. 1973: The regionalizing ritual. *Scottish Geographical Magazine* 89, 196–207.

FLEURE, H. J. 1919: Human regions. *Scottish Geographical Magazine* 35, 94–105.

FLOWERDEW, R. 1986: Three years in British geography. *Area* 18, 263–4.

—— 1989: Some critical views of modelling in geography. In B. Macmillan (ed.) *Remodelling Geography*. Oxford: Basil Blackwell, 245–54.

FOLKE, S. 1972: Why a radical geography must be Marxist. *Antipode* 4(2), 13–18.

—— 1973: First thoughts on the geography of imperialism. *Antipode* 5(3), 16–20.

FOORD, J. and GREGSON, N. 1986: Patriarchy: towards a reconceptualisation. *Antipode* 18, 186–211.

FOOTE, D. C. and GREER-WOOTTEN, B. 1968: An approach to systems analysis in cultural geography. *The Professional Geographer* 20, 86–90.

FORD, L. R. 1982: Beware of new geographies. *The Professional Geographer* 34, 131–5.

FORER, P. C. 1974: Space through time: a case study with New Zealand airlines. In E. L. Cripps (ed.), *Space-time concepts in urban and regional models*. London: Pion, 22–45.

FORRESTER, J. W. 1969: *Urban dynamics*. Cambridge, Mass.: MIT Press.

FOTHERINGHAM, A. S. 1981: Spatial structure and distance-decay parameters. *Annals of the Association of American Geographers* 71, 425–36.

—— and MACKINNON, R.D. 1989: The National Center for Geographic Information and Analysis. *Environment and Planning A* 21, 141–4.

FOUCAULT, M. 1972: *The archaeology of knowledge*. London: Tavistock Publications.

FREEMAN, T. W. 1961: *A hundred years of geography*. London: Gerald Duckworth.

—— 1977ff: *Geographers: biobibliographical studies*. London: Mansell.

—— 1979: The British school of geography. *Organon* 14, 205–16.

—— 1980a: *A history of modern British geography*. London: Longman.

—— 1980b: The Royal Geographical Society and the development of geography. In E. H. Brown (ed.), *Geography, yesterday and tomorrow*. Oxford: Oxford University Press, 1–99.

FULLER, G. A. 1971: The geography of prophylaxis: an example of intuitive schemes and spatial competition in Latin America. *Antipode* 3(1), 21–30.

GAILE, G. L. and WILLMOTT, C. J. (eds.) 1984: *Spatial statistics and models.* Dordrecht: D. Reidel.

—— and WILLMOTT, C. J. (eds.) 1989: *Geography in America.* Columbus: Merrill Publishing.

GALE, N. and GOLLEDGE, R. G. 1982: On the subjective partitioning of space *Annals of the Association of American Geographers* 72, 60–7.

GAMBLE, A. 1988: *The free economy and the strong state.* London Macmillan.

GARRISON, W. L. 1953: Remoteness and the passenger utilization of air transportation. *Annals of the Association of American Geographers* 43, 169.

—— 1956a: Applicability of statistical inference to geographical research. *Geographical Review* 46, 427–9.

—— 1956b: Some confusing aspects of common measurements. *The Professional Geographer* 8, 4–5.

—— 1959a: Spatial structure of the economy I. *Annals of the Association of American Geographers* 49, 238–9.

—— 1959b: Spatial structure of the economy II. *Annals of the Association of American Geographers* 49, 471–82.

—— 1960a: Spatial structure of the economy III. *Annals of the Association of American Geographers* 50, 357–73.

—— 1960b: Connectivity of the interstate highway system. *Papers and Proceedings, Regional Science Association* 6, 121–37.

—— 1962: Simulation models of urban growth and development. In K. Norborg (ed.), *IGU Symposium in Urban Geography*, Lund Studies in Geography B 24. Lund: C. W. K. Gleerup, 91–108.

—— 1979: Playing with ideas. *Annals of the Association of American Geographers* 69, 118–20.

GARRISON, W. L., BERRY, B. J. L., MARBLE, D. F., NYSTUEN, J. D. and MORRILL, R. L. 1959: *Studies of highway development and geographic change.* Seattle: University of Washington Press.

GARRISON, W. L. and MARBLE, D. F. 1957: The spatial structure of agricultural activities. *Annals of the Association of American Geographers* 47, 137–44.

—— (eds.), 1967a: *Quantitative geography. Part I: economic and cultural topics.* Northwestern University Studies in Geography, Number 13, Evanston, Illinois.

—— (eds.) 1967b: *Quantitative geography, Part II: physical and cartographic topics.* Northwestern University Studies in Geography, Number 14, Evanston, Illinois.

GATRELL, A. C. 1982: *Geometry in geography and the geometry of geography.* Discussion Paper 6, Department of Geography, University of Salford.

—— 1983: *Distance and space: a geographical perspective.* Oxford: Oxford University Press.

—— 1984a: The geometry of a research specialty: spatial diffusion modelling. *Annals of the Association of American Geographers* 74, 437–53.

—— 1984b: Describing the structure of a research literature: spatial diffusion modelling in geography. *Environment and Planning B: Planning and Design* 11, 29–45.

—— 1985: Any space for spatial analysis? In R. J. Johnston (ed.) *The future of geography.* London: Methuen, 190–208.

GATRELL, A. C. and LOVETT, A. A. 1986: The geography of hazardous waste disposal in England and Wales. *Area* 18, 275–83.

GATRELL, A. C. and SMITH, A. 1984: Networks of relations among a set of geographical journals. *The Professional Geographer* 36, 300–7.

GEARY, R. C. 1954: The contiguity ratio and statistical mapping. *The Incorporated Statistician* 5, 115–41.

GETIS, A. 1963: The determination of the location of retail activities with the use of a map transformation. *Economic Geography* 39, 1–22.

GETIS, A. and BOOTS, B. N. 1978: *Models of spatial processes.* Cambridge: Cambridge University Press.

GIBSON, E. 1978: Understanding the subjective meaning of places. In D. Ley and M. S. Samuels (eds.), *Humanistic geography: problems and prospects.* Chicago: Maaroufa Press, 138–54.

GIDDENS, A. 1981: *A critique of contemporary historical materialism.* London: Macmillan.

—— 1984: *The constitution of society.* Oxford: Polity Press.

GIER, J. and WALTON, J. 1987: Some problems with reconceptualising patriarchy. *Antipode* 19, 54–8.

GILBERT, A. 1988: The new regional geography in English- and French-speaking countries. *Progress in Human Geography* 12, 208–228.

GINSBURG, N. 1972: The mission of a scholarly society. *The Professional Geographer* 24, 1–6.

—— 1973: From colonialism to national development: geographical perspectives on patterns and policies. *Annals of the Association of American Geographers* 63, 1–21.

GLACKEN, C. J. 1956: Changing ideas of the habitable world. In W. L. Thomas (ed.), *Man's role in changing the face of the earth.* Chicago: University of Chicago Press, 70–92.

—— 1967: *Traces on the Rhodian shore: nature and culture in western thought from ancient times to the end of the eighteenth century.* Berkeley: University of California Press.

—— 1983: A late arrival in academia. In A. Buttimer, *The practice of geography.* London: Longman, 20–34.

GODDARD, J. and ARMSTRONG, P. 1986: The 1986 Domesday project. *Transactions, Institute of British Geographers* NS11, 279–89.

GOHEEN, P. G. 1970: *Victorian Toronto.* University of Chicago, Department of Geography, Research Paper 127.

GOLD, J. R. 1980: *An introduction to behavioural geography.* Oxford: Oxford University Press.

GOLLEDGE, R. G. 1969: The geographical relevance of some learning theories. In K. R. Cox and R. G. Golledge (eds.), *Behavioral problems in geography: a symposium.* Evanston: Northwestern University Studies in Geography 17, 101–45.

—— 1970: Some equilibrium models of consumer behavior. *Economic Geography* 46, 417–24.

—— 1980: A behavioral view of mobility and migration research. *The Professional Geographer* 32, 14–21.

—— 1981a: Misconceptions, misinterpretations, and misrepresentations of behavioral approaches in human geography. *Environment and Planning A* 13, 1325–44.

—— 1981b: A critical response to Guelke's 'Uncritical rhetoric'. *The Professional Geographer* 33, 247–51.

—— 1983: Models of man, points of view, and theory in social science. *Geographical Analysis* 15, 57–60.

GOLLEDGE, R. G. and AMEDEO, D. 1968: On laws in geography. *Annals of the Association of American Geography* 58, 760–74.

GOLLEDGE, R. G. and BROWN, L. A. 1967: Search, learning and the market decision process. *Geografiska Annaler* 49B, 116–24.

GOLLEDGE, R. G., BROWN, L. A. and WILLIAMSON, F. 1972: Behavioral approaches in geography: an overview. *The Australian Geographer* 12, 59–79.

GOLLEDGE, R. G. and COUCLELIS, H. 1984: Positivist philosophy and research in human spatial behavior. In T. F. Saarinen, D. Seamon and J. L. Sell (eds.) *Environmental perception and behavior: an inventory and prospect.* Chicago:

Department of Geography, University of Chicago, Research Paper 209, 179–90.
—— and RUSHTON, G. 1984: A review of analytic behavioural research in geography. In D. T. Herbert and R. J. Johnston (eds.) *Geography and the urban environment: progress in research and application*, volume 6. Chichester: John Wiley, 1–44.
—— and STIMSON, R. J. 1987: *Analytical Behavioural Geography*. London: Croom Helm.
—— and TIMMERMANS, H. (eds.) 1988: *Behavioural Modelling in Geography and Planning*. London: Croom Helm.
—— and RAYNER, J. N. (eds.) 1982: *Proximity and preference: problems in the multidimensional analysis of large data sets*. Minneapolis: University of Minnesota Press.
—— 1990: Applications of behavioural research on spatial problems: I Cognition. *Progress in Human Geography* 14
GOLLEDGE, R. G. *et al.* 1982: Commentary on 'The highest form of the geographer's art'. *Annals of the Association of American Geographers* 72, 557–8.
GOODSON, I. 1981: Becoming an academic subject: patterns of explanation and evolution. *British Journal of Sociology of Education* 2, 163–79.
GOUDIE, A. S. 1986a: *The human use of the environment*. Oxford: Basil Blackwell.
—— 1986b: The integration of human and physical geography. *Transactions, Institute of British Geographers* NS11, 464–7.
GOULD, P. R. 1963: Man against his environment: a game theoretic framework. *Annals of the Association of American Geographers* 53, 290–7.
—— 1966: On mental maps. Michigan Inter-University Community of Mathematical Geographers, Discussion Paper 9. Reprinted in R. M. Downs and D. Stea, 1973, *Image and environment*. London: Edward Arnold, 182–220.
—— 1969: Methodological developments since the fifties. In C. Board *et al.* (eds.) *Progress in Geography* 1, London: Edward Arnold, 1–50.
—— 1970a: Is *statistix inferens* the geographical name for a wild goose? *Economic Geography* 46, 439–48.
—— 1970b: Tanzania 1920–63: the spatial impress of the modernization process. *World Politics* 22, 149–70.
—— 1972: Pedagogic review. *Annals of the Association of American Geographers* 62, 689–700.
—— 1975: Mathematics in geography: conceptual revolution or new tool? *International Social Science Journal* 27, 303–27.
—— 1977: What is worth teaching in geography? *Journal of Geography in Higher Education* 1, 20–36.
—— 1978: Concerning a geographic education. In D. A. Lanegran and R. Palm (eds.), *An invitation to geography*. New York: McGraw Hill, 202–26.
—— 1979: Geography 1957–1977: the Augean period. *Annals of the Association of American Geographers* 69, 139–51.
—— 1980: Q-analysis, or a language of structure: an introduction for social scientists, geographers and planners. *International Journal of Man-Machine Studies* 12, 169–99.
—— 1981a: Letting the data speak for themselves. *Annals of the Association of American Geographers* 71, 166–76.
—— 1981b: Space and rum: an English note on espacien and rumian meaning. *Geografiska Annaler* 63B, 1–3.
—— 1985a: *The geographer at work*. London: Routledge & Kegan Paul.
—— 1985b: Will geographical self-reflection make you blind? In R. J. Johnston (ed.) *The future of geography*. London: Methuen, 276–90.
—— 1988: The only perspective: a critique of marxist claims to exclusiveness in geographical inquiry. In R. G. Golledge, H. Couclelis and P. R. Could (eds.)

A Ground for Common Search. Santa Barbara: The Santa Barbara Geographical Press, 1–10.

GOULD, P. R. and WHITE, R. 1974: *Mental maps*. Harmondsworth: Penguin Books.

—— and WHITE, R. 1986: *Mental maps* (second edition). London: George Allen & Unwin.

GRAHAM, E. 1986: The unity of geography: a comment. *Transactions, Institute of British Geographers* NS11, 464–7.

GRAHAM, J. 1988: Postmodernism and marxism. *Antipode* 20, 60–65.

GRANO, O. 1981: External influence and internal change in the development of geography. In D. R. Stoddart (ed.), *Geography, ideology and social concern*. Oxford: Blackwell, 17–36.

GRAVES, N. J. 1981: Can geographical studies be subsumed under one paradigm or are a plurality of paradigms inevitable? *Terra* 93, 85–90.

GRAY, F. 1975: Non-explanation in urban geography. *Area* 7, 228–35.

—— 1976: Selection and allocation in council housing. *Transactions, Institute of British Geographers* NS1, 34–46.

GREEN, N. P., FINCH, S. and WIGGINS, J. 1985: The 'state of the art' in Geographical Information Systems. *Area* 17, 295–301.

GREENBERG, D. 1984: Whodunit? Structure and subjectivity in behavioral geography. In T. F. Saarinen, D. Seamon and J. L. Sell (eds.) *Environmental perception and behavior: an inventory and prospect*. Chicago: Department of Geography, University of Chicago, Research Paper 209, 191–208.

GREER-WOOTTEN, B. 1972: *The role of general systems theory in geographic research*. Department of Geography, York University, Discussion Paper No. 3, Toronto.

GREGORY, D. 1976: Rethinking historical geography. *Area* 8, 295–9.

—— 1978a: *Ideology, science and human geography*. London: Hutchinson.

—— 1978b: The discourse of the past: phenomenology, structuralism, and historical geography. *Journal of Historical Geography* 4, 161–73.

—— 1980: The ideology of control: systems theory and geography. *Tijdschrift voor Economische en Sociale Geografie* 71, 327–42.

—— 1981: Human agency and human geography. *Transactions, Institute of British Geographers* NS6, 1–18.

—— 1982a: *Regional transformation and industrial revolution: a geography of the Yorkshire woollen industry*. London: Macmillan.

—— 1982b: Solid geometry: notes on the recovery of spatial structure. In P. R. Gould and G. Olsson (eds.), *A search for common ground*. London: Pion, 187–222.

—— 1985a: Suspended animation: the stasis of diffusion theory. In D. Gregory and J. Urry (eds.) *Social relations and spatial structures*. London: Macmillan, 296–336.

—— 1985b: People, places and practices: the future of human geography. In R. King (ed.) *Geographical futures*. Sheffield: The Geographical Association, 56–76.

—— 1989a: Areal differentiation and post-modern human geography. In D. Gregory and R. Walford (eds.) *Horizons in human geography*. London: Macmillan, 67–96.

—— 1989b: The crisis of modernity? Human geography and critical social theory. In R. Peet and N. J. Thrift (eds.) *New models in geography (Volume Two)*. London: Unwin Hyman, 348–85.

GREGORY, D. and LEY, D. 1988: Culture's geographies. *Environment and Planning D: Society and Space* 6, 115–6.

GREGORY, D. and URRY, J. 1985: Introduction. In D. Gregory and J. Urry (eds.) *Social relations and spatial structures*. London: Macmillan, 1–8.

GREGORY, K. J. 1985: *The nature of physical geography*. London: Edward Arnold.

GREGORY, S. 1963: *Statistical methods and the geographer*. London: Longman.

—— 1976: On geographical myths and statistical fables. *Transactions, Institute of British Geographers* NS1, 385–400.

GREGSON, N. 1986: On duality and dualism: the case of structuration and time geography. *Progress in Human Geography* 10, 184–205.

—— 1987a: The CURS initiative: some further comments. *Antipode* 19, 364–70.

—— 1987b: Structuration theory: some thoughts on the possibilities for empirical research. *Environment and Planning D: Society and Space* 5, 73–91.

GREGSON, N. and FOORD, J. 1987: Patriarchy: comments on critics. *Antipode* 19, 371–5.

GRIGG, D. B. 1977: E. G. Ravenstein and the laws of migration. *Journal of Historical Geography* 3, 41–54.

GROSSMAN, L. 1977: Man-environment relationships in anthropology and geography. *Annals of the Association of American Geographers* 67, 126–44.

GUDGIN, G. and TAYLOR, P. J. 1979: *Seats, votes and the spatial organisation of elections*. London: Pion.

GUELKE, L. 1971: Problems of scientific explanation in geography. *The Canadian Geographer* 15, 38–53.

—— 1974: An idealist alternative in human geography. *Annals of the Association of American Geographers* 14, 193–202.

—— 1975: On rethinking historical geography. *Area* 7, 135–8.

—— 1976: The philosophy of idealism. *Annals of the Association of American Geography* 66, 168–9.

—— 1977a: The role of laws in human geography. *Progress in Human Geography* 1, 376–86.

—— 1977b: Regional geography. *The Professional Geographer* 29, 1–7.

—— 1978: Geography and logical positivism. In D. T. Herbert and R. J. Johnston (eds.), *Geography and the urban environment: progress in research and applications*, 1. London: John Wiley, 35–61.

—— 1981a: Uncritical rhetoric: 'A classic disservice'. *The Professional Geographer* 33, 246–7.

—— 1981b: Idealism. In M. E. Harvey and B. P. Holly (eds.), *Themes in geographic thought*. London: Croom Helm, 133–47.

—— 1982: The idealist dispute in Anglo-American geography: a comment. *The Canadian Geographer* 26, 51–7.

GUTTING, G. 1980: Introduction. In G. Gutting (ed.), *Paradigms and revolutions*. Notre Dame, Indiana: University of Notre Dame Press, 1–22.

HABERMAS, J. 1972: *Knowledge and Human Interests*. London: Heinemann.

HACKING, I. 1983: *Representing and intervening*. Cambridge: Cambridge University Press.

HÄGERSTRAND, T. 1968: *Innovation diffusion as a spatial process*. Chicago: University of Chicago Press.

—— 1975: Space, time and human conditions. In A. Karlquist, L. Lundquist and F. Snickars (eds.) *Dynamic allocation of urban space*. Farnborough: Saxon House, 3–12.

—— 1977: The geographers' contribution to regional policy: the case of Sweden. In D. R. Deskins *et al.* (eds.), *Geographic humanism, analysis and social action: a half century of geography at Michigan*. Michigan Geographical Publications No. 17, Ann Arbor, 329–46.

—— 1982: Diorama, path and project. *Tijdschrift voor Economische en Sociale Geografie* 73, 323–39.

—— 1984: Presence and absence: a look at conceptual choices and bodily necessities. *Regional Studies* 18, 373–8.

HAGGETT, P. 1964: Regional and local components in the distribution of forested areas in southeast Brazil: a multivariate approach. *Geographical Journal* 130, 365–77.
—— 1965a: Changing concepts in economic geography. In R. J. Chorley and P. Haggett (eds.), *Frontiers in geographical teaching*. London: Methuen, 101–17.
—— 1965b: Scale components in geographical problems. In R. J. Chorley and P. Haggett (eds.), *Frontiers in geographical teaching*. London: Methuen, 164–85.
—— 1965c: *Locational analysis in human geography*. London: Edward Arnold.
—— 1967: Network models in geography. In R. J. Chorley and P. Haggett (eds.) *Models in geography*. London: Methuen, 609–70.
—— 1973: Forecasting alternative spatial, ecological and regional futures: problems and possibilities. In R. J. Chorley (ed.), *Directions in geography*. London: Methuen, 217–36.
—— 1978: The spatial economy. *Human geography: coming of age. American Behavioral Scientist* 22, 151–67.
HAGGETT, P. and CHORLEY, R. J. 1965: Frontier movements and the geographical tradition. In R. J. Chorley and P. Haggett (eds.), *Frontiers in geographical teaching*. London: Methuen 358–78.
—— and CHORLEY, R. J. 1967: Models, paradigms, and the new geography. In R. J. Chorley and P. Haggett (eds.), *Models in geography*. London: Methuen, 19–42.
—— and CHORLEY, R. J. 1969: *Network models in geography*. London: Edward Arnold.
—— and CHORLEY, R. J. 1989: From Madingley to Oxford. In B. Macmillan (ed.) *Remodelling Geography*. Oxford: Basil Blackwell, xv–xx.
HAGGETT, P. CLIFF, A. D. and FREY, A. 1977: *Locational analysis in human geography*. London: Edward Arnold.
HAGOOD, M. J. 1943: Development of a 1940 rural farm level of living index for counties. *Rural Sociology* 8, 171–80.
HAINES-YOUNG, R. 1989: Modelling geographical knowledge. In B. Macmillan (ed.) *Remodelling Geography*. Oxford: Basil Blackwell, 22–39.
HAINES-YOUNG, R. and PETCH, J. R. 1978: *The methodological limitations of Kuhn's model of science*. University of Salford, Department of Geography, Discussion Paper 8.
—— 1985: *Physical geography: its nature and methods*. London: Harper & Row.
HAINING, R. P. 1980: Spatial autocorrelation problems. In D. T. Herbert and R. J. Johnston (eds.), *Geography and the urban environment*, 3. Chichester: John Wiley, 1–44.
—— 1981: Analysing univariate maps, *Progress in Human Geography* 5, 58–78.
—— 1989: Geography and spatial statistics: current positions, future developments. In B. Macmillan (ed.) *Remodelling Geography*. Oxford: Basil Blackwell, 191–203.
HALL, P. 1974: The new political geography. *Transactions, Institute of British Geographers* 63, 48–52.
—— 1981a: *Great planning disasters*. London: Penguin.
—— 1981b: The geographer and society. *Geographical Journal* 147, 145–52.
—— 1982: The new political geography: seven years on, *Political Geography Quarterly* 1, 65–76.
HALL, P. *et al.* 1973: *The containment of urban England*. London: George Allen & Unwin.
HALL, P. G., JACKSON, P., MASSEY, D., ROBSON, B.T., THRIFT, N.J. and WILSON, A.G. 1987: Horizons and opportunities in research. *Area* 19, 266–72.
HALVORSON, P. and STAVE, B. M. 1978: A conversation with Brian J. L. Berry. *Journal of Urban History* 4, 209–38.
HAMILTON, F. E. I. 1974: A view of spatial behaviour, industrial organizations, and decision-making. In F. E. I. Hamilton (ed.), *Spatial perspectives on industrial*

organization and decision-making. London: John Wiley, 3–46.

HAMNETT, C. 1977: Non-explanation in urban geography: throwing the baby out with the bath water. *Area* **9**, 143–5.

HARE, F. K. 1974: Geography and public policy: a Canadian view. *Transactions, Institute of British Geographers* **63**, 25–8.

—— 1977: Man's world and geographers: a secular sermon. In D. R. Deskins *et al.* (eds.), *Geographic humanism, analysis and social action: a half century of geography at Michigan*. Michigan Geographical Publication No. 17, Ann Arbor, 259–73.

HARRIES, K. D. 1974: *The geography of crime and justice*. New York: McGraw Hill.

—— 1975: Rejoinder to Richard Peet: 'The geography of crime: a political critique.' *The Professional Geographer* **27**, 280–2.

—— 1976: Observations on radical versus liberal theories of crime causation. *The Professional Geographer* **28**, 100–13.

HARRIS, C. D. 1954a: The geography of manufacturing. In P. E. James and C. F. Jones (eds.), *American geography: inventory and prospect*. Syracuse: Syracuse University Press, 292–309.

—— 1954b: The market as a factor in the localization of industry in the United States. *Annals of the Association of American Geographers* **44**, 315–48.

—— 1977: Edward Louis Ullman, 1912–1976. *Annals of the Association of American Geographers* **67**, 595–600.

HARRIS, C. D. and ULLMAN, E. L. 1945: The nature of cities. *Annals of the American Academy of Political and Social Science* **242**, 7–17.

HARRIS, R. C. 1971: Theory and synthesis in historical geography. *The Canadian Geographer* **15**, 157–72.

—— 1977: The simplification of Europe overseas. *Annals of the Association of American Geographers* **67**, 469–83.

—— 1978: The historical mind and the practice of geography. In D. Ley and M. S. Samuels (eds.), *Humanistic geography: problems and prospects*. Chicago: Maaroufa Press, 123–37.

HARRISON, R. T. and LIVINGSTONE, D. N. 1982: Understanding in geography: structuring the subjective. In D. T. Herbert and R. J. Johnston (eds.), *Geography and the urban environment*, 5. Chichester: John Wiley, 1–40.

HART, J. F. 1982: The highest form of the geographer's art. *Annals of the Association of American Geographers* **72**, 1–29.

HARTSHORNE, R. 1939: *The nature of geography*. Lancaster, Pennsylvania: Association of American Geographers.

—— 1948: On the mores of methodological discussion in American geography. *Annals of the Association of American Geographers* **38**, 492–504.

—— 1954a: Political geography. In P. E. James and C. F. Jones (eds.), *American geography: inventory and prospect*. Syracuse: Syracuse University Press, 167–225.

—— 1954b: Comment on 'Exceptionalism in geography'. *Annals of the Association of American Geographers* **44**, 108–9.

—— 1955: 'Exceptionalism in geography' re-examined. *Annals of the Association of American Geographers* **45**, 205–44.

—— 1958: The concept of geography as a science of space from Kant and Humboldt to Hettner. *Annals of the Association of American Geographers* **48**, 97–108.

—— 1959: *Perspective on The Nature of Geography*. Chicago: Rand McNally.

—— 1972: Review of *Kant's concept of geography*. *The Canadian Geographer* **16**, 77–9.

—— 1979: Notes towards a bibliography of *The Nature of Geography*. *Annals of the Association of American Geographers* **69**, 63–76.

—— 1984: In *The Geographical Journal* **150**, 429.

HARVEY, D. 1967a: Models of the evolution of spatial patterns in geography. In R. J.

Chorley and P. Haggett (eds.), *Models in geography*. London: Methuen, 549–608.
—— 1967b: Editorial introduction: the problem of theory construction in geography. *Journal of Regional Science* 7, 211–16.
—— 1969a: *Explanation in geography*. London: Edward Arnold.
—— 1969b: Review of A. Pred, *Behavior and location part I. Geographical Review* 59, 312–14.
—— 1969c: Conceptual and measurement problems in the cognitive-behavioral approach to location theory. In K. R. Cox and R. G. Golledge (eds.), *Behavioral problems in geography: a symposium*. Northwestern University Studies in Geography 17, 35–68.
—— 1970: Behavioral postulates and the construction of theory in human geography. *Geographica Polonica* 18, 27–46.
—— 1972: Revolutionary and counter-revolutionary theory in geography and the problem of ghetto formation. *Antipode* 4(2), 1–13.
—— 1973: *Social justice and the city*. London: Edward Arnold.
—— 1974a: A commentary on the comments. *Antipode* 4(2), 36–41.
—— 1974b: Discussion with Brian Berry. *Antipode* 6(2), 145–8.
—— 1974c: What kind of geography for what kind of public policy? *Transactions, Institute of British Geographers* 63, 18–24.
—— 1974d: Population, resources and the ideology of science. *Economic Geography* 50, 256–77.
—— 1974e: Class-monopoly rent, finance capital and the urban revolution, *Regional Studies* 8, 239–55.
—— 1975a: Class structure in a capitalist society and the theory of residential differentiation. In R. Peel, M. Chisholm and P. Haggett (eds.), *Processes in physical and human geography: Bristol essays*. London: Heinemann, 354–69.
—— 1975b: The political economy of urbanization in advanced capitalist societies: the case of the United States. In G. Gappert and H. M. Rose (eds.), *The social economy of cities*. Beverly Hills: Sage Publications, 119–63.
—— 1975c: Review of B. J. L. Berry, *The human consequences of urbanization. Annals of the Association of American Geographers* 65, 99–103.
—— 1976: The marxist theory of the state. *Antipode* 8(2) 80–9.
—— 1978: The urban process under capitalism: a framework for analysis. *International Journal of Urban and Regional Research* 2, 101–32.
—— 1982: *The limits to capital*. Oxford: Blackwell.
—— 1984: On the history and present condition of geography: an historical materialist manifesto. *The Professional Geographer* 36, 1–11.
—— 1985a: *The urbanization of capital*. Oxford: Basil Blackwell.
—— 1985b: The geopolitics of capitalism. In D. Gregory and J. Urry (eds.) *Social relations and spatial structures*. London: Macmillan, 128–63.
—— 1985c: *Consciousness and the urban experience*. Oxford: Basil Blackwell.
—— 1987: Three myths in search of a reality in urban studies. *Environment and Planning D: Society and Space* 5, 367–76.
—— 1989a: *The Condition of Postmodernity*. Oxford: Basil Blackwell.
—— 1986b: From models to Marx: notes on the project to 'remodel' contemporary geography. In B. Macmillan (ed.) *Remodelling Geography*. Oxford: Basil Blackwell, 211–216.
—— 1989c: From managerialism to entrepreneurialism: the transformation of urban governance in late capitalism. *Geografiska Annaler* 71B, 3–17.
HARVEY, D. and SCOTT, A.J. 1989: The practice of human geography: theory and empirical specificity in the transition from Fordism to flexible accumulation. In W. Macmillan (ed.) *Remodelling geography*. Oxford: Basil Blackwell, 217–229.
HARVEY, M. E. and HOLLY, B. P. 1981: Paradigm, philosophy and geographic

thought. In M. E. Harvey and B. P. Holly (eds.), *Themes in geographic thought*. London: Croom Helm, 11–37.

HAY, A. M. 1978: Some problems in regional forecasting. In J. I. Clarke and J. Pelletser (eds.), *Régions géographique et régions d'amenagement*. Collection les hommes et les lettres, 7. Lyon: Editions Hermes.

—— 1979a: Positivism in human geography: response to critics. In D. T. Herbert and R. J. Johnston (eds.), *Geography and the urban environment: progress in research and applications*, 2. London: John Wiley, 1–26.

—— 1979b: The geographical explanation of commodity flow. *Progress in Human Geography* 3, 1–12.

—— 1985a: Scientific method in geography. In R. J. Johnston (ed.) *The future of geography*. London: Methuen, 129–42.

—— 1985b: Statistical tests in the absence of samples: a comment. *The Professional Geographer* 37, 334–8.

HAY, A. M. and JOHNSTON, R. J. 1983: The study of process in quantitative human geography. *L'Espace Geographique* 12, 69–76.

HAYNES, R. M. 1975: Dimensional analysis: some applications in human geography. *Geographical Analysis* 7, 51–68.

—— 1978: A note on dimensions and relationships in human geography. *Geographical Analysis* 10, 288–92.

—— 1982: *An introduction to dimensional analysis for geographers*. CATMOG 33, Geo Books, Norwich.

HAYTER, R. and WATTS, H. D. 1983: The geography of enterprise. *Progress in Human Geography* 7, 157–81 .

HELD, D. 1980: *Introduction to critical theory: Horkheimer to Habermas*. London: Hutchinson.

HERBERT, D. T. and JOHNSTON, R. J. 1978: Geography and the urban environment. In D. T. Herbert and R. J. Johnston (eds.), *Geography and the urban environment: progress in research and applications*, 1. London: John Wiley, 1–29.

HERBERTSON, A. J. 1905: The major natural regions, *Geographical Journal* 25, 300–10.

HEWITT, K. ed. 1983: *Interpretations of calamity*. London: George Allen & Unwin.

HILL, M. R. 1982: Positivism: a 'hidden' philosophy in geography. In M. E. Harvey and B. P. Holly (eds.) *Themes in geographic thought*. London: Croom Helm, 38–60.

HODGART, R. L. 1978: Optimizing access to public services:. a review of problems, models, and methods of locating central facilities. *Progress in Human Geography* 2, 17–48.

HOLT-JENSEN, A. 1988: *Geography: its history and concepts*. London: Harper & Row.

HOOK, J. C. 1955: Areal differentiation of the density of the rural farm population in the northeastern United States. *Annals of the Association of American Geographers* 45, 189–90.

HOOSON, D. J. M. 1981: Carl O. Sauer. In B. W. Blouet (ed.), *The origins of academic geography in the United States*. Hamden, Conn: Archon Books, 165–74.

HOUSE, J. W. 1973: Geographers, decision takers and policy makers. In M. Chisholm and B. Rodgers (eds.), *Studies in human geography*. London: Heinemann, 272–305.

HUCKLE, J. 1985: Geography and schooling. In R. J. Johnston (ed.) *The future of geography*. London: Methuen, 291–306.

HUDSON, R. 1983: The question of theory in political geography: outlines for a critical theory approach. In N. Kliot and S. Waterman (eds.) *Pluralism and political geography*. London: Croom Helm, 39–35.

—— 1988: Uneven development in capitalist societies. *Transactions, Institute of British Geographers* NS13, 484–96.

HUGGETT, R. J. 1980: *Systems analysis in geography*. Oxford: Oxford University Press.

HUGGETT, R. J. and THOMAS, R. W. 1980: *Modelling in geography*. London: Harper & Row.

ISARD, W. 1956a: *Location and space economy*. New York: John Wiley.

—— 1956b: Regional science, the concept of region, and regional structure. *Papers and Proceedings, Regional Science Association* 2, 13–39.

—— 1960: *Methods of regional analysis: an introduction in regional science*. New York: John Wiley.

—— 1975: *An introduction to regional science*. Englewood Cliffs, NJ: Prentice-Hall.

ISARD, W. *et al.* 1969: *General theory: social, political, economic and regional*. Cambridge, Mass: The MIT Press.

JACKSON, P. 1984: Social disorganization and moral order in the city. *Transactions, Institute of British Geographers* NS9, 168–80.

—— 1985: Urban ethnography. *Progress in Human Geography* 9, 157–76.

—— 1988: Definitions of the situation. In J. Eyles and D. M. Smith (eds.) *Qualitative Methods in Human Geography*. Cambridge: Polity Press, 49–74.

—— 1989: *Maps of meaning*. London: Unwin Hyman.

JACKSON, P. and SMITH, S. J. 1981: Introduction. In P. Jackson and S. J. Smith (eds.), *Social interaction and ethnic segregation*. London: Academic Press, 1–18.

—— 1984: *Exploring social geography*. London: George Allen & Unwin.

JACKSON, P., SMITH, S. J. and JOHNSTON, R. J. 1988: An equal opportunities policy for the IBG. *Area* 20, 279–80.

JAMES, P. E. 1942: *Latin America*. London: Cassell.

—— 1954: Introduction: the field of geography. in P. E. James and C. F. Jones (eds.), *American geography: inventory and prospect*. Syracuse: Syracuse University Press, 2–18.

—— 1965: The President's session. *The Professional Geographer* 17(4), 35–7.

—— 1972: *All possible worlds: a history of geographical ideas*. Indianapolis: The Odyssey Press.

JAMES, P. E. and JONES, C. F. (eds.) 1954: *American geography: inventory and prospect*. Syracuse: Syracuse University Press.

JAMES, P. E. and MARTIN, G. J. 1981: *All possible worlds: a history of geographical ideas* (2nd edn). New York: John Wiley.

JANELLE, D. G. 1968: Central-place development in a time-space framework. *The Professional Geographer* 20, 5–10.

—— 1969: Spatial reorganization: a model and concept. *Annals of the Association of American Geographers* 59, 348–64.

JOHNSON, J. H. and POOLEY, C. G. (eds.) 1982: *The structure of nineteenth-century cities*. London: Croom Helm.

JOHNSON, L. 1989: Geography, planning and gender. *New Zealand Geographer* 45, 85–91.

JOHNSTON, R. J. 1969: Urban geography in New Zealand 1945–1969. *New Zealand Geographer* 25, 121–35.

—— 1971: *Urban residential patterns: an introductory review*. London: G. Bell & Sons.

—— 1974: Continually changing human geography revisited: David Harvey: *Social Justice and the City*. *New Zealand Geographer* 30, 180–92.

—— 1976a: *The world trade system: some enquiries into its spatial structure*. London: G. Bell & Sons.

—— 1976b: Anarchy, conspiracy and apathy: the three 'conditions' of geography. *Area* 8, 1–3.

—— 1978a: *Multivariate statistical analysis in geography: a primer on the general linear model*. London: Longman.

—— 1978b: *Political, electoral and spatial systems*. London: Oxford University Press.

—— 1978c: Paradigms and revolutions or evolution: observations on human geography since the Second World War. *Progress in Human Geography* 2, 189–206.

—— 1979a: Urban geography: city structures. *Progress in Human Geography* 3, 133–8.

—— 1979b: *Geography and geographers: Anglo-American human geography since 1945* (1st edn), London: Edward Arnold.

—— 1980a: On the nature of explanation in human geography. *Transactions, Institute of British Geographers* NS5, 402–12.

—— 1980b: *City and society*. London: Penguin.

—— 1981a: Applied geography, quantitative analysis and ideology. *Applied Geography* 1, 213–9.

—— 1981b: Paradigms, revolutions, schools of thought and anarchy: reflections on the recent history of Anglo-American human geography. In B. W. Blouet (ed.), *The origins of academic geography in the United States*. Hamden, Conn.: Archon Books, 303–18.

—— 1982a: *Geography and the state*. London: Macmillan.

—— 1982b: On the nature of human geography. *Transactions, Institute of British Geographers* NS7, 123–5.

—— 1982c: On ecological analysis and spatial autocorrelation. In L. le Rouzic, (ed.), *L'autocorrelation spatiale*. Reims, Travaux de l'Institute de Géographie, 3–16.

—— 1983a: Resource analysis, resource management and the integration of human and physical geography. *Progress in Physical Geography* 7, 127–46.

—— 1983b: *Philosophy and human geography: an introduction to contemporary approaches* (1st. edn.). London: Edward Arnold.

—— 1983c: Texts, actors, and higher managers: judges, bureaucrats and the political organization of space, *Political Geography Quarterly* 2, 3–20.

—— 1983d: On geography and the history of geography. *History of Geography Newsletter* 3, 1–7.

—— 1984a: The political geography of electoral geography. In P. J. Taylor and J. W. House (eds.) *Political geography: recent advances and future directions*. London: Croom Helm, 133–48.

—— 1984b: *Residential segregation, the state and constitutional conflict in American urban areas*. London: Academic Press.

—— 1984c: The world is our oyster. *Transactions, Institute of British Geographers* NS9, 443–59.

—— 1984d: The region in twentieth century British geography. *History of Geography Newsletter* 4, 26–35.

—— 1984e: A foundling floundering in World Three. In M. Billinge, D. Gregory and R. Martin (eds.) *Recollections of a revolution*. London: Macmillan, 39–56.

—— 1984f: Quantitative ecological analysis in human geography: an evaluation of four problem areas. In G. Bahrenberg, M. Fischer and P. Nijkamp (eds.) *Recent developments in spatial data analysis*. Aldershot: Gower, 131–44.

—— 1985b: *The geography of English politics: the 1983 general election*. London: Croom Helm.

—— ed. 1985c: *The future of geography*. London: Methuen.

—— 1985d: To the ends of the earth. In R. J. Johnston (ed.) *The Future of Geography*. London: Methuen, 326–38.

—— 1986a: *On human geography*. Oxford: Basil Blackwell.

—— 1986b: Four fixations and the quest for unity in geography. *Transactions, Institute of British Geographers* NS11, 449–53.

—— 1986c: Placing politics. *Political Geography Quarterly* 5, s63–s78.

—— 1986d: Individual freedom and the world-economy. In R. J. Johnston and P. J. Taylor (eds.) *A world in crisis? geographical perspectives.* Oxford: Basil Blackwell, 173–95.

—— 1986e: The neighbourhood effect revisited: spatial science or political regionalism. *Environment and Planning D: Society and Space* 4, 41–56.

—— 1986f: *Philosophy and human geography: an introduction to contemporary approaches* (second edition). London: Edward Arnold.

—— 1986g: John L. Paterson: *David Harvey's Geography. Antipode* 18, 96–108.

—— 1986h: Understanding and solving American urban problems: geographical contributions? *The Professional Geographer* 38, 229–33.

—— 1987: Job markets and housing markets in the 'developed world'. *Tijdschrift voor Economische en Sociale Geografie* 78.

—— 1988: There's a place for us. *New Zealand Geographer* 44, 8–13.

—— 1989a: Philosophy, ideology and geography. In D. Gregory and R. Walford (eds.) *Horizons in Human Geography.* London: Macmillan, 48–66.

—— 1989b: *Environmental problems: nature, economy and state.* London: Belhaven Press.

—— 1990a: The challenge for regional geography: some proposals for research frontiers. In R. J. Johnston, J. Hauer and G.A. Hoekveld (eds.) *The challenge of regional geography.* London: Routledge, 124–41.

—— 1990b: Some misconceptions about conceptual issues. *Tijdschrift voor Economische en Sociale Geografie* 81, 14–18.

—— 1991: Territoriality and the state. In G. B. Benko (ed.) *Territoriality and the social sciences.* Ottawa: University of Ottawa Press.

JOHNSTON, R. J. and BRACK, E. V. 1983: Appointment and promotion in the academic labour market: a preliminary survey of British University Departments of Geography. *Transactions, Institute of British Geographers* NS8, 100–11.

JOHNSTON, R. J. and CLAVAL, P. (eds.) 1984: *Geography since the Second World War: an international survey.* London: Croom Helm.

JOHNSTON, R. J. and DOORNKAMP, J. C. (eds.) 1982: *The changing geography of the United Kingdom.* London: Methuen.

JOHNSTON, R. J. and GARDINER, V. (eds.) 1990: *The Changing Geography of the United Kingdom (Second edition).* London: Routledge.

JOHNSTON, R. J. and GREGORY, S. 1984: The United Kingdom. In R. J. Johnston and P. Claval (eds.), *Geography since the Second World War: an international survey.* London: Croom Helm, 107–31.

JOHNSTON, R. J. and HERBERT, D. T. 1978: Introduction. In D. T. Herbert and R. J. Johnston (eds.), *Social areas in cities: processes, patterns and problems.* London: John Wiley, 1–33.

JOHNSTON, R. J. and PATTIE, C. J. 1990: The regional impact of Thatcherism: attitudes and votes in Great Britain in the 1980s. *Regional Studies* 24.

JOHNSTON, R. J. and TAYLOR, P. J. (eds) 1986a: *A world in crisis? geographical perspectives.* Oxford: Basil Blackwell.

—— 1986b: Political geography: a politics of places within places. *Parliamentary Affairs* 39, 135–49.

—— and TAYLOR, P. J. (eds.) 1989: *A World in Crisis? (Second edition).* Oxford: Basil Blackwell.

—— and O'LOUGHLIN, J. 1987: The geography of violence and premature death. In Vayrynen, R. (ed.) *The quest for peace.* London: Sage Publications.

JONAS, A. 1988: A new regional geography of localities? *Area* 20, 101–10.

JONES, E. 1956: Cause and effect in human geography. *Annals of the Association of American Geographers* 46, 369–77.

—— 1980: Social geography. In E. H. Brown, (ed.), *Geography, yesterday and tomorrow*. Oxford: Oxford University Press, 251–62.

JONES, K. 1984: Geographical methods for exploring relationships. In G. Bahrenberg, M. M. Fischer and P. Nijkamp (eds.) *Recent developments in spatial data analysis*. Aldershot: Gower, 215–30.

JONES, L. V., LINDSEY, G. and COGGLESHALL, P. E. eds. 1982: *An assessment of research-doctorate programs in the United States: social and behavioral sciences*. Washington DC: National Academy Press.

KANSKY, K. J. 1963: *Structure of transportation networks*. Chicago: University of Chicago, Department of Geography, Research Paper 84.

KASPERSON, R. E. 1971: The post-behavioral revolution in geography. *British Columbia Geographical Series* 12, 5–20.

KATES, R. W. 1962: *Hazard and choice perception in flood plain management*. Chicago: University of Chicago, Department of Geography, Research Paper 78.

—— 1972: Review of *Perspectives on resource management*. *Annals of the Association of American Geographers* 62, 519–20.

—— 1987: The human environment: the road not taken, the road still beckoning. *Annals of the Association of American Geographers* 77, 525–34.

KATES, R. W. and BURTON, I. (ed.) 1985: *Geography, resources and environment* (two volumes). Chicago: University of Chicago Press.

KEEBLE, D. E. 1976: *Industrial location and planning in the United Kingdom*. London: Methuen.

KING, L. J. 1960: A note on theory and reality. *The Professional Geographer* 12(3), 4–6.

—— 1961: A multivariate analysis of the spacing of urban settlement in the United States. *Annals of the Association of American Geographers* 51, 222–3.

—— 1969a: The analysis of spatial form and relationship to geographic theory. *Annals of the Association of American Geographers* 59, 573–95.

—— 1969b: *Statistical analysis in geography*. Englewood Cliffs: Prentice-Hall.

—— 1976: Alternatives to a positive economic geography. *Annals of the Association of American Geographers* 66, 293–308.

—— 1979a: Areal associations and regressions. *Annals of the Association of American Geographers* 69, 124–8.

—— 1979b: The seventies: disillusionment and consolidation. *Annals of the Association of American Geographers* 69, 155–7.

KING, L. J. and CLARK, G. L. 1978: Government policy and regional development. *Progress in Human Geography* 2, 1–16.

KIRK, W. 1951: Historical geography and the concept of the behavioural environment. *Indian Geographical Journal* 25, 152–60.

—— 1963: Problems of geography. *Geography* 48, 357–71.

—— 1978: The road from Mandalay: towards a geographical philosophy. *Transactions, Institute of British Geographers* NS3, 381–394.

KISH, G. and WARD, R. 1981: A survival package for geography and other endangered disciplines. *Newsletter*, Association of American Geographers, 16, pp. 8,14.

KNOS, D. S. 1968: The distribution of land values in Topeka, Kansas. In B. J. L. Berry and D. F. Marble (eds.), *Spatial analysis*. Englewood Cliffs, NJ: Prentice-Hall, 269–89.

KNOX, P. L. 1975: *Social well-being: a spatial perspective*. London: Oxford University Press.

—— 1987: The social production of the built environment: architects, architecture and the post-modern city. *Progress in Human Geography* 11, 354–78.

KNOX, P. L. and AGNEW, J. A. 1989: *The geography of the world-economy*. London: Edward Arnold.

KNOX, P. L., BARTELS, E. H., BOHLAND, J. R., HOLCOMB, B. and JOHNSTON, R. J. 1988: *The United States: a contemporary human geography*. London: Longman.

KOFMAN, E. 1988: Is there a cultural geography beyond the fragments? *Area* 20, 85–7.

KOLLMORGEN, W. N. 1979: Kollmorgen as a bureaucrat. *Annals of the Association of American Geographers* 69, 77–89.

KUHN, T. S. 1962: *The structure of scientific revolutions*. Chicago: University of Chicago Press.

—— 1969: Comment on the relations of science and art. *Comparative Studies in Society and History* 11, 403–12.

—— 1970a: *The structure of scientific revolutions* (2nd edn). Chicago: University of Chicago Press.

—— 1970b: Logic of discovery or psychology of research? In I. Lakatos and A. Musgrave (eds.), *Criticism and the growth of knowledge*. Cambridge: Cambridge University Press, 1–23.

—— 1970c: Reflections on my critics. In I. Lakatos and A. Musgrave (eds.), *Criticism and the growth of knowledge*. Cambridge: Cambridge University Press, 231–78.

—— 1977: Second thoughts on paradigms. In F. Suppe (ed.), *The structure of scientific theories*. Urbana: University of Illinois Press, 459–82, plus discussion 500–17.

LABEDZ, L. 1977: Anarchism. In A. Bullock and O. Stallybrass (eds.), *The Fontana dictionary of modern thought*. London: Fontana, 22.

LAKATOS, I. 1978a: Falsification and the methodology of scientific research programmes. In J. Worrall and G. Currie (eds.), *The methodology of scientific research programmes, philosophical papers*, volume I. Cambridge: Cambridge University Press, 8–101.

—— 1978b: History of science and its rational reconstructions. In J. Worrall and G. Currie (eds.) *The methodology of scientific research programmes, philosophical papers*, volume 1. Cambridge: Cambridge University Press, 102–38.

LANGTON, J. 1972: Potentialities and problems of adapting a systems approach to the study of change in human geography. In C. Board *et al.* (eds.) *Progress in Geography* 4, London: Edward Arnold, 125–79.

—— 1984: The industrial revolution and the regional geography of England. *Transactions, Institute of British Geographers* NS9, 145–67.

LAPONCE, J. A. 1980: Political science: an import-export analysis of journals and footnotes. *Political Studies* 28, 401–19.

LASH, S. and URRY, J. 1987: *The end of organized capitalism*. Cambridge: Polity Press.

LAVALLE, P., McCONNELL, H. and BROWN, R. G. 1967: Certain aspects of the expansion of quantitative methodology in American geography. *Annals of the Association of American Geographers* 57, 423–36.

LAW, J. 1976: Theories and methods in the sociology of science: an interpretative approach. In G. Lemaine *et al.*, *Perspectives on the emergence of scientific disciplines*. The Hague: Mouton, 221–31.

LEACH, B. 1974: Race, problems and geography. *Transactions, Institute of British Geographers* 63, 41–7.

LEACH, E. R. 1974: *Lévi-Strauss*. London: Fontana.

LEE, R. 1985: The future of the region: regional geography as education for transformation. In R. King (ed.) *Geographical futures* Sheffield: The Geographical Association, 77–91.

—— 1984: Process and region in the A-level syllabus. *Geography* 69, 97–107.

LEE, Y. 1975: A rejoinder to 'The geography of crime: a political critique'. *The Professional Geographer* 27, 284–5.

324   Geography and Geographers

LEMAINE, G., *et al.* 1976: Introduction: problems in the emergence of new disciplines. In G. Lemaine *et al.* (eds.), *Perspectives on the emergence of scientific disciplines*. The Hague: Mouton, 1–73.

LEONARD, S. 1982: Urban managerialism: a period of transition. *Progress in Human Geography* 6, 190–215.

LEWIS, G. M. 1966: Regional ideas and reality in the Cis-Rocky Mountain West. *Transactions, Institute of British Geographers* 38, 135–50.

—— 1968: Levels of living in the Northeastern United States *c*. 1960: a new approach to regional geography. *Transactions, Institute of British Geographers* 45, 11–37.

LEWIS, J. and TOWNSEND, A. (eds.) 1989: *The north-south divide: regional change in Britain in the 1980s*. London: Paul Chapman.

LEWIS, P. W. 1965: Three related problems in the formulation of laws in geography. *The Professional Geographer* 17(5), 24–7.

LEWTHWAITE, G. R. 1966: Environmentalism and determinism: a search for clarification. *Annals of the Association of American Geographers* 56, 1–23.

LEY, D. 1974: *The black inner city as frontier outpost*. Washington DC: Association of American Geographers.

—— 1977a: The personality of a geographical fact. *The Professional Geographer* 29, 8–13.

—— 1977b: Social geography and the taken-for-granted world. *Transactions, Institute of British Geographers* NS2, 498–512.

—— 1978: Social geography and social action. In D. Ley and M. S. Samuels (eds.), *Humanistic geography: problems and prospects*. Chicago: Maaroufa Press, 41–57.

—— 1980: *Geography without man: a humanistic critique*. Oxford Research Paper 24, School of Geography, University of Oxford.

—— 1981: Behavioral geography and the philosophies of meaning. In K. R. Cox and R. G. Golledge (eds.), *Behavioral problems in geography revisited*. London: Methuen, 209–30.

—— 1983: *A social geography of the city*. New York: Harper & Row

LEY, D. and SAMUELS, M. S. 1978: Introduction: contexts of modern humanism in geography. In D. Ley and M. S. Samuels (eds.), *Humanistic geography: prospects and problems*. Chicago: Maaroufa Press, 1–18.

LICHTENBERGER, E. 1984: The German-speaking countries. In R. J. Johnston and P. Claval (eds.) *Geography since the Second World War: an international survey*. London: Croom Helm, 156–84.

LITTLE, J., PEAKE, L. and RICHARDSON, P. (eds) 1988: *Women in cities*. London: Macmillan.

LIVINGSTONE, D. N. 1984: Natural theory and neo-Lamarckism: the changing context of nineteenth century geography in the United States and Great Britain. *Annals of the Association of American Geographers* 74, 9–28.

LIVINGSTONE, D. N. and HARRISON, R. T. 1981: Immanuel Kant, subjectivism, and human geography: a preliminary investigation. *Transactions, Institute of British Geographers* NS6, 359–74.

LÖSCH, A. 1954: *The economics of location*. New Haven, Conn.: Yale University Press.

LOVERING, J. 1987: Militarism, capitalism and the nation-state: towards a realist synthesis. *Environment and Planning D: Society and Space* 5, 283–302.

LOWE, M. S. and SHORT, J. R. 1990: Progressive human geography. *Progress in Human Geography* 14.

LOWENTHAL, D. 1961: Geography, experience, and imagination: towards a geographical epistemology. *Annals of the Association of American Geographers* 51, 241–60.

—— (ed.) *George Perkins Marsh: man and nature*. Cambridge, Mass.: Harvard University Press.

—— 68: The American scene. *Geographical Review* **48**, 61–88.

—— 1975: Past time, present place: landscape and memory. *The Geographical Review* **65**, 1–36.

—— 1985: *The past is a foreign country*. Cambridge: Cambridge University Press.

LOWENTHAL, D. and BOWDEN, M. J. (eds.) 1975: *Geographies of the mind: essays in historical geosophy in honor of John Kirkland Wright*. New York: Oxford University Press.

LOWENTHAL, D. and PRINCE, H. C. 1965: English landscape tastes. *Geographical Review* **55**, 186–222.

LOWENTHAL, D. *et al*. 1973: Report of the AAG Task Force on environmental quality. *The Professional Geographer* **25**, 39–46.

LUKERMANN, F. 1958: Towards a more geographic economic geography. *The Professional Geographer* **10**(1), 2–10.

—— 1960a: On explanation, model, and prediction. *The Professional Geographer* **12**(1), 1–2.

—— 1960b: The geography of cement? *The Professional Geographer* **12**(4), 1–6.

—— 61: The role of theory in geographical inquiry. *The Professional Geographer* **13**(2), 1–6.

—— 1965: Geography; de facto or de jure. *Journal of the Minnesota Academy of Science* **32**, 189–96.

—— 1990: *The Nature of Geography*: Post hoc, ergo propter hoc? In J. N. Entrikin and S. D. Brunn (eds.) *Reflections on Richard Hartshorne's The Nature of Geography*. Washington: Association of American Geographers, 53–68.

LYNCH, K. 1960: *The image of the city*. Cambridge, Mass.: MIT Press.

McCARTY, H. H. 1940: *The geographic basis of American economic life*. New York: Harper & Brothers.

—— 1952: McCarty on McCarthy: the spatial distribution of the McCarthy vote 1952. Unpublished Paper, Department of Geography, State University of Iowa, Iowa City.

—— 1953: An approach to a theory of economic geography. *Annals of the Association of American Geographers* **43**, 183–4.

—— 1954: An approach to a theory of economic geography. *Economic Geography* **30**, 95–101.

—— 1958: Science, measurement, and area analysis. *Economic Geography* **34**, facing page 283.

—— 1979: Geography at Iowa. *Annals of the Association of American Geographers* **69**, 121–4.

McCARTY, H. H., HOOK, J. C. and KNOS, D. S. 1956: *The measurement of association in industrial geography*. Department of Geography, State University of Iowa, Iowa City.

McCARTY, H. H. and LINDBERG, J. B. 1966: *A preface to economic geography*. Englewood Cliffs, NJ: Prentice-Hall.

McDANIEL, R. and ELIOT HURST, M. E. 1968: *A systems analytic approach to economic geography*. Commission on College Geography, Publication 8, Association of American Geographers, Washington, DC.

McDOWELL, L. 1986a: Feminist geography. In R. J. Johnston, D. Gregory and D. M. Smith (eds.) *The dictionary of human geography*. Oxford: Basil Blackwell, 151–2.

—— 1986b: Beyond patriarchy: a class-based explanation of women's subordination. *Antipode* **18**, 311–21.

—— 1989: Women, gender and the organisation of space. In D. Gregory and R. Walford (eds.) *Horizons in human geography*. London: Macmillan, 136–51.

McDOWELL, L. and MASSEY, D. 1984: A woman's place? In D. Massey and J. Allen (eds.) *Geography matters!* Cambridge: Cambridge University Press, 128–47.

MACGILL, S. M. 1981: Liquefied energy gases in the UK: what price public safety? *Environment and Planning A* **13**, 339–54.
—— 1983: The Q-controversy: issues and nonissues. *Environment and Planning B: Planning and Design* **10**, 371–80.
MACKAY, J. R. 1958: The interactance hypothesis and boundaries in Canada: a preliminary study. *The Canadian Geographer* **11**, 1–8.
MACKENZIE, S. 1989: Restructuring the relations of work and life: women as environmental actors, feminism as geographic analysis. In A. Kobayashi and S. Mackenzie (eds.) *Remaking human geography*. Boston: Unwin Hyman, 40–61.
MACMILLAN, B. 1989a: Quantitative theory construction in human geography. In B. Macmillan (ed.) *Remodelling geography*. Oxford: Basil Blackwell, 89–107.
—— 1989b: Modelling through: an afterword to *Remodelling geography*. In B. Macmillan (ed.) *Remodelling geography*. Oxford: Basil Blackwell, 291–313.
McKINNEY, W. M. 1968: Carey, Spencer, and modern geography. *The Professional Geographer* **20**, 103–6.
McTAGGART, W. D. 1974: Structuralism and universalism in geography: reflections on contributions by H. C. Brookfield. *The Australian Geographer* **12**, 510–16.
MABOGUNJE, A. K. 1977: In search of spatial order: geography and the new programme of urbanization in Nigeria. In D. R. Deskins *et al.* (eds), *Geographic humanism, analysis and social action: a half century of geography at Michigan*. Michigan Geography Publications No. 17. Ann Arbor, 347–76.
MAGEE, B. 1975: *Popper*, London: Fontana.
MAGUIRE, D. J. 1989: The Domesday interactive videodisc system in geography teaching. *Journal of Geography in Higher Education* **13**, 55–68.
MAIR, A. 1986: Thomas Kuhn and understanding geography. *Progress in Human Geography* **10**, 345–70.
MANION, T. and WHITELEGG, J. 1979: Radical geography and Marxism. *Area* **11**, 122–4.
MANNERS, I. R. and MIKESELL, M. W. (eds.) 1974: *Perspectives on environment*. Commission on College Geography, Association of American Geographers, Washington.
MARCHAND, B. 1978: A dialectical approach in geography. *Geographical Analysis* **10**, 105–19.
MARCUS, M. G. 1979: Coming full circle: physical geography in the twentieth century. *Annals of the Association of American geographers* **69**, 521–32.
MARSHALL, J. U. 1985: Geography as a scientific enterprise. In R. J. Johnston (ed.) *The future of geography*. London: Methuen, 113–28.
MARTIN, A. F. 1951: The necessity for determinism. *Transactions, Institute of British Geographers* **17**, 1–12.
MARTIN, G. J. 1981: Ontography and Davisian physiography. In B. W. Blouet (ed.), *The origins of academic geography in the United States*. Hamden, Conn.: Archon Books, 279–90.
—— 1990: *The Nature of Geography* and the Schaefer-Hartshorne debate. In J. N. Entrikin and S. D. Brunn (eds.) *Reflections on Richard Hartshorne's The Nature of Geography*. Washington: Association of American Geographers, 69–88.
MARTIN, R. L. and OEPPEN, J. 1975: The identification of regional forecasting models using space-time correlation functions. *Transactions, Institute of British Geographers* **66**, 95–118.
MASSAM, B. H. 1976: *Location and space in social administration*. London: Edward Arnold.
MASSEY, D. 1975: Behavioral research. *Area* **7**, 201–3.
—— 1984a: *Spatial divisions of labour: social structures and the geography of production*. London: Macmillan.

—— 1984b: Introduction: geography matters. In D. Massey and J. Allen (eds.) *Geography matters! a reader*. Cambridge: Cambridge University Press, 1–11.

MASSEY, D. and MEEGAN, R. A. 1979: The geography of industrial reorganization. *Progress in Planning* 10, 155–237.

—— 1982: *The anatomy of job loss*. London: Methuen.

—— 1985: Introduction: the debate. In D. Massey and R. Meegan (eds.) *Politics and method: contrasting studies in industrial geography*. London: Methuen, 1–12.

MASTERMAN, M. 1970: The nature of a paradigm. In I. Lakatos and A. Musgrave (eds.), *Criticism and the growth of knowledge*. London: Cambridge University Press, 59–90.

MAY, J. A. 1970: *Kant's concept of geography: and its relation to recent geographical thought*. Department of Geography, University of Toronto, Research Publication 4, Toronto.

—— 1972: A reply to Professor Hartshorne. *The Canadian Geographer* 16, 79–81.

MAYER, H. M. 1954: Urban geography. In P. E. James and C. F. Jones (eds.), *American geography: inventory and prospect*. Syracuse: Syracuse University Press, 142–66.

MEAD, W. R. 1980: Regional geography. In E. H. Brown (ed.), *Geography, yesterday and tomorrow*. Oxford: Oxford University Press, 292–302.

MEADOWS, D. H. *et al*. 1972: *The limits to growth*. New York: Universal Books.

MEINIG, D. W. 1972: American wests: preface to a geographical introduction. *Annals of the Association of American Geographers* 62, 159–84.

—— 1978: The continuous shaping of America: a prospectus for geographers and historians. *The American Historical Review* 83, 1186–1217.

—— 1983: Geography as an art. *Transactions, Institute of British Geographers* NS8, 314–28.

MERCER, D. C. 1977: *Conflict and consensus in human geography*. Monash Publications in Geography No. 17, Clayton, Victoria, Australia.

—— 1984: Unmasking technocratic geography. In M. Billinge, D. Gregory and R. Martin (eds.) *Recollections of a revolution*. London: Macmillan, 153–99.

MERCER, D. C. and POWELL, J. M. 1972: *Phenomenology and related non-positivistic viewpoints in the social sciences*. Monash Publications in Geography, No. 1, Clayton, Victoria, Australia.

MEYER, D. R. 1972: Geographical population data: statistical description not statistical inference. *The Professional Geographer* 24, 26–8.

MIKESELL, M. W. 1967: Geographical perspectives in anthropology. *Annals of the Association of American Geographers* 57, 617–34.

—— 1969: The borderlands of geography as a social science. In M. Sherif and C. W. Sherif (eds.), *Interdisciplinary relationships in the social sciences*. Chicago: Aldine Publishing Company, 227–48.

—— (ed.) 1973: *Geographers abroad: essays on the prospects of research in foreign areas*. Chicago: Department of Geography, University of Chicago, Research Paper 152.

—— 1974: Geography as the study of environment: an assessment of some old and new commitments. In I. R. Manners and M. W. Mikesell (eds.), *Perspectives on environment*, Commission on College Geography, Association of American Geographers. Washington, DC, 1–23.

—— 1978: Tradition and innovation in cultural geography. *Annals of the Association of American Geographers* 68, 1–16.

—— 1981: Continuity and change. In B. W. Blouet (ed.), *The origins of academic geography in the United States*. Hamden, Conn.: Archon Books, 1–15.

—— 1984: North America. In R. J. Johnston and P. Claval (eds.) *Geography since the Second World War: an international survey*. London: Croom Helm, 185–213.

MITCHELL, B. and DRAPER, D. 1982: *Relevance and ethics in geography*. London: Longman.

MONTEFIORE, A. G. and WILLIAMS, W. M. 1955: Determinism and possibilism. *Geographical Studies* 2, 1–11.

MOODIE, D. W. and LEHR, J. C. 1976: Fact and theory in historical geography. *The Professional Geographer* 28, 132–6.

MOOS, A. I. and DEAR, M. J. 1986: Structuration theory in urban analysis: 1. theoretical exegesis. *Environment and Planning A* 18, 231–52.

MORGAN, M. A. 1967: Hardware models in geography. In R. J. Chorley and P. Haggett (eds.), *Models in geography*. London: Methuen, 727–74.

MORGAN, W. B. and MOSS, R. P. 1965: Geography and ecology: the concept of the community and its relationship to environment. *Annals of the Association of American Geographers* 55, 339–50.

MORRILL, R. L. 1965: *Migration and the growth of urban settlement*. Lund Studies in Geography, Series B, 24, Lund: C. W. K. Gleerup.

—— 1968: Waves of spatial diffusion. *Journal of Regional Science* 8, 1–18.

—— 1969: Geography and the transformation of society. *Antipode* 1(1), 6–9.

—— 1970a: *The spatial organization of society*. Belmont California: Wadsworth, 2nd edn. 1974.

—— 1970b: Geography and the transformation of society: part II. *Antipode* 2(1), 4–10.

—— 1974: Review of D. Harvey, *Social Justice and the City*. *Annals of the Association of American Geographers* 64, 475–7.

—— 1980: Productivity of American PhD-granting Departments of Geography. *The Professional Geographer* 32, 85–9.

—— 1981: *Political redistricting*. Resource Publications in Geography, Association of American Geographers, Washington, DC.

—— 1984: Recollections of the 'Quantitative Revolution's' early years: the University of Washington 1955–65. In M. Billinge, D. Gregory and R. Martin (eds.) *Recollections of a revolution*. London: Macmillan, 57–72.

—— 1985: Some important geographic questions. *The Professional Geographer* 37, 263–70.

MORRILL, R. L. and DORMITZER, J. 1979: *The spatial order: an introduction to modern geography*. North Scituate: Duxbury.

MORRILL, R. L. and GARRISON, W. L. 1960: Projections of interregional patterns of trade in wheat and flour. *Economic Geography* 36, 116–26.

MORRILL, R. L. and WOHLENBERG, E. H. 1971: *The geography of poverty in the United States*. New York: McGraw Hill.

MOSS, R. P. 1970: Authority and charisma: criteria of validity in geographical method. *South African Geographical Journal* 52, 13–37.

—— 1977: Deductive strategies in geographical generalization. *Progress in Physical Geography* 1, 23–39.

MOSS, R. P. and MORGAN, W. B. 1967: The concept of the community: some applications in geographical research. *Transactions, Institute of British Geographers* 41, 21–32.

MUIR, R. 1975: *Modern political geography*. London: Macmillan.

—— 1978: Radical geography or a new orthodoxy? *Area* 10, 322–7.

—— 1979: Radical geography and Marxism. *Area* 11, 126–127.

MULKAY, M. J. 1975: Three models of scientific development. *Sociological Review* 23, 509–26.

—— 1976: Methodology in the sociology of science: some reflections on the study of radio astronomy. In G. Lemaine *et al.* (eds.), *Perspectives in the emergence of scientific disciplines*. The Hague: Mouton, 207–20.

—— 1978: Consensus in science. *Social Science Information* 17, 107–22.

MULKAY, M. J., GILBERT, G. N. and WOOLGAR, S. 1975: Problem areas and research networks in science. *Sociology* 9, 187–203.

MULLER-WILLE, C. 1978: The forgotten heritage: Christaller's antecedents. In B. J. L. Berry (ed.), *The nature of change in geographical ideas*. de Kalb: Northern Illinois University Press, 37–64.

MUMFORD, L. 1956: Prospect. In W. L. Thomas (ed.) *Man's role in changing the face of the earth*. Chicago: University of Chicago Press, 1141–52.

MURDIE, R. A. 1969: *Factorial ecology of metropolitan Toronto 1951–1961*. Chicago: University of Chicago, Department of Geography, Research Paper 116.

MYRDAL, G. 1957: *Economic theory and underdeveloped regions*. London: Duckworth.

NATIONAL ACADEMY OF SCIENCES – NATIONAL RESEARCH COUNCIL 1965: *The science of geography*. Washington: NAS-NRC.

NEFT, D. 1966: *Statistical analysis for areal distributions*. Monograph 2, Regional Science Research Institute, Philadelphia.

NEWMAN, J. L. 1973: The use of the term 'hypothesis' in geography. *Annals of the Association of American Geographers* 63, 22–7.

NYSTUEN, J. D. 1963: Identification of some fundamental spatial concepts. *Papers of the Michigan Academy of Science*, Arts, and Letters, 48, 373–84. Reprinted in B. J. L. Berry and D. F. Marble (eds.), *Spatial analysis*. Englewood Cliffs, NJ: Prentice-Hall, 35–41.

—— 1984: Comment on 'Artificial intelligence and its applicability to geographical problem solving'. *The Professional Geographer* 36, 358–9.

ODUM, H. W. and MOORE, H. E. 1938: *American regionalism – a cultural-historical approach to national integration*. New York: H. Holt & Company.

OLSSON, G. 1965: *Distance and human interaction: a review and bibliography*. Regional Science Research Institute, Bibliography Series Number 2, Philadelphia.

—— 1969: Inference problems in locational analysis. In K. R. Cox and R. G. Golledge (eds.), *Behavioral problems in geography: a symposium*, Northwestern University Studies in Geography 17. Evanston, 14–34.

—— 1978: Of ambiguity or far cries from a memorializing mamafesta. In D. Ley and M. S. Samuels (eds.) *Humanistic geography*. London: Croom Helm, 109–20.

—— 1979: Social science and human action or on hitting your head against the ceiling of language. In S. Gale and G. Olsson (eds.) *Philosophy in geography*. Dordrecht: Reidel, 287–308.

—— 1982: —— In P. R. Gould and G. Olsson (eds.) *A search for common ground*. London: Pion, 223–31.

OPENSHAW, S. 1984a: *The modifiable areal unit problem*. CATMOG 38. Norwich: Geo Books.

—— 1984b: Ecological fallacies and the analysis of areal census data. *Environment and Planning* A16, 17–32.

—— 1986: *Nuclear power: siting and safety*. London: Routledge & Kegan Paul.

—— 1989: Computer modelling in human geography. In B. Macmillan (ed.) *Remodelling geography*. Oxford: Basil Blackwell, 70–88.

OPENSHAW, S., CARVER, S. and FERNIE, J. 1989: *Britain's nuclear waste: siting and safety*. London: Belhaven Press.

OPENSHAW, S., CHARLTON, M., CRAFT, A. W. and BIRCH, J. 1988: Investigation of leukaemia clusters by use of a geographical analysis machine. *The Lancet* 6 February, 272–3.

OPENSHAW, S., WYMER, C. and CRAFT, A. W. 1988: A Mark I geographical analysis machine for the automated analysis of point data sets. *International Journal of Geographical Information Systems*

OPENSHAW, S. and GODDARD, J. B. 1987: Some implications of the commodification of information and the emerging information economy for applied geographical analysis in the United Kingdom. *Environment and Planning A* 19, 1423–40.

OPENSHAW, S., STEADMAN, P. and GREEN, O. 1983: *Doomsday: Britain after nuclear attack*. Oxford: Basil Blackwell.

OPENSHAW, S. WYLMER, C. and CHARLTON, M. 1986: A geographical information and mapping system for the BBC Domesday optical discs. *Transactions, Institute of British Geographers* NS11, 296–304.

OWENS, P. L. 1984: Rural leisure and recreation research: a retrospective evaluation. *Progress in Human Geography* 8, 157–88.

O'RIORDAN, T. 1971a: Environmental management. In C. Board *et al.* (eds.), *Progress in Geography* 3. London: Edward Arnold, 173–231.

— 1971b: *Perspectives in resource management*. London: Pion.

— 1976: *Environmentalism*. London: Pion.

PACIONE, M. 1990a: Conceptual issues in applied urban geography. *Tijdschrift voor Economische en Sociale Geografie* 81, 3–13.

— 1990b: On the dangers of misinterpretation. *Tijdschrift voor Economische en Sociale Geografie* 81, 26–28.

PAHL, R. E. 1965: Trends in social geography. In R. J. Chorley and P. Haggett (eds.), *Frontiers in geographical teaching*. London: Methuen, 81–100.

— 1969: Urban social theory and research. *Environment and Planning* 1, 143–54. (Reprinted in R. E. Pahl 1970, *Whose City?*. London: Longman, 209–25.)

— 1975: *Whose city? and other essays*. Harmondsworth: Penguin Books (2nd edn).

— 1979: Socio-political factors in resource allocation. In D. T. Herbert and D. M. Smith (eds.) *Social problems and the city: geographical perspectives*. Oxford: Oxford University Press, 33–46.

PALM, R. 1979: Financial and real estate institutions in the housing market. In D. T. Herbert and R. J. Johnston (eds.), *Geography and the urban environment*, 2. Chichester John Wiley, 83–124.

PALM, R. and PRED, A. R. 1978: The status of American women: a time-geographic view. In D. Lanegran and R. Palm (eds.) *Invitation to geography* (second edition). New York: McGraw Hill, 99–109.

PAPAGEORGIOU, G. J. 1969: Description of a basis necessary to the analysis of spatial systems. *Geographical Analysis* 1, 213–15.

— (ed.) 1976: *Mathematical land use theory*. Lexington, Mass.: D. C. Heath.

PARKER, G. 1985: *Western geopolitical thought in the twentieth century*. London: Croom Helm.

PARKES, D. N. and THRIFT, N. J. 1980: *Times, spaces and places*. Chichester: John Wiley.

PARSONS, J. J. 1977: Geography as exploration and discovery. *Annals of the Association of American Geographers* 67, 1–16.

PATERSON, J. H. 1974: Writing regional geography. In C. Board *et al.* (eds.), *Progress in Geography* 6. London: Edward Arnold, 1–26.

PATERSON, J. L. 1985: *David Harvey's geography*. London: Croom Helm.

PATMORE, J. A. 1970: *Land and leisure*. Newton Abbott: David & Charles.

— 1983: *Recreation and resources: leisure patterns and leisure places*. Oxford: Basil Blackwell.

PATTERSON, T. C. 1986: The last sixty years: toward a social history of Americanist archaeology in the United States. *American Anthropologist* 88, 7–26.

PEACH, C. and SMITH, S. J. 1981: Introduction. In C. Peach, V. Robinson and S. J. Smith, (eds.), *Ethnic segregation in cities*. London: Croom Helm, 9–24.

PEET, J. R. 1971: Poor, hungry America. *The Professional Geographer* 23, 99–104.

— 1975a: Inequality and poverty: a marxist-geographic theory. *Annals of the Association of American Geographers* 65, 564–71.

— 1975b: The geography of crime: a political critique. *The Professional Geographer* 27, 277–80.

— 1976a: Further comments on the geography of crime. *The Professional Geo-*

grapher **28**, 96–100.

—— 1976b: Editorial: radical geography in 1976. *Antipode* **8**(3), inside cover.

—— 1977: The development of radical geography in the United States. *Progress in Human Geography* **1**, 240–63.

—— (ed.) 1978: *Radical geography*. London: Methuen.

—— 1979: Societal contradiction and marxist geography. *Annals of the Association of American Geographers* **69**, 164–9.

—— 1980: The transition from feudalism to capitalism. In J. R. Peet (ed.), *An introduction to marxist theories of underdevelopment*. Publication HG/14, Department of Human Geography, Australian National University (Canberra), 51–74.

—— 1985a: The social origins of environmental determinism. *Annals of the Association of American Geographers* **75**, 309–33.

—— 1985b: Radical geography in the United States: a personal history. *Antipode* **17**, 1–7.

—— 1989: World capitalism and the destruction of regional cultures. In R. J. Johnston and P. J. Taylor (eds.) *A World in Crisis?*. Oxford: Basil Blackwell, 175–99.

PEET, J. R. and LYONS, J. V. 1981: Marxism: dialectical materialism, social formation and the geographic relations. In M. E. Harvey and B. P. Holly (eds.), *Themes in geographic thought*. London: Croom Helm, 187–205.

PEET, J. R. and THRIFT, N. J. 1989: Political economy and human geography. In R. Peet and N. J. Thrift (eds.) *New Models in Geography (Volume One)*. London: Unwin Hyman, 3–27.

PELTIER, L. C. 1954: Geomorphology. In P. E. James and C. F. Jones (eds.), *American geography: inventory and prospect*. Syracuse: Syracuse University Press, 362–81.

PENNING-ROWSELL, E. C. 1981: Fluctuating fortunes in gauging landscape value. *Progress in Human Geography* **5**, 25–41.

PEPPER, D. 1984: *The roots of modern environmentalism*. London: Croom Helm.

—— 1987: Physical and human integration: an educational perspective. *Progress in Human Geography* **11**.

PEPPER, D. and JENKINS, A. 1983: A call to arms: geography and peace studies. *Area* **15**, 202–8.

—— (eds.) 1985: *The geography of peace and war.*. Oxford: Basil Blackwell.

PERRY, P. J. 1969: H.C. Darby and historical geography: a survey and review. *Geographische Zeitschrift* **57**, 161–77.

—— 1979: Beyond Domesday. *Progress in Human Geography* **3**, 40716.

PETCH, J. R. and HAINES-YOUNG, R. H. 1980: The challenge of critical rationalism for methodology in physical geography. *Progress in Physical Geography* **4**, 63–78.

PETER, L. and HULL, R. 1969: *The Peter principle*. London: Bantam Books.

PHILBRICK, A. K. 1957: Principles of areal functional organization in regional human geography. *Economic Geography* **33**, 299–366.

PHILLIPS, D. R. and JOSEPH, A. E. 1984: *Accessibility and utilization: perspectives on health care delivery*. London: Harper & Row.

PHILLIPS, M. and UNWIN, T. 1985: British historical geography: places and people. *Area* **17**, 155–64.

PICKLES, J. 1985: *Phenomenology, science and geography: spatiality and the human sciences*. Cambridge: Cambridge University Press.

—— 1986: *Geography and Humanism*. CATMOG 44, Norwich: Geo Books.

—— 1988: From fact-world to life-world: the phenomenological method and social science. In J. Eyles and D. M. Smith (eds.) *Qualitative methods in human geography*. Cambridge: Polity Press, 233–54.

PINCH, S. P. 1985: *Cities and services: the geography of collective consumption.* London: Routledge & Kegan Paul.

PIPKIN, J. S. 1981: Cognitive behavioral geography and repetitive travel. In K. R. Cox and R. G. Golledge (eds.), *Behavioral problems in geography revisited.* London: Methuen, 145–80.

PIRIE, G. H. 1976: Thoughts on revealed preferences and spatial behaviour. *Environment and Planning* A 8, 947–55.

PITTS, F. R. 1965: A graph theoretic approach to historical geography. *The Professional Geographer* 17(5), 15–20.

POCOCK, D. C. D. 1983: The paradox of humanistic geography. *Area* 15, 355–8.

POCOCK, D. C. D. and HUDSON, R. 1978: *Images of the urban environment.* London: Macmillan.

POIKER, T. K. 1983: The shining armor of the white knight. *The Professional Geographer* 35, 348–9.

POOLER, J. A. 1977: The origins of the spatial tradition in geography: an interpretation. *Ontario Geography* 11, 56–83.

POPPER, K. R. 1959: *The logic of scientific discovery.* London: Hutchinson.

—— 1967: Replies to my critics. In P. A. Schipp (ed.), *The philosophy of Karl Popper,* volume 2. La Salle, Indiana: Open Court Publishing Company, 961–97.

—— 1970: Normal science and its dangers. In I. Lakatos and A. Musgrave (eds.), *Criticism and the growth of knowledge.* London: Cambridge University Press, 51–8.

PORTEOUS, J. D. 1977: *Environment and behavior.* Reading, Mass.: Addison-Wesley.

—— 1985: Literature and humanist geography. *Area* 17, 117–22.

—— 1986: Bodyscape: the body-landscape metaphor. *The Canadian Geographer* 30, 2–1.

—— 1988: Topocide: the annihilation of place. In J. Eyles and D. M. Smith (eds.) *Qualitative methods in human geography.* Cambridge: Polity Press, 75–93.

PORTER, P. W. 1978: Geography as human ecology. *Human geography: coming of age. American Behavioral Scientist* 22, 15–40.

PORTER, P. W. and LUKERMANN, F. 1975: The geography of utopia. In D. Lowenthal and M. J. Bowden (eds.), *Geography of the mind: essays in historical geosophy.* New York: Oxford University Press, 197–224.

POWELL, J. M. 1970: *The public lands of Australia Felix: settlement and land appraisal in Victoria 1834–1891.* Melbourne: Oxford University Press.

—— 1971: Utopia, millenium and the cooperative ideal: a behavioral matrix in the settlement process. *The Australian Geographer* 11, 606–18.

—— 1972: *Images of Australia.* Monash University Publications in Geography No. 3, Clayton, Victoria, Australia.

—— 1977: *Mirrors of the New World: images and image-makers in the settlement process.* Folkstone: Dawson.

—— 1980a: Thomas Griffith Taylor 1880–1963. In T. W. Freeman and P. Pinchemel (eds.), *Geographers: biobibliographical studies,* volume 5. London: Mansell, 141–54.

—— 1980b: The haunting of Saloman's house: geography and the limits of science. *Australian Geographer* 14, 327–41.

—— 1981: Editorial comment: 'professional' geography into the eighties – ? *Australian Geographical Studies* 19, 228–30.

PRED, A. 1965a: The concentration of high value-added manufacturing. *Economic Geography* 41, 108–32.

—— 1965b: Industrialization, initial advantage, and American metropolitan growth. *Geographical Review* 55, 158–85.

—— 1967: *Behavior and location: foundations for a geographic and dynamic location theory. Part I.* Lund: C. W. K. Gleerup.

—— 1969: *Behavior and location: foundations for a geographic and dynamic location theory. Part II.* Lund: C. W. K. Gleerup.

—— 1973: Urbanization, domestic planning problems and Swedish geographic research. In C. Board *et al.* (eds.), *Progress in Geography* 5, London: Edward Arnold, 1–77.

—— 1972a: The choreography of existence: comments on Hägerstrand's time-geography and its usefulness. *Economic Geography* 53, 207–21.

—— 1977b: *City-systems in advanced economies.* London: Hutchinson.

—— 1979: The academic past through a time-geographic looking glass. *Annals of the Association of American Geographers* 69, 175–80.

—— 1981a: Production, family, and free-time projects: a time-geographic perspective on the individual and societal change in nineteenth century US cities. *Journal of Historical Geography* 7, 3–36.

—— 1981b: Of paths and projects: individual behavior and its societal context. In K. R. Cox and R. G. Golledge (eds.) *Behavioral problems in geography revisited.* London: Methuen, 231–55.

—— 1984a: From here and now to there and then: some notes on diffusions, defusions, and disillusions. In M. Billinge, D. Gregory and R. Martin (eds.) *Recollections of a revolution.* London: Macmillan, 86–103.

—— 1984b: Structuration, biography formation, and knowledge: observations on port growth during the late mercantile period. *Environment and Planning D: Society and Space.* 2, 251–76.

—— 1984c: Place as historically contingent process: structuration and the time-geography of becoming places. *Annals of the Association of American Geographers* 74, 279–97.

—— 1985: The social becomes the spatial and the spatial becomes the social. In D. Gregory and J. Urry (eds.) *Social relations and spatial structures.* London: Macmillan, 336–75.

—— 1986: *Becoming places, practice and structure: the emergence and aftermath of enclosures in the plains villages of southwestern Skane.* Oxford: Polity Press.

—— 1988: Lost words as reflections of lost worlds. In R. G. Golledge, H. Couclelis and P. R. Gould (eds.) *A Ground for Common Search.* Santa Barbara: The Santa Barbara Geographical Press, 138–47.

PRED, A. R. and KIBEL, B. M. 1970: An application of gaming simulation to a general model of economic locational processes. *Economic Geography* 46, 136–56.

PRED, A. and PALM, R. 1978: The status of American women: a time-geographic view. In D. A. Lanegran and R. Palm (eds.), *An invitation to geography* (2nd edn. New York: McGraw Hill, 99–109.

PRICE, D. G. and BLAIR, A. M. 1989: *The changing geography of the service sector.* London: Belhaven.

PRINCE, H. C. 1961–2: The geographical imagination. *Landscape* 11, 21–5.

—— 1971a: Real, imagined and abstract worlds of the past. In C. Board *et al.* (eds.), *Progress in Geography* 3, London: Edward Arnold, 1–86.

—— 1971b: America! America? Views on a pot melting 1. Questions of social relevance. *Area* 3, 150–3.

—— 1979: About half Marx for the transition from feudalism to capitalism. *Area* 11, 47–51.

PRUNTY, M. C. 1979: Clark in the early 1940s. *Annals of the Association of American Geographers* 69, 42–5.

PUDUP, M. B. 1988: Arguments within regional geography. *Progress in Human Geography* 12, 369–90.

QUAINI, M. 1982: *Geography and marxism*. Oxford: Blackwell.

RADFORD, J. P. 1981: The social geography of the nineteenth century US city. In D. T. Herbert and R. J. Johnston (eds.), *Geography and the urban environment*, 4. Chichester: John Wiley, 257–93.

RAVENSTEIN, E. G. 1885: The laws of migration. *Journal of the Royal Statistical Society* 48, 167–235.

RAWSTRON, E. M. 1958: Three principles of industrial location. *Transactions, Institute of British Geographers* 25, 135–42.

RAY, D. M., VILLENEUVE, P. Y. and ROBERGE, R. A. 1974: Functional prerequisites, spatial diffusion, and allometric growth. *Economic Geography* 50, 341–51.

REES, J. 1985: *Natural resources: allocation, economics and policy*. London: Methuen.

REES, P. H. and WILSON, A. G. 1977: *Spatial population analysis*. London: Edward Arnold.

REISER, R. 1973: The territorial illusion and behavioural sink: critical notes on behavioural geography. *Antipode* 5(3), 52–7.

RELPH, E. 1970: An inquiry into the relations between phenomenology and geography. *The Canadian Geographer* 14, 193–201.

—— 1976: *Place and placelessness*. London: Pion.

—— 1977: Humanism, phenomenology, and geography, *Annals of the Association of American Geographers* 67, 177–9.

—— 1981a: Phenomenology. In M. E. Harvey and B. P. Holly (eds.), *Themes in geographic thought*. London: Croom Helm, 99–114.

—— 1981b: *Rational landscapes and humanistic geography*. London: Croom Helm.

RENFREW, A. C. 1981: Space, time and man. *Transactions, Institute of British Geographers* NS6 257–78.

REYNOLDS, R. B. 1956: Statistical methods in geographical research. *Geographical Review* 46, 129–32.

RHIND, D. W. 1981: Geographical information systems in Britain. In N. Wrigley and R. J. Bennett (eds.), *Quantitative geography*. London: Routledge & Kegan Paul, 17–35.

—— 1986: Remote sensing, digital mapping and GIS: the creation of government policy in the UK. *Environment and Planning C: Government and Policy* 4, 91–100.

—— 1989: Computing, academic geography, and the world outside. In B. Macmillan (ed.) *Remodelling geography*. Oxford: Basil Blackwell, 177–90.

RHIND, D. W. and ADAMS, T. A. 1980: Recent developments in surveying and mapping. In E. H. Brown (ed.), *Geography, yesterday and tomorrow* (Oxford: Oxford University Press), 181–99.

RHIND, D. W. and HUDSON, R. 1981: *Land use*, London: Methuen.

RHIND, D. W. and MOUNSEY, H. 1989: The Chorley committee and 'Handling geographical information'. *Environment and Planning A* 21, 571–86.

RIDDELL, J. B. 1970: *The spatial dynamics of modernization in Sierra Leone*. Evanston, Ill.: Northwestern University Press.

ROBINSON, A. H. 1956: The necessity of weighting values in correlation analysis of area data. *Annals of the Association of American Geographers* 46, 233–6.

—— 1961: On perks and pokes. *Economic Geography* 37, 181–3.

—— 1962: Mapping the correspondence of isarithmic maps. *Annals of the Association of American Geographers* 52, 414–25.

ROBINSON, A. H. and BRYSON, R. A. 1957: A method for describing quantitatively the correspondence of geographical distributions. *Annals of the Association of American Geographers* 47, 379–91.

ROBINSON, A. H., LINDBERG, J. B. and BRINKMAN, L. W. 1961: A correlation and regression analysis applied to rural farm densities in the Great Plains. *Annals of the Association of American Geographers* 51, 211–21.

ROBINSON, M. E. 1982: Representation, misrepresentation, and 'uncritical rhetoric'. *The Professional Geographer* 34, 224–6.

ROBSON, B. T. 1969: *Urban analysis*. Cambridge: Cambridge University Press.

—— 1972: The corridors of geography. *Area* 4, 213–14.

—— 1982: Introduction. In B. T. Robson and J. Rees (eds.), *Geographical agenda for a changing world*. London: Social Science Research Council, 1–6.

—— 1984: A pleasant pain. In M. Billinge, D. Gregory and R. Martin (eds.) *Recollections of a revolution*. London: Macmillan, 104–6.

RODER, W. 1961: Attitudes and knowledge on the Topeka flood plain. In G. F. White (ed.), *Papers on flood problems*. Chicago: University of Chicago, Department of Geography, Research Paper 70, 62–83.

RODGERS, A. 1955: Changing locational patterns in the Soviet pulp and paper industries. *Annals of the Association of American Geographers* 45, 85–104.

ROONEY, J. F., ZELINSKY, W. and LOUDER, D. R. (eds.) 1982: *This remarkable continent: an atlas of United States and Canadian society and cultures*. College Station: Texas A and M University Press.

ROSE, C. 1987: The problem of reference and geographic structuration. *Environment and Planning D: Society and Space* 5, 93–112.

ROSE, D. 1987: Home ownership, subsistence, and historical change: the mining district of West Cornwall in the late nineteenth century. In N. J. Thrift and P. Williams (eds.) *Class and space: the making of urban society*. London: Routledge, 108–53.

ROSE, J. K. 1936: Corn yield and climate in the Corn Belt. *Geographical Review* 26, 88–102.

ROSS, R. S. J. 1983: Facing Leviathan: public policy and global capitalism. *Economic Geography* 59, 144–60.

ROTHSTEIN, J. 1958: *Communication, organization and science*. Colorado: Falcon's Wing Press.

ROWLES, G. D. 1978: Reflections on experiential field work. In D. Ley and M. S. Samuels (eds.), *Humanistic geography: problems and prospects*. London: Croom Helm, 173–93.

ROWNTREE, L., FOOTE, K. E. and DOMOSH, M. 1989: Cultural geography. In G. L. Gaile and C. J. Willmott (eds.) *Geography in America*. Columbus: Merrill, 209–17.

RUSHTON, G. 1969: Analysis of spatial behavior by revealed space preference. *Annals of the Association of American Geographers* 59, 391–400.

—— 1979: On behavioral and perception geography. *Annals of the Association of American Geographers* 69, 463–4.

SAARINEN, T. F. 1979: Commentary–critique of Bunting-Guelke paper *Annals of the Association of American Geographers* 69, 464–8.

SACK, R. D. 1972: Geography, geometry and explanation. *Annals of the Association of American Geographers* 62, 61–78.

—— 1973a: Comment in reply. *Annals of the Association of American Geographers* 63, 568–9.

—— 1973b: A concept of physical space in geography. *Geographical Analysis* 5, 16–34.

—— 1974a: The spatial separatist theme in geography. *Economic Geography* 50, 1–19.

—— 1974b: Chorology and spatial analysis. *Annals of the Association of American Geographers* 64, 439–52.

—— 1980: *Conceptions of space in social thought*. London: Macmillan.

—— 1983: Human territoriality: a theory. *Annals of the Association of American Geographers* 73, 55–74.

—— 1986: *Human territoriality: its theory and history*. Cambridge: Cambridge University Press.

SAMUELS, M. S. 1978: Existentialism and human geography. In D. Ley and M. S. Samuels (eds.), *Humanistic geography: problems and prospects*. Chicago: Maaroufa Press, 22–40.

SANDBACH, F. 1980: *Environment, ideology and policy*. Oxford: Blackwell.

SANTOS, M. 1974: Geography, marxism and underdevelopment. *Antipode* 6(3), 1–9.

SARRE, P. 1987: Realism in practice. *Area* 19, 3–10.

SARRE, P., PHILLIPS, D. and SKELLINGTON, R. 1989: *Ethnic Minority Housing: Explanations and Policies*. Aldershot: Avebury.

SAUER, C. O. 1925: The morphology of landscape. *University of California Publications in Geography* 2, 19–54.

—— 1941: Foreword to historical geography. *Annals of the Association of American Geographers* 31, 1–24.

—— 1956: The education of a geographer. *Annals of the Association of American Geographers* 46, 287–99.

—— 1956a: The agency of man on earth. In W. L. Thomas (ed.) *Man's role in changing the face of the earth*. Chicago: University of Chicago Press, 49–69.

—— 1956b: Retrospect. In W. L. Thomas (ed.) *Man's role in changing the face of the earth*. Chicago: University of Chicago Press, 1131–5.

SAUNDERS, P. and WILLIAMS, P. R. 1986: The new conservatism: some thoughts on recent and future developments in urban studies. *Environment and Planning D: Society and Space* 4, 393–9.

—— 1987: For an emancipated social science. *Environment and Planning D: Society and Space* 5, 427–30.

SAYER, A. 1979: Epistemology and conceptions of people and nature in geography. *Geoforum* 10, 19–44.

—— 1981: Defensible values in geography. In D. T. Herbert and R. J. Johnston (eds.), *Geography and the urban environment*, 4. Chichester: John Wiley, 29–56.

—— 1982: Explanation in economic geography. *Progress in Human Geography* 6, 68–88.

—— 1983: Notes on geography and the relationship between people and nature. In The London Group of the Union of Socialist Geographers, *Society and nature*. London, 47–57.

—— 1984: *Method in social science: a realist approach*. London: Hutchinson.

—— 1985: Realism and geography. In R. J. Johnston (ed.) *The future of geography*. London: Methuen, 159–73.

—— 1987: Hard work and its alternatives. *Environment and Planning D: Society and Space* 5, 395–9.

—— 1989a: The 'new' regional geography and problems of narrative. *Environment and Planning D: Society and Space* 7, 253–76.

—— 1989b: On the dialogue between humanism and historical materialism in geography. In A. Kobayashi and S. Mackenzie (eds.) *Remaking human geography*. Boston: Unwin Hyman, 206–226.

SAYER, A. and MORGAN, K. 1875: A modern industry in a declining region: links between method, theory and policy. In D. Massey and R. Meegan (eds.) *Politics and method: contrasting studies in industrial geography*. London: Methuen, 144–68.

SCHAEFER, F. K. 1953: Exceptionalism in geography: a methodological examination. *Annals of the Association of American Geographers* 43, 226–49.

SCOTT, A. J. 1982: The meaning and social origins of discourse on the spatial foundations of society. In P. R. Gould and G. Olsson (eds.), *A search for Common Ground*. London: Pion, 141–56.

—— 1985: Location processes, urbanization, and territorial development: an exploratory essay. *Environment and Planning A* 17, 479–501.

—— 1986: Industrialization and urbanization: a geographical agenda. *Annals of the Association of American Geographers* 76, 25–37.

—— 1988: *Metropolis*. Los Angeles: University of California Press.

SCOTT, A. J. and COOKE, P. N. 1988: The new geography and sociology of production. *Environment and Planning D: Society and Space* 6, 241–4.

SCOTT, A. J. and STORPER, M. eds. 1985: *Production, work, territory*. Boston: George Allen & Unwin.

SEAMON, D. 1987: Phenomenology and environment-behavior research. In G. T. Moore and E. Zube (ed.) *Advances in Environment, Behavior and Design*. New York: Plenum, 3–36.

SHANNON, G. W. and DEVER, G. E. A. 1974: *Health care delivery: spatial perspectives*. New York: McGraw Hill.

SHEPPARD, E. S. 1979: Gravity parameter estimation. *Geographical Analysis* 11, 120–33.

SHORT, J. R. 1984: *The urban arena: capital, state and community in contemporary Britain*. London: Macmillan.

SIDDALL, W. R. 1961: Two kinds of geography. *Economic Geography* 36, facing page 189.

SIMON, H. A. 1957: *Models of man: social and rational*. New York: John Wiley.

SINCLAIR, J. G. and KISSLING, C. C. 1971: A network analysis approach to fruit distribution planning. *Proceedings, Sixth New Zealand Geography Conference* Volume 1, Christchurch, 131–6.

SLATER, D. 1973: Geography and underdevelopment – 1. *Antipode* 5(3), 21–33.

—— 1975: The poverty of modern geographical enquiry. *Pacific Viewpoint* 16, 159–76.

SMAILES, A. E. 1946: The urban mesh of England and Wales. *Transactions and Papers, Institute of British Geographers* 11, 85–101.

SMITH, C. T. 1965: Historical geography: current trends and prospects. In R. J. Chorley and P. Haggett (eds.), *Frontiers in geographical teaching*. London: Methuen, 118–43.

SMITH, D. M. 1971: America! America? Views on a pot melting. 2. Radical geography – the next revolution? *Area* 3, 153–7.

—— 1973a: Alternative 'relevant' professional roles. *Area* 5, 1–4.

—— 1973b: *The geography of social well-being in the United States*. New York: McGraw Hill.

—— 1977: *Human geography: a welfare approach*. London: Edward Arnold.

—— 1979: *Where the grass is greener: living in an unequal world*. London: Penguin.

—— 1981: *Industrial location: an economic geographical analysis* (2nd edn). New York: John Wiley.

—— 1984: Recollections of a random variable. In M. Billinge, D. Gregory and R. Martin (eds.) *Recollections of a revolution*. London: Macmillan, 117–33.

—— 1985: The 'new blood' scheme and its application to geography. *Area* 17, 237–43.

—— 1986: UGC research ratings: pass or fail? *Area* 18, 247–9.

—— 1988a: Towards an intepretative human geography. In J. Eyles and D. M. Smith (eds.) *Qualitative Methods in Human Geography*. Cambridge: Polity Press, 255–67.

—— 1988b: On academic performance. *Area* 20, 3–13.

SMITH, N. 1979: Geography, science and post-positivist modes of explanation. *Progress in Human Geography* 3, 365–83.

—— 1984: *Uneven development: nature, capital and the production of space*. Oxford: Basil Blackwell.

—— 1986: On the necessity of uneven development. *International Journal of Urban and Regional Research* 10, 87–104.

—— 1987a: Danger of the empirical turn: The CURS initiative. *Antipode* **19**, 59–68.
—— 1987b: Rascal concepts, minimalizing discourse, and the politics of geography. *Environment and Planning D: Society and Space* **5**, 377–83.
—— 1990: Geography as museum: private history and conservative idealism in *The Nature of Geography*. In J. N. Entrikin and S. D. Brunn (eds.) *Reflections on Richard Hartshorne's The Nature of Geography*. Washington: Association of American Geographers, 89–120.
SMITH, S. J. 1984: Practicing humanistic geography. *Annals of the Association of American Geographers* **74**, 353–74.
—— 1988: Constructing local knowledge: the analysis of self in everyday life. In J. Eyles and D. M. Smith (eds.) *Qualitative Methods in Human Geography*. Cambridge: Polity Press, 17–38.
SMITH, T. R. 1984: Artificial intelligence and its applicability to geographical problem solving. *The Professional Geographer* **36**, 147–58.
SMITH, T. R. CLARK, W. A. V. and COTTON, J. 1984: Deriving and testing production system models of sequential decision-making behavior. *Geographical Analysis* **16**, 191–222.
SMITH, W. 1949: *An economic geography of Great Britain*. London: Methuen.
SOJA, E. W. 1968: *The geography of modernization in Kenya*. Syracuse: Syracuse University Press.
—— 1980: The socio-spatial dialectic. *Annals of the Association of American Geographers* **70**, 207–25.
—— 1985: The spatiality of social life: towards a transformative retheorization. In D. Gregory and J. Urry (eds.) *Social relations and spatial structures*. London: Macmillan, 90–127.
—— 1989: *Postmodern geographies*. London: Verso.
SPATE, O. H. K. 1957: How determined is possibilism? *Geographical Studies* **4**, 3–12.
—— 1960a: Quantity and quality in geography. *Annals of the Association of American Geographers* **50**, 477–94.
—— 1960b: Lord Kelvin rides again. *Economic Geography* **36**, facing page 1.
—— 1963: Letter to the editor. *Geography* **48**, 206.
—— 1989: Foreword. In F. W. Boal and D. N. Livingstone (eds.) *The Behavioural Environment*. London: Routledge, xvii–xx.
SPENCER, C. P. and BLADES, M. 1986: Pattern and process: a review essay on the relationship between geography and environmental psychology. *Progress in Human Geography* **10**, 230–48.
SPENCER, H. 1982: *A system of synthetic philosophy, volume 1 first principles* (4th edn). New York: Appleton.
SPENCER, J. E. and THOMAS, W. L. 1973: *Introducing cultural geography*. New York: John Wiley.
STAMP, L. D. 1946: *The land of Britain*. London: Longman.
—— 1966: Ten years on. *Transactions, Institute of British Geographers* **40**, 11–20.
STAMP, L. D. and BEAVER, S. H. 1947: *The British Isles*. London: Longman.
STEEL, R. W. 1974: The Third World: geography in practice. *Geography* **59**, 189–207.
—— 1982: Regional geography in practice. *Geography* **67**, 2–8.
STEGMULLER, W. 1976: *The structure and dynamics of theories*. New York: Springer-Verlag.
STEWART, J. Q. 1945: *Coasts, waves and weather*. Boston: Ginn & Co.
—— 1947: Empirical mathematical rules concerning the distribution and equilibrium of population. *Geographical Review* **37**, 461–85.

—— 1956: The development of social physics. *American Journal of Physics* 18, 239–53.

STEWART, J. Q. and WARNTZ, W. 1958: Macrogeography and social science, *Geographical Review* 48, 167–184.

—— 1959: Physics of population distribution. *Journal of Regional Science* 1, 99–123.

STODDART, D. R. 1965: Geography and the ecological approach: the ecosystem as a geographic principle and method. *Geography* 50, 242–51.

—— 1966: Darwin's impact on geography. *Annals of the Association of American Geographers* 56, 683–98.

—— 1967a: Growth and structure of geography. *Transactions, Institute of British Geographers* 41, 1–19.

—— 1967b: Organism and ecosystem as geographic models. In R. J. Chorley and P. Haggett (eds.), *Models in geography*. London: Methuen, 511–47.

—— 1975a: The RGS and the foundations of geography at Cambridge. *Geographical Journal* 141, 216–39.

—— 1975b: Kropotkin, Réclus and 'relevant' geography. *Area* 7, 188–90.

—— 1977: The paradigm concept and the history of geography. Abstract of a paper for the conference of the International Geographical Union Commission on the History of Geographic Thought, Edinburgh.

—— 1981a: The paradigm concept and the history of geography. In D. R. Stoddart (ed.), *Geography, ideology and social concern*. Oxford: Blackwell, 70–80.

—— 1981b: Ideas and interpretation in the history of geography. In D. R. Stoddart (ed.), *Geography, ideology and social concern*. Oxford: Blackwell 1–7.

—— 1986: *On geography: and its history*. Oxford: Basil Blackwell.

—— 1987: To claim the high ground: geography for the end of the century. *Transactions, Institute of British Geographers* NS12, 327–36.

—— 1990: Epilogue: homage to Richard Hartshorne. In J. N. Entrikin and S. D. Brunn (eds.) *Reflections on Richard Hartshorne's The Nature of Geography*. Washington: Association of American Geographers, 163–6.

STORPER, M. 1987: The post-Enlightenment challenge to Marxist urban studies. *Environment and Planning D: Society and Space* 5, 418–26.

STOUFFER, S. A. 1940: Intervening opportunities: a theory relating mobility and distance. *American Sociological Review* 5, 845–67.

SUMMERFIELD, M. A. 1983: Population, samples and statistical inference in geography. *The Professional Geographer* 35, 143–8.

SUPPE, F. 1977a: The search for philosophic understanding of scientific theories. In F. Suppe (ed.), *The structure of scientific theories*. Urbana: University of Illinois Press, 3–233.

—— 1977b: Exemplars, theories and disciplinary matrices. In F. Suppe (ed.), *The structure of scientific theories*. Urbana: University of Illinois Press, 473–99.

—— 1977c: Afterword – 1977. In F. Suppe (ed.), *The structure of scientific theories*. Urbana: University of Illinois Press, 617–730.

SVIATLOVSKY, E. E. and EELS, W. C. 1937: The centrographical method and regional analysis. *Geographical Review* 27, 240–54.

—— 1970: *Geography*. Englewood Cliffs, NJ: Prentice-Hall.

TAAFFE, E. J. 1974: The spatial view in context. *Annals of the Association of American Geographers* 64, 1–16.

—— 1979: In the Chicago area. *Annals of the Association of American Geographers* 69, 133–8.

TAAFFE, E. J., MORRILL, R. L. and GOULD, P.R. 1963: Transport expansion in underdeveloped countries: a comparative analysis. *Geographical Review* 53, 503–29.

TATHAM, G. 1953: Environmentalism and possibilism. In G. Taylor (ed.), *Geography in the twentieth century*. London: Methuen, 128–64.

TAYLOR, E. G. R 1937: Whither geography? a review of some recent geographical texts. *Geographical Review* **27**, 129–35.

TAYLOR, P .J. 1976: An interpretation of the quantification debate in British geography. *Transactions, Institute of British Geographers* NS1, 129–42.

—— 1978: Political geography. *Progress in Human Geography* **2**, 53–62.

—— 1979: 'Difficult-to-let', 'difficult-to-live-in', and sometimes 'difficult-to-get-out-of': an essay on the provision of council housing. *Environment and Planning* A **11**, 1305–20.

—— 1981: Factor analysis in geographical research. In R. J. Bennett (ed.), *European progress in spatial analysis.* London: Pion, 251–67.

—— 1981b: Geographical scales within the world-economy approach. *Review* **5(1)**, 3–11.

—— 1982: A materialist framework for political geography. *Transactions, Institute of British Geographers* NS7, 15–34.

—— 1985a: The geography of elections. In M. Pacione (ed.) *Progress in political geography.* London: Croom Helm, 243–72.

—— 1985b: *Political geography: world-economy, nation-state and community.* London: Longman.

—— 1985c: The value of a geographical perspective. In R. J. Johnston (ed) *The future of geography.* London: Methuen, 92–110.

—— 1986: An exploration into world-systems analysis of political parties. *Political Geography Quarterly* **5**, S5–S20.

—— 1987: History's dialogue: an exemplification from political geography. *Progress in Human Geography* **11**.

—— 1989: *Political geography: world-economy, nation-state and community (Second Edition).* London: Longman.

TAYLOR, P. J. and GUDGIN, G. 1976: A statistical theory of electoral redistricting. *Environment and Planning* A **8**, 43–58.

TAYLOR, P. J. and JOHNSTON, R. J. 1979: *Geography of elections.* Harmondsworth: Penguin Books.

—— 1985: The geography of the British state. In J. R. Short and A. M. Kirby (eds.) *The human geography of contemporary Britain.* London: Macmillan, 23–39.

THOMAN, R. S. 1965: Some comments on *The Science of Geography. The Professional Geographer* **17**(6), 8–10.

THOMAS, E. N. 1960: Areal associations between population growth and selected factors in the Chicago urbanized area. *Economic Geography* **36**, 158–70.

—— 1968: Maps of residuals from regression. In B. J. L. Berry and D. F. Marble (eds.), *Spatial analysis.* Englewood Cliffs, NJ: Prentice-Hall, 326–52.

THOMAS, E. N. and ANDERSON, D. L. 1965: Additional comments on weighting values in correlation analysis of areal data. *Annals of the Association of American Geographers* **55**, 492–505.

THOMAS, R. W. 1982: *Information statistics in geography*, Norwich: Geo Books.

THOMAS, W. L. (ed.) 1956: *Man's role in changing the face of the earth.* Chicago: University of Chicago Press.

THOMPSON, J. H. *et al.* 1962: Toward a geography of economic health: the case of New York state. *Annals of the Association of American Geographers* **52**, 1–20.

THORNES, J. B. 1989a: Geomorphology and grass roots models. In B. Macmillan (ed.) *Remodelling geography.* Oxford: Basil Blackwell, 3–21.

—— 1989b: Environmental systems. In M. J. Clark, K. J. Gregory and A. M. Gurnell (eds.) *Horizons in physical geography.* London: Macmillan, 27–46.

THRALL, G. I. 1985: Scientific geography. *Area* **17**, 254.

—— 1986: Reply to Felix Driver and Christopher Philo. *Area* **18**, 162–3.

THRIFT, N. J. 1977: *An introduction to time geography.* CATMOG 13, Norwich: Geo Books.

—— 1979: Unemployment in the inner city: urban problem or structural imperative? a review of the British experience. In D. T. Herbert and R. J. Johnston (eds.), *Geography and urban environment: progress in research and applications*, volume 2. London: John Wiley, 125–226.

—— 1981: Behavioural geography. In N. Wrigley and R. J. Bennett (eds.), *Quantitative geography*. London: Routledge & Kegan Paul, 352–65.

—— 1983a: On the determination of social action in space and time. *Environment and Planning D: Society and Space* 1, 23–57.

—— 1983b: Literature, the production of culture and the politics of place. *Antipode* 15, 12–23.

—— 1987: No perfect symmetry. *Environment and Planning D: Society and Space* 5, 400–7.

THRIFT, N. J. and PRED, A. R. 1981: Time geography: a new beginning. *Progress in Human Geography* 5, 277–86.

TIMMERMANS, H. and GOLLEDGE, R. G. 1990: Applications of behavioural research on spatial problems: II Preference and choice. *Progress in Human Geography* 14.

TIMMS, D. 1965: Quantitative techniques in urban social geography. In R. J. Chorley and P. Haggett (eds.), *Frontiers in geographical teaching*. London: Methuen, 239–65.

TOCALIS, T .R. 1978: Changing theoretical foundations of the gravity concept of human interaction. In B. J. L. Berry, (ed.), *The nature of change in geographical ideas*. de Kalb: Northern Illinois University Press, 65–124.

TOMLINSON, R. F. 1989: Geographic information systems and geographers in the 1990s. *The Canadian Geographer* 33, 290–8.

TOULMIN, S. E. 1970: Does the distinction between normal and revolutionary science hold water? In I. Lakatos and A. Musgrave (eds.), *Criticism and the growth of knowledge*. London: Cambridge University Press, 39–48.

TREWARTHA, G. T. 1973: Comments on geography and public policy. *The Professional Geographer* 25, 78–9.

TUAN, YI-FU 1971: Geography, phenomenology, and the study of human nature. *The Canadian Geographer* 15, 181–92.

—— 1974: Space and place: humanistic perspectives. In C. Board *et al.* (eds.), *Progress in Geography* 6, London: Edward Arnold, 211–52.

—— 1975a: Images and mental maps. *Annals of the Association of American Geographers* 65, 205–13.

—— 1975b: Place: an experiential perspective *Geographical Review* 65, 151–65.

—— 1976: Humanistic geography. *Annals of the Association of American Geographers* 66, 266–76.

—— 1977: *Space and place*. London: Edward Arnold.

—— 1978: Literature and geography: implications for geographical research. In D. Ley and M. S. Samuels (eds.), *Humanistic geography: prospects and problems*. Chicago: Maaroufa Press, 194–206.

—— 1978: *Landscapes of fear*. Oxford: Basil Blackwell.

—— 1982: *Segmented worlds and self*. Minneapolis: University of Minnesota Press.

—— 1984: *Dominance and affection*. New Haven: Yale University Press.

TULLOCK, G. 1976: *The vote motive*. London: Institute of Economic Affairs.

TURNER, B. L. 1989: The specialist-synthesis approach to the revival of geography: the case of cultural ecology. *Annals of the Association of American Geographers* 79, 88–100.

TURNER, B. L. and MEYER, W. B. 1985: The use of citation indices in comparing geography programs: an exploratory study. *The Professional Geographer* 37, 271–8.

ULLMAN, E. L. 1941: A theory of location for cities. *American Journal of Sociology* 46, 853–64.

—— 1953: Human geography and area research. *Annals of the Association of American Geographers* **43**, 54–66.

—— 1956: The role of transportation and the bases for interaction. In W. L. Thomas (ed.), *Man's role in changing the face of the earth*. Chicago: University of Chicago Press, 862–80.

UPTON, G. J. G. and FINGLETON, B. 1985: *Spatial data analysis by example: Volume 1: point pattern and quantitative data*. Chichester: John Wiley.

URLICH, D. U. 1972: Migrations of the North Island Maoris 1800–1840: a systems view of migration. *New Zealand Geographer* **28**, 23–35.

URLICH CLOHER, D. 1975: A perspective on Australian urbanization. In J. M. Powell and M. Williams (eds.), *Australian space, Australian time: geographical perspectives*. Melbourne: Oxford University Press, 104–59.

URRY, J. 1985: Space, time and the study of the social. In H. Newby *et al*. (eds.) *Restructuring Capital*. London: Macmillan, 21–40.

—— 1986: Locality research: the case of Lancaster. *Regional Studies* **20**, 233–42.

—— 1987: Society, space and locality. *Environment and Planning D: Society and Space* **5**, 435–44.

VAN DEN DAELE, W. and WEINGART, P. 1976: Resistance and receptivity of science to external direction: the emergence of new disciplines under the impact of science policy. In G. Lemaine *et al*. (eds.), *Perspectives on the emergence of scientific disciplines*. The Hague: Mouton, 247–75.

VAN DER LAAN, L. and PIERSMA, A. 1982: The image of man: paradigmatic cornerstone in human geography. *Annals of the Association of American Geographers* **73**, 411–26.

VAN DER WUSTEN, H. and O'LOUGHLIN, J. 1986: Claiming new territory for a stable peace: how geography can contribute. *The Professional Geographer* **38**, 18–27.

VAN PAASSEN, C. 1981: The philosophy of geography: from Vidal to Hägerstrand. In A. Pred and G. Tornquist (eds.), *Space and time in geography* (Lund: C. W. K. Gleerup), 17–29.

VANCE, J. E. 1970: *The merchant's world*. Englewood Cliffs, NJ: Prentice-Hall.

—— 1978: Geography and the study of cities. *Human Geography: Coming of Age. American Behavioral Scientist* **22**, 131–49.

VON BERTALANFFY, L. 1950: An outline of general systems theory. *British Journal of the Philosophy of Science* **1**, 134–65.

WAGNER, P. L. 1976: Reflections on a radical geography. *Antipode* **8**(3), 83–5.

WALBY, S. 1986: *Patriarchy at work*. Cambridge: Polity Press.

WALKER, R. A. 1981a: A theory of suburbanization. In M. J. Dear and A. J. Scott (eds.), *Urbanization and urban planning in capitalist societies*. London: Methuen, 383–430.

—— 1981b: Left-wing libertarianism, an academic disorder: a reply to David Sibley. *The Professional Geographer* **33**, 5–9.

—— 1989a: What's left to do? *Antipode* **21**, 133–65.

—— 1989b: Geography from the left. In G. L. Gaile and C. J. Willmott (eds.) *Geography in America*. Columbus: Merrill Publishing Company, 619–51.

WALKER, R. A. and STORPER, M. 1981: Capital and industrial location. *Progress in Human Geography* **5**, 473–509.

WALLACE, I. 1989: *The Global Economic System*. London: Unwin Hyman.

WALMSLEY, D. J. 1972: *Systems theory: a framework for human geographical enquiry*. Research School of Pacific Studies. Department of Human Geography Publication HG/7, Australian National University, Canberra.

—— 1974: Positivism and phenomenology in human geography. *The Canadian Geographer* **18**, 95–107.

WALMSLEY, D. J. and SORENSEN, A. D. 1980: What marx for the radicals? an Antipodean viewpoint. *Area* 12, 137–41.

WARD, D. 1971: *Cities and immigrants: a geography of change in nineteenth-century America.* New York: Oxford University Press.

WARF, B. 1986: Ideology, everyday life and emancipatory phenomenology. *Antipode* 18, 268–83.

—— 1988: The resurrection of local uniqueness. In R. G. Golledge, H. Couclelis and P. R. Gould (eds.) *A Ground for Common Search.* Santa Barbara: The Santa Barbara Geographical Press, 51–62.

WARNTZ, W. 1959a: *Toward a geography of price.* Philadelphia: University of Pennsylvania Press.

—— 1959b: Geography at mid-twentieth century. *World Politics* 11, 442–54.

—— 1959c: Progress in economic geography. In P. E. James (ed.), *New viewpoints in geography.* Washington: National Council for the Social Studies, 54–75.

—— 1968: Letter to the editor. *The Professional Geographer* 20, 357.

—— 1984: Trajectories and coordinates. In M. Billinge, D. Gregory and R. Martin (eds.) *Recollections of a revolution.* London: Macmillan, 134–52.

WATERMAN, S. 1985: Not just the milk and honey – now a way of life: Israeli human geography since the six-day war. *Progress in Human Geography* 9, 194–234.

—— and KLIOT, N. 1990: The political impact on writing the geography of Palestine–Israel. *Progress in Human Geography* 14.

WATKINS, J. W. N. 1970: Against 'normal science'. In I. Lakatos and A. Musgrave (eds.), *Criticism and the growth of knowledge.* London: Cambridge University Press, 25–38.

WATSON, J. D. 1968: *The double helix: a personal account of the discovery of the structure of DNA.* London: Weidenfeld & Nicolson.

WATSON, J. W. 1953: The sociological aspects of geography. In G. Taylor (ed.), *Geography in the twentieth century.* London: Methuen, 453–99.

—— 1955: Geography: a discipline in distance. *Scottish Geographical Magazine* 71, 1–13.

—— 1983: The soul of geography. *Transactions, Institute of British Geographers* NS8, 385–99.

WATSON, M. K. 1978: The scale problem in human geography. *Geografiska Annaler* 60B, 36–47.

WATTS, M. 1988: Deconstructing determinism. *Antipode* 20, 142–68.

—— 1989: The agrarian crisis in Africa: debating the crisis. *Progress in Human Geography* 13, 1–41.

WATTS, S. J. and WATTS, S. J. 1978: The idealist alternative in geography and history. *The Professional Geographer* 30, 123–7.

WEAVER, J. C. 1943: Climatic relations of American barley production. *Geographical Review* 33, 569–88.

—— 1954: Crop-combination regions in the Middle West. *Geographical Review* 44, 175–200.

WEBBER, M. J. 1972: *Impact of uncertainty on location.* Canberra: Australian National University Press.

—— 1977: Pedagogy again: what is entropy? *Annals of the Association of American Geographers* 67, 254–66.

WESTERN, J. S. 1978: Knowing one's place: 'the Coloured people' and the Group Areas Act in Cape Town. In D. Ley and M. S. Samuels (eds.), *Humanistic geography: problems and prospects.* Chicago: Maaroufa Press, 297–318.

WHEELER, P. B. 1982: Revolutions, research programmes and human geography. *Area* 14, 1–6.

WHITE, G. F. 1945: *Human adjustment to floods*. Chicago: University of Chicago, Department of Geography, Research Paper 29.

—— 1972: Geography and public policy. *The Professional Geographer* 24, 101–4.

—— 1973: Natural hazards research. In R. J. Chorley (ed.), *Directions in geography*. London: Methuen, 193–216.

—— 1985: Geographers in a perilously changing world. *Annals of the Association of American Geographers* 75, 10–16.

WHITE, P. E. 1985: On the use of creative literature in migration study. *Area* 17, 277–83.

WHITEHAND, J. W. R. 1970: Innovation diffusion in an academic discipline: the case of the 'new' geography. *Area* 2(3), 19–30.

—— 1984: The impact of geographical journals: a look at ISI data. *Area* 16, 185–7.

—— 1985: Contributors to the recent development and influence of human geography: what citation analysis suggests. *Transactions, Institute of British Geographers* NS10, 222–3.

WHITEHAND, J. W. R. and PATTEN, J. H. C. (eds.) 1977: *Change in the town*. *Transactions, Institute of British Geographers* 2(3).

WILLIAMS, P. R. 1978: Urban managerialism: a concept of relevance? *Area* 10, 236–40.

—— 1982: Restructuring urban managerialism: towards a political economy of urban allocation. *Environment and Planning A* 14, 95–106.

WILSON, A. G. 1967: A statistical theory of spatial distribution models. *Transportation Research* 1, 253–69.

—— 1970: *Entropy in urban and regional modelling*. London: Pion.

—— 1974: *Urban and regional models in geography and planning*. London: John Wiley.

—— 1976a: Catastrophe theory and urban modelling: an application to modal choice. *Environment and Planning A* 8, 351–46.

—— 1976b: Retailers' profits and consumers' welfare in a spatial interaction shopping model. In I. Masser (ed.), *Theory and practice in regional science*. London: Pion, 42–57.

—— 1978: Mathematical education for geographers. Department of Geography, University of Leeds, *Discussion Paper* 211, Leeds.

—— 1981a: *Catastrophe theory and bifurcation: applications to urban and regional systems*. London: Croom Helm.

—— 1981b: *Geography and the environment: systems analytical methods*. Chichester: John Wiley.

—— 1984: Making urban models more realistic: some strategies for future research. *Environment and Planning A* 16, 1419–32.

—— 1989a: Classics, modelling and critical theory: human geography as structured pluralism. In B. Macmillan (ed.) *Remodelling geography*. Oxford: Basil Blackwell, 61–9.

—— 1989b: Mathematical models and geographic theory. In D. Gregory and R. Walford (eds.) *Horizons in human geography*. London: Macmillan, 29–47.

WILSON, A. G. and BENNETT, R. J. 1985: *Mathematical methods in human geography and planning*. Chichester: John Wiley.

WILSON, A. G., REES, P. H. and LEIGH, C. 1977: *Models of cities and regions*. London: John Wiley.

WISE, M. J. 1975: A university teacher of geography. *Transactions, Institute of British Geographers* 66, 1–16.

—— 1977: On progress and geography. *Progress in Human Geography* 1, 1–11.

WISNER, B. 1970: Introduction: on radical methodology. *Antipode* 2, 1–3.

WOLCH, J. and DEAR, M. (editors) 1989: *The power of geography: how territory shapes social life*. Boston: Unwin Hyman.

WOLDENBERG, M. J. and BERRY, B. J. L. 1967: Rivers and central places: analogous systems? *Journal of Regional Science* 7, 129–40.

WOLF, L. G. 1976: Comments on the Harries-Peet controversy. *The Professional Geographer* 28, 196–8.

WOLPERT, J. 1964: The decision process in spatial context. *Annals of the Association of American Geographers* 54, 337–58.

—— 1965: Behavioral aspects of the decision to migrate. *Papers and Proceedings, Regional Science Association* 15, 159–72.

—— 1967: Distance and directional bias in inter-urban migratory streams. *Annals of the Association of American Geographers* 57, 605–16.

—— 1970: Departures from the usual environment in locational analysis. *Annals of the Association of American Geographers* 60, 220–9.

WOLPERT, J., DEAR, M. and CRAWFORD, R. 1975: Satellite mental health facilities. *Annals of the Association of American Geographers* 65, 24–35.

WOMEN AND GEOGRAPHY STUDY GROUP, 1984: *Geography and gender: an introduction to feminist geography*. London: Hutchinson.

WOOLDRIDGE, S. W. 1956: *The geographer as scientist*. London: Thomas Nelson.

WOOLDRIDGE, S. W. and EAST, W. G. 1958: *The spirit and purpose of geography*. London: Hutchinson.

WOOLGAR, S. W. 1976: The identification and definition of scientific collectivities. In G. Lemaine *et al.* (eds.), *Perspectives on the emergence of scientific disciplines*. The Hague: Mouton, 233–45.

WRIGHT, J. K. 1925: *The geographical lore of the time of the crusades: a study in the history of medieval science and tradition in western Europe*. New York: American Geographical Society.

—— 1947: Terrae incognitae: the place of imagination in geography. *Annals of the Association of American Geographers* 37, 1–15.

WRIGLEY, E. A. 1965: Changes in the philosophy of geography. In R. J. Chorley and P. Haggett (eds.), *Frontiers in geographical teaching*. London: Methuen, 3–24.

WRIGLEY, N. 1979: Developments in the statistical analysis of categorical data. *Progress in Human Geography* 3, 315–55.

—— 1984: Quantitative methods: diagnostics revisited. *Progress in Human Geography* 8, 525–35.

—— 1985: *Categorical data analysis for geographers and environmental scientists*. London: Longman.

WRIGLEY, N. and BENNETT, R. J. (eds.) 1981: *Quantitative geography: a British view*. London: Routledge & Kegan Paul.

WRIGLEY, N. and LONGLEY, P. A. 1984: Discrete choice modelling in urban analysis. In D. T. Herbert and R. J. Johnston (eds.) *Geography and the urban environment: progress in research and applications*, volume 6. Chichester: John Wiley, 45–94.

WRIGLEY, N. and MATTHEWS, S. 1986: Citation classics and citation levels in geography. *Area* 18, 185–94.

ZELINSKY, W. 1970: Beyond the exponentials: the role of geography in the great transition. *Economic Geography* 46, 499–535.

—— 1978: Introduction. *Human Geography: Coming of Age. American Behavioral Scientist* 22, 5–13.

—— 1973a: Women in geography: a brief factual report. *The Professional Geographer* 25, 151–65.

—— 1973b: *The cultural geography of the United States*. Englewood Cliffs, NJ: Prentice-Hall.

—— 1974: Selfward bound? Personal preference patterns and the changing map of American society. *Economic Geography* **50**, 144–79.

—— 1975: The demigod's dilemma. *Annals of the Association of American Geographers* **65**, 123–43.

ZELINSKY, W., MONK, J. and HANSON, S. 1982: Women and geography: a review and prospectus. *Progress in Human Geography* **6**, 317–66.

ZIPF, G. K. 1949: *Human behavior and the principle of least effort*. New York: Hafner.

General Index

Author Index